Cracking the AP
Statistics Exam

The Princeton Review

Cracking the AP
Statistics Exam

BY MADHURI S. MULEKAR

2002–2003 EDITION
RANDOM HOUSE, INC.
NEW YORK

www.PrincetonReview.com

Princeton Review Publishing, L.L.C.
2315 Broadway
New York, NY   10024
E-mail: booksupport@review.com

ISBN: 0-375-76232-9

AP and Advanced Placement are registered trademarks of the College Entrance Examination Board, which was not involved in the production of, and does not endorse, this book.

Editor: Jeff Soloway
Production Editor: Maria Dente
Production Coordinator: Stephen White

Manufactured in the United States of America.

9 8 7 6 5 4 3 2 1

2002–2003 Edition

ACKNOWLEDGMENTS

I would like to thank my spouse Satish Mulekar for his understanding, patience, and willingness to help during this project. I would not have been able to complete this project without his assistance in making time available for it.

CONTENTS

FOREWORD

WHAT IS THE PRINCETON REVIEW?

The Princeton Review is an international test preparation company with branches in all the major U.S. cities and several abroad. In 1981, John Katzman started teaching an SAT prep course in his parents' living room. Within five years The Princeton Review had become the largest SAT coaching program in the country.

The Princeton Review's phenomenal success in improving students' scores on standardized tests was (and is) due to a simple, innovative, and radically effective philosophy: Study the test, not what the test *claims* to test. This approach has led to the development of techniques for taking standardized tests based on the principles the test writers themselves use to write the tests.

The Princeton Review has found that its methods work not just for cracking the SAT, but for any standardized tests. We've already successfully applied our system to the GMAT, LSAT, MCAT, and GRE, to name just a few. Although in some ways the AP Statistics exam is a very different test from those mentioned above, in the end, a standardized test is a standardized test. This book uses our time-tested principle: Crack the system based on how the test is written.

We also offer books and online services that cover an enormous variety of education and career-related topics. If you're interested, check out our website at www.PrincetonReview.com.

PART

I

INTRODUCTION

1

ABOUT THE AP
STATISTICS EXAM

WHAT IS THE ADVANCED PLACEMENT PROGRAM?

The Advanced Placement (AP) program allows high school students to take college level courses and get college course credit. Approximately 14,000 schools worldwide offer AP courses to their students. In the year 2001, some 845,000 students worldwide took over 1.4 million AP exams. There are currently 35 different AP courses and plans to develop more.

The AP program is coordinated by an organization called the College Board. For each AP subject, the College Board appoints a Test Development Committee consisting of six teachers of the subject, three from colleges or universities and three from high schools. The Test Development Committee is responsible for developing the curriculum for the AP course and writing the AP exams. Once the exam is developed, the College Board hands it over to the Educational Testing Services (ETS), which prints and administers it. ETS also plays a role in developing the exam. ETS is the same organization that produces and administers the SAT and many other admissions exams.

The final AP exam grade is assigned on a five-point scale (5, 4, 3, 2, 1). To students making the required grade, many colleges and universities give credit for passing an introductory course in that subject. Each college has a different requirement. Some give credit only for grades 4 and 5, while others give credit for a 3 as well.

You can get more information on the AP program by checking out the College Board's website (www.collegeboard.org) and downloading the *AP Program Guide*.

WHAT IS AP STATISTICS?

AP Statistics exam is one of the more recent AP offerings. The first AP Statistics exam was given in May 1997. This course is equivalent to a one-semester, introductory, college course. The prerequisite for this course is simply a second year of algebra—no knowledge of calculus is required. The purpose of an AP Statistics course is to introduce students to major concepts and tools for collecting and analyzing data, and for making conclusions from their analysis. Active learning and communication are high priorities. The full course description is available on the College Board's website at www.collegeboard.org/ap/library.

WHO SHOULD TAKE AP STATISTICS?

The AP Statistics exam is recommended for any secondary student who is reasonably adept at mathematics and quantitative reasoning, and has successfully completed a second year course in algebra. Typically students take AP Statistics in their junior or senior year. The College Board points out the following:

- High school students planning to take a science course in their senior year can benefit by taking AP Statistics in their junior year.

- For students who are not taking a mathematics course in their senior year, AP Statistics offers an opportunity to continue to develop their quantitative skills.

- Since the only precursor for AP Statistics is a second-year course in algebra, students taking a pre-calculus course in their senior year can take AP Statistics concurrently.

- Many college majors, such as engineering, psychology, sociology, pre-med, and business, require at least an introductory course in statistics.

CURRICULUM

The curriculum for AP Statistics consists of four basic themes:

1. **Exploring Data:** observing patterns and departures from patterns.

2. **Planning a Study:** deciding what and how to measure.

3. **Anticipating Patterns:** producing models using probability and simulation.

4. **Statistical Inference:** confirming models.

The following is an outline of the major topics covered by the AP Statistics exam. The topics may be taught in a different order. Keep in mind that less emphasis is placed on actual arithmetic computation and more emphasis is placed on conceptual understanding and interpretation.

I.   Exploring Data: Observing patterns and departures from patterns

    A. Interpreting graphical displays of distributions of univariate data (dotplot, stemplot, histogram, cumulative frequency plot)
        1. Center and spread
        2. Clusters and gaps
        3. Outliers and other unusual features
        4. Shape

    B. Summarizing distributions of univariate data
        1. Measuring center: median, mean
        2. Measuring spread: range, interquartile range, standard deviation
        3. Measuring position: quartiles, percentiles, standardized scores (z-scores)
        4. Using boxplots
        5. The effect of changing units on summary statistics

    C. Comparing distributions of univariate data (dotplots, back-to-back stemplots, parallel boxplots)
        1. Comparing center and spread: within group, between group variation
        2. Comparing clusters and gaps
        3. Comparing outliers and other unusual features
        4. Comparing shapes

    D. Exploring bivariate data
        1. Analyzing patterns in scatterplots
        2. Correlation and linearity
        3. Least-squares regression line
        4. Residual plots, ouliers, and influential points
        5. Transformations to achieve linearity: logarithmic and power transformations

    E. Exploring categorical data: frequency tables
        1. Marginal and joint frequencies for two-way tables
        2. Conditional relative frequencies and association

II. Planning a Study: Deciding what and how to measure

    A. Overview of methods of data collection
        1. Census
        2. Sample survey
        3. Experiment
        4. Observational study

    B. Planning and conducting surveys
        1. Characteristics of a well-designed and well-conducted survey
        2. Populations, samples, and random selection
        3. Sources of bias in surveys
        4. Simple random sampling
        5. Stratified random sampling

C. Planning and conducting experiments
1. Characteristics of a well-designed and well-conducted experiment
2. Treatments, control groups, experimental units, random assignments, and replication
3. Sources of bias and confounding, including placebo effect and blinding
4. Completely randomized design
5. Randomized block design, including matched pairs design

D. Generalizability of results from observational studies, experimental studies, and surveys

III. Anticipating Patterns: Producing models using probability theory and simulation

A. Probability as relative frequency
1. "Law of large numbers" concept
2. Addition rule, multiplication rule, conditional probability, and independence
3. Discrete random variables and their probability distributions, including binomial
4. Simulation of probability distributions, including binomial and geometric
5. Mean (expected value) and standard deviation of a random variable, and linear transformation of a random variable

B. Combining independent random variables
1. Notion of independence versus dependence
2. Mean and standard deviation for sums and differences of independent random variables

C. The normal distribution
1. Properties of the normal distribution
2. Using tables of the normal distribution
3. The normal distribution as a model for measurements

D. Sampling distributions
1. Sampling distribution of a sample proportion
2. Sampling distribution of a sample mean
3. Central Limit Theorem
4. Sampling distribution of a difference between two independent sample proportions
5. Sampling distribution of a difference between two independent sample means
6. Simulation of sampling distributions

IV. Statistical Inference: Confirming models

A. Confidence intervals
1. The meaning of a confidence interval
2. Large sample confidence interval for a proportion
3. Large sample confidence interval for a mean
4. Large sample confidence interval for a difference between two proportions
5. Large sample confidence interval for a difference between two means (unpaired and paired)

B. Tests of significance
   1. Logic of significance testing, null and alternative hypotheses; *p*-values; one- and two-sided tests; concepts of type I and type II errors; concept of power
   2. Large sample test for a proportion
   3. Large sample test for a mean
   4. Large sample test for a difference between two proportions
   5. Large sample test for a difference between two means (unpaired and paired)
   6. Chi-square test for goodness of fit, homogeneity of proportions, and independence (one and two-way tables)

C. Special case of normally distributed data
   1. *t*-distribution
   2. Single sample *t*-procedures
   3. Two sample (independent and matched pairs) *t*-procedures
   4. Inference for the slope of least squares regression line

THE CALCULATOR

Regarding calculators on the AP Statistics exam, the College Board states the following:

"Each student is expected to bring to the exam a graphing calculator with statistical capabilities."

Note the word *expected*. Though the Test Development Committee makes some effort to develop tests that can be passed without using a graphing calculator, the truth is that you will be at a disadvantage if you don't have one. A good graphing calculator, such as the TI-83, (which is currently by far the most commonly used) will not save you time or prevent you from making minor arithmetic mistakes, but it will help compute descriptive statistics, such as standard deviation, correlation coefficient, and the equation of least squares regression line. It is also capable of making useful graphs, such as histograms, scatterplot graphs, and least squares regression lines. It goes without saying that these capabilities are extremely useful on the AP Statistics exam.

Make sure you are thoroughly familiar with the functioning capabilities of your calculator. Don't bring an unfamiliar calculator to the AP exam. During the months before your exam, practice using your calculator until you feel confident with it.

You should always remember that a graphing calculator is only a computational aid—it cannot answer problems for you. Use it carefully. Interpreting numerical answers given by the calculator is still *your* responsibility. The calculator cannot do it for you. Nonetheless, the calculator will definitely make your computation easier. So use it.

Certain types of calculators may be prohibited from use on exams, such as calculators with keyboards. This policy is updated as new and modified calculators enter the market. Refer to the College Board's policy (it's on the website) on the use of calculators on exams before purchasing one.

COMPUTER OUTPUTS

Due to time constraints during the exam, students are not expected to do extensive computations. For some questions, computer outputs are provided. Students are expected to make use of these outputs and interpret them correctly. Generally, only very standard, non-program-specific outputs are provided. During the weeks before the exam, get familiar with the outputs of statistical programs. Learn to read them, interpret them, and use them, so you won't be caught by surprise on the exam. When you encounter a question on the exam that comes with a computer output, be sure to read the entire question carefully before answering it, and be sure to use the given output. Do not start computing everything again—this will only waste precious time.

FORMAT OF THE AP STATISTICS EXAMINATION

An AP Statistics exam is made up of two parts: a Multiple Choice section and a Free Response section. The entire test lasts three hours.

- **Part I: Multiple Choice.** This part consists of 40 multiple-choice questions, each with five possible answers. Exactly one hour and 30 minutes is allotted for this part of the exam.

- **Part II: Free Response.** This part consists of six free-response questions, requiring not only that you perform the right computations but that you communicate your reasoning and justify your answer clearly. Exactly one hour and 30 minutes is allotted for this part of the exam. This Free Response section is further divided into two parts, Part A and Part B.

    Part A: Five free-response questions, on which you are instructed to spend about 65 minutes.

    Part B: The Investigative Task Question, on which you are told to spend about 25 minutes. This question typically consists of several parts, linking different areas of the curriculum together. As the name suggests, the Investigative Task Question invites you to investigate a situation and arrive at a solution. It might also require you to expand your statistics knowledge a bit beyond the course curriculum.

GRADING THE EXAM

The test is offered every year in May. Afterward, the Multiple Choice section is scored immediately by computer. The free-response questions, however, are scored by a group of high school and college teachers known as readers.

THE FREE-RESPONSE QUESTIONS

In early June, the readers gather in a designated location to grade the free-response questions. The Test Development Committee prepares the initial rubric for grading them. A select group of readers, known as table leaders, arrive at the reading site prior to the reading. After looking at sample answers from students, the table leaders further fine-tune the rubric. After the rubric is finalized, all readers arrive at the reading site and are trained by the table leaders on the use of the rubric in grading the exams. As a general rule, no reader is allowed to grade more than one question in a given exam. **Communication** and **clarity of solution** receive major emphasis in the grading.

Each question is graded on a 0 to 4 scale. The scores are defined as follows:
4 – Complete response
3 – Substantial response
2 – Developing response
1 – Minimal response
0 – No response or totally incorrect response

THE FINAL GRADE

In determining the final grade, the grades on the two sections are combined as follows:

- Part I: Multiple Choice. This part consists of 50 percent of the total grade. A correction factor is used to ensure that completely random guessing will not significantly improve your grade.

- Number of correct answers – 0.25 X (number of incorrect answers).

- Part II: Free Response Section. This part consists of 50 percent of the total grade.
    Part A: Consists of 75 percent of the Part II grade.
    Part B: Consists of 25 percent of the Part II grade.

The chief faculty consultant determines the final grade assignment. For determining grade distribution, the grade distributions of scores on past AP Statistics exams are taken into account. Some other data, such as validity studies, table leader reports, and grade distribution on equator questions are also considered. The total raw scores are then converted into the AP program's five-point scale, where each score is represented as follows:

> 5 – Extremely well qualified

> 4 – Well qualified

> 3 – Qualified

> 2 – Possibly qualified

> 1 – No recommendation

In 2001, 11.4 percent of students taking the AP Statistics exam scored a 5; 23.3 percent scored a 4; 24.9 percent scored a 3; 19.1 percent scored a 2; and 21.2 percent scored a 1.

SIGNING UP FOR THE EXAM

If you want to take an AP exam, first see your guidance counselor. He or she will direct you to your school's AP Coordinator, who is in charge of overseeing the AP programs, as well as collecting fees for the exams. If your school does not have a designated AP Coordinator, or you are the only student at your school interested in taking an AP exam, then you can take the AP exam through another school. Contact the College Board or visit its website to find a school in your area offering the exam. Note the following about exam fees:

- Each exam costs $78. Your school gets $7 out of the exam fees to cover administrative costs. If you're in acute financial need, check with your AP Coordinator or contact the College Board to ask about fee reduction credits.

- In some circumstances, if you cannot take a test at the regularly scheduled time, you can take an alternate exam offered at a different time. You may have to pay a surcharge of $40 to take an alternate exam.

- If you register for an exam but don't take it, your school is charged $13 and has the responsibility of deciding whether or not you get a refund for the rest of the fee. Once you begin taking an exam, the fee is nonrefundable.

THE COLLEGE BOARD'S SUGGESTED TIMETABLE FOR THOSE PLANNING TO TAKE THE AP STATISTICS EXAM

- **Far in advance:** Talk to your teachers about the requirements for enrolling in the course. Also, try to talk to other AP students to get an idea of what to expect.

- **January:** Talk to your statistics teacher and your guidance counselor. Discuss with them the possibility of taking the AP Statistics exam. If you decide to take it, then contact the AP Coordinator at your school or, if there is no AP Coordinator, contact the College Board to find the nearest school that offers the exam. At this point, you will be required to pay the exam fee and you can also provide the College Board with a list of colleges and universities to which you want your scores to be sent. If you need to make special arrangements because of a disability, you should also do so at this time.

- **Early March:** If you need to take the exam at another school, by now you should have made plans. If you haven't already done so, be sure to do it now.

- **March 25:** This is the postmark deadline for the College Board Services for Students with Disabilities (SSD) Eligibility Form, for students not currently receiving testing accommodations.

- **May 8, 2002, Afternoon:** AP Statistics exam is administered.

- **May 7, 2003, Afternoon:** AP Statistics exam is administered.

- **Early-to-mid June:** Reading of free-response questions.

- **June 15:** If you want your grades sent to colleges other than those you listed earlier in the application form, then you need to do so in writing by this date. This is also the last date for canceling your score.

- **Early July:** AP Grade Reports are released to the colleges you designated and sent to your home address and your school.

- **July 1:** At this point, you can call 888 308-0013 to get your score. This service costs $10.

WHAT TO BRING TO THE EXAM

- Two no. 2 pencils

- An eraser

- A calculator. A programmable calculator with statistical functions is allowed on both parts of the exam. The TI-83 is the most popular one. Refer to the calculator policy of the College Board for allowable calculators.

- A watch without an alarm or a calculator

- A photo ID, if you are taking the exam at a school other than your own

- A snack

WHAT YOU MAY NOT BRING TO THE EXAM

- Textbooks, notebooks, dictionaries, etc.

- Statistical tables. Do not bring your own copies of statistical tables. They are provided with both parts of the exam.

- Formula sheets. Formulas are provided with both tests. Look at the formula sheet provided in this book, and familiarize yourself with it.

- Any pieces of paper. All the papers needed for completing the exam are provided.

- Laptop computers.

- Cameras (to prevent you from copying the exam and taking it out with you).

- Portable stereos or radios.

- Walkie-talkies or two-way radios for communication (to prevent you from communicating exam questions with others).

- Any laser devices for data transfer (to prevent you from communicating with others).

NO CHEATING!

Refrain from doing anything that might make your exam proctor suspicious. You can be thrown out of the exam room or have your scores canceled if the proctor thinks you're cheating.

- Follow all instructions properly.

- Do not open the exam booklet and look at the questions before the exam begins.

- Do not try to talk to anybody other than the proctor once the exam begins. If you need something, ask the proctor, not the student next to you.

- Do not tear pages out of the test booklet.

- Do not try to sneak papers in or out of the exam room.

- Do not try to look at books, notebooks, etc.

- Do not try to exchange calculators, pencils, erasers, etc., with other students.

- Stop working on the exam when you are told.

- Do not try to give or receive answers from anybody.

- Do not behave in a disruptive manner, such as walking around and/or squirming too much in your seat.

- Do not wear noisy jewelry, such as bracelets, that jingle when you write.

- Refrain from doing anything that might be misinterpreted by the proctor as a signal to another student.

SPECIAL CIRCUMSTANCES

STUDENTS WITH DISABILITIES

You can request special testing conditions to accommodate a disability by contacting your AP Coordinator or the College Board before April 1. You'll need to have either a current Individualized Education Program (IEP) on file at your school, or a signed letter from an appropriate professional (a physician, a psychologist, etc.) describing the disability and verifying the need for special arrangements. Some of the options are listed below:

- Students with poor or no vision may take large-type tests or Braille tests.

- Students with poor vision and/or a disability that impedes writing may request the use of a reader/writer.

- Students with qualified disabilities may request to take the test at a more accommodating location.

Make sure your disability documentation is in order long before the test. If possible, take the test under the standard conditions. Once your documentation is in order, your score report will indicate "Certified Disability." Otherwise it will indicate "Non-Standard Administration." Admissions officers at colleges might frown upon "non-standard administration" test scores.

PROBLEMS ON TEST DAY

If you notice a misprint, inconclusive question, or any other error on the test (a blank page in the test, a missing question, unstapled test paper, etc.), then report it immediately to the proctor. If you believe the misprint or error on the test is critical, report the error to the College Board immediately after the test. But make sure the error has really occurred and you did not just misread or misunderstand the question. Note that the questions are reviewed over and again by the Test Development Committee, the Chief Faculty Consultant, and ETS representatives. Although not impossible, it is very unlikely that the test will contain serious mistakes.

After reading this chapter, you should be aware of the time limits for each section of the test. If your proctor does not give you the required time, contact your AP Coordinator immediately after the test. If that does not get you anywhere, contact your school principal. If you wait too long, you may be stuck with your score on the mistimed exam.

CANCELLING YOUR SCORE

If you think you really blew the exam, you can contact the College Board by June 15 and cancel your score, or request that your grade be withheld from the colleges you had listed on your application. Do not use this option unless you are absolutely sure that you did horribly. Even if you felt lost on some of the free-response questions, it's very likely that a lot of other students felt the same way. If most students did poorly on certain questions, the College Board will take that into consideration when assigning final grades.

GETTING MORE INFORMATION

If you have more questions about the AP Statistics exam or the AP program as a whole, you can contact the College Board directly at the following location:

AP Services
P.O. Box 6671
Princeton, NJ 08541-6671
Telephone: 888-CALL-4-AP or 609-771-7300
Teletypewriter (TTY): 609-882-4118
Fax: 609-530-0482
E-mail: apexams@info.collegeboard.org

The College Board's website (www.collegeboard.org) is an excellent source of information. There you can see or even download (for free) a detailed description of the AP Statistics exam with sample multiple-choice and free-response questions, student free-response questions and answers from years past, the most up-to-date calculator policy, and other useful tidbits.

Preparing for the AP Statistics Exam

IN THE MONTHS BEFORE THE TEST

It does not pay to wait until the last minute to study for the exam. A marathon cramming session the night before will most likely just leave you too tired to think clearly on the test. So start your review early—preferably months before the test. Starting early will give you plenty of time to identify the concepts that give you trouble and will enable you to ask your teacher for help. Try to review your AP Statistics material for half an hour to an hour three or four times a week. Study consistently, even if it's just for a short period at a time. That way you are more likely to understand and remember the material. Here are a few other tips on preparing for the exam:

- **Read this book:** It covers all the important information required for the AP Statistics exam and offers plenty of examples. As for the tests in the back of the book, either take them as timed practice runs for the AP exam itself, or go through them more slowly, using the questions as drills to help you refine your skills or to identify problems that you find difficult.

- **Read your textbook closely:** Pay particular attention to the discussion and the examples—don't just concentrate on the highlighted material.

PRACTICE

Nobody ever said statistics would be easy, but one thing will make it a lot easier—practice. Try to work on as many examples from your textbook as possible. It's also a good idea to get additional statistics books from the library and work on their examples. The more you practice reading and solving descriptive questions, the more comfortable you'll be with them, and the better you will do on the exam.

When you're doing a practice question, never stop after getting a numeric answer. Always try to interpret your answer in the context of the problem. It's not easy to explain answers to a statistics problem in nonstatistical terms, but it is important—and it is required. So, start early and practice as much as you can. The best way to learn something is by trying to explain it to somebody else. It is a good idea to work with a friend, so that both of you can take turns explaining the answers.

Go to the source

Get some old AP Statistics tests. The College Board releases the free-response part of the exam every year. These free-response sections and sample solutions are available for free on the College Board website at www.collegeboard.org/ap/statistics. Download the questions, try to answer them yourself, and then look at the solutions. Don't read the solutions first! Reading answers written by somebody else is not the same as trying to puzzle out the solutions yourself. You can watch an expert ice skater twirl around the rink all you want, but that is not going to make you a great figure skater. To skate like an expert, you need to get on your skates and practice the moves over and over. It's the same with statistics. You may fall flat on your face with the first few solutions you try, but practice will make all the difference.

The College Board releases the multiple-choice part of the exam to the public only once every five years. The last was in 1997; most likely, the 2002 exam will be the next to be released. Many teachers keep the released exams on file and use them for class tests or practice tests. You can purchase a copy from the College Board by calling or by heading to the "Shop" section on the College Board website. Practicing on a real released exam is a great way to build your confidence and refine your skills.

Many AP Statistics teachers throughout the country post their class materials, including projects and old tests, on the web. Try typing in "AP Statistics" on a good search engine. The teachers' test materials may not be as good as the College Board's, but they serve as additional practice.

Still more practice

Look for survey results or scientific articles published by your local newspaper or by newspapers or magazines on the web. Be critical of the articles. Try to identify the problem involved, the type of study used, the experimental units, the treatments, etc. Try to figure out what kind of statistical techniques were used to analyze the data and why. The first few cases might be difficult, but soon you'll be surprised at how well you understand what was done. You might even identify a mistake; if so, discuss the article with your statistics teacher.

Look at the graphs and charts included in the newspaper articles. For each graph, write a short summary, just three or four sentences, identifying different characteristics of the data presented.

WRITING TIPS

There is a big emphasis on communication in the AP Statistics exam. Even if you have a perfect numerical solution, unclear communication can prevent you from getting a high score on the question. Again, practice is the key. With every example you practice on, write down how you arrived at your answer, why you chose a particular technique, what your answer tells you, and so on.

In addition, practice summarizing the contents of newspaper articles—even nonstatistical or scientific articles. Writing is not as easy as you think. Do not take it for granted. Many students have trouble putting together three or four grammatically correct and meaningful sentences.

IN THE WEEK BEFORE THE TEST

- By now you should have collected several different practice tests from different sources, including this book and the College Board. During the last week, take these practice tests. Time yourself as though it were the real AP exam. You might even ask your statistics teacher to grade the tests.

- Spend some time studying every evening. There are four major sections in the AP Statistics curriculum. Review one section each evening. Then spend one evening reviewing free-response questions and one evening reviewing multiple-choice questions.

- Don't do anything out of the ordinary. This is not the time to start a new diet or exercise program!

- Familiarize yourself with the instructions for taking the exam so you won't have to waste time when you're actually taking it. You can find these instructions on the first page of the practice tests in this book.

ON THE DAY OF THE TEST

- Eat a reasonable breakfast. Do not overeat, which may make you drowsy, but definitely do not skip breakfast, either. Hunger pangs can prevent you from thinking straight.

- Use the bathroom before you enter the testing room. And avoid drinking beverages beforehand that will send you to the bathroom during the exam.

- Wear comfortable clothing.

WHAT TO BRING

Pack your bag the night before the exam. Don't forget the following:

- Several sharpened **no. 2 pencils** (with erasers).

- A **snack.** Eating a piece of fruit or a candy bar during the break will give you a much-needed energy boost.

- If you're taking the exam at a different school from your own, or if you're homeschooled, bring a **photo I.D.** and your secondary school code number (home-schoolers will be given a code on the testing day).

- Your **social security number.** While it's not mandatory for you to provide your social security number, it is used for identification and appears on your AP Grade Report.

- A **watch without a calculator.** If your watch has an alarm, turn it off.

- A **calculator.** As we discussed in the previous chapter, each student is expected to bring a graphing calculator with statistical capabilities. Powerbooks and portable computers, pocket organizers, and devices with typewriter-style (QWERTY) keyboards, electronic writing pads, or pen input devices are not allowed; but most graphing calculators currently on the market are acceptable. Non-graphing scientific calculators are permitted only if they have statistical capabilities.

FINALLY...

Relax. Even if you've just read this book carefully, you're probably better prepared than a lot of the other students. Stay positive, and remember—everyone else is at least as nervous as you are.

3

TEST-TAKING
STRATEGIES

TIPS FOR BOTH SECTIONS OF THE AP STATISTICS EXAM

Here are two things to keep in mind for both parts of the exam:

- **Statistical tables:** Statistical tables and formulas are provided for you in the exam booklets in both sections. A copy of those tables and formulas is available at the back of this book. In the months before the exam, familiarize yourself with them and practice using them.

- **Calculators:** You can use a graphical calculator with statistical capabilities on both sections of the exam. From the beginning of your statistics course, use just one calculator, and practice with it as much as you can. Being familiar with the capabilities of your calculator will save you time on the exam. And remember that many calculators have distribution functions, which can save you from spending time looking through the tables provided.

CRACKING THE MULTIPLE CHOICE SECTION

Section I of the AP Statistics exam consists of 40 multiple-choice questions, which you're given 90 minutes to complete. That works out to 2.25 minutes per question. This section is worth 50 percent of your grade.

All the multiple-choice questions will have a similar format; each will be followed by five answer choices. At times, it may seem that there could be more than one possible correct answer. There is only one! Remember that the committee members who write these questions are statistics teachers. So, when it comes to statistics, they know how students think and what kind of mistakes they make. In order to trap you, answers resulting from common mistakes are often included in the five answer choices.

THE ANSWER SHEET

For the Multiple Choice section, you write the answers not in the test booklet but on a separate answer sheet (very similar to the ones we've supplied in this book). Five oval-shaped bubbles follow the question number, one for each possible answer. Don't forget to fill in all your answers on the answer sheet—don't just mark them in the test booklet. Marks in the test booklet will not be graded. Also, make sure that your filled-in answers correspond to the correct question numbers.

SHOULD YOU GUESS?

Your score on the Multiple Choice section will be computed as follows:

$$\frac{\text{Number of correctly answered questions} - \frac{1}{4}(\text{Number of incorrectly answered questions})}{\text{Your score on the Multiple Choice section}}$$

In other words, you get one point for every correct answer and lose 0.25 points for every wrong answer. For every answer you skip, you get 0 points. The penalty of 0.25 points for every wrong answer is the College Board's system to prevent you from guessing randomly.

Does this mean you should never guess? Absolutely not! Of course, bubbling in the answers at random isn't going to help. But you can use Process of Elimination (POE) to rule out answer choices you know are wrong and increase your chances of guessing the right answer. Read all the answer choices carefully. Eliminate the ones that you know are wrong. If you only have one answer choice left, choose it, even if you're not completely sure why it's correct. Remember: Questions are graded by a computer, so it doesn't care how you arrived at the correct answer.

If, however, you've eliminated an answer choice or two, but you still have more than one possibility, then go ahead and guess. Eliminating even one answer choice means that your odds of choosing the correct answer have improved to the point where guessing is to your advantage.

THE TWO-PASS SYSTEM

Remember that you have about two and a quarter minutes per question on this section of the exam. Do not waste time by lingering too long over any single question. If you're having trouble, move on to the next question. After you finish all the questions, you can come back to the ones you skipped.

The best strategy is to go through the Multiple Choice section twice. The first time, do all the questions that you can answer fairly quickly, the ones where you feel confident about the correct answer. On this first pass, skip the questions that seem to require more thinking, or the ones you need to read two or three times before you understand them. Circle the questions that you've skipped in the question booklet so that you can find them easily in the second pass. You must be very careful with the answer sheet by making sure the filled-in answers correspond to the correct questions.

Once you have gone through all the questions, go back to the ones that you skipped in the first pass. But don't linger too long on any one question even in the second pass. Spending too much time wrestling over a hard question can cause two things to happen: One, you may run out of time and miss out on answering easier questions in the later part of the exam. Two, your anxiety might start building up, and this could prevent you from thinking clearly and make answering other questions even more difficult. If a question is too hard, just skip it and move on to another. It's perfectly fine not to answer every question on the test. Many people do this and still get high scores.

CRACKING THE FREE RESPONSE SECTION

Section II is worth 50 percent of your grade on the AP Statistics exam. This section is composed of two parts. Part I contains five free-response questions; Part II contains one longer free-response question known as the "investigative task." You're given a total of 90 minutes for this section. It's recommended that you spend the first 65 minutes on the first five questions, and the next 25 minutes on the investigative task. The investigative task question is worth twice as much as each of the other free-response questions.

COMMUNICATION

Remember that your answers to the free-response questions are graded by readers and not by computers. Communication is a very important part of AP Statistics. Compose your answers in precise sentences. Just getting the correct numerical answer is not enough. You should be able to explain your reasoning behind the technique that you selected and communicate your answer in the context of the problem. Even if the question does not explicitly say so, always explain and justify every step of your answer, including the final answer. Do not expect the graders to read between the lines. Explain everything as though somebody with no knowledge of statistics were going to read it. Be sure to present your solution in a systematic manner, using solid logic and appropriate language. And remember: Though you won't earn points for neatness, the graders can't give you a grade if they can't read and understand your solution!

USE ONLY THE SPACE YOU NEED

Do not try to fill up the space provided for each question. The space given is usually more than enough. The people who design the tests realize that some students write in big letters and some students make mistakes and need extra space for corrections. So if you have a complete solution, don't worry about the extra space. Writing more will not earn you extra credit. In fact, many students tend to go overboard and shoot themselves in the foot by making a mistake after they've already written the right answer.

READ THE WHOLE QUESTION!

Each question might have several subparts. Try to answer them all, and don't give up on the question if one subsection is giving you trouble. For example, if the answer to part (b) depends on the answer to part (a), but you think you got the answer to part (a) wrong, you should still go ahead and do part (b) using your answer to part (a) as required. Chances are that the grader will not mark you wrong twice, unless it is obvious from your answer that you should have discovered your mistake.

Use Common Sense

Always use your common sense in answering questions. For example, on one free-response question that asked students to compute the mean weight of newborn babies from given data, some students answered 70 pounds. It should have been immediately obvious that the answer was probably off by a decimal point. A 70-pound baby would be a giant! This is an important mistake that should be easy to fix. Some mistakes may not be so obvious from the answer. However, the grader will consider simple, easily recognizable errors (e.g., giving negative probabilities) to be very important.

Concepts Versus Computations

The AP Statistics exam, and particularly the Free Response section, emphasizes the understanding and communication of concepts, rather than routine computation. If you show a clear understanding of why you have selected a particular technique and how you plan to use it, but you make some minor arithmetic mistake, then most likely the grader will not subtract points. Suppose, for example, in doing a t-interval problem, you defined the parameter of interest, justified why using the t-interval was appropriate in this case, and checked all the assumptions correctly. Then you showed the correct formula for the margin of error and made the correct substitutions. But in doing the computation, you reversed the digits of the answer, and got 1.61 instead of 1.16, as follows:

$$95\% \text{ ME} = t_{0.025}(14)\frac{S}{\sqrt{n}} = 2.145\left(\frac{2.1}{\sqrt{15}}\right) = 1.61$$

This mistake is not so obvious from the answer. So, you then went ahead and computed your interval correctly, using the above margin of error, to get 14.75 ± 1.61, which gives $(13.14, 16.36)$. And finally, you explained and interpreted the answer correctly. In this case, since everything else was done perfectly, most likely your arithmetic error would be ignored and you would still get full credit for the question.

On the other hand, imagine the following scenario. While computing the probability under the normal curve, you make a mistake and get the wrong answer. Say you compute

$$P(X > 20) = P\left(Z > \frac{20 - 15}{2}\right) = P(Z > 2.5)$$

Then, you look up the number in the normal table and find that the probability corresponding to 2.5 is 0.9938. But instead of subtracting this figure from 1, you subtract it from 0.5 and get the answer −0.4938. This mistake will not be ignored, because students are expected to know that a probability value is *always* between 0 and 1. If you get a negative value or a value larger than 1 for probability, you are expected to realize your mistake immediately. No matter how perfect the rest of the solution is, such an easily identifiable error will not be ignored.

Think Like a Grader

When answering questions try to think about what kind of answer the grader is expecting. Look at past free-response questions and grading rubrics on the College Board website (www.collegeboard.org/ap/statistics). These examples will give you some idea of how the answers should be phrased. The graders are told to keep in mind that there are two aspects to the scoring of free-response answers: showing statistical knowledge and communicating that knowledge. Again, responses should be written as clearly as possible, in complete sentences. You don't need to show all the steps of a calculation, but you must explain how you got your answer and why you chose the technique you used. The following tables are scoring guidelines that the College Board gives to free-response graders on the AP Statistics exam (remember that each question is scored from 0 to 4).

	Statistical Knowledge	Communication
	• Identify the important components of the problem • Demonstrate the statistical concepts and techniques that result in the correct solution of the problem	• Explain clearly what you did to get the solution to the problem and why you chose a particular method • Give a clear statement of your conclusions
Expect this score on the question	**If you do this...**	**and do this...**
4	• Through your answer, show that you understand the problem's different statistical components • Correctly analyze the relations among the different components of the problem • Correctly use the appropriate statistical techniques • Make sure all your answers are reasonable	• Clearly explain your entire solution, not just the final answer • Describe your reasoning in getting that solution, using the correct terminology • Use the required numerical or graphical aids to explain your solution • State and check all appropriate assumptions for the statistical techniques used in your solution • Give a reasonable and complete conclusion
3	• With some minor exceptions, show an almost complete understanding of the problem's different components • Analyze the relations among the different components of the problem, with a few gaps • Use the appropriate statistical techniques • Give fairly reasonable answers, but with some computational errors	• Provide a clear but incomplete explanation of your choice of statistical techniques • Give a less-than-perfectly-organized explanation of the steps leading to your solution • Neglect a few conditions necessary for the techniques you use • Use graphical and numerical techniques to help justify your solution • Give a reasonable but somewhat incomplete conclusion
2	• Show some understanding of the problem's statistical components • Have trouble relating the different components • Use some statistical techniques correctly but omit or misuse others • Make some computational mistakes that result in unreasonable answers	• Give a vague explanation of your solution • Use inappropriate terminology • Give an explanation that is difficult to interpret • Use incomplete or ineffective graphical methods to support your solution • Totally neglect to use graphical methods to support your solution
1	• Show a limited understanding of the problem's components • Fail to identify some important components • Have difficulty organizing your solution • Use irrelevant information in your solution • Use statistical techniques incorrectly • Fail to use statistical techniques • Make arithmetic mistakes that result in unreasonable answers	• Give little explanation of your solution or methods • Give an unclear explanation of your solution or methods • Give an explanation that does not match your solution • Fail to use diagrams or graphical methods • Use graphical methods incorrectly • Forget to write a conclusion • Give an incorrect conclusion
0	• Show little or no understanding of the problem's statistical components	• Provide no explanation of any legitimate solution

Using the Calculator

Below is a brief outline of how to use the TI-83 calculator. You may need to refer to this section as you work through the examples later in the book. This is not a complete list of the useful functions of TI-83, but it does cover the functions used most often in an AP Statistics course. You may want to refer to your TI-83 manual for more options.

The most commonly used statistical features of the TI-83 are the following:

STAT

When you press the STAT button, you are then given three different options: EDIT, CALC, and TESTS.

1. **EDIT:** You can access these procedures using STAT → EDIT.

   - **Edit:** Use this option to access lists (similar to a spreadsheet) to create a new list of data or edit an existing list of data. There are six default columns, labeled L1, L2, L3, L4, L5, and L6.

     To enter data in a list: Suppose the data to be entered is 3, 5, –2, 6. Enter the data in a list using the following steps. The data will be saved automatically.

     > - To **ENTER** data in a list, say, L1
     > - Choose **STAT → EDIT**
     > - Press **ENTER**
     > - In the list titled L1, type 3
     > - Press **ENTER**
     > - Type 5
     > - Press **ENTER**
     > - Type (–)2
     > - Press **ENTER**
     > - Type 6
     > - Press **ENTER**

     To create a new list: Suppose you want to create a new list, named NEW, in addition to the 6 default lists. Use the following steps.

     > - Suppose you want to create a list between, say, L1 and L2
     > - Choose **STAT → EDIT**
     > - Press **ENTER**
     > - Put the cursor at the title of list L2
     > - Press 2nd → INS *A new column will be added to the left of L2.*
     > - Use the ALPHA (green) key and alphabet keys to label new column
     > - Press **ENTER**

     To access a list of names: Use 2nd → LIST

   - **SortA(:** Use this option to sort data in a given list in ascending (increasing) order. The sorted data will be saved in the same list.

- Enter data in a list, say, L1
- Choose **STAT** → **EDIT** → **SortA(**
- Press **ENTER**
- Enter the list name and right parenthesis to read SortA(L1)
- Press **ENTER**

- **SortD(:** Use this option to sort data in a given list in descending (decreasing) order. The sorted data will be saved in the same list.

- Enter data in a list, say, L1
- Choose **STAT** → **EDIT** → **SortD(**
- Press **ENTER**
- Enter the list name and right parenthesis to read SortD(L1)
- Press **ENTER**

- **ClrList:** Use this option to clear all data in a given list. This option is not for deleting a partial list. To delete a partial list, use the DEL key. This action will delete all numbers in a given column, but note—the deletion is not reversible.

- Suppose data is in a list, say, L1
- Choose **STAT** → **EDIT** → **ClrList**
- Press **ENTER**
- Enter the list name to read ClrList L1
- Press **ENTER**

2. **CALC:** You can access these procedures using **STAT** → **CALC**.

Use this option to get one or two variable summary statistics, the correlation coefficient, linear regression coefficients (slope and y-intercept), and regression using transformed variables. The steps for using these procedures are provided in chapter 4.

1:1-Var Stats: Use this option to compute summary statistics for one-variable (univariate) data. It gives the number of observations (n), mean $\left(\overline{X}\right)$, sum $\left(\sum X\right)$, sum of squares $\left(\sum X^2\right)$, sample standard deviation (S), population standard deviation (σ), median, quartiles $\left(Q_1 \text{ and } Q_3\right)$, minimum, and maximum.

2:2-Var Stats: Use this option to compute summary statistics for bivariate data. It gives the number of pairs of observations (n), mean $\left(\overline{X} \text{ and } \overline{Y}\right)$, sum $\left(\sum X \text{ and } \sum Y\right)$, sum of squares $\left(\sum X^2 \text{ and } \sum Y^2\right)$, sample standard deviation $\left(S_x \text{ and } S_y\right)$, population standard deviation $\left(\sigma_x \text{ and } \sigma_y\right)$, min and max for each variable, and sum of products $\left(\sum XY\right)$.

8:LinReg(*a*+*bx*): Use this option to get the correlation coefficient and least squares estimates for slope and *y*-intercept for linear regression.

9:LnReg: Use this option for logarithmic transformation to linearize a regression model.

ExpReg: Use this option for exponential transformation to linearize a regression model.

PwrReg: Use this option for fitting a power model using logarithmic transformation to linearize a regression model.

3. **TESTS:** Access these procedures using STAT $\rightarrow$ TESTS.

Procedures for creating confidence intervals and testing hypotheses are located under this option. The steps for using these procedures are provided in chapter 7.

1:Z-Test: Use this for a one-sample *z*-test for population mean (known population variance).

2:T-Test: Use this for a one-sample *t*-test for a population mean (unknown population variance).

3:2-SampZTest: Use this for a *z*-test for the difference between two population means (independent samples).

4:2-SampTTest: Use this for a *t*-test for the difference between two population means (independent samples, unknown population variances—equal and unequal).

5:1-PropZTest: Use this for a large-sample *z*-test for a population proportion.

6:2-PropZTest: Use this for a large-samples *z*-test for the difference between two population proportions (independent samples).

7:Zinterval: Use this for a one-sample *z*-confidence interval for a population mean (known population variance).

8:Tinterval: Use this for a one-sample *t*-confidence interval for a population mean (unknown population variance).

9:2-SampZInt: Use this for a *z*-confidence interval for the difference between two population means (independent samples).

0:2-SampTInt: Use this for a *t*-confidence interval for the difference between two population means (independent samples, unknown population variances—equal and unequal).

A:1-PropZInt: Use this for a large-sample *z*-confidence interval for a population proportion.

B:2-PropZInt: Use this for a large-samples *z*-confidence interval for the difference between two population proportions (independent samples).

C: x^2 −Test: Use this for a chi-square test for independence of two categorical variables.

E:LinRegTTest: Use this for a *t*-test for the slope of least squares regression line.

MATH

Under MATH there are four options, but the PRB option is the only one you'll need for AP Statistics. The steps for using these procedures are listed in chapter 6.

1. **PRB:** Access these procedures using MATH → PRB

    3:nCr: Use this option to get combinations.

    5:randInt(: Use this option to generate a set of integer random numbers from a specified range.

    randInt (*lower limit, upper limit, numbers to generate*)

    6:randNorm(: Use this option to generate a set of random numbers from a specified normally distributed population.

    randNorm (*Mean, standard deviation, numbers to generate*)

    7:randBin(: Use this option to generate a set of random numbers from a binomial population.

    randBin (*n, p, numbers to generate*)

MATRX

Under MATRX there are three options. The NAMES and EDIT options are the ones you'll need to use.

1. **NAMES:** Access this option as MATRX → NAMES

    Use this option to read an already-created matrix—for example, a matrix of expected counts created by a chi-square test of independence.

- Choose **MATRX → NAMES**

A list of matrix names with their respective dimensions will be displayed.

- Use the up and down arrows to move up and down the list. Highlight the name of the matrix to be read

- Press **ENTER** *The name of the selected matrix will be pasted in the window.*

- Press **ENTER** *The matrix will be listed in the window.*

---

2. **EDIT:** Use this option to create a new matrix or edit an existing one.

    To create a new matrix: Suppose you want to create the following 2×3 matrix.

$$A = \begin{bmatrix} 20 & 5 & 30 \\ 10 & 15 & 25 \end{bmatrix}$$

- Choose **MATRX** → **EDIT**
  A list of matrix names with their respective dimensions will be displayed.

- Use the up and down arrows to move up and down the list. Highlight the name of the matrix to be created, say, 1: [A]

- Create the appropriate dimensions for the matrix 2 > > 3

- Press **ENTER**

- ENTER 20

- Press **ENTER**

- ENTER 5

- Press **ENTER**

- ENTER 30

- Press **ENTER**

- ENTER 10

- Press **ENTER**

- ENTER 15

- Press **ENTER**

- ENTER 25

- Press **ENTER**

DISTR

Procedures for computing probabilities and cumulative probabilities for different distributions are listed under this option. The steps for using these procedures are provided in chapter 6. Access these procedures using 2nd → DISTR.

> **2:normalcdf(:** Use this option to find the area under any normal curve in a given range specified by a lower limit and an upper limit.
>
> normalcdf (*lower limit, upper limit, mean, standard deviation*)
>
> **3:invNorm(:** Use this option to find a z-score corresponding to the specified area (*p*) less than that of the z-score.
>
> invNorm (*p, mean, standard deviation*)
>
> **5:tcdf(:** Use this option to find the area under the *t*-distribution—for example, if you need to find a *p*-value for a *t*-test.
>
> tcdf (*lower limit, upper limit, mean, degrees of freedom*)
>
> **7: x^2 −cdf(:** Use this option to find the area under the chi-square distribution—for example, when you need to find a *p*-value for a chi-square test.
>
> x^2 −cdf (*lower limit, upper limit, degrees of freedom*)

0:binompdf(: Use this option to find the binomial probability of a specific outcome. $P(x) = \binom{n}{x} p^x (1-p)^{n-x}$

$$\text{binompdf } (n, p, x)$$

A:binomcdf(: Use this option to find the cumulative binomial probability of a specified outcome. $P(x \le x_o) = \sum_{x=0}^{x_0} \binom{n}{x} p^x (1-p)^{n-x}$

$$\text{binomcdf } (n, p, x_0)$$

D:geometpdf(: Use this option to find the geometric probability of a specific outcome. $P(x) = p(1-p)^{x-1}$

$$\text{geometpdf } (p, x)$$

E:geometcdf(: Use this option to find the cumulative binomial probability of specified outcomes. $P(x \le x_0) = \sum_{x=1}^{x_0} p(1-p)^{x-1}$

$$\text{geometcdf } (p, x_0)$$

Diagnostics

Use this option to get the calculator to display values for the correlation coefficient and coefficient of determination when executing regression models. You need to turn diagnostics on only once; it will stay on until you turn the diagnostics off.

- Choose 2nd → Catalogue → DiagnosticOn

STAT PLOT

Use this option to make a scatterplot, boxplot, histogram, regression line plot, and residual plot. The steps for making these graphs are given in chapter 4.

TIPS ON USING THE CALCULATOR WELL

The calculator is a valuable tool, but many students lose points by using it improperly or relying on it too heavily. Note that though the TI-83 is currently the most popular calculator, there are many others out on the market. You do not know if the readers grading your exam will be familiar with your particular calculator. Also, remember that readers come from both high schools and colleges. While most high school statistics classes use calculators, many colleges do not require specific calculators in their courses. It's quite possible that your answers will be graded by people unfamiliar with statistical calculators. So, **do not use calculator talk.** Explain your answer in plain English, using the appropriate statistical terminology. Imagine you're faced with the following question:

1. Suppose the time 8-to-12-year-olds spend on playing video games per week is normally distributed, with a mean of 15 hours and a standard deviation of 2 hours. What percent of children spend more than 20 hours per week playing video games?

   - If your answer to this question is just the number "0.0062," you will probably not get credit. First, you did not describe your reasoning for getting this number. Second, you failed to communicate your answer appropriately. Third, the question asks for a *percentage*.

   - If your answer to this question is just the number "0.62%," with no further explanation or description of the steps you used to get this number, you might or might not get any credit for the answer. It depends on whether the passage above constitutes the entire question or just a sub-question of the question, and how the answer to this sub-question is related to other sub-questions.

   - If your answer to this question is "normalcdf (20, 2000, 15, 2) = 0.0062"—again, you should not expect to get credit. Those who are familiar with the functions of a TI-83 calculator will understand your answer, but non-users will not understand your answer. Other calculators, such as Casio or HP, have different formats. This is what statistics teachers refer to as "calculator talk." Statistics teachers and, more importantly, statistics graders, do not like calculator talk.

   - You should explain your answer as follows:

     Let X = the time spent by 8-to-12-year-olds per week on playing video games.

     Then, $P(X > 20) = P\left(Z > \dfrac{20 - 15}{2}\right) = P(Z > 2.5) = 0.0062$

     Therefore, about 0.62 percent of 8-to-12-year-olds spend more than 20 hours per week playing video games.

This will constitute a complete and well-communicated answer, without calculator talk.

Your work versus the calculator's work

Do not reproduce calculator output just as is. Do not describe how you entered numbers in the calculator, or your sequence of keystrokes. This will not give you any advantage. When using confidence intervals or hypotheses testing procedures, do not copy input or output from the calculator screen. For example, take the following problem:

1. A random sample of 15 8-to-12-year-olds was selected. All selected children were monitored for six months and the number of hours they spent playing video games was recorded. The mean number of hours they spent playing video games was 14.75, with a standard deviation of 2.1 hours. Estimate the true mean time that 8-to-12-year-olds spend playing video games per week using a 95 percent confidence level.

- You might be tempted to copy the following from your TI-83 calculator.

Tinterval	Tinterval
Inpt: Stats	(13.587, 15.913)
$\overline{X}$: 14.75	$\overline{X}$: 14.75
Sx: 2.1	Sx: 2.1
n: 15	n: 15
C-Level: 95	
Calculate	

Do not give in to temptation. This is calculator talk. It is not a complete answer to the question. It will not receive any credit beyond the credit allowed for arithmetic computations.

- Suppose you give the following answer:

$$95\% \text{ ME} = t_{0.025}(14)\frac{S}{\sqrt{n}} = 2.145\left(\frac{2.1}{\sqrt{15}}\right) = 1.16$$

$$14.75 \pm 1.16 \text{ gives } (13.59, 15.91)$$

This is better than calculator talk, but it is still an incomplete answer. It provides the correct mechanics, but fails to provide the proper communication. What is the parameter of interest here? Why was the t-interval used? Why is the t-interval appropriate in this situation? Are the conditions required for using the t-interval satisfied? What does the answer tell us in the context of the situation described? All those questions need to be answered. The above answer might get you credit for correct mechanics but nothing else. It might be worth 1 point out of 4.

- Refer to chapter 7 to review the steps leading to a complete answer for constructing a confidence interval and testing a hypothesis.

Showing graphs

If you make plots on your calculator for, say, checking the conditions for a certain procedure used to answer a question, be sure to do more than just say that the graph shows that the required conditions were met. The grader has no way of knowing what graph you made, what your graph looked like, why you think the conditions were met, or whether you even looked at a graph. Copy the graph from your calculator screen onto your answer sheet, so that the grader can see what it is that you looked at when arriving at your answer. Discuss how you used the graph to make a decision. Even if your answer is wrong, you might get partial credit for using the correct reasoning. For example, you'd probably lose points for using the wrong graph, but you might get some credit for drawing the correct conclusion from the wrong graph.

A FEW MORE TIPS

- **Units of measurements:** Include units in all your computations and answers. You will probably not lose points for missing units, but you might gain an advantage by showing them. AP Statistics exams are graded holistically. The grader will look at the whole question before assigning a grade, and every little bit helps.

- **Conflicting arguments:** Read your entire answer after finishing the question. If your explanation has any conflicting arguments, it will reveal a lack of understanding of the material, and you will most likely lose points.

- **Parallel solutions:** Do not give parallel solutions. For example, students often realize that a t-test is an appropriate procedure in a given situation, but do not know which t-test to use. So they try to play it safe by giving both solutions (the matched and the independent samples case, for example). This is not a good strategy. In the exam, both the solutions will be graded, and the one with the lower score will be counted.

PART **II**

SUBJECT REVIEW

4

EXPLORING DATA

EXPLORING DATA: OBSERVING PATTERNS AND DEPARTURES FROM PATTERNS

Statistics is a science of data. We all use data to estimate unknown quantities, to make decisions, and to develop and implement policies. To draw any sensible conclusions from collected data, we need to summarize the data or examine the patterns that it forms. This chapter will discuss graphical and numerical techniques used to study data. In the **Multiple Choice section**, this topic appears in 8 to 12 out of 40 questions. In the **Free Response section**, this topic appears in 1 to 2 out of 6 questions.

COLLECTING DATA

Who collects data and what do we do with collected data?

- Businesses collect data on their products and on consumer behavior. For example, they might use the collected data to determine the marketability of new products.

- Real estate agents collect data on market trends and on the availability of certain types of properties. They might use the collected data to identify popular locations for first-time homebuyers.

- Physicians collect diagnostic data on their patients. They might use collected data to identify the appropriate treatment for a patient.

- Law enforcement officials collect data on criminal behavior and the frequency of certain crimes. They might use the collected data to determine where to increase police patrols.

All too often, the data collected is not in a form useful for decision-making. For example, imagine a polling group was conducting a telephone survey to estimate the percent of state residents in favor of the governor's new proposal. Five interviewers called 1,800 residents over a period of five days and recorded the result for each resident as "supports" or "does not support." So at the completion of the survey, the polling group had a list of 1,800 responses listed as "supports" or "does not support." What conclusion can we draw from this list? Unfortunately, nothing—until somebody takes the time to organize it.

To use collected data, it needs to be organized and summarized. The different methods for doing this are known as **descriptive methods**. Different descriptive methods might result in different outcomes, leading to different conclusions. Descriptive methods are useful for data presentation, data reduction, and summarization. The best method depends on the type of data being collected.

TYPES OF DATA

There are two types of data: quantitative and qualitative.

Data is considered **quantitative** if it is numeric in nature, i.e., if the measurements or observations are numbers. The height of oak trees, the number of students present in class, the amount of money received as tips, and the amount of rainfall per year are all examples of quantitative data.

Data is considered **qualitative** or **categorical** if it can be classified into different groups or categories. Birth month, shirt size, choice of soft drink, color of eyes, type of job, and marital status are all examples of qualitative categories.

Sometimes data that is numeric in nature can also be categorical. For example, birth month, when recorded as January, February, etc., is obviously categorical. But when birth month is recorded using numbers, such as 1 (for January), 2 (for February), ... 12 (for December), its categorical nature is not obvious, but it is still a categorical variable taking numerical values.

Quantitative data is often converted into categorical data, in order to simplify recording or analysis. For example, if we want to analyze household annual incomes, instead of recording individual incomes, we might form the following groups: "below $10,000," "$10,000 - $24,999.99," "$25,000 - $49,999.99," "$50,000 - $100,000," and "above $100,000" and record the group to which each household belongs.

By taking only one measurement on each object we get **univariate data**. By taking two measurements on each object we get **bivariate data**.

For example, measuring the heights of a group of children will result in a univariate data set of the heights of the children. On the other hand, if we measure the height and the weight of each child, then we will get a bivariate data set consisting of the heights and weights of the children.

TYPES OF DESCRIPTIVE METHODS

We use different descriptive methods depending on the type of data collected. Descriptive methods are divided into three basic categories:

- Tabular methods
- Graphical methods
- Numerical methods

Different descriptive methods explore different characteristics of data. As a result, the outcome may be different for each method, leading to different conclusions. Different conclusions should not be misunderstood as contradictory conclusions. In general, we cannot look at data from all possible angles using only one method. So it's best to use more than one when we're summarizing a data set, even if the different methods produce some overlap of information.

TABULAR METHODS

Collected data is generally not in an easily analyzable form. Therefore, it needs to be rearranged before analysis. The frequency distribution table is an important tabular method that facilitates the analysis of patterns of variation among observed data. Typically, the letter n is used to denote the size of the data, i.e., the number of observations in a data set.

- The **frequency** of an observation in a data set is the number of times that observation occurs in the data set. Frequency is denoted using the letter f.

- The **relative frequency** of an observation in a set with n observations is the ratio of

   the frequency to the total number of observations. It is denoted by rf, and $rf = \dfrac{f}{n}$.

- The **cumulative frequency** gives the number of observations less than or equal to a specified value. It is denoted by cf.

A **frequency distribution table** is a table giving all possible values of the data and their frequencies. The data points can be reported in one of two manners: grouped or ungrouped. Additionally, other columns—such as relative frequency and cumulative frequency, or the midpoints of groups, etc.—may be added to the frequency distribution table as needed. If the data points are reported as they occurred, giving a list of all values, then the table is an **ungrouped** frequency distribution table. If the data points are grouped by some scheme into certain categories, also known as **classes**, then the table is a **grouped** frequency distribution table.

Each group or class is defined by two limits, an **upper limit** and a **lower limit**. The data points taking values below the upper limit and above the lower limit fall within the group. The value that is halfway between the two endpoints of the class is known as the **class-mark** or **midpoint.**

While grouping data, we must define groups so that the entire range of data is covered and so that there are no overlapping groups. For example, consider the following groups used by one teacher to assign letter grades on tests:

Letter grade	Score on test
A	90 and above
B	80-87
C	70-82
D	60-69
F	Below 60

What is wrong with this grouping scheme?

- No grade will be assigned to those who score 88 and 89 on the test. These scores seem to have been forgotten.

- Those who score 80, 81, and 82 will get a B as well as a C. This couldn't be right!

Try to avoid such follies while grouping data.

- Groups should be non-overlapping.

- There should be no gaps between groups. However, it is possible that no data will belong to a certain group. Then the frequency for that group will be 0.

- Groups should cover the entire range of data. No data points should be left out.

It is not essential that all groups be of equal length, as long as the concept of varying group length is taken into account when comparing different data sets and making decisions. But making all groups equal in length certainly makes comparisons and decision-making easier. For example, suppose three teachers are using the following schemes to assign letter grades:

Letter grade	Score on test		
	Teacher I	Teacher II	Teacher III
A	Above 90	Above 90	Above 90
B	80-89	75-89	75-89
C	70-79	60-75	60-75
D	60-69	40-60	40-60
F	Below 60	Below 40	Below 40

Note that grade distributions for Teachers I and II will not be comparable, since the teachers used different grouping schemes. Although Teachers II and III are using unequal group sizes, both of them are using the same grouping scheme. The grade distributions for Teachers II and III will be comparable.

Example 1: The Student Government Association (SGA) at a university was interested in the amount students spend per month on housing. Since students who live in dorms pay a fixed housing fee per semester, it was decided not to include those students in the study. The SGA selected a sample of students living off-campus and collected data on their housing type and on the amount they spent per month on housing. The collected information is listed in the table below. The columns titled "Exp" (for "Expenditure") give the amount each student spent per month on housing. The columns titled "Type" gives each student's type of housing, classified as:

A = Apartment   C = Condominium   H = House   T = Townhouse

Exp	Type	Exp	Type	Exp	Type	Exp	Type	Exp	Type	Exp	Type	Exp	Type	Exp	Type
304	C	323	H	529	T	482	A	406	H	628	T	259	C	330	A
342	A	350	A	358	A	423	A	440	H	333	A	424	H	595	C
437	A	349	A	278	A	530	A	384	H	327	A	529	H	383	C
446	A	384	H	482	H	404	H	391	T	581	A	466	H	437	C
362	C	394	A	270	A	393	A	501	T	398	T	834	T	416	C
552	H	296	C	462	H	450	C	550	T	516	T	558	A	351	T
411	C	435	A	503	A	364	T	306	T	478	T	332	C	385	T
330	C	334	A	367	A	264	A	450	H	358	H	317	H	376	T
673	H	525	T	353	H	276	A	309	C	439	H	430	A	408	C
309	H	391	A	760	A	297	T	255	T	377	A	282	T	385	A

Table 1: Housing expenditure and type of housing data

Of course, all these numbers are useless unless we rearrange and summarize them in a meaningful fashion. Note that the data was collected for two variables, namely, type of housing and housing expenditure per month. Type of housing is a categorical variable, and housing expenditure is a quantitative variable.

The frequency distribution table for housing expenditure is as follows:

Housing Expenditure	Frequency f	Relative Frequency $rf = f/n$	Percentage $100\ rf$	Cumulative Frequency cf
250-299	9	0.11	11	9
300-349	14	0.17	17	23
350-399	20	0.25	25	43
400-449	14	0.17	17	57
450-499	7	0.09	9	64
500-549	7	0.09	9	71
550-599	5	0.06	6	76
600-649	1	0.01	1	77
650-699	1	0.01	1	78
700-749	0	0.00	0	78
750-799	1	0.01	1	79
800-849	1	0.01	1	80

Table 2: Frequency distribution for housing expenditure

Note that

- The housing expenditures are grouped into different classes. For the class "400-449," the number 400 defines the lower limit and the number 449 defines the upper limit.

- All classes are of length equal to 50.

- The class-mark is the halfway point for each class. For class "400-449," the class-mark is 424.5.

- The numbers in the frequency column add up to the total number of observations, $n = 80$.

- The numbers in the relative frequency column add up to 1. If there is a rounding-off error, the total may be slightly off, but it still should be very close to 1.

- The numbers in the percentage column add up to 100. If there is a rounding-off error, the total may not be exactly 100, but it should be very close.

- The last entry in the cumulative frequency column is equal to the total number of observations, $n = 80$.

We can interpret the numbers in this table as follows:

- The frequency for group 300-349 is 14. This means that 14 students from those interviewed spend $300 to $349 per month on housing.

- The relative frequency for group 300-349 is 0.17 and the percentage is 17. This means that 17 percent of students interviewed spend $300 to $349 per month on housing.

- The cumulative frequency for group 300-349 is 23. This means that 23 of the students interviewed spend less than or equal to $349 per month.

The frequency distribution table for housing type is as follows:

Type of Housing	Frequency f	Relative Frequency $rf = f/n$	Percentage $100\ rf$
Apartment	29	0.36	36
Condominum	14	0.18	18
House	19	0.24	24
Townhouse	18	0.23	23

Table 3: Frequency distribution for housing type

Again, note that

- The figures in the frequency column add up to the total number of observations, $n = 80$.

- The figures in the relative frequency column add up to 1. If there is a rounding-off error, the total may not be exactly 1, but it should be very close.

- The figures in the percentage column add up to 100. If there is a rounding-off error, the total may not be exactly 100, but it should be very close.

- For this categorical variable, there is no specific ordering of values. So, cumulative frequency is meaningless.

We can interpret the numbers in this table as follows:

- The frequency for Apartment is 29. This means that 29 of the students interviewed live in apartments.

- The relative frequency for Apartment is 0.36 and the percentage is 36. This means that 36 percent of students interviewed live in apartments.

GRAPHICAL METHODS

Presenting data in tables, as we did above, is not always useful and may fail to convey the message we want. A more appealing way to communicate is through graphs and charts. With today's technology, it has become much easier to generate useful charts and graphs. To summarize and describe qualitative data, bar charts and pie charts are particularly useful. To summarize and describe quantitative data, dotplots, boxplots, histograms, stemplots, and cumulative frequency charts are often employed. Time series plots are used to summarize data collected over time.

EXAMINING GRAPHS

We can describe the overall pattern of the distribution of a data set using the following three terms:

- The **center** of a distribution describes the point around which the data points are spread.

- The **spread** of a distribution describes how the data points are spread, using the range of data values and the vastness or narrowness of the spread.

- The **shape** of a distribution can be classified in a few different ways. Some distributions have simple shapes; others are more irregular. Some basic distribution shapes are described using the idea of symmetry.

  Symmetric distribution: If one half of the distribution is approximately a mirror image of the other half, then the distribution is described as symmetric. In other words, a symmetric distribution has the same number of observations on its greater half as it does on its lesser half. The distribution of scores on a fair exam is generally symmetric.

  Left-skewed distribution: If the lesser half of the distribution extends further out than its greater half, then the distribution is described as left-skewed. In other words, a left-skewed distribution has a longer left tail than right tail. There are more observations with higher values than there are with lower values. The distribution of scores on an easy exam is generally left-skewed, because there will be more students with higher scores and fewer with lower scores.

  Right-skewed distribution: If the greater half of a distribution extends further out than its lesser half, then the distribution is described as right-skewed. In other words, a right-skewed distribution has a longer right tail than left tail. The distribution of scores on a difficult test is generally right-skewed, because there will be more students with lower scores and fewer with higher scores.

The following three graphs show the three basic shapes of distributions:

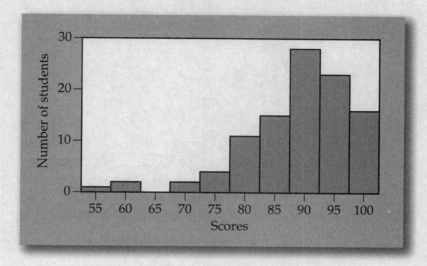

Figure 1: Left-skewed distribution

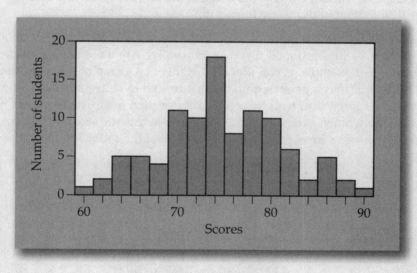

Figure 2: Symmetric distribution

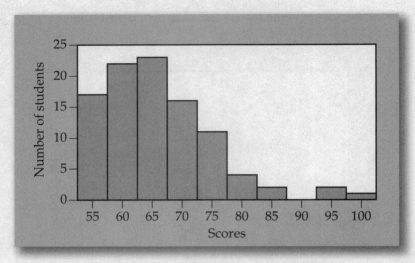

Figure 3: Right-skewed distribution

Patterns and deviations from patterns

When examining data, we should look for the overall pattern of the data and for striking deviations from the pattern. The following terms are important:

- **Clusters and gaps**: It's important to describe any significant data clusters and gaps. Are any observations grouped together unusually? Are there any significant gaps in the data? For example, if you plot the heights of a group of students, the plot is likely to peak at two separate points, with a trough in between. The reason for this is that women in general tend to be a bit shorter than men. The first peak corresponds to the women's most common height, whereas the second peak corresponds to the men's most common height. Look at the following figure:

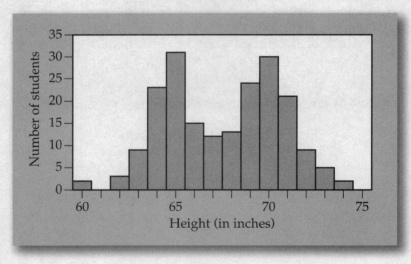

Figure 4: Distribution of student heights

- **Outliers**: An outlier is an observation that is different from the rest of the data. For example, imagine a class in which most of the students scored between 60 and 98 on a test. But one student scored 18. This score is an outlier, because it's so much different from most of the others. In a distribution of the salary of employees of any company, the salary of the highest official is typically an outlier. Consider the following distribution, which shows the salaries of employees at one company.

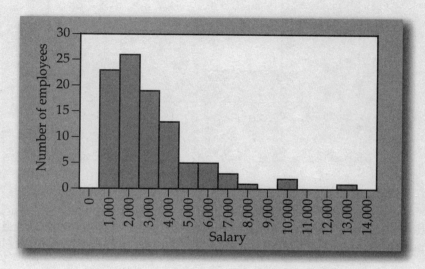

Figure 5: Distribution of salaries

Note that the distribution is highly skewed. A few employees on the higher end earn much more than the rest of the employees. Those higher observations are outliers, since they deviate so much from the rest.

GRAPHICAL METHODS FOR CATEGORICAL DATA: BAR CHART AND PIE CHART

Bar charts

Bar charts are very common. Economists use them to display financial data. The business section of any newspaper usually has at least one bar chart. A bar chart can have either horizontal or vertical bars. Bar charts look very similar to histograms (see below), but are used only for categorical data.

This is how to make one:

- Draw horizontal X and vertical Y axes.

- On the horizontal axis, mark the categories of the variable at equal intervals.

- Scale the vertical axis in order to plot frequencies, relative frequencies, or percentages.

- Note that the above two lines would give a vertical bar chart. For a horizontal bar chart, transpose the X-axis and Y-axis.

- For each category, draw a bar whose height (or whose length, for horizontal bars) is equal to the data plotted, frequency, relative frequency, percentage, etc.

Example 2: Create a bar chart summarizing the data on housing type in Table 1.

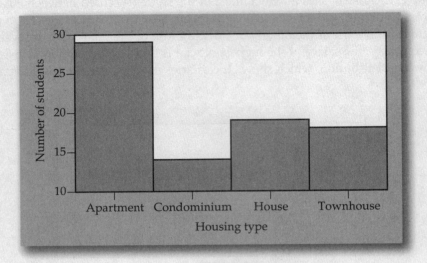

Figure 6: Bar chart for type of housing data

The bar chart above clearly shows that an apartment is the most popular type of accommodation among these students. There's not much difference in preference between houses and townhouses, with houses leading townhouses by a narrow margin. The least number of students live in condominiums.

How do we read a bar chart?

- Each bar indicates a different category.

- The height of a frequency bar chart indicates how often that category occurred in the data set. For example, the first bar in the above bar chart corresponds to "apartment." The height of this graph can be read off of the vertical axis as 29. This means that 29 students out of all those interviewed live in apartments.

Pie chart

A pie chart displays the groups formed by a data set. It is commonly used to describe the different spending categories of a budget, for example. Businesses use pie charts to display the various components of their entire production output. For example, a paper company producing copying paper, notebook paper, trifolds, etc., could use a pie chart to describe what proportion of its entire production is made up by each of these products.

This is how to make a pie chart:

- Prepare a frequency distribution table.

- Compute the percentages for each category.

- Equate one percentage point to an angle of 3.6 degrees. For each category compute Angle = 3.6 × percentage.

- Draw a circle of the desired size and then draw one radius within the circle to be used as a starting point.

- Form "slices" of the pie with sizes equal to the corresponding angles computed earlier.

- Go all the way around the circle.

Example 3: Create a pie chart summarizing the housing type data in Table 1.

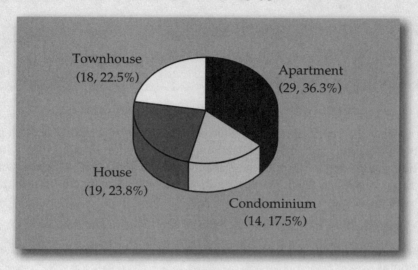

Figure 7: Pie chart for housing type

This pie chart shows clearly that the highest percent of students live in apartments.
How do we read a pie chart?

- Each piece of the pie corresponds to one category.

- The category corresponding to the largest piece is the one that occurs most often.

GRAPHICAL METHODS FOR QUANTITATIVE DATA: DOTPLOT, STEMPLOT, HISTOGRAM, CUMULATIVE FREQUENCY CHART, AND TIME SERIES PLOT

Dotplots

This is one of the easiest plots to make, but it's most effective for smaller data sets. If the data set is too large, then the dotplot will be very cluttered. For large data sets, it's best to group the data and create a histogram.

This is how to make a dotplot:

- Draw a horizontal line (the X-axis) to indicate the data range.

- Scale the line to accommodate the entire range of data.

- Mark a dot for each observation in the appropriate place above the scaled line.

- If more than one observation has the same value, then add dots one above the other.

Example 4: Create a dotplot for the housing expenditure data in Table 1.

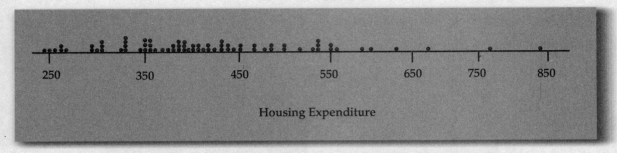

Figure 8: Dotplot for the housing expenditure data

This dotplot shows that the distribution of housing expenditure is right-skewed, with possibly a few outliers on the higher end, i.e., a few students paying a lot more for housing than what most of the others spend. The expenditures ranged from $250 a month to almost $850 a month, with most of the amounts in the range of $250 to $550. The distribution is centered around $425 a month.

How do we read a dot plot?

- Each dot on the plot indicates the location of the value of the data point.

- For any data point, we can look directly down at the scale to determine the value of the point.

We can use the dotplot to determine:

- How the data points are spread.

- What kind of shape the points make collectively.

- Where the center of the distribution is—in other words, where this picture of dots is likely to balance if it were held on an outstretched finger.

Stemplots

Stemplots, also known as stem-and-leaf plots, are also commonly used. When turned on its side, a stemplot resembles a histogram. One advantage of using a stemplot is that it preserves the identity of each data point, but for very large data sets a stemplot is inconvenient to use.

This is how to make a stemplot:

- Separate each observation into two parts. The left-most part of each observation is called the **stem** and the remaining part is called the **leaf**. There is no definite rule for determining where to make the division. Use a scheme that gives a reasonable number of stems. Too few stems can distort the picture by hiding patterns, while too many stems can distort the picture by diluting patterns. For example, if you have a sample of 80 numbers between 1 and 99, you may want to divide the data into groups of 10. So for stems, you might choose the first digit of each number in the sample (0,1,2,3,4,5,6,7,8,9). If the sample was of 80 numbers between 1 and 49, you might want to make 10 stems by writing in the first digit of every number twice (0,0,1,1,2,2,3,3,4,4). The first occurrence of each 1 would be the stem for all numbers from 10 to 14; the second occurrence of each 1 would be the stem for all numbers between 15 and 19. The first occurrence of each 2 would be the stem for all numbers from 10 to 14; the second occurrence of each 2 would be the stem for all numbers between 15 and 19; and so on.

- Draw a vertical line more toward the left side of the page to separate the stems from the leaves.

- Write all possible stems in increasing order on the left of the line, making sure that the entire range of the data is covered.

- For each observation, write in the leaf to the right of the corresponding stem, on the right side of the vertical line.

- Write in all leaves for the same stem in sequence.

Example 5: Create a stemplot for the housing expenditure data in Table 1.

Stemplot of housing expenditure data
N = 80   Leaf Unit = 10

Stem	Leaves
2	556777899
3	0000122233334444
3	5555666778888899999
4	000112233333344
4	566788
5	00122224
5	5589
6	2
6	7
7	
7	6
8	3

Figure 9: Stemplot for the housing expenditure data

This stemplot shows that the distribution of housing expenditure is right-skewed, with possibly a few outliers on the higher end. The expenditures ranged from $250 a month to almost $850 a month, with most of the amounts in the range of $250 to $550 per month. The distribution is centered around approximately $425 a month.

How do we read a stemplot?

- The numbers on the left of the vertical line are stems, one for each class or group of data. In this stemplot, notice that there are two 3s and two 4s and so on. The first of each pair of stems corresponds to the lower half of a group of each hundred dollars spent per month and the second stem of the pair corresponds to the higher half of each hundred. For example, in the pair of 5s, the first 5 corresponds to the expenditure between $500 and $549 per month, while the second 5 corresponds to the expenditure between $550 and $599 per month.

- The numbers on the right of the vertical line are leaves. Each stem has a different number of leaves, indicating the frequency of that class. For example, stem 2 has nine leaves, which means nine observations belong to this stem. In other words, nine students pay $250-$299 per month for housing.

- Each leaf indicates a single observation. Four leaves with value 0 on stem 3 indicate that four students spend $300-$309 per month on housing.

- The lower stem 7 has no leaves. It means that no interviewed student pays between $700 and $749 per month for housing.

We can use the stemplot to determine:

- How all the leaves are spread. To do this, we might turn the graph on its side, with the stems at the bottom.

- What kind of shape the leaves make collectively.

- Where the center of this data set is—in other words, where this picture of stems and leaves would balance if it were turned on its side, with the stems at the bottom, and held on an outstretched finger.

Histograms

This is probably the most popular form of displaying data. It looks like a stemplot on its side. Unlike the stemplot and dotplot, the histogram is useful for displaying large data sets. For very small data sets, however, a histogram might fail to show a pattern, so a dotplot or stemplot would be more appropriate.

Another disadvantage of the histogram is that, due to grouping, the pattern of data within each group is lost. For example, suppose the frequency of a letter grade A (score 90 and above) is 18. From a histogram it would not be possible to tell how the grades of those 18 students are spread within the range of 90 to 100. All of them could be at 90, or all could be at 100, or they could be evenly spread from 90 to 100. Once grouped, data points lose their individuality.

A histogram can be drawn for ungrouped as well as grouped data. It can use categories such as frequencies, relative frequencies, and percentages.

This is how to make one:

- Create groups of equal length.

- Draw the X-axis and the Y-axis.

- Scale the X-axis to accommodate all the data groups.

- Scale the Y-axis to accommodate the range of frequencies used (or relative frequencies, or percentages).

- Draw bars of heights equal to the corresponding frequencies (or relative frequencies, or percentages) and add a label for each group. Draw the bars next to each other, without any gaps.

Example 6: Create a histogram to describe the housing expenditure data in Table 1.

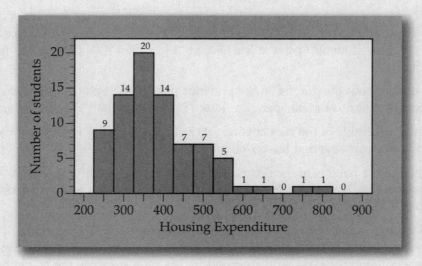

Figure 10: Frequency histogram of housing expenditure data

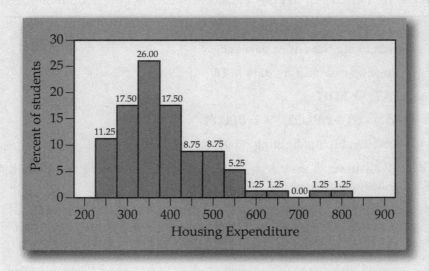

Figure 11: Percent histogram of housing expenditure data

Both these graphs show that the distribution of housing expenditure is right-skewed. In other words, more students spend lower amounts for housing, while fewer students pay higher amounts for housing. The expenditures ranged from about $250 per month to $850 per month. The expenditures seem to be centered around $350 per month.

How do we read a histogram?

- Each bar represents a different group or class. There is only one bar for each class.

- The classes are placed on the X-axis in numerically increasing order, just like on a number line.

- The height of a bar in a frequency histogram corresponds to the frequency of that class. For example, the height of the first bar of Figure 10 is equal to 9. This indicates that nine students spend at least $250 but less than $300 per month on housing.

- Note that on both the graphs on the previous page, there's one gap with no bar. This means that no student spends at least $700 but less than $750 on housing.

- The total of heights of the bars beyond 700 in Figure 10 is $0 + 1 + 1 = 2$. This means that two students spend at least $700 per month on housing.

- The total of the heights of the second and third bars in Figure 10 is $14 + 20 = 34$. This means that 34 students spend at least $300, but less than $400, per month on housing.

- Percentage frequency or relative frequency histograms can be read similarly. In a relative frequency histogram, the height of the bar reflects the relative frequency corresponding to the class. In the percent frequency histogram, the height of the bar reflects the percent frequency that corresponds to the class.

You can also use your calculator to draw a histogram. Here's how to do it on the TI-83.

TI-83:
Making a histogram using the entire data set:

- Enter the housing expenditure data in L1

- Choose **STAT** → **EDIT**

- Choose **2nd** → **STAT PLOT** → 1: **PLOT1**

- Turn the plot1 On by highlighting it (selecting it)

- Out of six available choices, select "histogram" by highlighting the figure that looks like a histogram

- Enter Xlist: L1

- Enter Freq: 1

  (a) To let calculator determine classes:

- Choose **ZOOM** → 9: **ZOOMSTAT** → **TRACE** >>
  (b) To use classes of your choice:

- Choose **WINDOW**

- Enter the required numbers in the window

  WINDOW
  Xmin = 250
  Xmax = 850
  Xscl = 50 (group width)

Ymin = -1
Ymax = 20 (highest frequency)
Yscl = 1 (depends on frequency)
Xres = 1

- Choose **GRAPH** → **TRACE**

Making a histogram from a frequency distribution table:

- Enter class midpoints into L1

- Enter frequencies into L2

- Choose **2nd** → **STAT PLOT** → 1: **PLOT1**

- Turn the plot1 On by highlighting the figure that looks like a histogram

- Out of six available choices, select "histogram" by highlighting it

- Enter Xlist: L1

- Enter Freq: L2

- Choose **WINDOW**

- Enter the required numbers in the window

  WINDOW
  Xmin = *enter minimum value*
  Xmax = *enter maximum value*
  Xscl = *enter group width*
  Ymin = -1
  Ymax = *enter highest frequency*
  Yscl = 0 (for no occurences)
  Xres = 1

- Choose **GRAPH** → **TRACE**

Cumulative frequency chart

The cumulative frequency for any group is the frequency for that group plus the frequencies of all groups of smaller observations. The cumulative frequency chart is also known as the **Ogive Chart**. A cumulative frequency chart is typically *S*-shaped.

Here's how to draw cumulative distribution charts:

- Draw the X-axis and the Y-axis.

- Scale the X-axis to accommodate the range of all groups.

- Scale the Y-axis from 0 to *n* for a cumulative frequency chart (from 0 to 1 for a relative cumulative frequency chart and from 0 to 100 for a percentage cumulative frequency chart).

- On the X-axis, mark the upper boundary of each group.

- Place a marker at the height equal to the cumulative frequency for that group above the upper boundary for each group. Connect all the markers.

Example 7: Create a cumulative frequency chart to describe the housing expenditure data in Table 1.

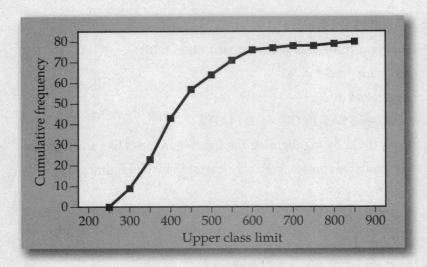

Figure 12: Cumulative frequency chart for the housing data

Note that the line's steep climb in the beginning combined with its tapering off at the higher end of the graph indicates that the distribution is right-skewed.

How do we read a cumulative frequency chart?

- From any point on the graph, we can draw a vertical line to read the X-value from the X-axis and a horizontal line to read the Y-value from the Y-axis. For example, take the third point from the bottom. Draw a vertical line to read X. It's about 350. Then draw a horizontal line to read Y. It's about 23 or 24. This tells us that about 23 (or 24) students spend less than $350 per month on housing.

- Since a total of 80 students were interviewed, we can also say that about 80 − 23 = 57 (or 80 − 24 = 56) students spend at least $350 per month on housing.

- The steepness of the line is an indicator of the shape of the distribution. Refer to the following graph, which shows cumulative frequency lines for left-skewed, symmetric, and right-skewed distributions. Note that for the right-skewed distribution, the curve increases quickly in the beginning but then steadies in the later part. For the left-skewed distribution, the curve increases slowly in the beginning, but then steeply later on.

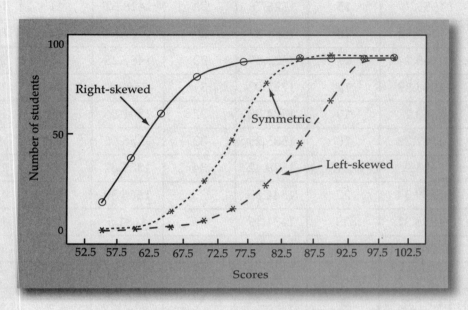

Figure 13: Comparison of cumulative frequency charts

Time series plot

Sometimes data is collected over a specified time period. For example, we might measure the amount of profit per month for the last financial year, the daily temperatures for the last five years, the number of students present in class every day for a month, etc. A plot of such data to show changes in a certain variable over time is known as a time series plot.

Here's how to make one:

- Draw the X-axis and the Y-axis.
- Scale the X-axis to accommodate the range of time in the study.
- Scale the Y-axis to accommodate the range of measurements collected.
- Plot the data in the sequence in which it was collected over time, and then connect the points.

Example 8: The owner of a small store is interested in the store's revenue trend over the last year. She collects weekly revenue data from her records. The data is given below.

Week	Revenue	Week	Revenue	Week	Revenue	Week	Revenue
1	1436.33	14	1309.14	27	1475.74	40	1462.19
2	1559.7	15	1526.76	28	1418.67	41	1490.28
3	1482.52	16	1588.37	29	1431.63	42	1623.12
4	1648.14	17	1623.49	30	1460.25	43	1676.18
5	1596.39	18	1732.92	31	1595.1	44	1579.41
6	1360.2	19	1574.98	32	1501.56	45	1421.73
7	1717.28	20	1585.25	33	1456.46	46	1378.4
8	1615.9	21	1579.42	34	1383.87	47	1327.11
9	1559.34	22	1544.85	35	1666.59	48	1611.77
10	1898.31	23	1431.19	36	1681.5	49	1530.62
11	1781.11	24	1559.41	37	1586.48	50	1419.27
12	1306.31	25	1342.61	38	1750.58	51	1377.12
13	1388.8	26	1452.74	39	1339.98	52	1504.47

Table 4: Revenue generated per week

Make a time series plot for this data.

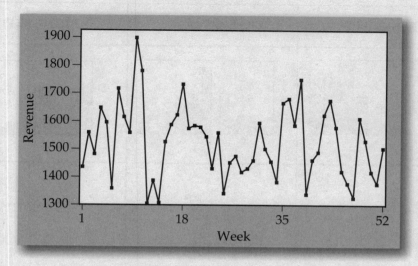

Figure 14: Time series plot of revenue generated per week

This plot shows that, in general, the revenue is fluctuating. It increased for the first 10 weeks and then dropped suddenly. The revenue for the next three weeks was low, but picked up steadily until about the 18th week. After that, the revenue fluctuated a lot, with a slight downward trend.

How do we read a time series plot?

- The horizontal axis gives the sequence of events.

- The position of each point is evaluated relative to the position of adjoining points.

The table on the following page shows different graphs summarizing the scores of students on an easy exam, a fair exam, and a difficult exam. Examine the graphs carefully to see how the symmetry or the skewedness affects the shape of the different types of graphs. If you know how symmetric or skewed distributions look, then you can determine the nature of the distribution by examining the graphs. Note that box plots are discussed later in this chapter.

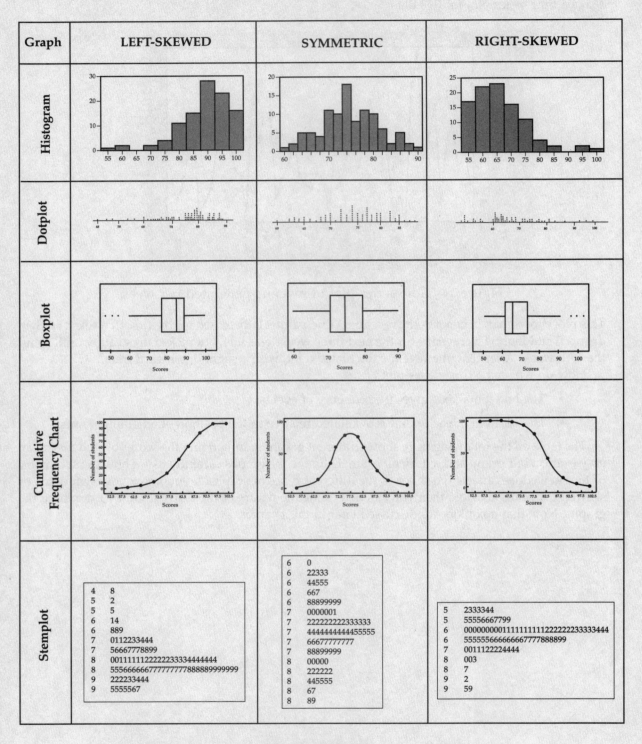

Table 5: Comparison of shapes for different graphs

SUMMARIZING DISTRIBUTIONS OF UNIVARIATE DATA

First, two important terms: The **population** is the entire group of individuals in a study. The **sample** is the part of the population that is actually studied.

For example, when a shopper buys a bag of a dozen oranges, he might squeeze one or two to determine how fresh they are. In this case, the entire bag of oranges constitutes the population, and the one or two oranges inspected constitute the sample.

GRAPHICAL SUMMARIES

Graphical summary measures are a good way of conveying information. But they are also very subjective. Two researchers can take the same data and convey completely different messages just by manipulating the layout of a graph. So, you have to be careful when reading graphs.

The following two graphs display a business's revenue in the last calendar year.

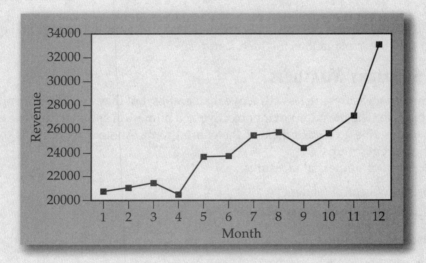

Figure 15: Revenue generated over one calendar year

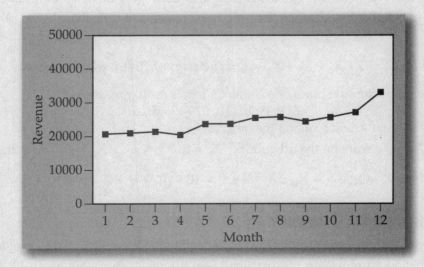

Figure 16: Revenue generated over one calendar year

- The first graph gives the impression that the revenue increased dramatically over the last calendar year.

- The second graph gives the impression that the revenue increased steadily but only slightly.

A closer inspection of the scale on the Y-axis tells a different story. Both the graphs are displaying *exactly the same revenue data*. The only difference is that one has a more extended scale than the other. But the impressions, they leave with the viewer are totally distinct.

When examining a graphical summary of univariate data, use the following three measures to describe the data:

- Center

- Spread

- Shape

In addition, you should always note any clustering of data, any gaps in the data, and any outliers. If possible, try to provide explanations for such features.

NUMERICAL SUMMARY MEASURES

Numerical summary measures are less attractive than graphs, but they are also more reliable because they're less subjective. The most important objective of a numerical summary measure is to provide a single value to describe a characteristic of the entire group. Another objective is to facilitate the comparison of different groups.

There are three types of numerical measures:

- Measures of central tendency

- Measures of variation (spread)

- Measures of position

REVIEW OF SUMMATION NOTATION

A Greek capital letter Σ (read as "Sigma") is used to indicate the sum of a set of measurements. For example, if we denote the first through the fifth measurements of something by $X_1, X_2, X_3, X_4, X_5,$ then

$$\sum_{i=1}^{5} X_i = X_1 + X_2 + X_3 + X_4 + X_5 = \text{the sum of first 5 measurements}$$

Example 9: The following list shows one student's scores on 10 quizzes.

$$8, 9, 0, 10, 10, 8, 7, 9, 10, 5$$

What is this student's total score on the quizzes?

Solution: Let X_i = the score on the ith quiz. So $X_1 = 8$, $X_2 = 9$, ... $X_{10} = 5$. Then, the total score is

$$\sum_{i=1}^{10} X_i = X_1 + X_2 + \cdots + X_{10} = 8 + 9 + 0 + 10 + 10 + 8 + 7 + 9 + 10 + 5 = 76$$

MEASURES OF CENTRAL TENDENCY

Measures of central tendency determine the central point of a set of data, or the point around which all the measurements are scattered. The two main measures of central tendency are the mean and the median.

Mean: The arithmetic mean (often called the **average**) is the most commonly used measure of the center of a set of data. The mean can be described as a data set's center of gravity, the point at which the whole group of data balances. Unlike the median, the mean is affected by extreme or outlier measurements. One very large or very small measurement can pull the mean up or down.

- The population mean is denoted by Greek letter μ (read as "mu"). It is computed

  as $\mu = \dfrac{\sum\limits_{i=1}^{N} X_i}{N}$ where N = the number of measurements in the population.

- The sample mean is generally denoted by an English letter with a bar on top, such as $\overline{X}$ (read as 'X bar') or $\overline{Y}$ (read as 'Y bar'). It is computed as $\overline{X} = \dfrac{\sum\limits_{i=1}^{n} X_i}{n}$

  where n = the number of measurements in the sample.

Median: The median is another commonly used measure of central tendency. The median is the point at which half of the measurements have a value at or below the median, and half have a value at or above the median. The median is not affected by outlier measurements. Therefore, for skewed data sets or data sets containing outliers, it's best to use the median rather than the mean to measure the center of the data.

Let's denote the median as M. Use the following steps to determine the median:

- Suppose there are n measurements in a data set.

- Arrange the measurements in increasing order of value, i.e., from smallest to largest.

- Compute $l = \dfrac{n+1}{2}$

- Then the median M = the value of the lth measurement.

Note that if the data set contains an odd number of measurements, then the median belongs to the data set. But if the data set contains an even number of measurements, then the median does not belong to the data set. It is instead the mean of the middle two measurements. For example, if a data set contains five measurements, then the median is the third smallest (or third largest) measurement. But if the data set contains six measurements, then the median is the mean of the third smallest and the fourth smallest measurements.

MEASURES OF VARIATION

Measures of variation (or "measures of spread") summarize the spread of a data set. They describe how measurements differ from each other and/or from their mean. The three most commonly used measures of variation are range, interquartile range, and standard deviation.

Range: The range is the difference between the largest and the smallest measurement in a data set.

$$R = \text{Range} = \text{Largest measurement} - \text{smallest measurement}$$

Range is the simplest of the measures of spread, and is very easy to compute and understand. But it is not a reliable measure, since it depends only on two extreme measurements and does not take into account the values of the remaining measurements.

Interquartile range: The interquartile range (IQR) is the range of the middle 50 percent of the data, the difference between the third quartile (Q_3) and the first quartile (Q_1). (Quartiles are defined below under measures of position.)

$$IQR = Q_3 - Q_1$$

Interquartile range is not affected by outliers.

Standard deviation: Standard deviation is a better measure of variation than range is. Unlike range, standard deviation takes into account each and every measurement. The square of the standard deviation is known as variance.

- A lower case Greek letter σ (read as 'sigma') is used to denote a population standard deviation. So σ^2 denotes a population variance. The population standard deviation is defined as

$$\sigma = \sqrt{\frac{\sum_{i=1}^{N}(X_i - \mu)^2}{N}}$$

- The letter S is used to denote a sample standard deviation. So S^2 denotes a sample variance. The sample standard deviation is defined as

$$S = \sqrt{\frac{\sum_{i=1}^{n}(X_i - \overline{X})^2}{n-1}}$$

To avoid problems with rounding off errors, use the equivalent computational form.
Computational form of sample standard deviation:

$$S = \sqrt{\frac{\sum_{i=1}^{n} X_i^2 - \frac{\left(\sum_{i=1}^{n} X_i\right)^2}{n}}{n-1}}$$

Where

$\sum_{i=1}^{n} X_i^2$ = Sum of the squared observations (square each observation and add).

$\left(\sum_{i=1}^{n} X_i\right)^2$ = Square of the sum of the observations (add all observations and then square the sum).

Note that $\sum_{i=1}^{n} X_i^2 \neq \left(\sum_{i=1}^{n} X_i\right)^2$ in general. A simple example can demonstrate this.

Let $X_1 = 8$, $X_2 = 9$, and $X_3 = 5$.
Then

$$\sum_{i=1}^{n} X_i^2 = 8^2 + 9^2 + 5^2 = 64 + 81 + 25 = 170 \text{ and } \left(\sum_{i=1}^{n} X_i\right)^2 = (8+9+5)^2 = 22^2 = 484$$

- Note that standard deviation is measured in the same units as data values are measured in, while variance is measured in squared units of the data values. For example, suppose the standard deviation of a set of housing expenditure data is 110 and the variance is 12,100. The associated units of measurement would be the following: standard deviation $S = 110$ dollars, and variance $S^2 = 110^2 = 12,100$ squared dollars (or dollars 2).

- Standard deviation is used as a measure of distance between any measurement and the mean of the data set. For example, a measurement can be described as being so many standard deviations above or below the mean. (See the discussion of z-scores, below).

- A standard deviation (or variance) of 0 indicates no change in the measurements. For example, if a student scores 8, 8, 8, and 8 on all four quizzes, then the standard deviation of the scores is 0.

- Standard deviation is the positive square root of variance. Since variance is a squared quantity, it is *always* a positive number. So if your computation gives you a negative value for variance, go back and check your work.

- A larger standard deviation (and consequently, variance) indicates a larger spread among the measurements. For example, two students score the following on their quizzes:

Student A: 8, 9, 4, 8, 6, 8, 7, 9, 10, 5 $S_A = 1.897$

Student B: 7, 8, 6, 6, 6, 6, 7, 5, 5, 7 $S_B = 0.949$

The dotplots and boxplots (we'll discuss boxplots in more detail later in the chapter) of scores for the two students are given below. Compare the spread of the scores from the plots. Both graphs show that the scores for student A are more spread out (they span a larger range) than the scores for student B. So it makes sense that the scores for student A have a larger standard deviation than that for student B.

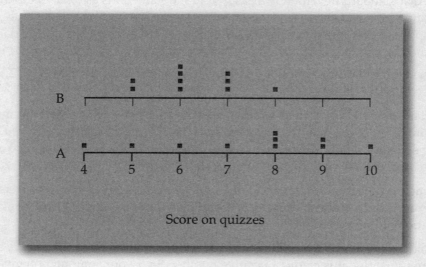

Figure 17: Dotplot of students' scores on quizzes

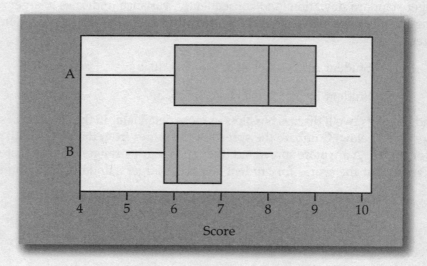

Figure 18: Boxplot of students' scores on quizzes

MEASURES OF POSITION

These measures are used to describe the position of a measurement with respect to the rest of measurements in the data set. Quartiles, percentiles, and standardized scores (z-scores) are the most commonly used measures of position. In order to compute quartiles and percentiles, but not to compute z-scores, the data must be sorted by value.

Quartiles: Quartiles divide a data set into four equal parts.

Q_1 : First quartile. The number such that at most 25 percent of the data values are at or below it and at most 75 percent of the data values are at or above it.

Q_2 : Second quartile, same as the median. A number such that at most 50 percent of the data values are at or below it, and at most 50 percent of data values are at or above it.

Q_3 : Third quartile. A number such that at most 75 percent of the data values are at or below it, and at most 25 percent of data values are at or above it.

In other words, 25 percent of the data is below Q_1, 25 percent is between Q_1 and Q_2, 25 percent is between Q_2 and Q_3, and 25 percent is above Q_3. Refer to the discussion of percentiles for instructions on how to compute quartiles.

Percentiles: Percentiles divide a data set into 100 equal parts. For each data set, there are 99 percentiles, denoted by P_1, P_2, $\cdots$, P_{99}.

P_k = The kth percentile, which is the number such that at most k percent of the data values are at or below it and at most $(100-k)$ percent of the data values are at or above it.

For example, P_{95} is the 95th percentile, which means that at most 95 percent of data values are at or below P_{95} and at most 5 percent of data values are at or above P_{95}. Note that $P_{25} = Q_1$, $P_{50} = Q_2 = M$, and $P_{75} = Q_3$.

- Suppose there are n measurements in a data set.

- Suppose we are interested in determining the kth percentile.

- Arrange all measurements in increasing order of value, i.e., from the smallest to the largest.

- Compute $l = \dfrac{(n+1)k}{100}$

- The percentile P_k = the value of the measurement in the lth observation when counted from the lowest measurement.

Standardized scores or **z-scores:** Standardized scores, commonly known as z-scores, are independent of the units in which the data values are measured. Therefore, they are useful when comparing observations from different data sets measured on different scales. They are computed as:

$$z\text{-score} = \frac{\text{measurement} - \text{mean}}{\text{standard deviation}}$$

A z-score gives the distance between the measurement and the mean in terms of the number of standard deviations. A negative z-score indicates that the measurement is smaller than the mean; a positive z-score indicates that the measurement is larger than the mean.

Example 10: Suppose a teacher gave her students a test. The class average was 74 and the standard deviation was 6. Suppose student A got an 88 and student B got a 70.

$$\text{Student A:} \quad z\text{-score} = \frac{\text{measurement} - \text{mean}}{\text{standard deviation}} = \frac{88 - 74}{6} = 2.33$$

Student A scored 2.33 standard deviations above the class average.

$$\text{Student B:} \quad z\text{-score} = \frac{\text{measurement} - \text{mean}}{\text{standard deviation}} = \frac{70 - 74}{6} = -0.67$$

Student B scored 0.67 standard deviations below the class average.

Note that student B scored closer to the class average than student A.

Example 11: The mean and the standard deviation of the daily high temperatures for two cities are given below:

City	Mean	Standard deviation
South Bend	80	12
North Bend	84	4

Yesterday, both cities reported a high temperature of 95 degrees. Which city had the more unusually high temperature?

Solution: Since the mean daily high temperature at South Bend is 80 degrees—which is lower than the mean daily high temperature at North Bend (84 degrees)—we are tempted to say that 95 degrees is more unusually high at South Bend. But that would be wrong, since it does not take into account the spread of the temperatures at these two cities.

Compute z-scores for both cities:

$$\text{South Bend:} \quad z\text{-score} = \frac{\text{measurement} - \text{mean}}{\text{standard deviation}} = \frac{95 - 80}{12} = 1.25$$

$$\text{North Bend:} \quad z\text{-score} = \frac{\text{measurement} - \text{mean}}{\text{standard deviation}} = \frac{95 - 84}{4} = 2.75$$

Ninety-five degrees Fahrenheit is 1.25 standard deviations above the average in South Bend, whereas it is 2.75 standard deviations above the average in North Bend. This means that 95 degrees Fahrenheit was more unusually high in North Bend.

Example 12: A small used car dealer wanted to get an idea of how many cars her dealership sells per day. Listed below is the number of cars per day sold over a two-week period.

14	9	23	7	11	23	17
11	3	24	21	2	20	20

Compute:

    (a) the mean number of cars sold per day

    (b) the range of cars sold per day

    (c) the standard deviation of the number of cars sold per day

    (d) the median number of cars sold per day

    (e) the first and third quartiles of the number of cars sold per day

    (f) the interquartile range of the number of cars sold per day

    (g) the 90th percentile of the number of cars sold per day

Solution:

    (a) Let X = the number of cars sold on a given day.

$\sum X = 14 + 9 + \cdots + 20 = 205$, and the number of observations = $n = 14$

The sample mean is $\overline{X} = \dfrac{\sum X}{n} = \dfrac{205}{14} = 14.64$ customers

On the average she sells 14.64 cars per day.

    (b) The smallest number is 2 and the largest number is 24. On the best day, her dealership sold 24 cars, and on the worst day it sold only 2 cars.

R = largest measurement − smallest measurement = $24 - 2 = 22$

The range of the number of cars sold is 22.

    (c) To compute the standard deviation, first compute the sum of squares as shown below.

$$\sum X^2 = 14^2 + 9^2 + \cdots + 20^2 = 3{,}745$$

As shown above, $\sum X = 205$ and $n = 14$. So,

$$S = \sqrt{\dfrac{\sum\limits_{i=1}^{n} X_i^2 - \dfrac{\left(\sum\limits_{i=1}^{n} X_i\right)^2}{n}}{n-1}} = \sqrt{\dfrac{3{,}745 - \dfrac{(205)^2}{14}}{14-1}} = 7.5611 \text{ customers}$$

    (d) To find the median, first arrange the data in increasing order.

$$2, 3, 7, 9, 11, 11, 14, 17, 20, 20, 21, 23, 23, 24$$

Compute:

$$l = \dfrac{n+1}{2} = \dfrac{14+1}{2} = 7.5$$

So the median is the value of the 7.5th observation, i.e., the average of the 7th and the 8th observations. When counted from the smallest observation, 7th observation = 14 and the 8th observation = 17, and M = Median = (14 + 17) / 2 = 15.5

On half of the days, less than 15.5 cars were sold per day, and on the other half of the days more than 15.5 cars were sold per day.

(e) To find the first quartile, i.e., the 25th percentile, compute:

$$l = \frac{(n+1)k}{100} = \frac{(14+1)25}{100} = 3.75$$

So, the first quartile (Q_1) is the value of the 3.75th observation.

When counted from the smallest observation, the 3rd observation = 7 and the 4th observation = 9. Interpolating between the 3rd and 4th observation for the 3.75th observation we get

$$Q_1 = \text{first quartile} = 7 + (9 - 7)(3.75 - 3) = 8.5$$

On at most 25 percent of the days, 8.5 or fewer cars were sold per day, and on the remaining 75 percent of the days, 8.5 or more cars were sold per day.

To find the third quartile, i.e., the 75th percentile, compute:

$$l = \frac{(n+1)k}{100} = \frac{(14+1)75}{100} = 11.25$$

So, the third quartile (Q_3) is the value of the 11.25th observation.

When counted from the smallest observation, the 11th observation = 21 and the 12th observation = 23. Interpolating between the 11th and 12th observation for the 11.25th observation we get

$$Q_3 = \text{third quartile} = 21 + (23 - 21)(11.25 - 11) = 21.5$$

On at most 75 percent of the days, 21.5 or fewer cars were sold per day, and on the remaining 25 percent of the days, 21.5 or more cars were sold per day.

The middle 50 percent of the days fall in the range of 8.5 to 21.5 cars sold.

(f) Interquartile range = IQR = $Q_3 - Q_1 = 21.5 - 8.5 = 13$

(g) To find the 90th percentile (P_{90}), compute:

$$l = \frac{(n+1)k}{100} = \frac{(14+1)90}{100} = 13.5$$

So, the 90th percentile is the value of the 13.5th observation, and when counted from the smallest observation, the 13th observation = 23 and the 14th observation = 23.

Interpolating between the 13th and 14th observation for the 13.5th observation, we get

$$P_{90} = \text{90th percentile} = 23$$

On at most 90 percent of the days, 23 or fewer cars were sold per day, and on the remaining 10 percent of the days, 23 or more cars were sold per day.

TI-83:

- Enter data in L1
- Choose **STAT** $\rightarrow$ **CALC** $\rightarrow$ 1: 1-Var Stats
- Press **ENTER**
- Choose 2nd $\rightarrow$ 1 (to get L1) 1-Var Stats L1
- Press **ENTER**

Note: This option gives output that contains the following

$\overline{X}, \sum X, \sum X^2, S, \sigma, n, Min, Q_1, M, Q_3, Max$

Scroll down using the down arrow to read the entire output.

BOXPLOTS

A boxplot, also known as a box-and-whiskers plot, is a graphical data summary based on measures of position. It is useful for identifying outliers.

Here's how to make one:

- Draw a horizontal number line.

- Scale the number line to cover the range of observations.

- Draw a rectangular box above the line from the first quartile to the third quartile (Q_1 to Q_3).

- Draw a vertical line at the median, dividing the box into two compartments.

- Compute "whisker" length = 1.5 IQR

- Compute L = $Q_1 - 1.5 IQR$

- Compute U = $Q_3 + 1.5 IQR$

- Make a lower whisker by drawing a line from the lower (left-most) wall of the box at Q_1 to the farthest observation greater than or equal to L.

- Make an upper whisker by drawing a line from the upper (right most) wall of the box at Q_3 to the farthest observation less than or equal to U.

- Plot any points with values smaller than L or larger than U in their respective places above the number line beyond the whiskers.

How do we read a box plot?

- Any points below the lower (left-most) whisker are identified as outliers on the lower end.

- Any points above the higher (right-most) whisker are identified as outliers on the higher end.

- The length of the box indicates the IQR, i.e., the range of the middle 50 percent of data, when the data is arranged in increasing order of value.

- The length of the lower whisker shows the spread of the smallest 25 percent of data, when the data is arranged in increasing order of value.

- The length of the first compartment of the box shows the spread of the next smallest 25 percent of data.

- The length of the second compartment of the box shows the spread of the third smallest 25 percent of data.

- The length of the upper whisker shows the spread of the largest 25 percent of data.

- Compare the lengths of four parts to compare the respective spread of the data. Use the information about spread to determine the shape of the distribution.

Example 13: Make a boxplot for the car sales data given in the previous example.

Solution: As shown earlier, for the car sales data,

$$Q_1 = 8.5, M = 15.5, \text{ and } Q_3 = 21.5$$

$$\text{IQR} = Q_3 - Q_1 = 21.5 - 8.5 = 13$$

$$\text{Compute L} = Q_1 - 1.5 IQR = 8.5 - 1.5(13) = -11$$

$$\text{Compute U} = Q_3 + 1.5 IQR = 21.5 + 1.5(13) = 41$$

- Draw a box from 8.5 to 21.5

- Draw a divider in the box at 15.5

- Draw a whisker from 8.5 to 2 (lowest observation within the range of L)

- Draw a whisker from 21.5 to 24 (highest observation within the range of U)

- There are no observations beyond L and U

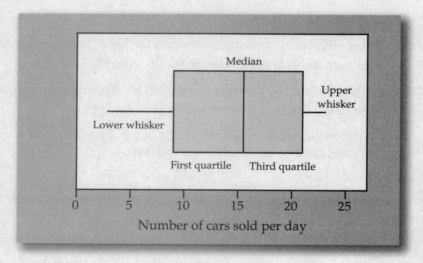

Figure 19: Boxplot of the number of cars sold per day

The longer lower whisker and the longer lower box indicate that the distribution of the number of cars sold per day has a slightly longer left tail, i.e., the distribution is slightly left-skewed. There are no outliers.

Example 14: Make a box plot of the housing expenditure data given in the first example of this chapter.

Solution: Compute summary measures as follows:

$$M = \$392 \text{ per month}$$

$$Q_1 = \$333.25 \text{ per month and } Q_3 = \$465 \text{ per month}$$

$$\text{IQR} = 465 - 333.25 = 131.75$$

$$\text{L} = Q_1 - 1.5 IQR = 333.25 - 1.5(131.75) = 135.25$$

$$\text{U} = Q_3 + 1.5 IQR = 465.4 + 1.5(131.75) = 662.63$$

Note that the lowest housing expenditure (255) is higher than L. So there are no outliers on the lower side. Also note that the highest housing expenditure (834) is larger than U. So, there is at least one outlier on the higher side. The box plot below identifies three outliers on the higher side. This means that there are three students with exceptionally high housing expenditures compared to the rest of the students. The distribution is right-skewed because of these outliers.

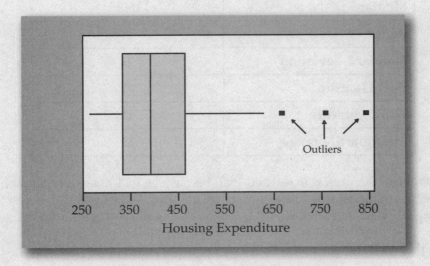

Figure 20: Boxplot of housing expenditure data

THE EFFECT OF CHANGING UNITS ON SUMMARY MEASURES

Let $X_1, X_2, \cdots, X_n$ be n observations. If we added a constant (a) to each observation or multiplied each observation by a number (b, b $\neq$ 0), then how will the summary measures change? The following chart shows the effect of changing the units.

Summary measure	$Y_i = X_i + a$	$Y_i = bX_i$
Mean	Mean(Y) = Median(X) + a	Mean(Y) = b Mean(X)
Median	Median(Y) = Median(X) + a	Median(Y) = b Median(X)
Range	Range(Y) = Range(X) *Range is unaffected*	Range(Y) = b Range(X)
Standard deviation	Standard deviation(Y) = Standard deviation(X) *Standard deviation is unaffected*	Standard deviation(Y) =|b| Standard deviation(X)
Quartiles	Quartiles(Y) = Quartiles(X) + a	Quartiles(Y) = b Quartiles(X)
Interquartile range	IQR(Y) = IQR(X) *IQR is unaffected*	IQR(Y) = b IQR(X)

Example 15: A college professor gave a test to his students. The test had five questions, each worth 20 points. The summary statistics for the students' scores on the test are as follows:

Mean	62
Median	60
Range	45
Standard deviation	8
First Quartile	71
Third Quartile	48
Interquartile range	23

After grading the test, the professor realized that, because he had made a typographical error in question number 2, no student was able to answer the question. So he decided to adjust the students' scores by adding 20 points to each one. What will be the summary statistics for the new, adjusted scores?

Solution: Note that each student's score will increase by 20 points.

Summary statistics for adjusted scores	
Mean	62 + 20 = 82
Median	60 + 20 = 80
Range	45 (unaffected)
Standard deviation	8 (unaffected)
First Quartile	71 + 20 = 91
Third Quartile	48 + 20 = 68
Interquartile range	23 (unaffected)

Example 16: The summary statistics for the property tax per property collected by one county are as follows:

Summary statistics for property tax	
Mean	12,000
Median	8,000
Range	30,000
Standard deviation	5,000
First Quartile	14,000
Third Quartile	5,000
Interquartile range	9,000

This year, county residents voted to increase property taxes by 2 percent, in order to support the local school system. What will be the summary statistics for the new, increased property taxes?

Solution: Note that each property owner will pay 2 percent more in taxes. So the new taxes will be:

$$\text{new tax} = 1.02 \, (\text{old tax})$$

Summary statistics for increased property taxes	
Mean	1.02 (12,000) = 12,240
Median	1.02 (8,000) = 8,160
Range	1.02 (30,000) = 30,600
Standard deviation	1.02 (5,000) = 5,100
First Quartile	1.02 (14,000) = 14,280
Third Quartile	1.02 (5,000) = 5,100
Interquartile range	1.02 (9,000) = 9,180

COMPARING DISTRIBUTIONS OF UNIVARIATE DATA

When comparing distributions of two or more groups, use the following criteria:

- Compare the centers of the distributions.

- Compare the spreads of the distributions. Consider the differences in the spread of data within each group as well as the differences between groups.

- Compare clusters of measurements and gaps in measurements.

- Compare outliers and any other unusual features.

- Compare the shapes of the distributions.

Example 17: A department store wants to compare the optical scanners it's currently using with the new models of scanners. These new models are not perfect, however—they occasionally have trouble reading the bar codes on labels. The store manager decides to compare the number of reading errors made by the old scanners to the number of reading errors made by the new models. She selects a group of 50 items and runs them through each of the scanners 20 times and then records the number of errors made. The data is shown in the following table.

Scanner	Number of reading errors per group of 50 items
Old	6, 3, 4, 4, 6, 3, 5, 3, 1, 5, 3, 2, 5, 5, 4, 8, 4, 7, 3, 3
New	2, 3, 3, 1, 2, 1, 2, 3, 1, 2, 2, 2, 4, 0, 1, 3, 2, 0, 2, 2

Display these data graphically so that the number of reading errors by the old and new scanners can be easily compared. Based on the examination of your graphical display, write a few sentences comparing the number of errors by the old and new scanners.

Solution: Use any one of the following graphical displays.

- **Parallel dotplots,** showing the errors made by both scanners. Parallel dotplots can be used to compare two or more data sets. Using the same scale, draw a dotplot for each data set. Label each line appropriately.

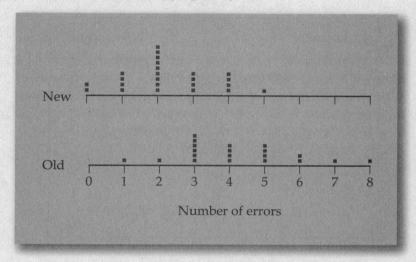

Figure 21: Parallel dotplots showing the number of errors by old and new scanners

- **Parallel boxplots** showing the errors made by both scanners. Parallel boxplots can be used to compare two or more data sets. Using the same scale, draw a boxplot for each data set. Label each boxplot appropriately.

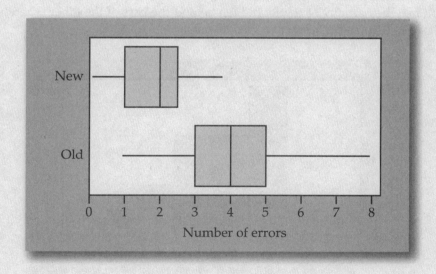

Figure 22: Parallel boxplots showing the number of errors by old and new scanners

- **Back-to-back stemplots,** showing the errors made by both scanners, using the same stems. Back-to-back stemplots can be used to compare only two data sets. Put the common stems in the middle. On one side of the stems make a stemplot for one data set. On the other side of the stems, make a stemplot for the other data set.

Old scanner		New scanner
Leaves	Stems	Leaves
0	0	00
0	1	0000
0	2	000000000
000000	3	0000
0000	4	0
0000	5	
00	6	
0	7	
	8	

Figure 23: Back-to-back stemplots

- **Two histograms,** showing the errors made by both scanners. Although not incorrect, this is not a great option. Be sure to use the same scale for both histograms—otherwise the comparison would not be valid. The problem with using two histograms is that we cannot lay one histogram over the other, since the bars of one graph may be partially or totally hidden behind the bars of the other. Therefore, we have to display the histograms side by side.

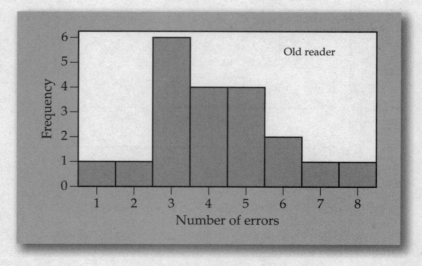

Figure 24: Histogram showing the number of errors made by the old scanner

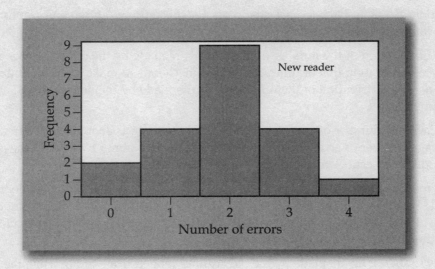

Figure 25: Histogram showing the number of errors made by the new scanner

- **Parallel frequency polygons**. A frequency polygon is a graph showing the frequency of different values of a random variable. It is also known as a **line graph**. Basically, it can be drawn by connecting the midpoints of the tops of each bar of a histogram. Parallel frequency polygrams can be used to compare two or more data sets. Using the same scale, draw a line graph for each data set. Use different symbols to indicate different groups. Include the appropriate legend for correct identification.

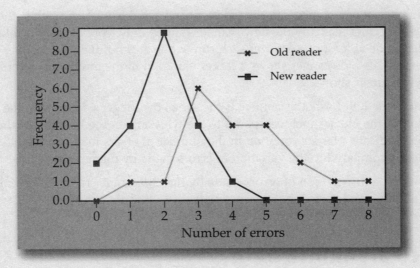

Figure 26: Line graph showing the number of errors by the old and new scanners

Examining parallel dotplots, back-to-back stemplots, two histograms, or two line graphs gives us the following information about the data:

- The distribution of the number of reading errors made by the old scanner is right-skewed, indicating that at times the old scanner tends to make a large number of errors. The distribution of the number of errors made by the new scanner is almost symmetric.

- The average number of errors made by the old scanner is about four, whereas the average number of errors made by the new scanner is about two. So on the average, the new scanner tends to make fewer mistakes.

- The median number of errors made by the old scanner is about four, while that made by the new scanner is about two. So with the new scanner, 50 percent of the time at most two errors were made; whereas with the old scanner, 50 percent of the time more than four errors were made.

- The number of errors made by the old scanner ranged from 1 to 8, while the number of errors made by the new scanner ranged only from 0 to 4. The old scanner made at least one error in each run, while at times the new scanner read flawlessly. The old scanner shows a larger variation in the number of errors than the new scanner shows.

The examination of the parallel boxplots gives us the following information about the data:

- The median number of errors made by the old scanner is about four, while that made by the new scanner is about two. So with the new scanner, 50 percent of the time at most two errors were made; whereas with the old scanner, 50 percent of the time more than four errors were made.

- The number of errors made by the old scanner ranged from 1 to 8, while the number of errors made by the new scanner ranged only from 0 to 4. The old scanner made at least one error in each run, while at times the new scanner read flawlessly. The old scanner shows a larger variation in the number of errors than the new scanner shows.

- Although the IQR for both scanners is the same, the longer whiskers on the boxplot for the old scanner, compared to the whiskers on the boxplot for the new scanner, indicate a larger variation in the number of errors made by the old scanner as compared to the variation in errors made by the new one.

- Although the distribution of errors made by the old scanner is right-skewed, there were no outliers detected in either boxplot.

EXPLORING BIVARIATE DATA

Bivariate data is data on two different variables collected from each item in a study.

We often want to investigate a relation between two quantitative variables. If two different quantitative variables have a linear relation, then we can measure the strength of that relation by gathering data on the two variables from each item in a study. For example, we might want to know the relation between:

- High school students' scores on the midterm and their scores on the final exam

- College students' SAT or ACT scores and their GPA when they graduate
- The price of crude oil and the price of gasoline each month
- The daily temperature and the atmospheric pressure at a given location
- Advertising expenditure and the number of sales generated
- The weight of a car and its miles per gallon of gas

There are two commonly used measures to summarize the relation between two variables. A **scatterplot** is a graphical summary measure; the **correlation coefficient** is a numerical summary measure.

SCATTERPLOT

A **scatterplot** is used to describe the nature, degree, and direction of the relation between two variables X and Y, where (X, Y) gives a pair of measurements, i.e., a bivariate quantitative data. Here's how to make one:

- Draw an X-axis and a Y-axis.
- Scale the X-axis to accommodate the range of data for the first variable.
- Scale the Y-axis to accommodate the range of data for the other variable.
- For each pair of measurements, mark the point on the graph where the (unmarked) lines of the X and Y values cross.

Here's what a scatterplot can tell us about the two variables:

- **Nature**: A scatterplot tells us whether the nature of the relation between the two variables is linear or non-linear. A linear relation is one that can be described using a straight line.

- **Direction**: The scatterplot will show whether the Y-value increases or decreases as the X increases.

    If a scatterplot shows an increasing or upward trend, then it indicates a positive relation between the two variables. For example, the relation between the heights of fathers and the heights of their sons is a positive relation. Taller fathers tend to have taller sons.

    If a scatterplot shows a decreasing or downward trend, then it indicates a negative relation between the two variables. For example, the relation between the weight of a car and its gas mileage is a negative relation. Heavier cars tend to get lower gas mileage.

- **Degree**: If the trend of the data can be described with a line or a curve, then the spread of the data values around the trend describes the degree (or strength) of the relation between the two.

    If a scatterplot shows less scattered points, i.e., points very close to the linear trend, then it indicates a strong relation between the two variables.

    If a scatterplot shows more scattered points, then it indicates a weaker relation between the two variables.

    If a scatterplot shows points scattered without any apparent pattern, then it indicates no relation between the two variables.

The following scatterplots show various degrees of relation between the two variables.

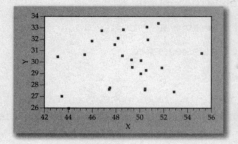

Figure 27: No relation between X and Y

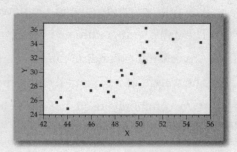

Figure 28: Linear relation between X and Y

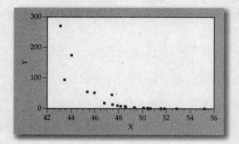

Figure 29: Nonlinear relation between X and Y

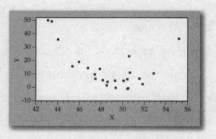

Figure 30: Nonlinear relation between X and Y

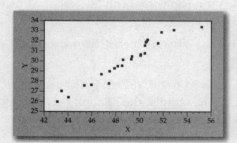

Figure 31: Strong positive linear relation between X and Y

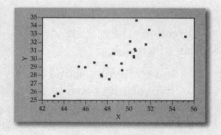

Figure 32: Weaker positive linear relation between X and Y

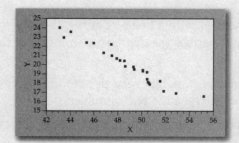

Figure 33: Strong negative linear relation between X and Y

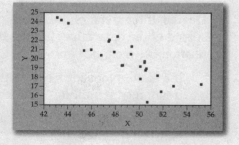

Figure 34: Weaker negative linear relation between X and Y

Example 18: At the graduation ceremony of a large university, a random sample of 50 father-son pairs was selected, and the heights of the fathers and sons were measured. Below is a scatterplot of the data collected.

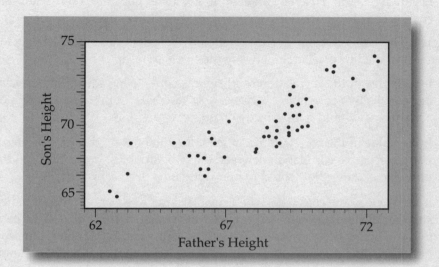

Figure 35: Scatterplot of the heights of fathers and the heights of their sons

Notice from the plot that there is an increasing relation between the father's height and the son's height. The relation is fairly strong and linear. In general, taller fathers have taller sons, though that's not necessarily true for every father-son pair selected.

CORRELATION COEFFICIENT

Like other graphical measures, scatterplots are subject to interpretation. Correlation coefficients are numerical (not graphical) measures used to judge the linear relation between two variables.

Pearson's correlation coefficient (also known simply as "the correlation coefficient") is a numeric measure of the degree and direction of the linear relation between two quantitative variables. The Pearson's correlation coefficient between two variables X and Y computed from a population is denoted by ρ (read as "rho"), whereas the correlation coefficient between two variables computed from a sample is denoted by r.

$$-1 \leq r \leq +1 \text{ always}$$

Here's what the correlation coefficient tells us:

- **Direction**: The positive or negative sign of the correlation coefficient describes the direction of the linear relation between the two variables.

  A positive value of the correlation coefficient indicates a positive relation between X and Y. This means that as X increases, Y also increases linearly. For example, the relation between the heights of fathers and the heights of their sons is a positive relation. Taller fathers tend to have taller sons. A scatterplot of such data will show an increasing or upward linear trend.

A negative value of the correlation coefficient indicates a negative relation between X and Y. This means that as X increases, Y decreases linearly. For example, the relation between the weight of a car and its gas mileage is a negative relation. Heavier cars tend to get lower gas mileage. A scatterplot of such data will show a decreasing or downward linear trend.

- **Degree**: The numeric value of the correlation coefficient describes the degree (or strength) of the linear relation between the two variables.

  If the value of the correlation coefficient is equal to +1, then it indicates a perfect positive correlation between two variables. In this case, all the points in a scatterplot would fall perfectly on an increasing line.

  If the value of the correlation coefficient is equal to −1, then it indicates a perfect negative correlation between the two variables. In this case, all the points in a scatterplot would fall perfectly on a decreasing line.

  If the value of the correlation coefficient is closer to +1 or −1, then it indicates a stronger relation between two variables of interest. For example, if the correlation coefficient between X and Y is 0.68, whereas the correlation coefficient between X and Z is 0.82, then X and Z have a stronger relation than X and Y.

  If the value of the correlation coefficient is closer to 0, then it indicates a weaker relation between the two variables. For example, if the correlation coefficient between X and Y is −0.86, whereas the correlation coefficient between X and Z is −0.75, then X and Y have a stronger relation than X and Z.

  Ignoring the positive or negative sign, the higher values of the correlation coefficient indicate stronger relations. For example, if the correlation coefficient between X and Y is 0.68, whereas the correlation coefficient between X and Z is −0.75, then X and Z have a stronger relation than X and Y.

The correlation coefficient is computed as

$$r = \frac{SS_{xy}}{\sqrt{(SS_{xx})(SS_{yy})}}$$

where n = the number of pairs of measurements.

SS_{xx} is the numerator of the variance of x-values, which is computed as

$$SS_{xx} = \sum X^2 - \frac{(\sum X)^2}{n}$$

SS_{yy} is the numerator of the variance of y-values, which is computed as

$$SS_{yy} = \sum Y^2 - \frac{(\sum Y)^2}{n}$$

SS_{xy} is the numerator of the covariance of x and y-values, which is computed as

$$SS_{xy} = \sum XY - \frac{(\sum X)(\sum Y)}{n}$$

Example 19: A sample of 12 father and son pairs was selected at random. The heights (in inches) of the selected father-son pairs are listed below.

Height of father (X)	Height of son (Y)
66	66
68	67
66	65
66	67
67	68
67	65
67	67
68	70
69	70
70	70
71	72
73	74

Compute the correlation coefficient between the heights of the fathers and the heights of their sons. Interpret the computed value.

Solution: First let's make a scatterplot to determine the nature of the relation between the two variables.

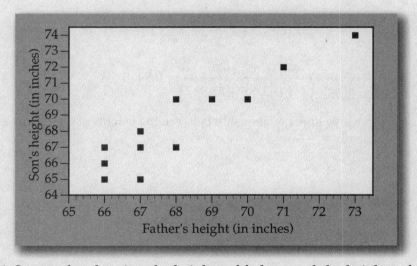

Figure 36: Scatterplot showing the heights of fathers and the heights of their sons

TI-83:

To make a scatterplot:

- Enter *X*-values into L1

- Enter corresponding *Y*-values into L2

- Choose **2nd → STAT PLOT → 1: Plot1**

- Turn the plot on by highlighting On

- Choose scatterplot by highlighting the picture of a scatterplot under Type

- Enter Xlist: L1

- Enter Ylist: L2

- Select type of marking from 3 available marks

- Choose **ZOOM → 9:ZoomStat**

- Use TRACE option to trace points in the scatterplot

The scatterplot shows a positive linear relation between the heights of the fathers and the heights of their sons. Now let's compute the correlation coefficient.

There are $n = 12$ pairs of measurements.

$$\sum X = 66 + 68 + \cdots + 73 = 818 \qquad\qquad \sum X^2 = 66^2 + 68^2 + \cdots + 73^2 = 55,814$$

$$\sum Y = 66 + 67 + \cdots + 74 = 821 \qquad\qquad \sum Y^2 = 66^2 + 67^2 + \cdots + 74^2 = 56,257$$

$$\sum XY = 66(66) + 68(67) + \ldots + 73(74) = 56,028$$

$$SS_{xx} = \sum X^2 - \frac{(\sum X)^2}{n} = 55,814 - \frac{(818)^2}{12} = 53.667$$

$$SS_{yy} = \sum Y^2 - \frac{(\sum Y)^2}{n} = 56,257 - \frac{(821)^2}{12} = 86.917$$

$$SS_{xy} = \sum XY - \frac{(\sum X)(\sum Y)}{n} = 56,028 - \frac{(818)(821)}{12} = 63.167$$

This gives, $r = \dfrac{SS_{xy}}{\sqrt{(SS_{xx})(SS_{yy})}} = \dfrac{63.167}{\sqrt{(53.667)(83.917)}} = 0.9413$

There is a very strong positive linear relationship between the heights of the fathers and the heights of their sons.

TI-83:

To compute the correlation coefficient:

- Enter X-values into L1
- Enter corresponding Y-values into L2
- Choose **2nd** → **CATALOG** → **DiagnosticOn**

Note: This step is needed only the very first time. Once the diagnostics are turned on, omit this step.

- Choose **STAT** → **CALC** → **8: LinReg(a + bx)**
- Enter L1, L2   LinReg(a + bx) L1,L2
- Press **ENTER**

TI-83:

To get summary statistics for bivariate data:

- Enter X-values into L1
- Enter corresponding Y-values into L2
- Choose **STAT** → **CALC** → **2: 2-Var Stats**
- Enter L1, L2   2-Var Stats L1,L2
- Press **ENTER**

This option will provide

$$\overline{X}, \sum X, \sum X^2, S_X, \sigma_X, n,$$
$$\overline{Y}, \sum Y, \sum Y^2, S_Y, \sigma_Y$$
$$\sum XY, \min X, \max X, \min Y, \max Y$$

Use the up arrow and down arrow to scroll up and down the list.

In a scatterplot, when this bivariate data is plotted, or other bivariate data with a linear relation, it shows a sort of elliptical cloud of points. Lengthwise, the cloud is centered at $\overline{X}$ and spread approximately in the range of $\left(\overline{X} - 3S_x, \overline{X} + 3S_x\right)$. Widthwise (or heightwise), the cloud is centered at $\overline{Y}$ and spread approximately in the range of $\left(\overline{Y} - 3S_y, \overline{Y} + 3S_y\right)$. The inclination of the cloud is determined by the correlation coefficient (or, equivalently, by the slope of the line, as discussed on the next page).

LEAST SQUARES REGRESSION LINE

Once we have established that the two variables are related to each other, we are often interested in estimating or quantifying the relation between the two variables. Such an estimation can be useful for predicting the corresponding values of one variable for known values of the other variable.

A **linear regression model** or **linear regression equation** is an equation that gives a straight line relationship between two variables.

The linear relation between two variables is given by the following equation for the regression line:

$$Y = \beta_0 + \beta_1 X + e$$

Where

- Y is the **dependent variable** or **response variable**.

- X is the **independent variable** or **explanatory variable**.

- β_0 is the **Y-intercept**. It is the value of Y for $X = 0$.

- β_1 is the **slope** of the line. It gives the amount of change in Y for every unit change in X.

- e is the random error or residual. It is the difference between the observed and predicted value. For example, suppose that, using some weather models, the weather station predicted that today's highest temperature would be 75 degrees Fahrenheit. At the end of the day the highest temperature recorded was 78 degrees. Here the predicted temperature is 75 degrees while the observed temperature is 78 degrees. The difference $78 - 75 = 3$ is the error. In this case, the y day's high temperature was underpredicted.

The **predicted value** of Y for a given value of X is denoted by y. It is computed using the estimated regression line

$$y = a + bx$$

Where

$a = \hat{\beta}_0 = $ The estimated slope of the regression line.
And

$b = \hat{\beta}_1 = $ The estimated Y-intercept of the regression line.

Error or residual = $e = (y - \hat{y}) = $ observed value of Y for a given value X – predicted value of Y for a given value X.

The **least squares regression line** is a line that minimizes the error sum of squares (SSE). It is also known as the line of best fit. The least squares estimates of Y-intercept and slope are given as follows:

$$\hat{\beta}_1 = b = \frac{SS_{xy}}{SS_{xx}} \quad \text{and} \quad \hat{\beta}_0 = a = \overline{Y} - b\overline{X}$$

A line estimated using least squares estimates of the Y-intercept and the slope has the smallest error sum of squares. Any other line will have larger error sum of squares. This means that on the average, this line is likely to give estimates closer to the actual values than any other line. The error sum of squares (SSE) is computed as

$$SSE = \sum e_i^2 = \sum (y_i - \hat{y}_i)^2 = SS_{yy} - bSS_{xy}$$

The line of best fit will always pass through the point $(\overline{X}, \overline{Y})$.

The coefficient of determination measures the percent of variation in Y-values explained by the linear relation between X and Y-values. In other words, it measures the percent of variation in Y-values attributable to the variation in X-values. It is denoted by R^2 (R-square). It can be shown that, for a linear regression, R^2 is equal to the square of the Pearson's correlation coefficient. Note that $0 \le R^2 \le 1$ always.

Example 20: A random sample of 10 office assistants hired within the last six months was selected from a large company. For each selected office assistant, his or her experience (in months) at the time of hire and starting salary were recorded. The data is given in the table below.

Experience (in months)	Starting salary (in 1000 dollars)
5	28
12	34
2	24
0	19
2	24
10	32
5	25
1	20
10	29
5	26

(a) Compute the slope for the line of best fit. Interpret it.

(b) Compute the Y-intercept of the line of best fit. Interpret it.

(c) Find the least squares regression line to estimate starting salary using experience.

(d) Plot the line of best fit in the scatterplot.

(e) Predict the starting salary for an office assistant with six months of prior experience.

(f) What is the residual when predicting the starting salary of an assistant with 12 months of experience?

(g) Compute the coefficient of determination. Interpret it.

Solution: In this example, note that the starting salary depends on the worker's experience. Therefore, starting salary is the dependent variable and experience is the independent variable. There are 10 pairs of measurements. The scatterplot of the data is as follows:

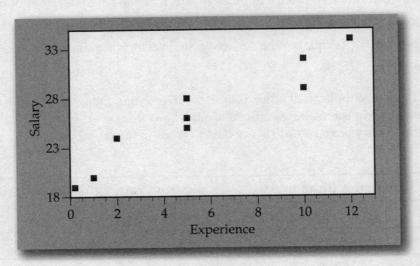

Figure 37: Scatterplot showing starting salary and experience of office assistants

The scatterplot shows that there is a fairly strong positive linear relationship between the starting salary of office assistants and their prior experience.

From the data compute:

$n = 10$

$\sum X = 52$ $\sum X^2 = 428$

$\sum Y = 261$ $\sum Y^2 = 7{,}019$

$\sum XY = 1{,}529$

$$SS_{xx} = 428 - \frac{(52)^2}{10} = 157.6 \qquad SS_{yy} = 7{,}019 - \frac{(261)^2}{10} = 206.9$$

$$SS_{xy} = 1{,}529 - \frac{(52)(261)}{10} = 171.8$$

(a) Compute the estimated slope.

$$\hat{\beta}_1 = b = \frac{SS_{xy}}{SS_{xx}} = \frac{171.8}{157.6} = 1.09 \text{ is the estimated slope of the line of best fit.}$$

For every month's additional experience at the time of hiring, the starting salary increases on the average (or approximately) by $1,090.

(b) Compute the estimated Y-intercept.

$\hat{\beta}_0 = a = \overline{Y} - b\overline{X} = 26.1 - 1.09(5.2) = 20.43$ is the estimated Y-intercept of the line of best fit. The approximate (or average) starting salary of inexperienced (experience = 0 months) office assistants is $20,432.

(c) The equation of the least squares regression line (or line of best fit) is

Starting salary = 20.432 + 1.09. (Experience.)

(d) The following scatterplot shows the line of best fit superimposed on it.

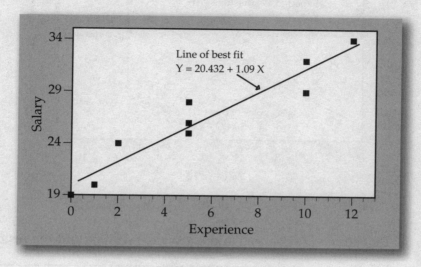

Figure 38: Line of best fit

(e) The office assistant has 6 months of prior experience. For $X = 6$ months
Starting salary = 20.432 + 1.09 Experience = 20.432 + 1.09 (6) = 26.972.
The estimated starting salary for an office assistant with 6 months of prior experience is $26,972.

(f) The data shows that an office assistant with 12 months of experience received
$34,000 as a starting salary. The predicted salary is 20.432 + 1.09(12) = 33.512, i.e.,
$33,512. So, the residual = observed − predicted = 34,000 − 33,512 = 488.
It means this office assistant received $488 more than the expected starting salary.

(g) The correlation coefficient is $r = \dfrac{SS_{xy}}{\sqrt{(SS_{xx})(SS_{yy})}} = \dfrac{171.8}{\sqrt{(157.6)(206.9)}} = 0.9514$

So, the coefficient of determination = $R^2 = (0.9514)^2 = 0.9052$, i.e., 90.52%.

About 90.52 percent of the variation among starting salaries is attributable to prior experience. So there is still about 9.5 percent of variation among salaries that remains unexplained. It may be due to some other factors, such as education, gender, the person the assistant is working for, etc.

The following plot shows the observed Y-value, the line of best fit, and the residual for one pair of data.

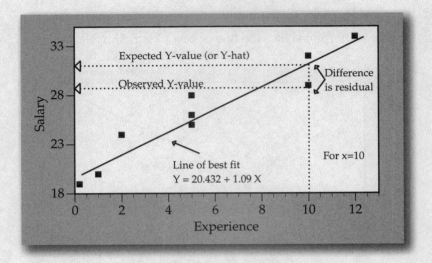

Figure 39: Plot showing observed and expected *Y*-values and the residual

---

TI-83:

To compute least squares estimates of the slope and *Y*-intercept:

- Enter *X*-values into L1

- Enter corresponding *Y*-values into L2

- Choose **STAT** → **CALC** → **8: LinReg(a + bx)**

- Enter L1, L2   LinReg(a + bx) L1,L2

- Press **ENTER**

TI-83:

To get a regression line superimposed on a scatterplot:

- Enter *X*-values into L1

- Enter corresponding *Y*-values into L2

- Choose **STAT** → **CALC** → **8: LinReg(a + bx)**

- Enter L1, L2, Y1

- LinReg(a + bx) L1,L2,Y1

- *To get* Y1, *use the following sequence of commands.*

Choose VARS → Y-VARS → 1: Function → 1: Y1

- Press **ENTER**

- Press **ENTER**

OUTLIERS AND INFLUENTIAL POINTS

As discussed earlier, an **outlier** is an observation that is different from the rest of the data—in other words, an observation that does not conform to the general trend. An **influential observation** is an observation that affects the summary statistic. Some outliers are influential, while others are not. If there is a considerable difference between the correlation coefficients computed with and without a specific observation, then that observation is considered influential. The same can be said about the line of best fit. If the estimates of the line of best fit change considerably when including or excluding a point, then that point is an influential observation.

Look at the following plots for examples of outlier points:

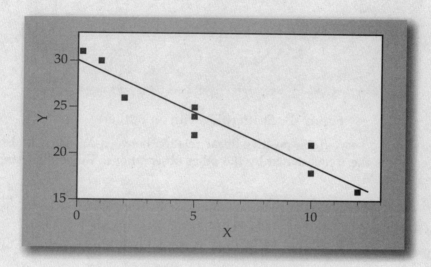

Figure 40: Scatterplot showing no outlier

This scatterplot shows no outlier. It demonstrates a fairly strong positive linear relation between X and Y.

$r = -0.951$

$R^2 = 0.905$ or 90.5%

The line of best fit is

$Y = 29.57 - 1.09X$

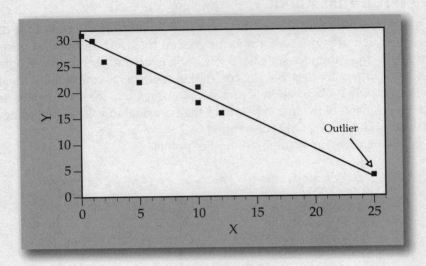

Figure 41: Scatterplot with an outlier

This scatterplot shows a very strong positive linear relation between X and Y. It also shows one outlier, which confirms the trend shown by the other observations. This outlier strengthens the relation between X and Y.

$r = -0.982$

$R^2 = 0.964$ or 96.4%

The line of best fit is

$Y = 29.31 - 1.03X$

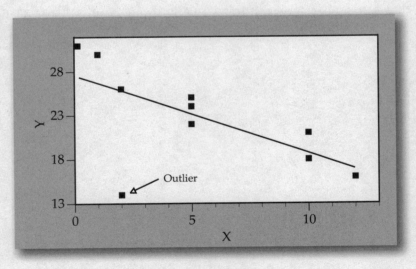

Figure 42: Scatterplot with an outlier

This scatterplot shows a fairly strong positive linear relation between X and Y. But it also shows one outlier, which opposes the trend of the other observations. This outlier weakens the strength of the relation between X and Y.

$r = -0.643$

$R^2 = 0.414$ or 41.4%

The line of best fit is

$Y = 27.21 - 0.86X$

RESIDUAL PLOTS

A **residual plot** is a plot of residuals versus the predicted values of Y. This type of plot is used to assess the fit of the model. A residual plot should show residuals randomly distributed. If the residual plot shows any patterns or trends, it is an indication that the linear model is not a good fit for the data.

Example 21: Refer to the earlier example of the office assistants. Compute the predicted values and the residual for each observed X-value.

Experience (in months) X	Starting Salary (in 1000 dollars) Y	Predicted Salary $\hat{Y} = 20.432 + 1.09X$	Residual $e = Y - \hat{Y}$
5	28	25.882	2.118
12	34	33.512	0.488
2	24	22.612	1.388
0	19	20.432	−1.432
2	24	22.612	1.388
10	32	31.332	0.668
5	25	25.883	−0.882
1	20	21.522	−1.522
10	29	31.332	−2.332
5	26	25.882	0.118

Make a residual plot by plotting the residual values on the Y-axis and the predicted values on the X-axis.

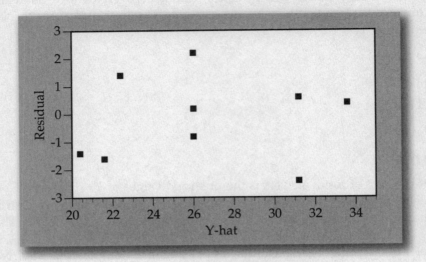

Figure 43: Residual plot of starting salary and experience

Note that all the residual values are scattered randomly around the line of 0. The absence of any trends or patterns indicates that the linear model is a good fit for this data.

TI-83:

- Enter X values into L1

- Enter corresponding Y-values into L2

- Choose **STAT** $\rightarrow$ **CALC** $\rightarrow$ **8: LinReg(a + bx)**

- Enter L1, L2, Y1   LinReg(a + bx) L1, L2, Y1 *To get Y1, use the following sequence of commands.*

- Choose **VARS** $\rightarrow$ **Y-VARS** $\rightarrow$ **1: Function** $\rightarrow$ **1: Y1** Press **ENTER**

This will store the regression equation in Y1.

- Press **ENTER** to compute residuals for the above estimated line

- Create a new column for residuals titled RESDL

- Take the cursor to this new column title. This will allow you to define the column. Enter L2-Y1(L1) This command will fill the column titled RESDL with residuals.

To plot the computed residuals:

- Choose Y=

- In this screen, deselect regression equation \Y1

- In this screen, set \Y2 = 0

- Choose **2nd** $\rightarrow$ **STAT PLOT** $\rightarrow$ **2: Plot2**

- Press **ENTER**

- Turn Plot2 On by highlighting it

- Choose scatterplot by highlighting the picture of a scatterplot under Type
- Enter Xlist: L1
- Enter Ylist: RESDL
- Select type of marking from 3 available marks
- Choose **ZOOM** → **9:ZoomStat**
- Use **TRACE** option to trace points in the scatterplot

TRANSFORMATIONS TO ACHIEVE LINEARITY

Always do a scatterplot of the data to examine the nature of the relation between the two variables. You should also examine the fit of the linear model by using a residual plot. If either one of these plots indicates that the linear model might not be appropriate for the data, then there are two options available: You can either use **nonlinear models** or use **transformation** to achieve linearity. Square root transformation and logarithmic transformation are the most commonly used transformations.

For example, if the data seems to have a relation of the nature $Y = aX^b$, then we can take a logarithm of both sides to get $\ln(Y) = \ln(a) + b\ln(X)$. This gives the equation of a straight line—in other words, a linear relation.

After the variables have been transformed, we can then use them to make a model. For example, we could take the natural log of all Y-values ($Z = \ln(Y)$) or the square root of all Y-values ($Z = \sqrt{Y}$). Then we would fit the model for Z as a function of X. When using a fitted model for predictions, remember to transform the predicted values back to the original scale using a reverse transformation.

For example, when using the transformation $Z = \ln(Y)$ to get $\hat{Z} = a + bX$, you would need to use the reverse transformation of $\hat{Y} = \exp\hat{Z}$ for predictions. If using the transformation $Z = \sqrt{Y}$ to get $\hat{Z} = a + bX$, you would need to use the reverse transformation of $\hat{Y} = \left(\hat{Z}\right)^2$ for predictions.

Here are some examples of transformations:

- The **log transformation** ($Z = \ln(Y)$) is used to linearize the regression model when the relationship between Y and X suggests a model with a consistently increasing slope.

- The **square root transformation** ($Z = \sqrt{Y}$) is used when the spread of observations increases with the mean.

- The **reciprocal transformation** ($Z = 1/Y$) is used to minimize the effect of large values of X.

- The **square transformation** ($Z = Y^2$) is used when the slope of the relation consistently decreases as the independent variable increases.

> **TI-83:**
> **To use power transformation**
>
> This procedure will fit the model equation $Y = aX^b$ to the data using transformed values of $\ln(X)$ and $\ln(Y)$. In other words, the line $\ln(Y) = \ln(a) + b \ \ln(X)$ will be fitted to the data.
>
> - Enter X-values into L1
> - Enter corresponding Y-values into L2
> - Choose **STAT** $\rightarrow$ **CALC** $\rightarrow$ **A: PwrReg**
> - Enter L1, L2   PwrReg L1,L2
> - Press **ENTER**

> **TI-83:**
> **To use logarithmic transformation**
>
> This procedure will fit the model equation $Y = a + b \ \ln(X)$ to the data using transformed values of $\ln(X)$ and Y-values. In other words, line $Y = a + b \ \ln(X)$ will be fitted to the data.
>
> - Enter X-values into L1
> - Enter corresponding Y-values into L2
> - Choose **STAT** $\rightarrow$ **CALC** $\rightarrow$ **9: LnReg**
> - Enter L1, L2   LnReg L1,L2
> - Press **ENTER**

> **TI-83:**
> **To use exponential transformation**
>
> This procedure will fit the model equation $Y = ab^X$ to the data using the X-values and the transformed values of $\ln(Y)$. In other words, the line $\ln(Y) = \ln(a) + X \ \ln(b)$ will be fitted to the data.
>
> - Enter X-values into L1
> - Enter corresponding Y-values into L2
> - Choose **STAT** $\rightarrow$ **CALC** $\rightarrow$ **0: ExpReg**
> - Enter L1, L2   ExpReg L1,L2
> - Press **ENTER**

Example 22: A mathematics teacher is studying the relationship between the time children spend on computational drills and their scores on a particular standardized test. She divides students into 10 different groups. Each group spends a particular amount of time on computational drills. All students take the same standardized tests after the computational drills. Their average score on the standardized test and the time they spent on computational drills are recorded in the table on the next page.

Time (in minutes)	Mean Score
25	45
30	56
50	68
60	87
75	89
80	96
100	105
110	112
125	118
130	126

In this example, the scores on the standardized tests depend on the time spent on the computational drills. So time is the independent variable and the score on the test is the dependent variable. A scatterplot of the data and the residual plot for a linear fit are given below.

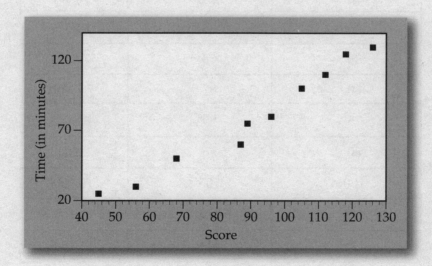

Figure 44: Scatterplot for score versus time

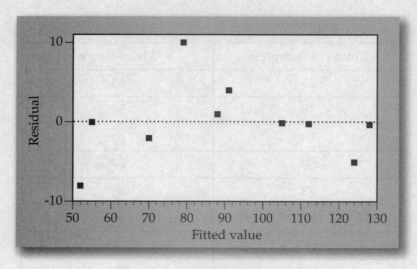

Figure 45: Residual plot for score versus time

Note that the scatterplot shows a slight curvature. Also note that the residual plot shows a nonrandom pattern, indicating that the line model is not a good fit for this data. Let's try a square root transformation. First, take the square root of the time.

Time (in minutes)	Mean Score	$\sqrt{\text{Time}}$
25	45	5.0000
30	56	5.4772
50	68	7.0711
60	87	7.74601
75	89	8.6603
80	96	8.9443
100	105	10.0000
110	112	11.1803
125	118	11.1803
130	126	11.4018

Table 6: Transformed data

Now, let's make a scatterplot of score versus square root of time. Also fit a line using square root of time as an independent variable and score as a dependent variable. Make a residual plot for the fit.

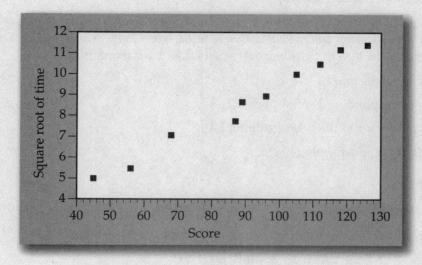

Figure 46: Scatterplot of transformed data

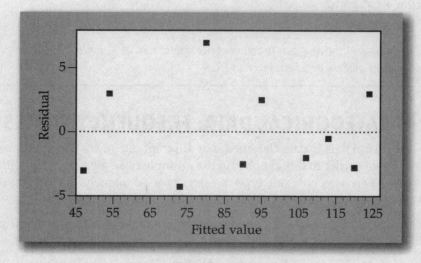

Figure 47: Residual plot for line fitted to transformed data

Now the scatterplot shows a linear pattern. The residual plot shows no pattern, just randomly scattered residuals, which indicates that a line fit is good. The estimated line of best fit is

$$\text{Score} = -11.2 + 11.8 \sqrt{\text{Time}}$$

With

$$R^2 = 0.984 \text{ or } 98.4\%$$

Suppose we are interested in predicting the mean score of students who do computational drills for 60 minutes. Then we would calculate

$$\text{Score} = -11.2 + 11.8 \sqrt{\text{Time}} = -11.2 + 11.8 \sqrt{60} = 80.2$$

EXPLORING CATEGORICAL DATA: FREQUENCY TABLES

Remember that categorical data is data classified into different categories. We computed a frequency table for categorical data earlier in this chapter, in the example regarding students' different types of housing. In that case, there was only one type of category used, namely, type of housing.

Data can also be classified into two categories simultaneously. For example:

- Students might be classified by gender (male or female) and their student status (freshman, sophomore, junior, or senior).

- Senators might be classified by party affiliation (Democrat or Republican) and their vote on a specific bill (yea or nay).

- Teachers might be classified by the type of college they belong to (Arts & Sciences, Engineering, Education, or Business) and their position (assistant professor, associate professor, or professor).

- Items produced by a factory might be classified by their batch number and their quality status (defective or non-defective).

- Car accidents might be classified by the number of vehicles involved and the cause of the accident.

MARGINAL AND JOINT FREQUENCIES OF TWO-WAY TABLES

Suppose data is classified by two different criteria. If the classification criterion 1 has r number of categories and the classification criterion 2 has c number of categories, then the classification of data results in a table with r rows and c columns.

A table of data classified by r categories of classification criterion 1 and c categories of classification criterion 2 is known as an $r \times c$ **contingency table**.

Suppose 200 students were classified by gender and academic major. The data resulted in a 2×4 contingency table, shown below.

		Academic Major			
		Arts	Sciences	Engineering	Education
Gender	Female	35	15	5	25
	Male	10	40	50	20

Table 7: 2 x 4 Contingency table

The table shows that

- 35 female students are majoring in arts
- 10 male students are majoring in arts
- 15 female students are majoring in sciences

The figures above are joint frequencies of respective categories. The **joint frequency** of two categories is the frequency with which two categories, one from each of the two classification criteria, occur together.

Let's compute row totals and column totals:

		Academic Major				Row Totals
		Arts	Sciences	Engineering	Education	
Gender	Female	35	15	5	25	80
	Male	10	40	50	20	120
Column Totals		45	55	55	45	200

Table 8: 2 x 4 Contingency table with row and column totals

This table shows that

- There are 80 female students in this study.

- There are 120 male students in this study.

- Out of the 200 students in this study, 45 are majoring in arts subjects.

- Out of the 200 students in this study, 55 are majoring in science subjects.

- Out of the 200 students in this study, 55 are majoring in engineering subjects.

- Out of the 200 students in this study, 45 are majoring in education subjects

These row and column totals give the marginal frequencies for these two categories. The **marginal frequency** is the frequency with which each category occurs.

CONDITIONAL RELATIVE FREQUENCIES AND ASSOCIATION

From the above contingency table we can see that

- Among female students, 35/80 or 43.75 percent are majoring in arts subjects. In other words, the conditional percentage of arts majors among female students is 43.75 percent.

- Among male students, 50/120 or 41.67 percent are majoring in engineering subjects. In other words, the conditional percentage of engineering majors among male students is 41.67 percent.

- Among science majors, 15/55 or 27.27 percent are females. In other words, the conditional percentage of female students among the science majors is 27.27 percent.

- Among education majors, 20/45 or 44.44 percent are males. In other words, the conditional percentage of male students among the education majors is 44.44 percent.

The **conditional relative frequency** is the relative frequency of one category given that the other category has occurred. This frequency is used to determine whether there is an association between the two classification criteria. To measure the degree of relation between two quantitative variables, we use the concept of correlation, which we discussed above. On the other hand, to measure the degree of relation between two *categorical* variables, we use the concept of **association**.

If the data above shows a tendency for students of one particular gender to prefer a particular academic major, then we can say that there is an association between gender and academic major. If there is no association between the two classification criteria, then the expected number of measurements in a given cell of the contingency table is equal to

$$\frac{(\text{row total})(\text{column total})}{\text{total number of measurements}}$$

For example, if there is not an association between gender and the academic major of students, then the expected number of female students majoring in sciences would be $\frac{(80)(55)}{200} = 22$. We can compare the expected frequency with the observed frequency to determine if there is an association between the two categories.

- For female students majoring in sciences

    Expected cell count = 22 > observed cell count = 15

    So we can say that there is a negative association between being female and majoring in science. In other words, fewer females tend to choose an academic major in the sciences than would be expected if there were no association between gender and academic major.

- For male students majoring in engineering

    Expected cell count = $\frac{(120)(55)}{200} = 33$ < observed cell count = 50

    So we can say that there is a positive association between being male and majoring in engineering. In other words, more males tend to choose an academic major in engineering than we would expect if there were no association between gender and academic major.

5

PLANNING A STUDY

PLANNING A STUDY

If you want to draw valid conclusions from a study, you must collect the data according to a well-developed plan. This plan must include the question or questions to be answered, as well as an appropriate method of data collection and analysis. This chapter will discuss various techniques for planning a study. In the **Multiple Choice section**, this topic appears in 4 to 6 out of 40 questions. In the **Free Response section**, this topic usually appears in 1 out of 6 questions.

OVERVIEW OF METHODS OF DATA COLLECTION

TERMS AND CONCEPTS

- A **population** is the entire group of individuals in a study.

- A **frame** is a list of all members of the population. For example, a list of all account holders in a bank, a list of participants in the Boston Marathon in the year 2001, etc.

- A **sample** is the part of the population that is actually being examined.

- A **sample survey** is the process of collecting information from a sample. Information obtained from the sample is usually used to make an inference about a population parameter.

- A **census** is the process of collecting information from all the units in a population. It is feasible to do a census if the population is small and the process of getting information does not destroy or modify units of the population. For example, if a school principal wants to know the educational background of the parents of all the children in his school, he can gather this information from every one of the school children.

As the following examples exhibit, a census is very often not a viable method for collecting information. A census is often too costly or too time consuming, and sometimes damaging to the population being studied.

- A political advisor to a candidate for governor wants to determine how much support his candidate has in the state. Suppose the state has 4,000,000 eligible voters. It would clearly be too time consuming to contact each and every voter in this state, and even if it was accomplished, by the time the census was finished, the level of support for the candidate might have changed and the information collected would be useless.

- Suppose an environmentalist is interested in determining the amount of toxins in a lake. Using a census would mean emptying the lake and testing all the water in the lake—obviously not a good way to gather information!

- A manufacturer of light bulbs is interested in determining the mean lifetime of 60-watt bulbs produced by his factory. Using a census would mean burning all the light bulbs produced in the factory and measuring their lifetimes—again, a census would not be practical here.

EXPERIMENTS AND OBSERVATIONAL STUDIES

An **experiment** is a planned activity that results in measurements (data or observations). In an experiment, the experimenter creates differences in the variables involved in the study and then observes the effects of such differences on the resulting measurements. For example, suppose a team of engineers at an automotive factory runs cars at different predetermined and controlled speeds and then crashes the cars at a specific site. Then, the engineers measure the damage to the cars' bumpers. In this example, the team of engineers creates the differences in the environment by running the cars at different speeds.

An **observational study** is an activity in which the experimenter merely plays a role of an observer noting the differences among variables and observing their effects on measurements. The experimenter does not contribute to the creation of these differences. For example, suppose an engineering student collects information from car accident reports filed by the local Police Department. The reports tell the student how fast the cars were traveling when the crashes occurred and how much damage was done to the cars' bumpers. In this example the experimenter (the student) has no control over the variable speed of the car—she does not contribute to the creation of differences among speeds, as the team of engineers did in the previous example. The student merely observes the differences in speeds, as recorded in the reports, and the results of the crashes as measured by the amount of damage to the bumpers.

Experiments are the preferred method of collecting data, but unfortunately, in some situations it is simply impossible to conduct an experiment. Sometimes we must instead use an observational study. For example:

- To study the effect of smoking on people's lungs, an experiment would require one group of people to smoke and another group not to smoke. But it is clearly unethical to ask some people to smoke so that the damage to their lungs can be measured.

- Certain inherited traits affect patients' reaction to medicine. But it is not possible to randomly assign genetic traits to different patients; they are born with those traits. An experiment in this situation would be impossible.

One of the problems with observational studies is that their results are often not extendable to a population, because many observational studies use samples that aren't truly representative of the population, such as volunteers or hospitalized patients. These samples might simply be easiest to obtain. This problem can be solved by making observations on hospitalized as well as non-hospitalized patients.

PLANNING AND CONDUCTING SURVEYS

GETTING SAMPLES

There are different methods of getting a sample from the population. Some sampling methods are better than the others. **Biased sampling** methods result in values that are systematically different from the population values, or systematically favor certain outcomes. **Judgmental sampling, samples of convenience,** and **volunteer samples** are some of the methods that generally result in biased outcomes. Sampling methods that are based on a probabilistic selection of samples, such as simple random sampling, generally result in unbiased outcomes.

BIASED SAMPLES

Judgmental sampling makes use of a non-random approach to determine which item of the population is to be selected in the sample. The approach is entirely based on the judgment of the person selecting the sample. For example, jury selection from an available pool of jurors is not a random process. Lawyers from both parties use their judgment to decide who shall be selected. The result may be a biased jury, i.e., a selection of jurors with specific opinions.

Using a **sample of convenience** is another method that results in biased outcomes. Samples of convenience are too easy to obtain. For example, suppose a real estate agent wants to estimate the mean selling price of houses in a Chicago suburb. To save time, he looks up the selling prices of houses sold in the last three months in the subdivision where he lives. Using his own subdivision may have saved him time, but the sample is not representative of all the houses in that suburb.

Volunteer samples, in which the subjects themselves choose to be part of the sample, may also result in biased outcomes. For example, imagine that a local television station decides to do a survey about a possible tax increase to support the local school system. A telephone number is provided and respondents are asked to call and register their opinions by pressing 1 if they support the tax increase and 2 if they don't. The television station then counts the number of 1s and 2s to determine the degree of support for the tax increase. But the station may well have inadvertently introduced bias into the results. Only those who feel very strongly about the tax increase (either for or against) are likely to call the number and register their opinions, and therefore the sample may not reflect the true feelings of the whole population.

Simple Random Sampling

Simple random sampling is a process of obtaining a sample from a population in which each member has an equal chance of being selected. In this type of sample, there is no bias, or preference for one outcome over another. Simple random samples, also known just as "random samples," are obtained in two different ways:

1. **Sampling with replacement from a finite population.** An example is the process of selecting cards from a deck, provided that you return each card before the next is drawn. With this scheme, the chance of selection remains the same for all cards drawn—namely, 1 out of 52. If you didn't replace the first card before drawing the second, then the chance of selecting a particular second card would be higher (1 out of 51) than the chance of selecting the first one (1 out of 52). When two cards are drawn with replacement, the probability of selecting two particular cards in a row is $(1/52)(1/52) = 0.0003698$, and is the same regardless of the cards selected.

2. **Sampling without replacement from an infinite population** (or a population that is simply very large compared to the sample size). For example, selecting 2 voters from a list of 200,000 registered voters in a city. Here, the population size (200,000) is quite large compared to the sample size (2). Note that when you're sampling without replacement, the available population size decreases as you continue sampling, but since the population size is so large compared to the sample size, the change in the chance of a particular person getting selected is negligible for practical purposes. The chance of selecting the first voter is one out of 200,000 (that is, 0.000005). Since the sample is being selected without replacement, the chance of selecting the second voter increases slightly, to one out of 199,999 (that is 0.000005000025). But this isn't much of a difference. The chance of selecting 2 voters out of 200,000 *without* replacement is $(0.000005)(0.000005000025) = 2.5000125E-11$; whereas the chance of selecting 2 out of 200,000 *with* replacement is $(0.000005)(0.000005) = 2.5E-11$. So for all practical purposes, the chance of selection is the same.

How to select a simple random sample

To select a simple random sample from a population, we need to use some kind of chance mechanism. Here are some examples:

- Imagine prizes offered at a baseball game. A portion of each ticket collected at the stadium entrance is put in a large box. About halfway through the game, all the ticket stubs in the box are mixed thoroughly. Then a pre-specified number of ticket stubs are picked from the box. The persons sitting in the selected seats (as identified by the ticket stubs) receive prizes.

- Suppose there are 40 students in a class. The teacher asks each student to write his or her name on a separate (but identical) piece of paper and drop it in a box. The teacher then mixes thoroughly all the pieces in the box and selects one piece at random, without looking at the name, of course. The student whose name appears on the selected piece of paper is designated as the class representative.

- A teacher wants to select a few students for a project, so she asks each child to toss a coin. Those whose tosses result in "heads" are selected for the project.

- A kindergarten teacher wants to select five children out of 50 to perform a song at the holiday party. The teacher puts two kinds of lollypops in a jar, five of them red and the rest green. He then asks each child to take one lollypop from the jar without looking at it. The five children that pick a red lollypop are selected to sing.

The same random result can be achieved by using random number tables. A portion of a random number table is given below:

96410	96335	55249	16141	61826	57992	21382	33971	12082	91970
26284	92797	33575	94150	40006	54881	13224	03812	70400	45585
75797	18618	90593	54825	64520	78493	92474	32268	07392	73286
48600	65342	08640	78370	10781	58660	77819	79678	67621	74961
82468	15036	79934	76903	48376	09162	51320	84504	39332	26922

To demonstrate the use of random number tables, let us again consider the example of the kindergarten teacher. He could number the children using two digit numbers: 01, 02, 03, ..., 50. He would then start anywhere in the random number table and read each pair of numbers sequentially (it doesn't matter whether he reads vertically or horizontally). But the teacher is selecting from only 50 children. So he should ignore 00 and the numbers from 51 to 99. Suppose he began at the fourth line. Then he would get 48, 60, 06, 53, 42, 08, 64, 07, and so on. The child numbered 48 would be selected. The number 60 in the sequence would be ignored. The next selected child would be number 06. Number 53 in the sequence would be ignored, and so on. As a result, children numbered 48, 06, 42, 08, and 07 would be selected to participate in the program.

Computer programs and calculators can generate random numbers.

TI-83:

- Choose **MATH** → **PRB** → **5: randInt(1,50,5)**

  Enter the range of numbers from which to select and the total number of random numbers to generate. Separate the two numbers by a comma.

  Note: The first and second numbers indicate the range of numbers from which to select, and the third number indicates the number of random numbers to generate. In this case the calculator will generate 5 numbers between 1 and 50.

OTHER METHODS OF RANDOM SAMPLING

Besides simple random sampling, there are other sampling procedures that make use of a random phenomenon to get a sample from a population.

- In a **systematic sampling** procedure, the first item is selected at random from the first k items in the frame, and then every k^{th} item is included in the sample. This method is popular among biologists, foresters, environmentalists, and marine scientists.

- In **stratified random sampling,** the population is divided into groups called strata (the singular is "stratum") and a simple random sample is selected from each stratum. Strata are homogeneous groups of population units—that is, units in a given stratum are similar in some characteristics, while those in different strata differ in those characteristics. For example, students in a university can be grouped into strata by their major. If a population is divided into homogeneous strata, then stratified sampling can be useful in reducing variation.

- In **proportional sampling,** the population is divided into groups called strata, and a simple random sample of size proportional to the stratum size is selected from each stratum. The selection of members of Congress in the U.S. House of Representatives is a good example of proportional sampling; the U.S. Senate, on the other hand, is an example of stratified sampling.

- In **cluster sampling,** a population is divided into non-homogeneous groups called clusters, and a simple random sample is obtained from some clusters, but not necessarily all.

BIAS IN SURVEYS

For a survey to produce reliable results, it must be properly designed and conducted. Samples should be selected using a proper randomization technique. A non-random selection will limit the generalizability of the results. Furthermore, interviewers should be trained in proper interviewing techniques. The attitude and behavior of the interviewer should not lead to any specific answers, since this would result in a biased outcome. Questions should be carefully worded, as the wording of a question can affect the response, and leading questions should be avoided.

Sampling error is a variation inherent in any survey. Even if a survey is repeated using the same sample size and the same questionnaires, the outcome will be different, if only slightly.

SOURCES OF BIAS IN SURVEYS

A survey is biased if it systematically favors certain outcomes.

- **Response bias** is caused by the behavior of the interviewer or respondent. For example, if high school children are asked in the presence of their parents whether they've ever smoked a cigarette, then they are likely to lie. It is possible to reduce response bias by carefully training interviewers and supervising the interview process.

- **Non-response bias** may occur if the person selected for an interview cannot be contacted or refuses to answer.

- **Undercoverage bias** may occur if part of the population is left out of the selection process. For example, if you conduct a telephone survey, individuals without a telephone are left out of the selection process. In the United States, almost 98 percent of households have a telephone, so only a small percent of the population would be left out of a telephone survey. But in many African countries, less than four percent of households have telephones, and those that do are often affluent. A telephone survey there would give biased results. In every U.S. census, a certain percent of the population is missed due to undercoverage. This undercoverage tends to be higher in poorer sections of large cities.

- **Wording effect bias** may occur if confusing or leading questions are asked. For example, imagine an interviewer who says, "The American Dental Association recommends brushing your teeth three times a day. How often do you brush your teeth every day?" The respondents will feel compelled to give an answer of three or more, even if they don't brush their teeth that often. So the responses are likely to be higher than the true average of the population. In this situation, the wording effect bias could be reduced or avoided by simply asking, "How often do you brush your teeth every day?"

PLANNING AND CONDUCTING EXPERIMENTS

TERMS AND CONCEPTS

- A **response** or a **dependent variable** is the variable to be measured in the experiment. An **explanatory** or **independent variable** is a variable that attempts to explain the differences in responses. For example, a dentist is interested in studying the duration of the effects of different amounts of anesthesia. In this case the "amount of anesthesia" is the explanatory variable and the "duration of the effect" is the response variable.

- An **experimental unit** is the smallest unit of the population to which a treatment is applied. In the above example, each patient receiving a dose of anesthesia is an experimental unit. An **observational unit** is the smallest unit for which the measurements are taken. If the observational units are people or animals, they are commonly referred to as "subjects." For example, two different pesticides are to be used to control bugs on pecan trees. Some trees are sprayed with pesticide A and some with pesticide B. After a certain time, a few pecans are selected from each sprayed tree and inspected for infestation. In this situation, each tree is an experimental unit, while each pecan is an observational unit.

- A **confounding variable** is a variable whose effect on the response cannot be separated from the effect of the explanatory variable. For example, an education student is interested in studying the effect of parental involvement in children's education on the level of achievement of those children in school. It is possible that children with lower parental involvement are also from less educated families. If so, the level of parental involvement will be confounded with the parents' education level. If the experiment is not conducted properly, it will not be possible to separate the effect of parental involvement on children's achievement from the effect of the parents' education level on the children's achievement. In properly constructed experiments, an experimenter tries to control confounding variables. Confounding can be an even more serious problem in observational studies, since the experimenter has no control over the confounding variables.

- A **factor** is a variable whose effect on the response is of interest in the experiment. Factors are of two types: quantitative and qualitative. When studying the effect of education level (as defined by less than high school, high school, undergraduate, and graduate) on the achievement of children, the factor "education level" is a qualitative (or "categorical") factor. When studying the effect of a car's speed on its stopping distance, the factor "speed" is a quantitative variable. It is possible to redefine quantitative variables into categorical variables. For example, to study the effect of income level on spending power, we can categorize annual incomes by grouping them into "less than 10,000," "10,000 – 24,999," "25,000 – 49,999," "50,000 – 99,999," and "100,000 and above."

- **Levels** are the values of a factor used in the experiment. An experiment can have one or more factors. The number of levels used in the experiment may differ from factor to factor. **Treatments** are the factor-level combinations used in the experiment. If the experiment has only one factor, then all the levels of that factor are considered treatments of the experiment.

For example, suppose that there is only one medicine on the market for controlling anxiety level. But then two pharmaceutical companies come up with new medicines. A doctor is interested in comparing the effectiveness of the current medicine with that of the two new medicines. Here "anxiety-controlling medicine" is the only factor of interest. There are three levels of this medicine, which become three treatments, namely, "current medicine," "new medicine A," and "new medicine B."

Now suppose the doctor also wants to determine the effect of two types of breathing exercises along with the medicines. Let us call the exercises "Exec1" and "Exec2". Now this experiment has two factors, one at three levels and one at two levels, as shown in the table on the next page.

Factor	Anxiety controlling medicine	Breathing exercises
Number of levels	3	2
Levels	Current medicine	Exce1
	New medicine	
	New medicine B	Exce2

Then, as defined earlier, all the factor-level combinations become treatments. So there are $3 \times 2 = 6$ treatments of interest to the doctor. They are the following:

1. "Current medicine" and "Exec1"

2. "New medicine A" and "Exec1"

3. "New medicine B" and "Exec1"

4. "Current medicine" and "Exec2"

5. "New medicine A" and "Exec2"

6. "New medicine B" and "Exec2"

A **control group** is a group of experimental units similar to all the other experimental units except that it is not given any treatment. A control group is used to establish the baseline response expected from experimental units if no treatment is given. For example, the doctor from the example above might want to know what will happen to the anxiety level of patients if no treatment at all (medicine or breathing exercises) is prescribed.

A **placebo group** is a control group that receives a placebo in experiments involving medicines. A placebo is a medicine that looks exactly like the real medicine, but does not contain any active ingredients. The patients will not be able to tell the placebo and the real medicine apart by looking at them. People who do not receive any medicine sometimes have different responses from those who receive a placebo. It seems that just the comforting thought of taking medicine has some effect on patients, even when they are not receiving any active ingredients. In other words, simply knowinhÙof the presence or absence of an active ingredient can have an effect on a patient's reaction.

SINGLE-BLIND AND DOUBLE-BLIND EXPERIMENTS

Similarly, it is possible that measurements will be biased if the person taking the measurements knows whether a patient received a placebo or not. **Blinding technique** is used in medical experiments to prevent such a bias. The blinding technique can be used in two different fashions: double blinding and single blinding. In a **single-blind experiment**, either the patient does not know which treatment he or she is receiving or the person measuring the patient's reaction does not know which treatment was given. In a **double-blind experiment,** both the patient and the person measuring the patient's reaction does not know which treatment the patient was given.

Double-blind experiments are preferred, but in certain situations they simply can't be conducted. For example, in an experiment designed to compare the drop in cholesterol level produced by a certain medication to that produced by going on a particular diet, the patients always know which treatment they are given. You can't hide from them the fact that they have been subjected to a medication or a low-cholesterol diet! So the double-blind experiment would not be possible. But a single-blind experiment would be possible, since the lab technician measuring the patients' cholesterol level does not need to know which treatment the patients have been getting.

RANDOMIZATION

The technique of randomization is used to average out the effects of extraneous factors on responses. In other words, it balances the effects of factors you cannot see.

- If each experimental unit is supposed to receive only one treatment, then which experimental unit receives which treatment should be determined randomly. For example, in the experiment above that compares three anxiety-controlling medicines, the doctor should use some kind of randomization mechanism (such as one of the methods described earlier) to decide which participating patient should get which one of the three medicines.

- If each experimental unit is supposed to receive all treatments, then the order of treatments should be determined randomly for each experimental unit. Suppose the doctor is interested in comparing the effects of all three medicines on each patient. Then for each patient, the doctor should use some kind of randomization mechanism to decide the order in which the three medicines will be given. All participating patients will be given all three medicines, with some washout period in between the administration of each medicine. But the order in which the three medicines are given will differ with each patient: Some will get "current medicine" first, then "new medicine A," and then "new medicine B." Others will get "new medicine B" first, then "current medicine," and then "new medicine A," and so on.

BLOCKING

The technique of **blocking** is used to control the effects of known factors—factors that you *can* see. A **block** is a group of homogeneous experimental units. Experimental units in a block are similar in certain characteristics, whereas those in different blocks differ in those characteristics. For example, a doctor might suspect that the effect of a certain medicine is different on women than on men. The doctor could then control this potentially confounding factor by separating patients into two groups by gender. There would then be two blocks, male and female. Blocking may reduce unwanted variation in responses, thus allowing the experimenter to see more clearly those differences in responses due to treatments. Essentially, blocking is another way of describing stratification. In the scenario described above in which three medical treatments are given to each patient, each patient is acting as a block. So, the number of blocks is equal to the number of patients.

REPLICATION

Replication refers to the process of giving a certain treatment numerous times in an experiment, or of applying it to a number of different experimental units. Replication reduces chance variation among results. It also allows us to estimate chance variation among results. In the example of comparing three medicines to control anxiety, suppose the doctor prescribes each of three medicines to each patient. If the responses of the three patients were different, then we would not know whether the differences were true effects of medicines or due just to chance. Could differences among the patients have lead to differences in their responses? Yes, it is possible, but we could not know. What if the doctor were to prescribe each medicine to more than one patient? Each patient could receive one of three treatments selected at random. Then, on the average, the three groups of patients would likely be similar. As the differences among patients are averaged out, the effect of treatment differences will stand out.

Would all patients receiving the same treatment have the same responses? No, not likely. Then how can we explain the differences among the responses of patients receiving the same treatment? The differences are due simply to chance variation among results. Without replication, it would not be possible to estimate this chance variation.

COMPLETELY RANDOMIZED DESIGN

In a completely randomized design, treatments are assigned randomly to all experimental units or experimental units are assigned randomly to all treatments. This design can compare any number of treatments. There are advantages in having an equal number of experimental units for each treatment, but this is not necessary.

Example 1: Suppose a doctor is interested in comparing the anxiety-controlling drug out on the market now (let's call it "current medicine") with two new drugs ("new medicine A" and "new medicine B"). A group of patients from a local clinic is available for the experiment. Design an experiment to compare the effects of these three drugs.

Solution: In this experiment, there is one factor of interest with three levels.

- Factor of interest: anxiety-controlling medicines
- Number of levels: 3
- Treatments: "current medicine," "new medicine A," and "new medicine B"
- Experimental unit: each patient
- Response variable: the anxiety level measured for each patient

Use the group of patients available from the local clinic and design the experiment as follows:

- Measure the anxiety level of each patient.
- Use a randomization scheme to divide the patients into three groups. For example, throw a six-sided die for each patient. If the numbers 1 or 2 show, then assign the patient to group 1; if the numbers 3 or 4 show, assign the patient to group 2; otherwise, assign to group 3. Or fill a jar with blue, red, and green beads, with the total number of beads equal to the total number of participating patients. Ask each patient to take out one bead without looking in the jar. If the patient selects a blue bead, assign that patient to group 1; if the patient selects a red bead, assign to group 2; if the patient selects a green bead, assign to group 3.
- Prescribe current medicine to all patients in group 1.
- Prescribe new medicine A to all patients in group 2.
- Prescribe new medicine B to all patients in group 3.

- After a designated time period, measure the anxiety level of each patient.

- Compare the results.

This scheme can also be described using the following diagram:

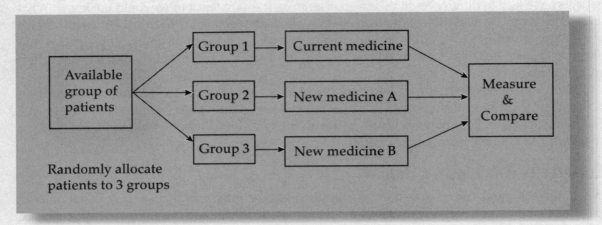

Figure 1: Schematic diagram of a completely randomized experiment

RANDOMIZED BLOCK DESIGN

If the treatments are the only systematic differences present in the experiment, then the completely randomized design is best for comparing the responses. But often there are other factors affecting responses. Unless they are controlled, the results will be biased. As we discussed earlier, one way to control the effects of known extraneous factors is to form groups of similar units called blocks. In a randomized block design, all treatments are grouped by certain characteristics to form homogeneous blocks, and then a completely randomized design is applied within each block. The blocking of experimental units allows the experimenter to remove systematic differences in responses due to a known factor, and leads to more precise conclusions from the experiment.

If there are only two treatments to be compared in the presence of a blocking factor, then you should use a **randomized paired comparison design**. This can be designed in two different ways.

- Form two or more blocks of experimental units. Each block should be matched by some characteristic. Within each block, toss a coin to assign two treatments to two experimental units randomly. In other words, both treatments will be applied within each block, with each experimental unit receiving only one treatment. Since both experimental units are similar to each other except for the treatment received, the differences in responses can be attributed to the differences in treatments. This type of experiment is called a **matched-pairs design.**

- Alternatively, each experimental unit can be used as its own block. Assign both treatments to each experimental unit, but in random order. To control the effect of the order of treatment, randomly determine the order. With each experimental unit, toss a coin to decide if the order of treatments should be "treatment 1 → treatment 2," or "treatment 2 → treatment 1." Since both treatments are assigned to the same experimental unit, the individual effects of experimental units are nullified, and the differences in responses can be attributed to the differences in treatments.

Example 2: Suppose a doctor wants to compare the anxiety-controlling drug currently on the market ("current medicine") with two new drugs ("new medicine A" and "new medicine B"). A group of patients from a local clinic is available for the experiment. All three drugs are known to have different effects on men and women. Design an experiment to compare the effects of the three drugs.

Solution: In this experiment, there are two factors of interest, anxiety-controlling medicine and patient's gender. Of these two factors, anxiety-controlling medicine is a treatment, whereas patient's gender is a blocking factor. Patient responses may be different because of the treatment administered or because of the patient's gender. Separate the available group of patients by gender, so that block 1 consists only of men and block 2 only of women. Now, within each block all the patients are similar (same gender).

Measure the anxiety level of each participating patient. For each male patient, randomly assign one of the three treatments. For example, use a random number table to get one-digit random numbers. Assign numbers {1, 2, 3} to group 1, numbers {4, 5, 6} to group 2, numbers {7, 8, 9} to group 3, and ignore number 0. Then draw a random number for each patient. Separate the patients into three groups depending on the number they've drawn. Prescribe current medicine to patients in group 1, new medicine A to patients in group 2, and new medicine B to patients in group 3. After a designated time, measure the anxiety level of each patient. Repeat this procedure for all female patients. When finished, compare the results. The following schematic diagram describes the design.

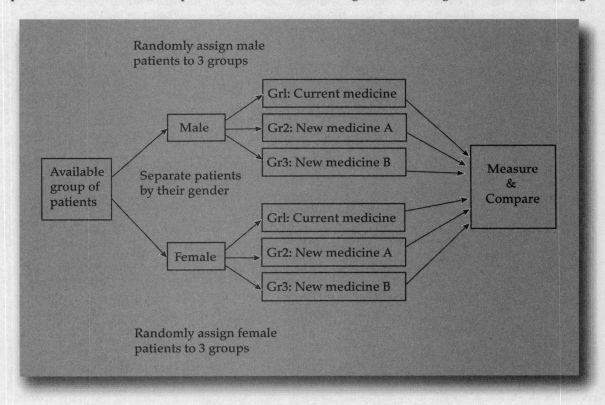

Figure 2: Schematic diagram of a randomized block design

Alternatively, the same experiment could be conducted as follows:

- Separate the available group of patients by gender, so that block 1 consists only of men and block 2 only of women. Administer all three medicines to each patient one at a time, with a washout period in between. Determine the order in which the medicines are to be given using a randomization scheme. For example, use a random number table to get random one-digit numbers. Assign number 1 to the current medicine, number 2 to new medicine A, number 3 to new medicine B, and ignore numbers 0, 4, 5, 6, 7, 8, 9. Get two distinct random numbers for each patient to determine the order of medicines. For example, suppose the first patient draws {3, 1}. First, measure this patient's anxiety level. Then give the patient new medicine A, and after a designated time, measure the patient's anxiety level. Then after a period of "washout" time, measure the patient's anxiety level again, administer the current medicine, and afterward, measure the anxiety level. Again, after another period of washout time, measure the patient's anxiety level, administer new medicine B, and measure the anxiety level. The order of medicines given will differ for each patient, depending on the random numbers drawn. Compare the results for all three medicines, as well as for both genders.

- Here we have two sets of blocks. Gender defines one set of blocks and each patient becomes a block by itself. The following schematic diagram describes the design.

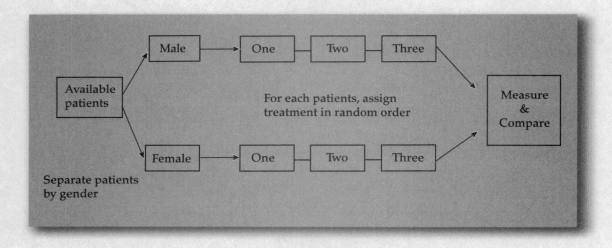

Figure 3: Schematic diagram of a randomized block design

MATCHED-PAIRS DESIGN

Example 3: A local sickle cell association offers programs to educate people about sickle cell disease. The director of the association is interested in assessing the program's effect on the participants' knowledge about the disease.

(a) Design an experiment to assess the effectiveness of this educational program.

(b) Explain why this is a matched-pairs experiment.

Solution:

(a) Prepare a test consisting of questions about sickle-cell disease. Select a random sample of participants enrolled in the program. At the beginning of the program, administer the test to all selected participants. Let's call this the pre-test. Record the results of the pre-test. Then let all the participants complete the program. Afterward, administer the same test again. Let's call this the post-test. Record the results of the post-test. Finally, compare the results of the pre-test to the post-test.

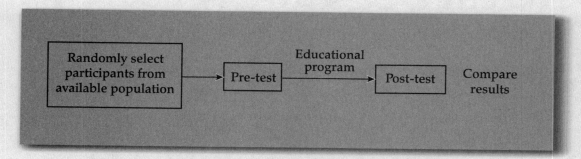

Figure 4: Schematic diagram of a matched-pairs design

(b) This is a matched-pairs design because the results of the two tests are matched by person. In this experiment, each participant's pre-test results are compared to the same participant's post-test results. A comparison of the pre-test results of one participant with the post-test results of another participant would be meaningless.

6

ANTICIPATING PATTERNS

ANTICIPATING PATTERNS: PRODUCING MODELS USING PROBABILITY AND SIMULATION

This chapter will discuss how to use probability as a tool to judge the distribution of data under a given model. In the **Multiple Choice section**, this topic appears in 8 to 12 out of 40 questions. In the **Free Response section**, this topic appears in 1 or 2 out of 6 questions.

PROBABILITY

Words referring to probability or chance are commonly used in conversation. For example, we often come across statements like these:

- It is likely to rain today, so please take your umbrella with you.

- It was an easy test; I'll probably get an A on it.

- The Yankees have a much better chance of winning than the Mets.

Words like "probably," "likely," and "chance" carry similar meanings in conversation. They all convey uncertainty. By using probability, we can also make a numerical statement about uncertainty. For example, bank managers can never know exactly when their depositors will make a withdrawal or exactly how much they'll withdraw. Managers also know that though most loans they've granted will be paid back, some of them will result in defaults—but they can't know exactly which ones. In other words, a variety of outcomes is possible, and therefore bank managers can never know exactly how much money the bank will have at any given moment in the future. However, the bankers can use the rules of probability and their past experience to make a reasonable estimation, and then use that estimation when making business decisions.

What Is "Probability"?

Probability is a measure of the likelihood of an event. Consider a fair coin toss. What makes this coin toss "fair"? We call it fair if the chance of the coin's showing heads when flipped is the same as its chance of showing tails—in other words, if there is a 50 percent chance of its showing heads and a 50 percent chance of its showing tails. Suppose we tossed the coin twice and got two heads. Does that mean this coin toss was not fair? What if we toss the coin three times? What do we expect to happen? Let's toss a coin 5, 10, 15, 20, 25, and more times and count the number of heads. Then we can calculate the probability of getting heads in a toss and plot that figure on a graph.

$$P(\text{heads in a toss}) = \frac{\text{Number of heads}}{\text{Number of tosses}}$$

$$\text{Percent of heads} = \frac{\text{Number of heads}}{\text{Number of tosses}} \times 100$$

The following table lists the results of one such experiment, and the plot shows them graphically.

Number of tosses	Number of heads	P(heads)	Percent of heads	Number of tosses	Number of heads	P(heads)	Percent of heads
2	0	0	0	35	17	0.48571	48.571
3	2	0.66667	66.667	40	18	0.45	45
4	3	0.75	75	45	18	0.4	40
5	5	1	100	50	23	0.46	46
6	3	0.5	50	60	32	0.53333	53.333
7	5	0.71429	71.429	70	29	0.41429	41.429
8	5	0.625	62.5	80	34	0.425	42.5
9	7	0.77778	77.778	90	48	0.53333	53.333
10	4	0.4	40	100	49	0.49	49
15	10	0.66667	66.667	150	74	0.49333	49.333
20	9	0.45	45	200	106	0.53	53
25	12	0.48	48	500	264	0.528	52.8
30	17	0.56667	56.667	1000	508	0.508	50.8

Table 1: Number of heads shown in different numbers of tosses

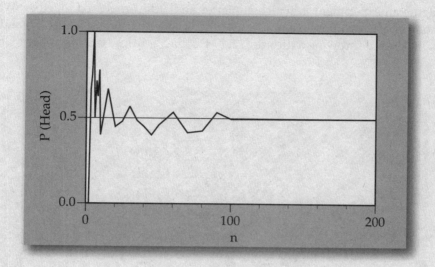

Figure 1: *P*(heads) estimated from different numbers of tosses

Notice that as the number of tosses increases, the percent of times that the coin lands on heads gets closer and closer to 50 percent. In other words, in the long run the relative frequency of getting heads in the toss approaches 0.5, which is what we expected it to be. This relative frequency reflects the concept of probability. In fact, in the long run, the relative frequency of the occurrence of any specific event will always approach the expected value, also known as the probability.

SAMPLE SPACE

Any process that results in an observation or an outcome is an experiment. An experiment may have more than one possible outcome. A set of all possible outcomes of an experiment is known as a **sample space**. It is generally denoted using the letter S.

- Tossing a coin may result in one of two possible outcomes, "heads" or "tails." Therefore, the sample space of tossing a coin is

$$S = \{Heads, Tails\}$$

- Throwing a die may result in one of six possible outcomes. The resulting sample space is

$$S = \{1, 2, 3, 4, 5, 6\}$$

- Tossing two coins may result in one of four possible outcomes. We can indicate the outcome of each of the two tosses by using a pair of letters, the first letter of which indicates the outcome of tossing the first coin and the second letter the outcome of tossing the second coin. H is for heads and T for tails. Then the resulting sample space is

$$S = \{(H, H), (H, T), (T, H), (T, T)\}$$

The outcomes listed in a sample space are never repeated, and no outcome is left out. Two events are said to be equally likely if one does not occur more often than the other. For example, the six possible outcomes for a throw of a die are equally likely.

A **tree diagram** representation is useful in determining the sample space for an experiment. For example, imagine an experiment in which a quarter and a die are tossed together. What are all the possible outcomes? The two possible outcomes of tossing a quarter are heads (H) and tails (T). The six possible outcomes of throwing a die are 1, 2, 3, 4, 5, and 6. Below is a tree diagram of the possible outcomes:

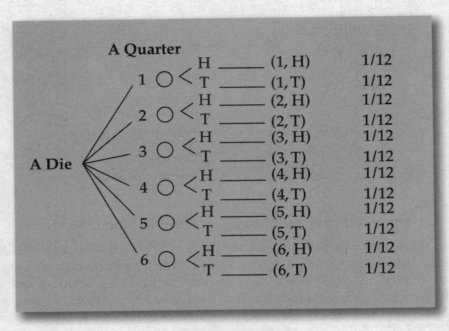

Figure 2: Tree diagram

Looking at the tree diagram, it is easy to see that the sample space is

S = {(H, 1), (H, 2), (H, 3), (H, 4), (H, 5), (H, 6),
(T, 1), (T, 2), (T, 3), (T, 4), (T, 5), (T, 6)}

The first letter of each pair represents the outcome of tossing the coin and the second represents the outcome of throwing the die. All 12 outcomes are equally likely. Therefore, the probability of each outcome is $\frac{1}{12}$.

It is common practice to use capital letters to indicate an event. For example, one may define

A = getting an even number when a die is thrown = {2, 4, 6}

B = getting two heads when two coins are tossed simultaneously = {(H, H)}

The probability of an event is generally denoted by a capital "P" followed by the name of the event in parentheses: P(the event). If all the events in a sample space are equally likely, then by using the concept of relative frequency, we can compute the probability of an event as

$$P(\text{an event}) = \frac{\text{Number of outcomes that lead to the event}}{\text{Total number of possible outcomes}}$$

Applying this to the events defined early—A (getting an even number in the toss of a die) and B (getting two heads when two coins are tossed)—we get:

- $P(A) = \dfrac{3}{6} = \dfrac{1}{2} = 0.5$. The probability of getting an even number when a six-sided die is thrown is 0.5. In other words, there is a 50 percent chance of getting an even number when a six-sided die is thrown.

- $P(B) = \dfrac{1}{4} = 0.25$. The probability of getting two heads when two coins are tossed simultaneously is 0.25. In other words, there is a 25 percent chance of getting two heads when two coins are tossed simultaneously.

BASIC PROBABILITY RULES AND TERMS

There are two rules that all the probabilities must satisfy:

- **Rule 1:** For any event A, the probability of A is always greater than or equal to 0 and less than or equal to 1.

$$0 \le P(A) \le 1$$

- **Rule 2:** The sum of the probabilities for all possible outcomes in a sample space is always 1.

As a result, we can say the following:

- If an event can never occur, its probability is 0. Such an event is known as an **impossible event.**

- If an event must occur every time, its probability is 1. Such an event is known as a **sure event.**

The **odds in favor of an event** is a ratio of the probability of the occurrence of an event to the probability of the non-occurrence of that event.

$$\text{Odds in favor of an event} = \frac{P(\text{event A occurs})}{P(\text{event A does not occur})}$$

or

$$P(\text{Event A occurs}) : P(\text{Event A does not occur})$$

Example 1: When tossing a die, what are the odds in favor of getting the number 2?
Solution: When tossing a die,

$$P(\text{getting the number 2}) = \frac{1}{6} \text{ and}$$

$$P(\text{not getting the number 2}) = P(\text{getting the numbers 1, 3, 4, 5, or 6}) = \frac{5}{6}.$$

Thus, the odds in favor of getting the number 2 are $\dfrac{1}{6} : \dfrac{5}{6}$ or 1 to 5 (or 1:5).

More terms

The **complement** of an event is the set of all possible outcomes in a sample space that does not lead to the event. The complement of an event A is denoted by A'.

The **union** of events A and B is the set of all possible outcomes that lead to at least one of two events A and B. The union of events A and B is denoted by $(A \cup B)$ or (A or B).

The **intersection** of events A and B is the set of all possible outcomes that lead to both events A and B. The intersection of events A and B is denoted by $(A \cap B)$ or (A and B).

Disjoint or **mutually exclusive events** are events that have no outcome in common. In other words, they cannot occur together.

A **conditional event**: A given B is a set of outcomes for event A that occurs if B has occurred. It is indicated by (A | B) and reads "event A given B."

Two events A and B are considered **independent** if the occurrence of one event does not depend on the occurrence of the other.

Independence versus dependence

Imagine that you shuffle a standard deck of cards and then draw a card at random. The chance of your getting an ace is the same across all four suits (hearts, clubs, diamonds, and spades). In other words, the likelihood of your getting an ace does not depend on the suit of the card. So we can say that the events "getting an ace" and "getting a particular suit" are independent.

Now consider a doctor examining patients in an emergency room. The likelihood of a patient being diagnosed for a knee injury is higher if that patient is a football player, because football players are more likely to suffer knee injuries than nonfootball players. Therefore the event "knee injury" depends on the event "football player."

The following Venn diagrams describe some of the terms previously discussed.

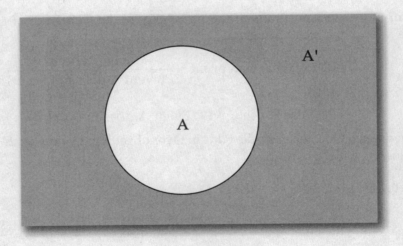

Figure 3: Event A and its complement

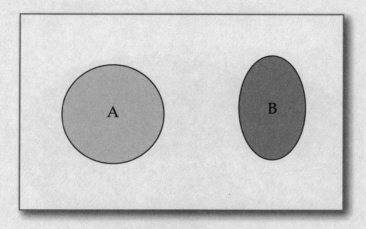

Figure 4: Disjoint events A and B

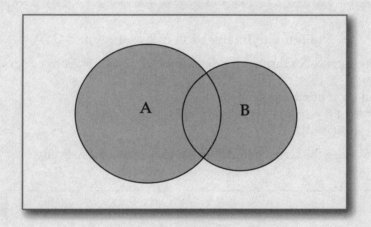

Figure 5: Union of events A and B

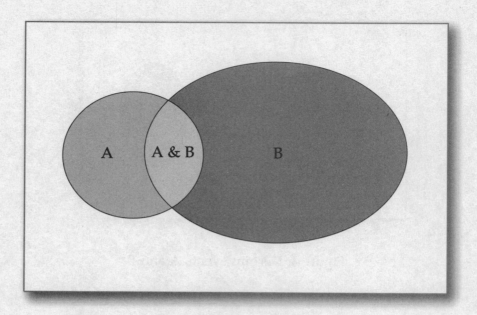

Figure 6: Intersection of events A and B

Example 2: the sample space for throwing a die is S = {1, 2, 3, 4, 5, 6}. Suppose events A, B, and C are defined as follows:

    A = Getting an even number = {2, 4, 6}

    B = Getting at least 5 = {5, 6}

    C = Getting at most 3 = {1, 2, 3}

Solution: How do we use the terms defined above to describe these events?

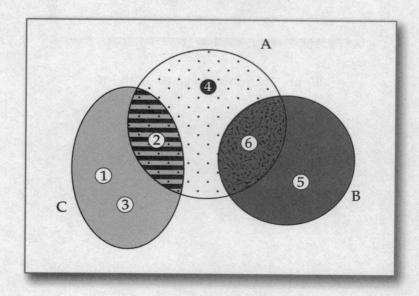

Figure 7: Venn diagram

- **Probability:** $P(A) = \dfrac{3}{6} = 0.5$, $P(B) = \dfrac{2}{6} = 0.33$, and $P(C) = \dfrac{3}{6} = 0.5$

- **Complement:** A' = getting an odd number = {1, 3, 5}

$$P(A') = \frac{3}{6} = 0.5$$

B' = getting a number less than 5 = {1, 2, 3, 4}

$$P(B') = \frac{4}{6} = 0.66$$

C' = getting a number larger than 3 = {4, 5, 6}

$$P(C') = \frac{3}{6} = 0.5$$

- **Union:** $(A \cup B)$ = Getting an even number or a number greater than or equal to 5 or both.

$$= \{2,\ 4,\ 5,\ 6\}$$

$$P(A \cup B) = \frac{4}{6} = 0.667$$

$(A \cup C)$ = Getting an even number or a number less than or equal to 3 or both.

$$= \{1,\ 2,\ 3,\ 4,\ 6\}$$

$$P(A \cup C) = \frac{5}{6} = 0.833$$

$(B \cup C)$ = Getting a number that is at most 3 or at least 5 or both.

$$= \{1,\ 2,\ 3,\ 5,\ 6\}$$

$$P(B \cup C) = \frac{5}{6} = 0.833$$

- **Intersection:** $(A \cap B)$ = Getting an even number that is at least 5 = {6}

$$P(A \cap B) = \frac{1}{6} = 0.167$$

$(A \cap C)$ = Getting an even number that is at most 3 = {2}

$$P(A \cap C) = \frac{1}{6} = 0.167$$

$(B \cap C)$ = Getting a number that is at most 3 and at least 5 = { }

$$P(B \cap C) = \frac{0}{6} = 0.000$$

In other words, B and C are disjoint or mutually exclusive events.

- **Conditional event:** $(A \mid C)$ = Getting an even number given that the number is at most 3 = {2}

$$P(A \mid C) = \frac{1}{3}$$

$(A \mid B)$ = Getting an even number given that the number is at least 5 = {6}

$$P(A \mid B) = \frac{1}{2}$$

MORE PROBABILITY RULES

- **Complement**: The probability of the complement of an event A is given by
$$P(A') = 1 - P(A)$$

- **Union** (Addition rule): The probability of the union of two events A and B is given by
$$P(A \cup B) = P(A) + P(B) - P(A \cap B)$$

If the events A and B are disjoint, then $P(A \cap B) = 0$

$$P(A \cup B) = P(A) + P(B)$$

- **Intersection** (Multiplication rule): For events A and B defined in a sample space S
$$P(A \cap B) = P(A) \cdot P(B \mid A) \text{ and } P(A \cap B) = P(B) \cdot P(A \mid B)$$

- **Conditional probabilities:** The symbol $P(A \mid B)$ indicates the probability that event A will occur given that event B has occurred. It is read as "probability of A given B."

$$P(A \mid B) = \frac{P(A \cap B)}{P(B)}$$

- **Independence**: Two events A and B are independent if and only if
$$P(A \mid B) = P(A) \text{ or } P(B \mid A) = P(B)$$

In other words, two events A and B are independent if and only if

$$P(A \cap B) = P(A) \cdot P(B)$$

Example 3: Imagine that you shuffle a standard deck of 52 cards and draw a card at random. Let

D = diamond	C = club	
H = heart	S = spade	
J = jack	Q = queen	K = king

Then

$$S = \{D1, ..., D10, DJ, DQ, DK, C1, ..., C10, CJ, CQ, CK$$
$$H1, ..., H10, HJ, HQ, HK, S1, ..., S10, SJ, SQ, SK\}$$

Suppose we define the following events:

$$A = \text{Getting an ace} = \{D1, C1, H1, S1\}$$

$$B = \text{Getting a diamond} = \{D1, ..., D10, DJ, DQ, DK\}$$

$$C = \text{Getting a club} = \{C1, C2, ..., CJ, CQ, CK\}$$

Then

- $P(A) = \dfrac{4}{52}$, $P(B) = \dfrac{13}{52}$, and $P(C) = \dfrac{13}{52}$

- $A' = \text{Getting a non-ace card}$

- $P(A') = 1 - P(A) = 1 - \dfrac{4}{52} = \dfrac{48}{52}$

- $B' = \text{Getting a card other than any diamond}$

- $P(B') = 1 - P(B) = 1 - \dfrac{13}{52} = \dfrac{39}{52}$

- $(A \cap B) = \text{Getting an ace of diamonds} = \{D1\}$

$$P(A \cap B) = \frac{1}{52}$$

Events A and B are not disjoint, since an ace of diamonds (D1) is a common outcome for both the events.

- $(B \cap C) = \text{Getting a card that is a club and a diamond} = \{\ \}$

$$P(B \cap C) = 0$$

The events B and C are disjoint, since no outcome is common to them. Each card in a deck belongs to only one suit.

- $(A \cup B) = \text{Getting an ace or a diamond or both}$

$$\{D1, ..., D10, DJ, DQ, DK, C1, H1, S1\}$$

$$P(A \cup B) = \frac{16}{52}$$

Alternatively,

$$P(A \cup B) = P(A) + P(B) - P(A \cap B)$$
$$= \frac{4}{52} + \frac{13}{52} - \frac{1}{52}$$
$$= \frac{16}{52}$$

- $P(B \cup C)$ = Getting a diamond or a club or both

$$= \{D1, \ldots, D10, \; DJ, \; DQ, \; DK, \; C1, \ldots, C10, \; CJ, \; CQ, \; CK\}$$

$$P(B \cup C) = \frac{26}{52}$$

Alternatively, since B and C are disjoint, $P(B \cap C) = 0$. Therefore,

$$P(B \cup C) = P(B) + P(C)$$
$$= \frac{13}{52} + \frac{13}{52}$$
$$= \frac{26}{52}$$

- $(A \mid B)$ = Getting an ace given that a diamond has been drawn = $\{D1\}$

$$P(A \mid C) = \frac{1}{13}$$

Alternatively,

$$P(A \mid B) = \frac{P(A \cap B)}{P(B)} = \frac{1/52}{13/52} = \frac{1}{13}$$

Note that $P(A \mid B) = P(A)$. Therefore, events A and B are independent.

Example 4: Seventy-five percent of people who purchase hair dryers are women. Of these women purchasers of hairdryers, 30 percent are over 50 years old. What is the probability that a randomly selected hair dryer purchaser is a woman over 50 years old?

Solution: Let us define the events as follows:

W = The purchaser of a hair dryer is a woman.
F = The purchaser of a hair dryer is over 50 years old.

It is known that $P(W) = 0.75$ and $P(F \mid W) = 0.30$.
Thus,

$$P(W \cap F) = P(F \mid W) \cdot P(W) = 0.30(0.75) = 0.225$$

There is a 22.5 percent chance that a randomly selected hair dryer purchaser is a woman over 50 years old.

Example 5: An insurance agent knows that 70 percent of her customers carry adequate collision coverage. She also knows that of those who carry adequate coverage, 5 percent have been involved in accidents, and of those who do not carry adequate coverage, 12 percent have been involved in accidents. If one of her clients gets involved in an auto accident, then what is the probability that the client does not have adequate insurance coverage?

Solution: Let us define events as follows:

A = Client carries adequate coverage
B = Client is involved in an auto accident

We need to find $P(A'|B)$, which equals $\dfrac{P(A'\cap B)}{P(B)}$

It is known that

$P(A)$ = Probability that a client carries adequate coverage = 0.70

$P(B|A)$ = Probability that a client carrying adequate coverage is involved in an auto accident = 0.05

$P(B|A')$ = Probability that a client without enough coverage is involved in an auto accident = 0.12

The probability that a client is not carrying enough insurance and gets involved in an auto accident is

$$P(A'\cap B) = P(B|A') \cdot P(A')$$
$$= 0.12(1-0.70)$$
$$= 0.036$$

and the probability that a randomly selected client is involved in an auto accident is

$$P(B) = P(B|A') \cdot P(A) + P(B|A') \cdot P(A')$$
$$= 0.05(0.70) + 0.12(1-0.70)$$
$$= 0.071$$

Therefore,

$$P(A'|B) = \frac{P(A'\cap B)}{P(B)} = \frac{0.036}{0.071} = 0.507$$

There is a 50.7 percent chance that this client does not carry adequate insurance.

Example 6: The local Chamber of Commerce conducted a survey of one thousand randomly selected shoppers at a mall. For all shoppers, "gender of shopper," and "items shopping for" was recorded. The data collected is summarized in the following table.

Gender	Items shopping for			
	Clothing	Shoes	Other	Total
Male	75	25	150	250
Female	350	230	170	750
Total	425	255	320	1000

If a shopper is selected at random from this mall,

(a) What is the probability that the shopper is a female?

(b) What is the probability that the shopper is shopping for shoes?

(c) What is the probability that the shopper is a female shopping for shoes?

(d) What is the probability that the shopper is shopping for shoes given that the shopper is a female?

(e) Are the events "female" and "shopping for shoes" disjoint?

(f) Are the events "female" and "shopping for shoes" independent?

Solution:

(a) What is the probability that the shopper is a female?

$$P = P(\text{Female}) = \frac{750}{1000} = 0.75$$

(b) What is the probability that the shopper is shopping for shoes?

$$P(\text{Shopping for shoes}) = \frac{255}{1000} = 0.25$$

(c) What is the probability that the shopper is a female shopping for shoes?

$$P(\text{Female} \cap \text{Shopping for shoes}) = \frac{230}{1000} = 0.23$$

(d) What is the probability that the shopper is shopping for shoes given that the shopper is a female?

$$P(\text{Shopping for shoes} \mid \text{Female}) = \frac{P(\text{Shopping for shoes} \cap \text{Female})}{P(\text{Female})}$$

$$= \frac{0.23}{0.75}$$

$$= 0.3067$$

(e) Are the events "female" and "shopping for shoes" disjoint?

There are 230 females shopping for shoes, or

$P(\text{Female} \cap \text{Shopping for shoes}) = 0.23 \neq 0$. Therefore the events "female" and "shopping for shoes" are not disjoint.

(f) Are the events "female" and "shopping for shoes" independent?

$P(\text{Shopping for shoes} \mid \text{Female}) = 0.3067$ and $P(\text{Shopping for shoes}) = 0.255$, which means $P(\text{Shopping for shoes} \mid \text{Female}) \neq P(\text{Shopping for shoes})$. Therefore, events "female" and "shopping for shoes" are not independent.

RANDOM VARIABLES AND THEIR PROBABILITY DISTRIBUTIONS

A **variable** is a quantity whose value varies from subject to subject. Examples include height (which varies from person to person), the number of e-mail messages you receive per day (which changes from day to day), the number of patients examined by a doctor per day (which changes from day to day), the number of home runs hit in a season by members of a baseball team (which varies from player to player), the hair color of students in a class (which varies from student to student), and the altitude of an airplane in flight (which varies from minute to minute).

A **probability experiment** is an experiment whose possible outcomes may be known but whose exact outcome is a random event and cannot be predicted with certainty in advance. If the outcome of a probability experiment takes a numerical value, then the outcome is a **quantitative variable**. A **random variable** is a numeric outcome of a probability experiment. Random variables are usually denoted using capital letters, such as X or Y. Sometimes two or more variables are denoted using the same letter but different subscripts, such as X_1 and X_2.

There are two types of random variables, discrete and continuous:

- A **discrete random variable** is a quantitative variable that takes a countable number of values. The following are all discrete random variables: the number of e-mail messages received per day, the number of home runs per batter, the number of red blood cells per sample of blood, the number of students present in class per day, and the number of customers served by a bank teller per hour. Note that between any two possible values of a discrete random variable, there is a countable number of possible values. You may receive 10 e-mail messages a day, or 12 messages a day, but you can never receive 12.5 messages in one day, or 12.6324 messages.

- A **continuous random variable** is a quantitative variable that can take all the possible values in a given range. A person's weight is a good example. A person can weigh 150 pounds, or 155 pounds, or any weight between those two, including 151.5 pounds or 153.23487 pounds. Other examples of continuous random values are the height attained by a plane, the amount of rainfall in a city per day, the amount of gasoline pumped into a car's gas tank, the weight of a newborn baby, and the amount of water flowing through a dam per hour.

THE PROBABILITY DISTRIBUTIONS OF DISCRETE RANDOM VARIABLES

A **probability distribution of a discrete random variable** or a **discrete probability distribution** is a table, list, graph, or formula giving all possible values taken by a random variable and their corresponding probabilities.

Let X be a random variable taking values $x_1, x_2, \cdots, x_n$ with respective probabilities $P(x_1), P(x_2), \cdots, P(x_n)$. Then $\left\{ \left(x_1, P(x_1) \right), \left(x_2, P(x_2) \right), \cdots, \left(x_n, P(x_n) \right) \right\}$ gives a valid probability distribution if:

- $0 \le P(x_i) \le 1$ for all $i = 1, 2, \cdots, n$, and

- $\sum_{i=1}^{n} P(x_i) = 1$

If $\left\{ (x_1, P(x_1)), (x_2, P(x_2)), \cdots, (x_n, P(x_n)) \right\}$ gives a valid probability distribution, then the probability that random variable X takes values less than or equal to the specified value gives the **cumulative distribution function (CDF)**.

$$\text{CDF} = P(X \le x_k) = \sum_{i=1}^{k} P(X = x_i) \text{ for all } k = 1, 2, \ldots, n$$

Random Variable X	Probability $P(X = x)$	Cumulative Probability $P(X \le x_k)$
x_1	$P(x_1)$	$P(x_1)$
x_2	$P(x_2)$	$P(x_1) + P(x_2)$
x_3	$P(x_3)$	$P(x_1) + P(x_2) + P(x_3)$
$\vdots$	$\vdots$	$\vdots$
x_n	$P(x_n)$	$P(x_1) + P(x_2) + \ldots + P(x_n) = 1$

Table 2: Cumulative probability distribution of a discrete random variable

MEAN OF A DISCRETE RANDOM VARIABLE

The mean μ of a discrete random variable X is also known as the **expected value**. It is denoted by $E(X)$ and is computed by multiplying each value of the random variable by its probability and then adding over the sample space.

$$\mu = E(X) = \sum_{i=1}^{n} x_i P(x_i)$$

VARIANCE OF A DISCRETE RANDOM VARIABLE

The variance of a discrete random variable is defined as the sum of the product of squared deviations of the values of the variable from the mean and the corresponding probabilities.

$$\sigma^2 = \sum_{i=1}^{n} \left(x_i - \mu \right)^2 P(x_i)$$

But this formula is not convenient for computation. Mathematically, it is equivalent to the following formula, which is easier to use.

$$\sigma^2 = \left[\sum_{i=1}^{n} x_i^2 P(x_i) \right] - \mu^2$$

Remember that standard deviation is simply the square root of variance.

Example 7: Sophia was recently promoted to assistant manager at a small women's clothing store. One of her duties is to fill out order forms for women's shirts, which come in sizes 6, 7, 8, 9, 10, 11, and 12. She would like to determine how many shirts of each size to order. At first she thought of ordering exactly the same number of shirts from each of the available sizes, but then she decided against doing that, since there might be a greater demand for certain sizes than for others. She looked up sales receipts from the past three months and summarized the information as follows:

Shirt size	6	7	8	9	10	11	12
Number sold	85	122	138	154	177	133	92

(a) Prepare a probability distribution of the number of shirts sold for each size.

(b) What is the probability that a randomly selected customer will request a shirt of size at least 11?

(c) Compute the expected shirt size of a random shopper and the standard deviation of the shirt size.

(d) If Sophia plans to order a total of 1,000 shirts, how many shirts of size 8 should she order?

Solution: (a) The total number of shirts sold is 901. Using this information we can compute the probability of each shirt size being sold. For example, the probability of selling size 6 is $85/901 = 0.09$. The random variable here (X) is the shirt size, and it takes values 6, 7, 8, 9, 10, 11, and 12. Both the table and the graph below give the probability distribution of the number of shirts sold for each size.

Probability distribution of shirt size:

Shirt size	$P(x)$
6	0.09
7	0.14
8	0.15
9	0.17
10	0.20
11	0.15
12	0.10

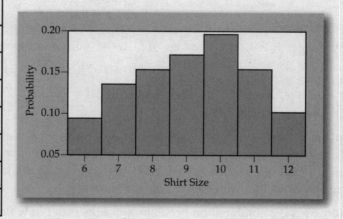

Table 3: Probability distribution of shirt size

Figure 8: Probability distribution of shirt size

This probability distribution shows that 9 percent of the customers bought size 6 shirts, 14 percent bought size 7 shirts, and so on.

(b) P(a customer will request a shirt of size at least 11)

$$= P(\text{shirt size} = 11 \text{ or } 12)$$

$$= P(\text{shirt size} = 11) + P(\text{shirt size} = 12)$$

$$= 0.15 + 0.10$$

$$= 0.25$$

(c) The expected shirt size:

$$\mu = E(x) = 6(0.09) + 7(0.14) + 8(0.15) + 9(0.17) + 10(0.20) + 11(0.15) + 12(0.10) = 9.09$$

The standard deviation of shirt size:

$$\sigma = \sqrt{6^2(0.09) + 7^2(0.14) + \cdots + 12^2(0.10) - 9.09^2} = \sqrt{86.02 - 82.63} = 1.84$$

(d) Suppose Sophia plans to a order total of 1,000 shirts.

From the probability distribution, $P(\text{shirt size} = 8) = 0.15$.

Therefore she needs to order $1000(0.15) = 150$ shirts of size 8.

COMBINATIONS

A **combination** is the number of ways r items can be selected out of n items if the order of selection is *not* important. It is denoted by $\begin{pmatrix} n \\ r \end{pmatrix}$, which reads as "$n$ choose r," and is computed as

$$\begin{pmatrix} n \\ r \end{pmatrix} = \frac{n!}{r!(n-r)!}$$

For any integer $n \geq 0$, $n!$ is read as "n factorial" and is computed as

$$n! = n(n-1)(n-2)(n-3)\ldots3(2)1$$

For example, $3! = 3(2)1 = 6$ and $5! = 5(4)3(2)1 = 120$
Note that $0! = 1$ and $1! = 1$

Example 8: A teacher wants to choose two students to represent the class in a competition. She finds that there are five students in the class who meet the eligibility criteria: Tom, Mary, Jan, Becky, and Pat. Since all five are eligible, she decides to select two at random. In how many different ways can this teacher select two students out of five students?

Solution: This is a combination problem, since the order in which two students get selected does not matter. The following list gives all the possible ways in which two students can be selected from Tom, Mary, Jan, Becky, and Pat. Note that, since the order of selection is immaterial, selecting Tom and Mary is the same as selecting Mary and Tom.

1. Tom and Mary	6. Mary and Becky
2. Tom and Jan	7. Mary and Pat
3. Tom and Becky	8. Jan and Becky
4. Tom and Pat	9. Jan and Pat
5. Mary and Jan	10. Becky and Pat

There are 10 different ways to select 2 students out of 5 when the order of selection is not important. Using the combination function, we can find this number without having to list all the possibilities. The combination is as follows: $\binom{5}{2} = \frac{5!}{2!(5-2)!} = \frac{120}{2(6)} = 10$

TI-83:

- Type the number 5 in the window
- Choose **MATH** → **PRB** → **3: nCr**
- Press **ENTER**
- Type the number 2 5 nCr 2
- Press **ENTER**

BINOMIAL DISTRIBUTION

A good example of a distribution of discrete random variables is the binomial distribution. A binomial distribution occurs in an experiment that possesses the following properties:

- There are n repeated trials
- All trials are identical and independent
- Each trial has two possible outcomes, in general known as "success" and "failure"
- P(success in a given trial) = p
- P(failure in a given trial) = $1 - p$

The binomial variable X:

$$X = \text{the number of successes in } n \text{ trials}$$
$$= 0, 1, 2, \ldots, n$$

$$P(x \text{ successes in } n \text{ trials}) = \binom{n}{x} p^x (1-p)^{n-x}$$

Mean of the binomial random variable:

$$\mu = E(X) = np$$

Variance of the binomial random variable:

$$\sigma^2 = np(1-p)$$

Some examples of a binomial random variable:

- A quality control inspector takes a random sample of 20 items from a large lot, inspects each item, classifies each as defective or non-defective, and counts the number of defective items in the sample.

- A telephone survey asks 400 area residents, selected at random, if they support the new gasoline tax increase. The answers are recorded as "yes" or "no." The number of persons answering "yes" is recorded.

- Consider families with three children. The number of girls out of the three children of each family is recorded.

- A certain medical procedure is performed on 15 patients who are not related to each other. The number of successful procedures is recorded.

- A homeowner buys 20 azalea plants from a nursery. The number of plants that survive at the end of the year is recorded.

The shape of the binomial distribution depends on the value of p. The distribution spreads from 0 to n. The following graphs show different binomial distributions:

For $p = 0.2$, the binomial distribution is right skewed with mean $\mu = 10(0.2) = 2$. In general, as p gets closer to 0 the binomial distribution becomes more right skewed.

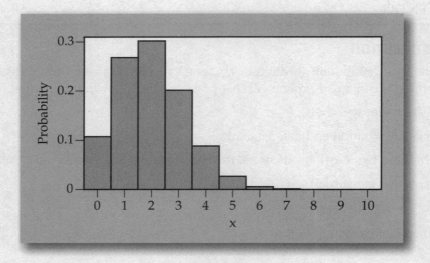

Figure 9: Binomial distribution with $n = 10$ and $p = 0.2$

For $p = 0.5$, the binomial distribution is symmetric with mean $\mu = 10(0.5) = 5$.

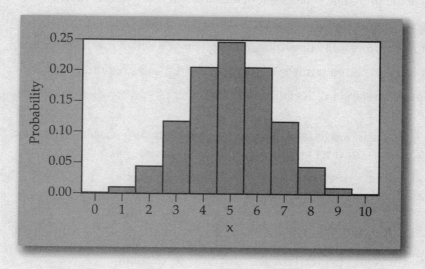

Figure 10: Binomial distribution with $n = 10$ and $p = 0.5$

For $p = 0.8$, the binomial distribution is left skewed with mean $\mu = 10(0.8) = 8$. In general as p gets closer to 1 the binomial distribution becomes more left skewed.

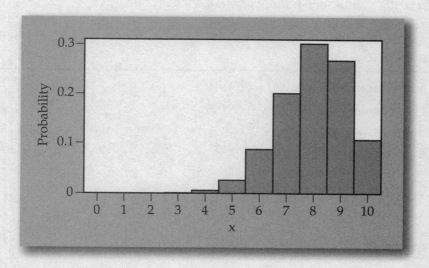

Figure 11: Binomial distribution with $n = 10$ and $p = 0.8$

Example 9: Suppose a family eats frequently at a nearby fast food restaurant. There are three possible toys (a car, a top, or a yo-yo) given with the kids' meals. The toys are placed in the meal bags at random. Suppose this family buys a kid's meal at this restaurant on four different days.

(a) What is the probability that 3 out of 4 meals will come with a yo-yo?

(b) What is the probability that at most 2 meals will come with a yo-yo?

(c) What is the probability of getting at least 3 yo-yos with 4 meals purchased?

(d) What is the expected number of yo-yos when 4 meals are purchased?

(e) Compute the standard deviation of the number of yo-yos when 4 meals are purchased.

Solution:

(a) Each kid's meal purchased is viewed as a trial with two possible outcomes, "yo-yo" or "no yo-yo". Let us consider getting a "yo-yo" as a success. Then

$p = P$(getting a yo-yo with a meal) $= 1/3$.
Since 4 meals were purchased, there are 4 trials ($n = 4$). Then

$$P(3 \text{ meals out of 4 with a yo-yo}) = \binom{4}{3}\left(\frac{1}{3}\right)^3\left(1-\frac{1}{3}\right)^{4-3} = 4(0.037)(0.667) = 0.0988$$

This is how you would get the probability with your calculator:

TI-83:

- Choose **2nd** → **DISTR** → **0: binompdf(**

- Enter n, p, x values in that order separated by a comma.

$$\text{binompdf}(4,1/3,3)$$

- Press **ENTER**

(b) P(at most 2 meals with a yo-yo) $= P(0) + P(1) + P(2)$

This is a cumulative probability, $P(x \leq 2)$.

$$P(\text{no yo-yo}) = P(x=0) = \binom{4}{0}\left(\frac{1}{3}\right)^0\left(1-\frac{1}{3}\right)^{4-0} = 0.1975$$

$$P(\text{one yo-yo}) = P(x=1) = \binom{4}{1}\left(\frac{1}{3}\right)^1\left(1-\frac{1}{3}\right)^{4-1} = 0.3951$$

$$P(\text{two yo-yos}) = P(x=2) = \binom{4}{2}\left(\frac{1}{3}\right)^2\left(1-\frac{1}{3}\right)^{4-2} = 0.2963$$

$$
\begin{aligned}
P(\text{at most 2 meals with a yo-yo}) &= P(0) + P(1) + P(2)\\
&= 0.1975 + 0.3951 + 0.2963\\
&= 0.8889
\end{aligned}
$$

Here's how you'd get this cumulative probability with your calculator:

TI-83:

- Choose **2nd** → **DISTR** → **A: binomcdf(**

- Enter n, p, x values in that order, separated by a comma.

$$\text{binomcdf}(4, 1/3, 3)$$

- Press **ENTER**

(c) $P(\text{at least 3 meals with a yo-yo}) = P(3) + P(4)$

$$= 0.0988 + \binom{4}{4}\left(\frac{1}{3}\right)^4\left(1 - \frac{1}{3}\right)^{4-4}$$

$$= 0.0988 + 0.0123$$

$$= 0.1111$$

(d) $E(X) = np = 4\left(\frac{1}{3}\right) = \frac{4}{3} = 1.33$

On the average we expect to get 1.33 yo-yos when 4 meals are purchased.

(e) Standard deviation is $\sigma = \sqrt{np(1-p)} = \sqrt{4\left(\frac{1}{3}\right)\left(1 - \frac{1}{3}\right)} = 0.9428$

Simulating a binomial distribution

Let's simulate the situation in the previous example using a six-sided die. Designate the outcomes as follows:

- Getting a 1 and 2 on the die means getting a yo-yo with the meal. The probability of getting a number 1 or 2 is $2/6 = 1/3$.

- Getting one of the remaining number (3, 4, 5, or 6) means getting a different toy (not a yo-yo) with the meal. The probability of getting a 3, 4, 5, or 6 is $4/6 = 2/3$.

Since the family is purchasing four meals, roll the die four times. Each roll represents a meal purchased. Based on the outcome for each roll, determine the toy received with the meal using the above scheme. For example, imagine that the first set of four rolls resulted in the numbers (4, 3, 2, 6). This means that only the third meal came with a yo-yo, while the remaining three meals came with other toys. So from this set of four meals purchased, the family got only one yo-yo. Note that the family received one yo-yo. Repeat this procedure (that of rolling the die four times and noting the number of yo-yos received out of four meals) 100 times. The results of one such simulation are listed below:

$$1, 1, 2, 1, 1, 1, 2, 1, 1, 1, 1, 2, 0, 0, 1, 0, 1, 1, 2, 1, 2, 0, 3, 1, 0,$$
$$0, 1, 3, 4, 1, 2, 1, 2, 2, 1, 0, 1, 1, 1, 0, 2, 2, 2, 0, 0, 1, 0, 3, 2, 2,$$
$$0, 1, 0, 1, 2, 1, 2, 1, 1, 0, 1, 1, 2, 1, 1, 2, 2, 3, 0, 2, 1, 2, 3, 2, 1,$$
$$1, 2, 0, 1, 3, 2, 1, 1, 1, 1, 1, 2, 1, 2, 2, 2, 2, 3, 1, 2, 2, 1, 1, 2, 1$$

This data shows that the first set of four meals resulted in getting one yo-yo, the second also resulted in one, the third resulted in two, and so on. The outcome zero means that the family got no yo-yos with the purchase of four meals; the number 4 means the family got a yo-yo with each of the four meals purchased. Now summarize the data as follows:

Number of meals out of 4 with a yo-yo	Simulated count
0	16
1	45
2	31
3	7
4	1
Total	100

Table 4: Frequency distribution of number of meals with a yo-yo

Using these simulated results, we can estimate the probabilities and the expected value.

(a) P(getting 3 meals with a yo-yo) = 7 out of 100 = 0.07

(b) P(getting at most 2 meals with a yo-yo)

$$= P(0, 1, \text{ or } 2 \text{ meals with a yo-yo})$$
$$= 92 \text{ out of } 100$$
$$= 0.92$$

(c) P(getting at least 3 meals with a yo-yo)

$$= P(3 \text{ or } 4 \text{ meals with a yo-yo})$$
$$= 8 \text{ out of } 100$$
$$= 0.08$$

(d) Expected number of yo-yos per 4 meals

$$= [0(16) + 1(45) + 2(31) + 3(7) + 4(1)]/100$$
$$= 132/100$$
$$= 1.32$$

GEOMETRIC DISTRIBUTION

Another example of a distribution of discrete random variables is the geometric distribution. The geometric distribution occurs in an experiment where repeated trials possess the following properties:

- The trials are repeated until the first success is observed.

- All trials are identical and independent.

- Each trial has two possible outcomes, in general known as "success" and "failure."

- P(success in a given trial) = p.

- P(failure in a given trial) = $1 - p$.

The geometric random variable X:

   X = the number of trials required to obtain the first success

   $= 0, 1, 2, \ldots$

   $P(x$ trials needed until the first success is observed $= p^x (1-p)^{x-1}$

Mean of the binomial random variable:

$$\mu = E(X) = \frac{(1-p)}{p}$$

Variance of the binomial random variable:

$$\sigma^2 = \frac{(1-p)^2}{p}$$

Some examples of the geometric random variable:

- A worker opening oysters to look for pearls counts the number of oysters he has to open until he finds the first pearl.

- A supervisor at the end of an assembly line counts the number of non-defective items produced until he finds the first defective one.

- An electrician inspecting cable one yard at a time for defects counts the number of yards he inspects before he finds a defect.

Example 10: Let's go back to the example of the fast food restaurant. Again, there are three possible toys (a car, a top, a yo-yo) given with the kids' meals, and the toys are placed in the meal bags at random. Suppose the kid in the family has his heart set on getting a yo-yo, so the family will buy him kid's meals until they get one with a yo-yo in it.

   (a) Find the probability that the family will have to buy 3 meals to get a yo-yo.

   (b) Find the probability that the family will have to buy 5 meals to get a yo-yo.

   (c) What is the expected number of meals needed to get a yo-yo?

Solution: Each kid's meal purchased is viewed as a trial with two possible outcomes, "yo-yo" or "no yo-yo". Let us consider getting a "yo-yo" as a success. So,

   $p = P$(getting a yo-yo with a meal) = 1/3

   (a) P(having to purchase 3 meals before getting a yo-yo)

   = P(no yo-yo in first 2 meals) P(yo-yo with the 3rd meal)

   $= (1-p)(1-p)p$

   $= (1-p)^2 p$

   $= \left(1 - \frac{1}{3}\right)^2 \left(\frac{1}{3}\right)$

   $= 0.148$

> **TI-83:**
>
> - Choose **2nd →DISTR →D: geompdf(**
> - Enter p, x values in that order separated by a comma.
>
> $$\text{geompdf}(1/3,3)$$
>
> - Press **ENTER**

(b) P(having to purchase 5 meals before getting a yo-yo)

$$= (1-p)^4 p$$
$$= \left(1 - \frac{1}{3}\right)^4 \left(\frac{1}{3}\right)$$
$$= 0.0658$$

(c) The expected number of meals to get a yo-yo = $E(X) = \dfrac{(1-p)}{p} = \dfrac{1-1/3}{1/3} = 2$

Simulating a geometric distribution

Consider the earlier example of purchasing kids' meals. Let's simulate the situation using a six-sided die. Designate the outcomes as follows:

- Getting a 1 and 2 on the die means getting a yo-yo with the meal. The probability of getting a number 1 or 2 is $2/6 = 1/3$.

- Getting one of the remaining numbers (3, 4, 5, or 6) means getting a different toy (not a yo-yo) with the meal. The probability of getting a 3, 4, 5, or 6 is $4/6 = 2/3$.

Since the family will purchase meals till they get a yo-yo, roll the die until the number 1 or 2 shows. Each roll represents a meal purchased. Count the number of rolls it takes to get number 1 or 2. For example, the first set of rolls resulted in faces with numbers (4, 3, 6, 5, 6, 2). This means that the sixth meal came with a yo-yo, while the first five meals came with different (non-yo-yo) toys. So in this set, the family had to purchase six meals to get one yo-yo. Suppose the next set of rolls resulted in (5, 5, 1). In this case, the family had to purchase only three meals to get a yo-yo. Roll 100 of these sets. From each set, note the number of meals the family had to purchase to get a yo-yo. The results of one such simulation are listed below:

> 6, 3, 2, 1, 8, 1, 3, 3, 2, 2, 2, 1, 3, 1, 2, 1, 7, 2, 9, 1, 1, 2, 2, 2, 7,
> 6, 2, 1, 1, 2, 1, 3, 2, 1, 1, 4, 5, 1, 2, 5, 1, 2, 5, 5, 2, 1, 2, 3, 2, 2,
> 3, 2, 2, 1, 1, 2, 1, 3, 2, 4, 3, 1, 3, 2, 1, 4, 1, 2, 2, 1, 3, 2, 2, 1, 2,
> 3, 3, 4, 7, 1, 1, 3, 2, 1, 3, 4, 3, 3, 4, 1, 2, 1, 2, 1, 1, 1, 1, 2, 1, 1

This shows that the first set resulted in the family's purchasing six meals to get a yo-yo; the second time, it took the family three meals to get a yo-yo; the third time, it took the family just two meals. Now summarize the results as follows:

Number of meals purchased before getting a yo-yo	1	2	3	4	5	6	7	8	9
Simulated count	34	32	17	6	4	2	3	1	1

Table 5: Frequency distribution of the number of meals purchased before getting a yo-yo

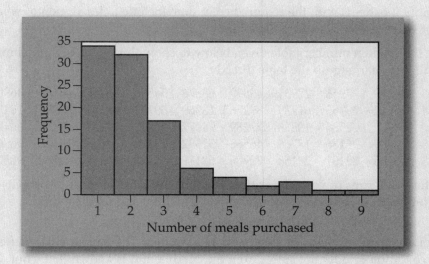

Figure 12: Probability distribution of the number of meals purchased

Using these simulated results, we can estimate the following probabilities:

(a) P(having to purchase 3 meals to get a yo-yo) = 17 out of 100 = 0.17.

(b) P(having to purchase 5 meals to get a yo-yo) = 4 out of 100 = 0.04.

(c) Expected number of meals needed to get a yo-yo

= The mean number of meals needed to get a yo-yo

= [1(34) + 2(32) + 3(17) + 4(6) + 5(4) + 6(2) + 7(3) + 8(1) + 9(1)] / 100 = 2.43

On average, you would have to purchase 2.43 meals before you got a yo-yo.

Note on binomial and geometric distributions

- In the binomial distribution, the number of trials (the number of meals purchased) is fixed, and the number of successes (the number of yo-yos received with a set of meals purchased) is a random event.

- In the geometric distribution, the number of successes (you need to get just one yo-yo) is fixed, by the number of trials required to get the success (the number of meals purchased before getting one yo-yo), which is a random event.

Example 11: Suppose a large research hospital is interested in recruiting patients with a specific medical condition for an experiment. Overall, 4 in every 10 patients visiting this hospital suffer from this condition. The physician in charge of the project wants to determine the mean number of patients he needs to examine before he can identify 2 patients with this condition.

(a) Describe how you would use a table of random numbers to carry out a simulation for determining the number of patients the doctor needs to examine before he can identify 2 patients with the required condition. Include a description of what each digit will represent in your simulation.

(b) Use the random number table given below to show three runs of your simulation. Do this by marking up the table directly.

56085	31590	73956	27931	49899	68676	54570	95456	43655	46907
96254	15612	29355	61739	89226	18360	69722	46304	61735	10436
96880	54319	72584	10836	77289	74077	74042	27133	53459	66476
77295	82889	96136	17766	46568	31392	14120	64658	14620	90969
65508	98265	82101	29153	72906	68119	48288	16211	96864	90572

(c) Perform 100 runs of your simulation. Find the expected number of patients the doctor needs to interview before he finds 2 with the required condition.

Solution:

(a) With each patient, there are two possible outcomes: The patient either suffers from the condition or does not suffer from the condition. It is known that 4 out of every 10 patients visiting this hospital suffer from this condition. This means that the probability that a randomly selected patient will suffer from the condition is

$$\frac{4}{10} = 0.4$$

i.e., $p = 0.4$

Consider one-digit random numbers, 0 through 9. Designate numbers 1, 2, 3, 4 (any four will do) as patients with the condition and numbers 0, 5, 6, 7, 8, 9 (the remaining numbers) as patients without the condition. Start at the beginning of the first line of the random number chart. Each number represents a patient being examined. Classify each number as representing either "patient with condition" or "patient without condition." Stop when the second "patient with condition" is identified. Count the number of patients examined until 2 are found with the condition.

(b) Begin the first simulation in the first row and the second simulation in the successive row.

5̶ 6̶ 0̶ 8̶ 5̶   3̲1̲ 590   73956   27931   49899   68676   54570   95456

9̶ 6̶ 2̲ 5̲ 4̲   15612   29355   61739   89226   18360   69722   46304

The first run shows that a total of 7 patients were examined before 2 with the condition were identified.

The second run shows that a total of 5 patients were examined before 2 with the specific condition were identified.

(c) The frequency distribution of a sample of 100 runs of the above-described simulation is given below. Another simulation of 100 runs would result in slightly different counts, of course.

Number of patients examined to find two with the condition	Simulated count
2	39
3	27
4	15
5	7
6	6
7	3
8	1
9	2

Table 6: Frequency distribution of the number of patients examined to find two with the condition

E(Number of patients examined to identify 2 with the condition)

$$= [2(39) + 3(27) + 4(15) + 5(7) + 6(6) + 7(3) + 8(1) + 9(2)] / 100$$
$$= 3.37$$

On the average 3 to 4 patients will be examined to find 2 with the required condition.

Continuous Random Variables and Their Probability Distributions

Recall that a continuous random variable takes all possible values in a given range. For example, the distance traveled by a car using one gallon of gas, waiting time at the checkout counter of a grocery store, and the amount of water released through Hoover Dam on a given day. Occasionally, when the discrete variable takes lots of values, it is treated as a continuous variable.

The probability distribution of a continuous random variable or **the continuous probability distribution** is a graph or a formula giving all possible values taken by a random variable and the corresponding probabilities. It is also known as the **density function**.

Let X be a continuous random variable taking values in the range (a, b). Then

- The area under the density curve is equal to the probability, i.e., $a \leq L \leq U \leq b$.

- $P(L < X < U)$ = the area under the curve between L and U.

- The total probability under the curve = 1.

- The probability that X takes a specific value is equal to 0, i.e., $P(X = x_0) = 0$.

The cumulative distribution function (CDF) of a random variable X is $P(X < x_0)$ for any $a < x_0 < b$. It is equal to 0 for any $x_0 < a$, and it is equal to 1 for any $x_0 > b$.

Example 12: The following graph gives the distribution of the yearly amount of rainfall in Rainy City.

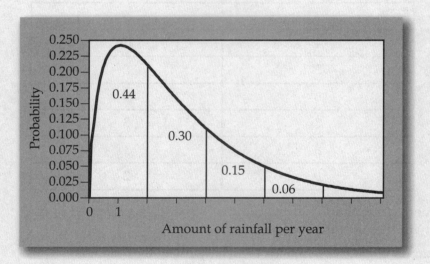

Figure 13: Probability distribution of amount of rainfall per year

In a randomly selected year,

    (a) What is the probability that Rainy City got more than 8 inches of rain?

    (b) What is the probability that Rainy City got between 2 and 6 inches of rain?

    (c) What is the probability that Rainy City got exactly 2 inches of rain?

    (d) What is the probability that Rainy City got at most 6 inches of rain?

Solution: Let X = the amount of rain per year in Rainy City.

(a) P(Rainy City got more than 8 inches of rain)

$$= P(X > 8) = 1 - P(X < 8) = 1 - [0.44 + 0.30 + 0.15 + 0.06] = 1 - 0.95 = 0.05$$

(b) P(Rainy City got between 2 and 6 inches of rain)

$$= P(2 < X < 6) = 0.30 + 0.15 = 0.45$$

(c) P(Rainy City got exactly 2 inches of rain) = 0

(d) P(Rainy City got at most 6 inches of rain)

$$= P(X \leq 6) = 0.44 + 0.30 + 0.15 = 0.89$$

THE NORMAL DISTRIBUTION

The discovery of the normal distribution is credited to Karl Gauss. It is also known as the bell-curve or Gaussian distribution. This is the most commonly used distribution in statistics because it closely approximates the distributions of many different measurements.

If a random variable X follows a normal distribution with mean μ and standard deviation σ, then it is denoted by $X \sim N(\mu, \sigma)$. The density function is given as follows:

$$f(x; \mu, \sigma) = \frac{1}{\sigma\sqrt{2\pi}} \exp\left\{-\frac{1}{2}\left(\frac{x - \mu}{\sigma}\right)^2\right\}, \quad -\infty < x < \infty, \quad -\infty < \mu < \infty, \text{ and } \sigma^2 > 0$$

The **standard normal** is the normal distribution with a mean of 0 and a variance of 1. The density function of the standard normal is given by $f(z) = \dfrac{1}{\sqrt{2\pi}} \exp\left\{-\dfrac{1}{2}z^2\right\}, \quad -\infty < z < \infty$

Any normal random variable can be transformed to the standard normal using the relation

$$Z = \frac{X - \mu}{\sigma}, \text{ which means } X \sim N(\mu, \sigma) \quad \Rightarrow \quad Z = \frac{X - \mu}{\sigma} \sim N(0,1)$$

and

$$Z \sim N(0,1) \quad \Rightarrow \quad X = Z\sigma + \mu \sim N(\mu, \sigma)$$

The value of variable Z computed as $Z = \dfrac{X - \mu}{\sigma}$ for any specific value of X is known as the **z-score**. For example, suppose $X \sim N(10, 2)$. The z-score for $X = 12.5$ is then

$$Z = \frac{X - \mu}{\sigma} = \frac{12.5 - 10}{2} = 1.25$$

PROPERTIES OF THE NORMAL DISTRIBUTION

The normal distribution has the following characteristics:

- It is continuous.
- It is symmetric around its mean.
- It is bell-shaped or mound-shaped.
- Mean = median = mode.
- The curve approaches the baseline (horizontal axis) on both sides of the mean without ever touching or crossing it.
- Most of the distribution lies within three standard deviations of the mean.
- It has two inflection points: One at $\mu - \sigma$ and one at $\mu + \sigma$.
- The location of the distribution on the number line depends on the mean of the distribution. See the following graphs.
- The shape of the distribution depends on the standard deviation. A normal distribution with a larger standard deviation is more flat, while one with a smaller standard deviation is more peaked. See the following graphs.

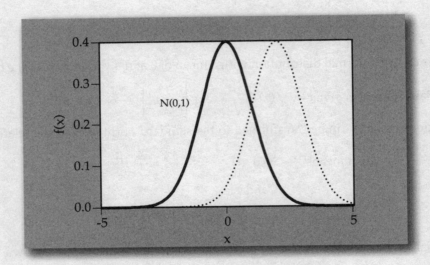

Figure 14: Normal distributions with different means

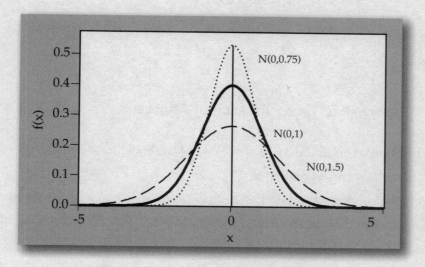

Figure 15: Normal distributions with different variances

USING THE NORMAL DISTRIBUTION TABLE

If the random variable X follows a normal distribution with mean μ and variance standard deviation σ, then the random variable $Z = \dfrac{X - \mu}{\sigma}$ follows a standard normal distribution, i.e., a normal distribution with mean 0 and variance 1.

To find the area under the standard normal distribution, i.e., a normal distribution with mean 0 and variance 1, you can simply look at the standard normal probability table, which is given to you with the AP exam and is also reprinted at the back of this book. To find the area under the curve (in other words, the probability) for any normal distribution other than the standard normal, we can make use of the following relation:

$$\text{If } X \sim N(\mu, \sigma), \text{ then } Z = \frac{X - \mu}{\sigma} \sim N(0,1)$$

Using this relation, we can tranform X to Z and then use the tables available for the standard normal distribution. Note that for any normal distribution:

- Approximately 68 percent of the area under the curve lies between $\mu - \sigma$ and $\mu + \sigma$

- Approximately 95 percent of the area under the curve lies between $\mu - 2\sigma$ and $\mu + 2\sigma$

- Approximately 99.73 percent (almost all) of the area under the curve lies between $\mu - 3\sigma$ and $\mu + 3\sigma$

Example 13:

   (a) Find $P(Z < 1.27)$.

   (b) Find $P(Z < 0.82)$.

   (c) Find $P(0.82 < Z < 1.27)$.

   (d) Find $P(Z > 1.27)$.

   (e) Find the 95th percentile of the standard normal distribution.

Solution:

   (a) Refer to the normal probability table at the end of the book.

- Go down to the row corresponding to "1.2"

- Go across to the column corresponding to "0.07"

- Read the number in the cross-section of the row for "1.2" and the column for "0.07"

- It says that $P(Z < 1.27) = 0.8980$

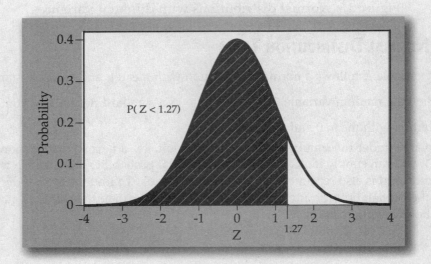

Figure 16: Shaded area under the standard normal distribution shows $P(Z < 1.27)$

TI-83:

- Choose **2nd** $\rightarrow$ **DISTR** $\rightarrow$ **2: normalcdf**

- Enter *lower bound*, *upper bound*, μ, and σ values in that order, separated by a comma. The lower bound should be negative infinity ($-\infty$), but you can simulate that by using any number beyond 5 standard deviations from the mean.

- Normalcdf(-5, 1.27, 0, 1)

- Press **ENTER**

(b) To find the $P(Z < 0.82)$, read the number in the cross-section of row for "0.8" and column for "0.02" We see that $P(Z < 0.82) = 0.7939$.

(c) $P(0.82 < Z < 1.27) = P(Z < 1.27) - P(Z < 0.82)$

$$= 0.8980 - 0.7939$$
$$= 0.1041$$

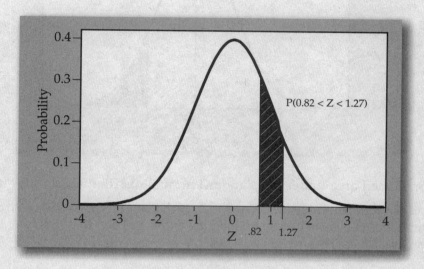

Figure 17: Shaded area under the standard normal distribution shows $P(0.82 < Z < 1.27)$

TI-83:

- Choose **2nd** → **DISTR** → **2: normalcdf(**
- Enter *lower bound, upper bound,* m, and s values in that order separated by a comma.
- normalcdf

$$(0.82, 1.27, 0, 1)$$

- Press **ENTER**

(d) $P(Z > 1.27) = 1 - P(Z < 1.27)$

$$= 1 - 0.8980$$
$$= 0.1020$$

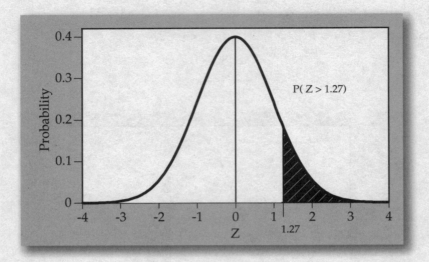

Figure 18: Shaded area under the standard normal distribution shows $P(Z > 1.27)$

(e) To find the 95th percentile means to find z_0 such that $P(Z < z_0) = 0.95$. To do this, we can simply use the table backward. Find the number closest to 0.95 among the probability values. Then we get $z_0 = 1.645$.

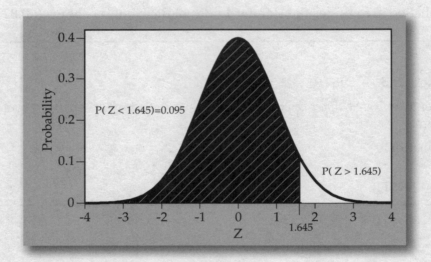

Figure 19: z-score such that $P(Z < z\text{-score}) = 0.95$

TI-83:

- Choose **2nd** → **DISTR** → **3: invNorm(**
- Enter *probability below* z_0, μ, and σ values in that order separated by a comma.

  $$\text{invNorm}(0.95, 0, 1)$$

- Press **ENTER**

Example 14: Suppose $X \sim N(10,2)$. Find

   (a) $P(X < 12.28)$

   (b) $P(6.72 < X < 12.28)$

   (c) Find x_0 such that $P(X > x_0) = 0.15$

Solution: (a) $P(X < 12.28) = P\left(Z < \dfrac{12.28 - 10}{2}\right) = P(Z < 1.14) = 0.8729$

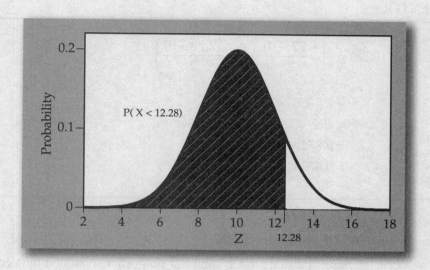

Figure 20: Shaded area shows $P(x < 12.28)$

$P(X < 12.28)$ is the same as $P(Z < 1.14)$ where $X \sim N(10, 2)$ and $Z \sim N(0, 1)$.

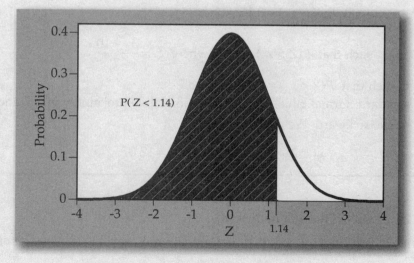

Figure 21: Shaded area shows $P(Z < 1.14)$

TI-83:

- Choose **2nd** → **DISTR** → **2: normalcdf(**

- Enter *lower bound*, *upper bound*, μ, and σ values in that order separated by a comma. Simulate $-\infty$ for the lower bound by using any number beyond 5 standard deviations of the mean.

$$\text{normalcdf}(0, 12.28, 10, 2)$$

- Press **ENTER**

(b) $P(6.72 < X < 12.28) = P\left(\dfrac{6.72 - 10}{2} < Z < \dfrac{12.28 - 10}{2} \right)$

$$= P(-1.64 < Z < 1.14)$$
$$= P(Z < 1.14) - P(Z < -1.64)$$
$$= 0.8729 - 0.0505$$
$$= 0.8224$$

TI-83:

- Choose **2nd** → **DISTR** → **2: normalcdf(**

- Enter *lower bound*, *upper bound*, μ, and σ values in that order separated by a comma.

$$\text{normalcdf}(6.72, 12.28, 10, 2)$$

- Press **ENTER**

(c) To find x_0 such that $P(X > x_0) = 0.15$

i.e., to find z_0 such that $P(Z > z_0) = 0.15$, where $z_0 = \dfrac{x_0 - 10}{2}$

or find z_0 such that $P(Z < z_0) = 1 - 0.15 = 0.85$

Use the standard normal table, look for the cumulative probability of .85, and then read the table backward. We get $z_0 = 1.04$

$$x_0 = 2z_0 + 10 = 2(1.04) + 10 = 12.07$$

TI-83:

- Choose **2nd** → **DISTR** → **3: invNorm(**

- Enter *probability below* z_0, μ, and σ values in that order, separated by a comma.

$$\text{invNorm}(0.85, 10, 2)$$

- Press **ENTER**

THE NORMAL DISTRIBUTION AS A MODEL FOR MEASUREMENTS

The normal distribution is commonly used to describe a variety of measurements.

Example 15: At the end of the semester, a teacher determines the percent grade earned by students, taking into account all homework, test, and project scores. These student scores are normally distributed, with a mean of 75 and a standard deviation of 8.

(a) If a 90-80-70-60 scheme is used to determine the letter grades of students, what percent of students earned an A?

(b) If a 90-80-70-60 scheme is used to determine the letter grades of students, what percent of students earned a B?

(c) If the teacher decides to give As to the top 10 percent of the class, then what is the cut-off point for an A?

(d) If the teacher decides to give Bs to the next 20 percent of the class, then what is the cut-off point for a B?

Solution: Remember that the grades are normally distributed with $\mu = 75$ and $\sigma = 8$.

(a) In the 90-80-70-60 scheme, a grade of 90 or better earns an A.

Compute $P(X \geq 90)$

$$P(X \geq 90) = P\left(Z \geq \frac{90-75}{8} \right) = P(Z \geq 1.875) = 1 - P(Z < 1.875) = 1 - 0.9696 = 0.0304$$

Therefore, 3.04 percent of the class got As.

TI-83:

- Choose **2nd** $\rightarrow$ **DISTR** $\rightarrow$ **2: normalcdf(**

- Enter *lower bound, upper bound*, μ, and σ values in that order, separated by a comma. Simulate an upper bound of ∞ by using any number beyond 5 standard deviations from the mean.

  normalcdf(90, 130, 75, 8)

- Press **ENTER**

(b) In the 90-80-70-60 scheme, a grade of 80 or better but less than 90, earns a B.

Compute $P(80 \leq X < 90)$

$$
\begin{aligned}
P(80 \leq X < 90) &= P\left(\frac{80-75}{8} \leq Z < \frac{90-75}{8} \right) \\
&= P(0.625 \leq Z < 1.875) \\
&= P(Z < 1.875) - P(Z < 0.625) \\
&= 0.9696 - 0.7340 \\
&= 0.2356
\end{aligned}
$$

Therefore, 23.56 percent of the class got Bs.

TI-83:

- Choose **2nd** → **DISTR** → **2: normalcdf(**
- Enter *lower bound*, *upper bound*, μ, and σ values in that order, separated by a comma.

$$\text{normalcdf}(80, 90, 75, 8)$$

- Press **ENTER**

(c) The teacher decides to give As to the top 10 percent of the class.

Find x_0 such that $P(x \geq x_0) = 0.10$

$$P(x \geq x_0) = 0.10 \text{ which means } P(z \geq z_0) = 0.10 \text{ where } z_0 = \frac{x_0 - 75}{8}$$

Therefore $P(z < z_0) = 0.90$ gives $z_0 = 1.28$

Therefore $x_0 = 1.28(8) + 75 = 85.24$

Therefore, any student with a percent grade of 85.24 or better gets an A.

TI-83:

- Choose **2nd** → **DISTR** → **3: invNorm(**
- Enter *probability below* z_0, μ, and σ values in that order separated by a comma.

$$\text{invNorm}(0.90, 75, 8)$$

- Press **ENTER**

(d) The teacher decides to give Bs to the next 20 percent of the class. This means that 30 percent of the students are above the cut-off point for the grade B (all A students and all B students).

Find x_0 such that $P(x \geq x_0) = 0.30$

$$P(x \geq x_0) = 0.30 \text{ means that } P(z \geq z_0) = 0.30 \text{ where } z_0 = \frac{x_0 - 75}{8}$$

Therefore $P(z < z_0) = 0.70$ which gives $z_0 = 0.524$

Therefore $x_0 = 0.524(8) + 75 = 79.19$

Therefore, any student with a grade of 79.19 or higher, but lower than 85.24, gets a B.

TI-83:

- Choose **2nd** → **DISTR** → **3: invNorm(**
- Enter *probability below* z_0, μ, and σ values in that order separated by a comma.

$$\text{invNorm}(0.70, 75, 8)$$

- Press **ENTER**

COMBINING INDEPENDENT RANDOM VARIABLES

Sometimes we are interested in linear combinations of independent random variables. If we know the mean and the variance of two random variables, we can determine the mean and the variance of a linear combination of these variables. Suppose X is a random variable with mean μ_X and variance σ_X^2. Suppose Y is a random variable with mean μ_Y and variance σ_Y^2. The two variables X and Y are independent.

Random Variable	Mean	Variance	
X	μ_X	σ_X^2	} Independent
Y	μ_Y	σ_Y^2	

Now consider a linear combination of random variables $aX + bY$, where a and b are constants. Then $aX + bY$ is also a random variable, with mean $\mu_{aX+bY} = a\mu_X + b\mu_Y$ and variance $\sigma_{aX+bY}^2 = a^2\sigma_X^2 + b^2\sigma_Y^2$. The following are specific cases:

Random Variable	Mean	Variance
aX	$a\mu_X$	$a^2\sigma_X^2$
$X+b$	$\mu_X + b$	σ_X^2
$aX+b$	$a\mu_X + b$	$a^2\sigma_X^2$
$X+Y$	$\mu_X + \mu_Y$	$\sigma_X^2 + \sigma_Y^2$
$X-Y$	$\mu_X - \mu_Y$	$\sigma_X^2 + \sigma_Y^2$
$aX - bY$	$a\mu_X - b\mu_Y$	$a^2\sigma_X^2 + b^2\sigma_X^2$

If X and Y are normally distributed, then a linear combination of the two will also be normally distributed.

Example 16: A company markets 16-ounce bottles of jam. The mean amount of jam per bottle is 16 ounces, with a standard deviation of 0.1 ounces. The mean weight of the glass bottles holding the jam is 5 ounces, with a standard deviation of 0.5 ounces.

(a) What is the mean weight of a filled bottle?

(b) What is the standard deviation of the weight of a filled bottle?

(c) When shipped to stores, 12 bottles are packed randomly in each box. What is the mean and standard deviation of the weights of these random groupings of 12 bottles?

(d) The mean weight of the empty boxes is 50 ounces, with a standard deviation of 4 ounces. What is the mean weight and the standard deviation of the weights of the filled boxes?

(e) If the amount of jam per bottle, the weight of the bottles (with their lids), and the weight of the boxes are approximately normally distributed, what percent of boxes will weigh more than 320 ounces?

Solution: Let A = the amount of jam per bottle

B = the weight of jars (with lids)

C = the weight of a box packed with 12 bottles

It is known that

$$\mu_A = 16 \text{ ounces}, \ \sigma_A = 0.1 \text{ ounces, and}$$

$$\mu_B = 5 \text{ ounces}, \ \sigma_B = 0.5 \text{ ounces}.$$

(a) Let W = weight of a filled bottle = weight of bottle content + weight of a bottle (with its lid)

Therefore the mean weight of a filled bottle is

$$\mu_W = \mu_A + \mu_B = 16 + 5 = 21 \text{ ounces}$$

(b) The standard deviation of the weight of a filled bottle is

$$\sigma_W = \sqrt{\sigma_A^2 + \sigma_B^2} = \sqrt{0.1^2 + 0.5^2} = 0.5099 \approx 0.51 \text{ ounces}$$

(c) Twelve bottles are grouped together randomly. Let G = total weight of a group of 12 bottles.

The mean weight of the group = $\mu_G = 12\mu_W = 12(21) = 252$ ounces

The standard deviation of the weight of the group is

$$\sqrt{12^2 \sigma_W^2} = \sqrt{12^2 (0.51)} = 8.57 \text{ ounces}$$

(d) Let E = the weight of an empty box

C = the weight of a packed box = G + E

The mean weight of a packed box is $\mu_C = \mu_G + \mu_E = 252 + 50 = 302$ ounces.

The standard deviation of the weights of the packed boxes is

$$\sigma_C = \sqrt{\sigma_G^2 + \sigma_E^2} = \sqrt{8.57^2 + 4^2} = 9.46 \text{ ounces}$$

(e) Since all weights are approximately normally distributed, $C \sim N(302, 9.46)$. Therefore

$$P(C > 302) = P\left(Z > \frac{302 - 320}{9.46}\right) = P(Z > 1.90) = 1 - P(Z < 1.90) = 0.0287$$

2.87 percent boxes will weigh more than 320 ounces.

SAMPLING DISTRIBUTIONS

TERMS AND CONCEPTS

- A **parameter** is a descriptive numerical measure of a population. For example, a student's GPA is computed using grades from all his or her courses, and therefore, GPA is a parameter.

- A **statistic** is a numerical descriptive measure of a sample. An example is the percent of votes received by a presidential candidate. Generally, not every eligible voter votes in a presidential election. Therefore, the president is elected based on the support received from a sample of the eligible voters who vote, and so the percent is a statistic. If, however, every eligible voter does vote, then the percent of votes received would be a parameter.

- The **sampling distribution** is the probability distribution of a statistic. Different samples of the same size from the same population will result in different statistic values. Therefore, a statistic is a random variable. Any table, list, graph, or formula giving all possible values a statistic can take and their corresponding probabilities gives a sampling distribution of that statistic.

- The **standard error** is the standard deviation of a statistic.

CENTRAL LIMIT THEOREM

The following is one of the most important theorems in statistics:
Regardless of the shape of the population, if a sufficiently large random sample of size n is taken from the population, then the sample mean is approximately normally distributed, with mean

$$\mu_{\overline{X}} = \mu \text{ and standard deviation } \sigma_{\overline{X}} = \frac{\sigma}{\sqrt{n}}$$

Basically, the Central Limit Theorem tells us the following:
Regardless of the shape of the population, as the sample size n increases:

- The shape of the distribution of $\overline{X}$ becomes more symmetric and bell-shaped (more normal).

- The center of the distribution of $\overline{X}$ remains at μ.

- The spread of the distribution of $\overline{X}$ decreases and the distribution becomes more peaked.

How large a sample size is needed to get an approximately normal distribution of $\overline{X}$ depends on the shape of the population distribution. In most cases, a sample size of 30 or larger is large enough to achieve an approximately normal distribution. However, in the case of very skewed populations, larger sample sizes might be needed.

Example 17: The GPAs of graduating students at a large university are normally distributed, with a mean GPA of 2.8 and a standard deviation of 0.5. A random sample of 50 students is taken from all the graduating students.

(a) Find the probability that the mean GPA of the sampled students is above 3.0.

(b) Find the probability that the mean GPA of sampled students is between 2.7 and 3.0.

Solution: Sample size 50 is sufficiently large for us to assume approximate normality for the sampling distribution of $\overline{X}$ with $\mu_{\overline{X}} = 2.8$ and $\sigma_{\overline{X}} = \sqrt{0.5^2/50} = 0.071$. In other words, $\overline{X} \sim N(2.8, 0.071)$

$$= P(\overline{X} > 3.0)$$
$$= P\left(Z > \frac{3.0 - 2.8}{0.071}\right)$$

(a) P(the mean GPA of the sampled students is above 3.0)

$$= P(Z > 2.82)$$
$$= 0.0024$$

There is less than a 1 percent chance (0.24 percent) that the mean GPA of the 50 sampled students will exceed 3.0.

(b) P(the mean GPA of sampled students is between 2.7 and 3.0)

$$= P(2.7 < \overline{X} < 3.0)$$
$$= P\left(\frac{2.7 - 2.8}{0.071} < Z < \frac{3.0 - 2.8}{0.071}\right)$$
$$= P(-1.41 < Z < 2.82)$$
$$= 0.9183$$

There is almost a 92 percent chance that the mean GPA of the 50 sampled students will be between 2.7 and 3.0.

SAMPLING DISTRIBUTION OF A SAMPLE PROPORTION

Consider a population with a proportion of successes (for example, "yes" answers to the question "Do you support the president's policies?") equal to p. Take a random sample of size n from this population and compute the sample proportion $\hat{p}$. Note that $\hat{p}$ estimates p. Different samples of size n will result in different $\hat{p}$ values. Therefore, $\hat{p}$ is a random variable. The probability of occurrence differs among the different $\hat{p}$ values. Some values of $\hat{p}$ are more likely to occur than others. All possible values of $\hat{p}$ along with their corresponding probabilities give the sampling distribution of $\hat{p}$. For a sufficiently large n, the sampling distribution of $\hat{p}$ is approximately normal, with mean

$$\mu_{\hat{p}} = p \text{ and standard deviation } \sigma_{\hat{p}} = \sqrt{\frac{p(1-p)}{n}}$$

SAMPLING DISTRIBUTION OF A SAMPLE MEAN

Consider a population with a mean equal to μ. Take a random sample of size n from this population and compute the sample mean $\overline{X}$. Note that $\overline{X}$ estimates μ. Different samples of size n will result in different $\overline{X}$ values. Therefore, $\overline{X}$ is a random variable. The probability of occurrence differs among the different $\overline{X}$ values. Some values of $\overline{X}$ are more likely to occur than others. All the possible values of $\overline{X}$ along with their corresponding probabilities give the sampling distribution of $\overline{X}$. For a sufficiently large n, the sampling distribution of $\overline{X}$ is approximately normal, with mean

$$\mu_{\overline{X}} = \mu \text{ and standard deviation } \sigma_{\overline{X}} = \frac{\sigma}{\sqrt{n}}$$

SAMPLING DISTRIBUTION OF A DIFFERENCE BETWEEN TWO INDEPENDENT SAMPLE PROPORTIONS

Consider two populations with proportions of successes equal to p_1 and p_2, respectively. Imagine that we want to find the difference in population proportions $(p_1 - p_2)$. Take independent random samples of sizes n_1 and n_2, respectively, from these populations and compute the respective sample proportions $\hat{p}_1$ and $\hat{p}_2$. Note that $(\hat{p}_1 - \hat{p}_2)$ estimates $(p_1 - p_2)$. Different samples of sizes n_1 and n_2 will result in different $(\hat{p}_1 - \hat{p}_2)$ values. Therefore, $(\hat{p}_1 - \hat{p}_2)$ is a random variable. The probability of occurrence differs among the different $(\hat{p}_1 - \hat{p}_2)$ values. Some values of $(\hat{p}_1 - \hat{p}_2)$ are more likely to occur than others. All the possible values of $(\hat{p}_1 - \hat{p}_2)$ along with their corresponding probabilities give the sampling distribution of $(\hat{p}_1 - \hat{p}_2)$. For sufficiently large sample sizes, the sampling distribution of $(\hat{p}_1 - \hat{p}_2)$ is approximately normal, with mean $\mu_{(\hat{p}_1 - \hat{p}_2)} = (p_1 - p_2)$ and standard deviation

$$\sigma_{(\hat{p}_1 - \hat{p}_2)} = \sqrt{\frac{p_1(1-p_1)}{n_1} + \frac{p_2(1-p_2)}{n_2}}$$

SAMPLING DISTRIBUTION OF A DIFFERENCE BETWEEN TWO INDEPENDENT SAMPLE MEANS

Consider two populations with means equal to μ_1 and μ_2, respectively. Imagine that we want to find the difference in population means $(\mu_1 - \mu_2)$. Take independent random samples of sizes n_1 and n_2, respectively, from these populations and compute the respective sample means $\overline{X}_1$ and $\overline{X}_2$. Note that $(\overline{X}_1 - \overline{X}_2)$ estimates $(\mu_1 - \mu_2)$. Different samples of size n_1 and n_2 will result in different $(\overline{X}_1 - \overline{X}_2)$ values. Therefore, $(\overline{X}_1 - \overline{X}_2)$ is a random variable. The probability of occurrence differs among the different $(\overline{X}_1 - \overline{X}_2)$ values. Some values of $(\overline{X}_1 - \overline{X}_2)$ are more likely to occur than others. All the possible values of $(\overline{X}_1 - \overline{X}_2)$ along with their corresponding probabilities give the sampling distribution of $(\overline{X}_1 - \overline{X}_2)$. For sufficiently large n_1 and n_2, the sampling distribution of $(\overline{X}_1 - \overline{X}_2)$ is approximately normal, with mean $\mu_{(\overline{X}_1 - \overline{X}_2)} = (\mu_1 - \mu_2)$ and standard deviation

$$\sigma_{(\overline{X}_1 - \overline{X}_2)} = \sqrt{\frac{\sigma_1^2}{n_1} + \frac{\sigma_2^2}{n_2}}$$

7

STATISTICAL INFERENCE

STATISTICAL INFERENCE: CONFIRMING MODELS

Important information about a population of interest is often unknown, but we can take samples from the population and gather and summarize the information from the samples. Such summary statistics can then be used to

- Estimate unknown population characteristics
- Make inferences about unknown population characteristics

This chapter will discuss the use of estimation and statistical inference in order to solve the types of problems you'll see on the AP Statistics exam. In the **Multiple Choice section**, this topic appears in 12 to 16 out of 40 questions. In the **Free Response section**, this topic appears in 2 to 3 out of 6 questions.

PARAMETERS AND STATISTICS

In a telephone survey conducted by a local newspaper, four hundred randomly selected residents of a county on the Gulf of Mexico were asked, "Are you in favor of spending tax money on measures to prevent the erosion of private beaches?" The answers were recorded as "yes," "no," or "no opinion." The newspaper found that 76 percent of respondents were against spending tax money to support private beaches. This percentage, known as a statistic, was calculated from the information obtained from a random sample of county residents and not the entire population of that county. But it still provides a reasonable estimate for the unknown parameter, namely, the percentage of *all* county residents who oppose such action.

- A **parameter** is a characteristic of a population. The mean annual household income in the state of California, the percentage of voters in favor of a certain presidential candidate in the state of Florida, and the variance of the amount of sugar per can of a specific brand of soda are all examples of parameters, i.e., numbers describing respective populations.

- A **statistic** is a number computed from the sample. Generally, a statistic is used to estimate an unknown parameter and make an inference about it. A statistic does not depend on the unknown parameter. The mean annual household income computed from 500 randomly selected households in the state of California, the percentage of voters in favor of a certain presidential candidate in a sample of 385 randomly selected voters in the state of Florida, and the variance of the amount of sugar per can of a specific brand of soda in 12 randomly selected cans are all examples of statistics.

ESTIMATION

Generally, population characteristics (parameters) are unknown. To estimate them, we take samples from the population and use information from those samples to make our best guess. This procedure of guessing an unknown parameter value using the observed values from samples is known as an **estimation process**. A specific guess or value computed from a sample is known as an **estimate**. To estimate the mean annual income per resident of Los Angeles County, we would probably use the mean annual income per resident of any random sample of residents of Los Angeles County. The sample mean would estimate the unknown population mean. Similarly, if we were interested in estimating the proportion of voters in favor of a candidate in the state of Louisiana, then we would use the proportion of voters in favor of this candidate from any random sample of voters from Louisiana. Again, the sample proportion would estimate the population proportion.

There are two estimation methods:

- **Point estimation** gives a single value as an estimate of the unknown parameter and makes no allowance for the uncertainty of the value's accuracy.

- **Interval estimation** recognizes the uncertainty of the estimate's accuracy and compensates for it by specifying a range of values around the estimate within which the population parameter may actually lie.

For example, Paul is planning a trip to Florida during his spring break. He collects information about the trip and prepares a budget. Using the collected information, he concludes, "This trip will cost me $1,000, give or take $100." Paul is expecting the cost of his trip to be somewhere between $900 and $1,100. Since he does not know all the exact costs for the different components of this trip, his estimation procedure does not guarantee that the actual cost of the trip will be within the estimated range, but still he believes that there is a very good chance that it will be within those limits. His estimated cost of $1,000 is a point estimate of the unknown cost of the trip. The range of $100 around the point estimate of the cost is known as the **margin of error**. The estimated range of cost ($900, $1,100) is an **interval estimate** of the cost of his trip.

POINT ESTIMATION

Consider a population with unknown parameter θ. Let $X_1, X_2, ..., X_n$ be a random sample from this population. A point estimator $\hat{\theta}$ of θ is a statistic computed from the sample. It means that $\hat{\theta}$ is a function of $X_1, X_2, ..., X_n$. Some examples are listed below:

- If θ is the unknown population mean μ, then $\hat{\theta} = \overline{X}$. In other words, the sample mean $\overline{X}$ is an estimator for μ. It is computed from the sampled data as

$$\overline{X} = \frac{(X_1 + X_2 + ...X_n)}{n}$$

For example, the mean family income computed from a random sample of families from Miami estimates the mean family income in Miami.

- If θ is the unknown population proportion p, then $\hat{\theta} = \hat{p}$. In other words, the sample proportion $\hat{p}$ is an estimator for p. It is computed from the sampled data as

$$\hat{p} = \frac{\text{Number of favorable occurrences}}{\text{Sample size}}$$

For example, the proportion of children on free lunches obtained from a random sample of 100 children in a certain county's education system estimates the proportion of children on free lunches in the entire education system of that county.

- If θ is the unknown population variance σ^2, then $\hat{\theta} = S^2$. The sample variance S^2 is an estimator for σ^2. It is computed from the sampled data as

$$S^2 = \frac{\sum_{i=1}^{n} \left(X_i - \overline{X}\right)^2}{n-1}$$

The variance in the fat content of 2 percent milk computed from 15 randomly selected gallons of milk estimates the variance in the fat content of all the 2 percent milk bottled by that dairy.

- If θ is the unknown difference in population means $\left(\mu_1 - \mu_2\right)$, then $\hat{\theta} = \left(\overline{X}_1 - \overline{X}_2\right)$. The difference in sample means $\left(\overline{X}_1 - \overline{X}_2\right)$ is an estimator for $\left(\mu_1 - \mu_2\right)$. It is computed from the sampled data as

$$\left(\overline{X}_1 - \overline{X}_2\right) = \left[\frac{(X_{11} + X_{12} + ...X_{1n_1})}{n_1}\right] - \left[\frac{(X_{21} + X_{22} + ...X_{2n_2})}{n_2}\right]$$

For example, if we are interested in estimating the difference in the mean lifespan of two brands of tires, then we could use the difference in the mean lifespan of randomly selected samples of these two brands of tires.

- If θ is the unknown difference in population proportions $(p_1 - p_2)$, then $\hat{\theta} = (\hat{p}_1 - \hat{p}_2)$.
  The difference in sample proportions $(\hat{p}_1 - \hat{p}_2)$ is an estimator for $(p_1 - p_2)$.

  It is computed from the sampled data as

$$(\hat{p}_1 - \hat{p}_2) = \left[\frac{\text{Favorable occurrences in sample 1}}{\text{Size of sample 1}}\right] - \left[\frac{\text{Favorable occurrences in sample 2}}{\text{Size of sample 2}}\right]$$

For example, to estimate the difference in the proportion of women graduating with a degree in engineering at two major universities in Alabama, we could use the difference in those proportions computed from two randomly selected samples of engineering students from those universities.

SAMPLING DISTRIBUTION OF A STATISTIC

As seen from these examples, the statistic $\hat{\theta}$ is a function of random variables. Therefore, it is a random variable itself. Different samples will result in different estimates. How close or how far can these estimates be from the true value? We can answer this question by studying the distribution of the estimates. The **sampling distribution** of a statistic is the distribution of estimates (values taken by the statistic) from all possible samples of the same size from the same population.

Example 1: Suppose a student is interested in estimating p, the probability of getting heads when a penny is tossed. Suppose she tosses a penny 50 times and gets 24 heads. This sample of 50 tosses gives her an estimated probability $(\hat{p})$ of $\frac{24}{50} = 0.48$. So the student decides to see what happens if she repeats the experiment. The histogram summarizes the results of 100 such experiments, each of 50 tosses:

Estimated P(heads)	Number of samples giving this estimate	Estimated P(heads)	Number of samples giving this estimate
0.32	1	0.50	14
0.34	2	0.52	10
0.36	3	0.54	16
0.38	3	0.56	5
0.40	5	0.58	5
0.42	6	0.60	2
0.44	6	0.62	3
0.46	6	0.64	2
0.48	11	0.66	0

Table 1: Distribution of P(heads) estimated from 50 tosses

This table gives a sampling distribution of a certain statistic, i.e., the probability of getting heads as estimated from 50 tosses of a penny.

Although an estimator is a random variable, we would like to get estimates close to the actual value. Three criteria used to evaluate the desirability of a point estimator are

- The center of the distribution of estimates as measured by the mean.

- The spread of the distribution of estimates as measured by the standard deviation.

- The shape of the distribution.

Let us look at a histogram of the sampling distribution given in the above example. This will help us describe the center, spread, and shape of the sampling distribution.

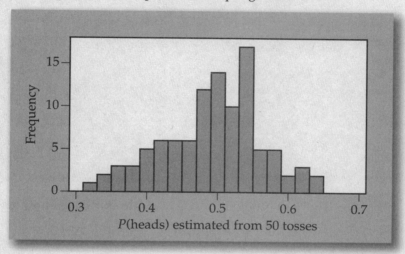

Figure 1: Sampling distribution of P(heads) for a 2001 penny

- The estimates are distributed around 0.5.

- The estimates range from about 0.32 to 0.64.

- The sampling distribution is slightly left skewed.

- From the above sampling distribution we can see that approximately 86 percent of the estimates are between 0.40 and 0.60.

PROPERTIES OF A STATISTIC

The center of a statistic's distribution

The property of **unbiasedness** refers to the idea that a statistic is expected to give values centered around the unknown parameter value. The bias of a statistic $\hat{\theta}$ is defined as

$$\text{Bias}(\hat{\theta}) = E(\hat{\theta}) - \theta$$

where $E(\hat{\theta})$ gives the mean of the sampling distribution of $\hat{\theta}$.

A statistic is unbiased if the mean of the sampling distribution of $\hat{\theta}$ is equal to the true value of the parameter θ. Bias measures the average accuracy of a statistic. A statistic with lower bias is considered more accurate. For an unbiased statistic, bias is equal to 0. A biased statistic has a systematic tendency to give estimates other than the actual value.

The spread of a statistic's distribution

The property of **efficiency** refers to the degree of variation in a statistic's values. Suppose more than one unbiased statistic is available to estimate an unknown parameter. The statistic with a smaller variance (or standard deviation) is considered to be more efficient. Such a statistic is more likely to give values closer to the unknown parameter value—in other words, more precise estimates.

Example 2: Consider a scale. Before you weigh yourself, you generally make sure that the pointer is at zero on the scale. Why? What happens if the needle points to 5 pounds (not 0) before you even step on it? In that case, for any item that you weigh, the scale is probably going to give a weight of 5 pounds more than the actual weight of the item. We refer to this as a biased scale. The following dotplots show the true weight of an item and its weight estimated from repeated weighings on four different scales.

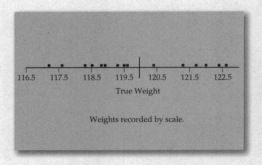

Scale A: Unbiased and less efficient

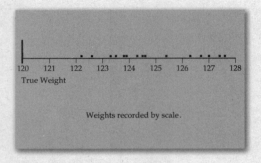

Scale B: Biased and less efficient

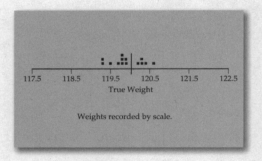

Scale C: Unbiased and more efficient

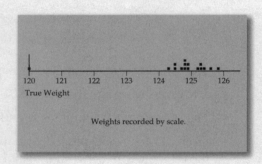

Scale D: Biased and more efficient

Figure 2: Properties of a statistic

Note that all the weights measured using scales A and C are scattered around the true weight, whereas all the weights measured using scales B and D are scattered around some value higher than the true weight. So the scales B and D have a tendency to systematically overweigh items. Therefore, scales B and D are biased, whereas scales A and C are unbiased.

The weights measured by scales A and B are spread more widely than the weights measured by scales C and D. Therefore, scales C and D are more efficient than scales A and B.

Consistency

The property of **consistency** also refers to the spread of a statistic's values. However, this property is mainly used in reference to the size of the sample taken to produce the statistic. Typically, standard deviation is used to measure the spread of the sampling distribution of a statistic. A lower standard deviation means more consistent values of statistic will be expected from different samples of the same size from the same population. Note that, as the sample size gets larger, more information about the population becomes available, and estimated values are expected to get closer to the unknown parameter value. In other words, the larger the sample, the better the estimator.

INTERVAL ESTIMATION AND THE CONFIDENCE INTERVAL

Another method of estimating an unknown parameter, besides point estimation, is interval estimation. This method gives us an interval around the statistic within which we expect the parameter to belong. One type of interval used to estimate parameters is the **confidence interval.**

The measure of our confidence in an estimate in terms of probability is called the **confidence coefficient**. The **confidence level** is that same probability written as a percentage. It is a common practice to indicate the confidence coefficient using this notation: $(1 - \alpha)$. We can consider α as the probability that we are *not* confident that the interval contains the parameter value, due to overestimation or underestimation. For example, if we are 95 percent confident about our estimation procedure, then the confidence coefficient is 0.95, the confidence level is 95 percent, and $\alpha = 0.05$. The general form of the confidence interval is (LCL, UCL), where LCL = Lower Confidence Limit and UCL = Upper Confidence Limit. The probability statement associated with the $(1 - \alpha)$ 100 percent confidence interval to estimate parameter θ is

$$P(LCL < \theta < UCL) = 1 - \alpha$$

This statement is associated with the method, and not with a specific interval constructed using a specific sample. So the true parameter value may or may not be in a specific interval constructed using one specific sample.

The maximum possible distance around the parameter value within which we expect the statistic to fall is known as the **margin of error** (ME). It can also be described as the maximum possible error in estimating the unknown parameter value with a given confidence level.

For confidence intervals based on symmetric distributions, such as normal and *t*, the LCL and UCL are generally equidistant from the statistic value. In other words:

$$LCL = Statistic - ME \text{ and } UCL = Statistic + ME$$

Therefore, the length or width of the confidence interval is given by (UCL – LCL) = 2ME. However, this is not true for confidence intervals constructed using skewed distributions, such as χ^2 and F. The true **meaning of the confidence level** is that, in repeated sampling, $(1 - a)$ 100 percent of the intervals constructed from random samples of the same size will contain the true parameter value.

INFERENCE: TESTS OF SIGNIFICANCE

Statistical inference is the process of analyzing data from a sample population in order to answer a specific question or make a decision. Imagine that, last month, a statewide poll showed that 65 percent of state residents supported the governor. This week, a widely circulated newspaper reported that the governor had approved some shady financial deals. With the election approaching, the governor's advisors need to know what effect the news had on the governor's popularity.

Specifically, has her support dropped from 65 percent as estimated by the last poll?

How can we answer this question? The best way is to take another random sample of state residents and estimate the governor's current statewide support by computing the percent of the sample still in favor of the governor. If this percentage is 65 percent or higher then there is no evidence that the scandal had an adverse effect. If this percentage is lower than 65 percent then the question is

- Is the decrease significant?

Or

- Is it attributable simply to chance, since there is a margin for error in this survey? (*Remember*, we are making a decision based on the sampled data, *not* the entire population.)

How much decrease can be attributed to chance? To determine that, we need to take into account the likelihood of the percentage of the sample in favor of the governor being the same as the percentage of the entire state being in favor. Here we are interested in making a decision about $p =$ the proportion of residents in favor of the governor. Obviously, due to lack of time, it is not possible to contact all residents of the state, so we poll a random sample of state residents and compute $\hat{p}$.

- Suppose $\hat{p} = 0.64$. Can the drop in the governor's popularity be dismissed as being due to a chance variation or does the new poll show evidence of a true drop in popularity?

- Suppose $\hat{p} = 0.63$. Can this result be dismissed as being due to a chance variation or can it be considered evidence of a true drop in popularity?

- Suppose $\hat{p} = 0.62$. Can this result be dismissed as being due to a chance variation or can it be considered evidence of a true drop in popularity?

- Suppose $\hat{p} = 0.61$. Can this result be dismissed as being due to a chance variation or can it be considered evidence of a true drop in popularity?

- Suppose $\hat{p} = 0.60$. Can this result be dismissed as being due to a chance variation or can it be considered evidence of a true drop in popularity?

At what point do we cease considering the difference to be the result of a chance variation in the data and start believing that the governor's support has decreased? It all depends on the likelihood of our estimates. We can determine the likelihood by examining the probability that a specific sample result will occur assuming that the real statewide support for the governor has stayed at 0.65. If different samples of the same size are taken, then the estimated proportion $\hat{p}$ will change from sample to sample. Some values are more likely to occur than others. So we need to know which values are less likely to occur in a sample if the percent of support has remained unchanged. In other words, we need to know the sampling distribution of $\hat{p}$. Let's simulate it.

Assume that the proportion of voters supporting the governor is still 0.65. Then we can simulate the situation by drawing repeated samples of, say, size 500. Imagine that each sample gives a different proportion. For example, the first sample results in a $\hat{p} = 0.61$; the second sample results in a $\hat{p} = 0.63$; the third sample results in a $\hat{p} = 0.67$, and so on. A histogram of 1,000 of these estimated proportions is as follows:

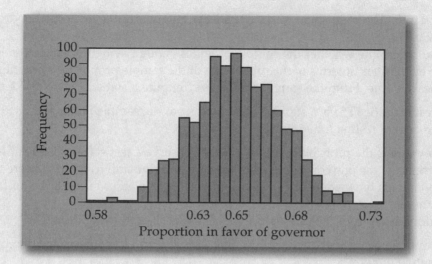

Figure 3: Sampling distribution of the proportion of voters supporting the governor

This histogram shows that a sample proportion closer to 0.65 is most likely to occur, while values further from 0.65 are increasingly less likely to occur. For example, from this simulated data we can estimate

- $P(\hat{p} \leq 0.63) = 0.177$. Note that to get this value, we have to add the frequency on the chart for $\hat{p} = 0.63$ to the frequencies for all $\hat{p}$ values lower than 0.63.

- $P(\hat{p} \leq 0.60) = 0.006$. Again, note that to get this value, we have to add the frequency on the chart for $\hat{p} = 0.60$ to the frequencies for all $\hat{p}$ values lower than 0.60.

Suppose our sample of 500 residents gives $\hat{p} = 0.60$. Our simulation results indicate that if 65 percent of the residents from the entire state still support the governor, then a sample of 500 is not very likely to give $\hat{p} = 0.60$ or lower. If we obtain a result of $\hat{p} = 0.60$, then we should conclude that support for the governor has probably decreased.

TESTING A HYPOTHESIS

The process described above, of decision-making about the value of a population parameter using information collected from a random sample, is known as **testing a hypothesis.**

A **hypothesis** (the plural is "hypotheses") is a claim or a statement about a parameter value. A hypothesis is always a statement about a population characteristic, and not about a sample. There are two types of hypotheses.

- The **null hypothesis** is a statement that is assumed to be true until proven otherwise. Sometimes it is described as the status quo statement about the parameter. The null hypothesis is denoted by H_0.

- The **alternative hypothesis** is a statement about the parameter that must be true if the null hypothesis is false. Sometimes it is described as the research hypothesis. The alternative hypothesis is denoted by H_1 or H_a.

In the above example, we would define:

- H_0: $p = 0.65$ (The proportion of state residents in favor of the governor is still 0.65.)

- H_a: $p < 0.65$ (The proportion of state residents in favor of the governor has dropped below 0.65.)

The goal is to determine whether the sample provides enough evidence for us to reject the null hypothesis. The evidence is in terms of the probability of the sample proportion occurring assuming the null hypothesis is true. From the sampled data, we compute a statistic value and a p-value.

- The **test statistic (TS)** is a statistic computed from the sampled data and used in the process of testing a hypothesis.

- The **p-value** is the probability that we would observe a test statistic value at least as extreme as the one computed from the sample if the null hypothesis were true. The p-value is the evidence we will use in deciding whether to reject the null hypothesis.

Using the information from the sample, we make one of the following decisions:

- The sample provides enough evidence to reject the null hypothesis and accept the alternative hypothesis; or

- Because of the lack of evidence, we do not reject the null hypothesis. (Note that failing to reject the null hypothesis does not imply accepting the null hypothesis.)

POSSIBLE ERRORS

Using the sampled data does not guarantee that our decision is correct. Since our decision is based on the sample and not on the entire population, it's possible for us to make the wrong decision. There are two scenarios that could lead to an error.

Suppose the truth is that the null hypothesis is correct. Using our data, we have made one of the following decisions:

- To reject the null hypothesis and accept the alternative hypothesis. Obviously, in this case we have made the wrong decision. **Error.**

- To fail to reject the null hypothesis. **Correct decision.**

Suppose the truth is that the alternative hypothesis is true. Using our data, we have made one of the following decisions:

- To reject the null hypothesis and accept the alternative hypothesis. **Correct decision.**

- To fail to reject the null hypothesis. This is obviously the wrong decision. **Error.**

The **Type I error** is the error of rejecting the null hypothesis when it is true. The probability of a type I error occurring is denoted by α.

The **Type II error** is the error of failing to reject the null hypothesis when it is false. The probability of type II error is denoted by β.

For a given sample size, we cannot control both type I and type II errors. If we try to reduce one type of error, the other type of error will increase. Also, keep in mind that in certain tests, it's more important to reduce one type of error than the other. For example, when trying a defendant, the null hypothesis is that the defendant is not guilty. The legal system considers the type I error (reject the null hypothesis when the null hypothesis is true—in other words, to convict an innocent defendant) to be worse than the type II error (fail to reject the null when the alternative hypothesis is true—in other words, acquit a guilty defendant), because our judicial system believes that it's more important to protect an innocent person than to punish a guilty person.

		True Situation	
		Null hypothesis is true	Alternative hypothesis is true
Decision	Reject null hypothesis	Type I error P(type I error) = α	Correct decision P(Correct decision) = 1 - β = Power of the test
	Fail to reject null hypothesis	Correct decision P(Correct decision) = 1 - α	Type II error P(Type II error) = β

Table 2: Two types of errors

Example 3: A pharmaceutical company claimed on television ads that its new medicine could prevent the common cold. Soon afterward, a consumer protection group started receiving complaints from consumers that the medicine did not perform as advertised. The consumer protection group decided to investigate the company's claim.

(a) Which decision by the consumer protection group might lead to the type I error?

(b) Which decision by the consumer protection group might lead to the type II error?

Solution: The consumer protection group decided to test the following set of hypotheses:
H_0: The medicine prevents the common cold, as advertised.
H_a: The medicine does not prevent the common cold.

(a) Concluding that the medicine does not prevent the common cold when it does will lead to the type I error.

(b) Concluding that the medicine does prevent the common cold when it does not will lead to the type II error.

Example 4: Most students enroll in courses with the intention of completing them. But after taking into account their mid-term grades, some students will consider dropping a course. In other words, they want to decide whether to

H_0: Complete the course.
H_a: Drop the course.

(a) Which decision by a student may lead to the type I error?

(b) Which decision by a student may lead to the type II error?

Solution:

    (a) Dropping a course when the student should have completed it.

    (b) Staying in a course when the student should have dropped it.

The **power of the test** for a test of fixed α significance is the probability that the null hypothesis will be rejected when a particular alternative value of the parameter is true. For a specific alternative,

$$\text{Power of a test} = 1 - P(\text{type II error})$$

A good test has a high power. Also note that

- The power of a test increases as the sample size increases.
- The power of a test increases as the type I error rate (α) increases.
- The power of a test increases as the distance between the true parameter value and the hypothesized value increases.

THE REJECTION AND NON-REJECTION REGIONS

The entire set of the possible values of a test statistic can be divided into two regions: the rejection region and the non-rejection region. The **rejection region (RR)** is the set of test statistic values for which we should reject the null hypothesis. It is also known as the **critical region (CR)**. The set of test statistic values for which we should fail to reject the null hypothesis is called the **non-rejection region**. The size of the rejection region is equal to α. The value of a test statistic that gives the boundary between the rejection and the non-rejection region is known as the **critical value (CV)**.

The location of the rejection region is determined by the nature of the alternative hypothesis, such as $\mu < 10$, $\mu > 10$, or $\mu \neq 10$. We can use three different types of tests, as defined by the location of the rejection region:

- **Left-tailed test:** In a left-tailed test, "too-small" values of the statistic as compared to the hypothesized parameter value lead to the rejection of the null hypothesis. Therefore, the entire rejection region falls in the left tail of the sampling distribution of the test statistic.

For example, a brewery markets bottles labeled "net contents 12 oz." A consumer advocacy group suspects that the average content of the bottles is lower than that printed on the labels and decides to investigate. The group is interested in testing H_0: $\mu = 12$ oz. against H_a: $\mu < 12$ oz., where $\mu =$ the mean amount filled per bottle. This is a left-tailed test. Too-small values of the sample mean will result in the rejection of the null hypothesis and the acceptance of the alternative hypothesis. So the rejection region is located in the left tail of the sampling distribution.

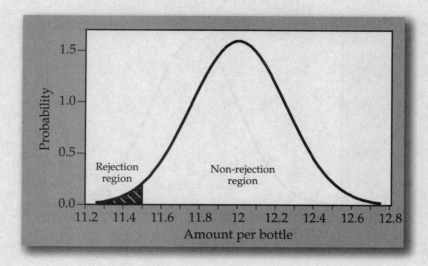

Figure 4: Rejection region for a left-tailed test

- **Right-tailed test:** In a right-tailed test, "too-large" values of the statistic as compared to the hypothesized parameter value lead to the rejection of the null hypothesis. Therefore, the entire rejection region falls in the right tail of the sampling distribution of the test statistic.

For example, a manufacturer of steel beams used in construction claims that the breaking strength of its beams is at least 500 psi. The engineering firm interested in using these beams decides to check out the claim. The firm will use the beams only if the strength exceeds 500 psi. It is interested in testing $H_0: \mu = 500$ psi against $H_a: \mu > 500$ psi, where $\mu =$ the mean breaking strength of beams. This is a right-tailed test. Too-large values of the sample mean will result in the rejection of the null hypothesis and the acceptance of the alternative hypothesis. So, the rejection region is located in the right tail of the sampling distribution.

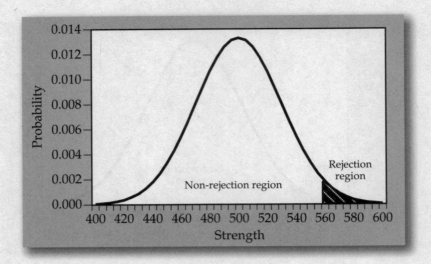

Figure 5: Rejection region for a right-tailed test

- **Two-tailed test:** In a two-tailed test, "too-small" or "too-large" values of the statistic as compared to the hypothesized parameter value lead to the rejection of the null hypothesis. Therefore, the rejection region falls in both tails of the sampling distribution of the test statistic. It's generally divided equally, half in the left tail and half in the right.

For example, students in my class are interested in determining if the new golden dollar is a fair coin—in other words, if, when tossed, it has a 50 percent chance of landing on heads and a 50 percent chance of landing on tails. To evaluate its fairness, the students decide to toss a golden dollar 100 times and count the number of heads. They are interested in testing H_0: $p = 0.50$ against H_a: $p \neq 0.50$, where $p =$ the proportion of heads. This is a two-tailed test. Too-large or too-small proportions of heads in 100 tosses will result in the rejection of the null hypothesis and the acceptance of the alternative hypothesis. So the rejection region is located in both tails of the sampling distribution, half in the left and half in the right.

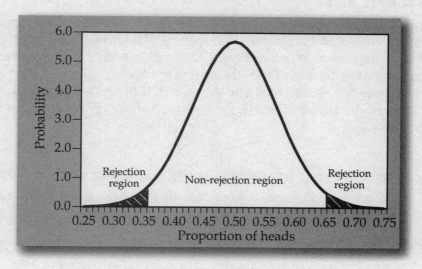

Figure 6: Rejection region for a two-tailed test

DETERMINING THE CRITICAL VALUE

The terms "too-small" and "too-large" are vague. How do we decide which values are too large and which are too small? The answer is simple: Values of the test statistic beyond the critical values are considered too large or too small. The critical value is determined based on how much risk of rejecting the true null hypothesis the investigator is willing to take. For example:

- In a **right-tailed test**, when the investigator is willing to take a 5 percent risk (i.e., $\alpha = 0.05$) of rejecting a true null hypothesis, the rejection region is formed by the largest values of the test statistic with a probability of occurrence totaling 0.05. In that case, the test statistic value above which 5 percent of the possible values are under the sampling distribution becomes the critical value.

- In a **two-tailed test**, when the investigator is willing to take a 5 pecent risk of rejecting a true null hypothesis, the rejection region is formed by the largest and smallest values of the test statistic with a probability of occurrence totaling 0.05. Therefore, the entire rejection region is divided equally into two parts, one in the left tail and the other in the right tail. The size of each part of the rejection region equals $\alpha/2$ (here, 0.025). In this case, there are two critical values. The test statistic value below which the bottom 2.5 percent of the sampling distribution lies becomes one critical value, and the test statistic value above which the top 2.5 percent of the sampling distribution lies becomes the other critical value.

Making a decision based on a two-sided confidence interval is equivalent to testing a two-sided hypothesis, in that a two-sided confidence interval gives a non-rejection region for a two-tailed test. Similarly, making a decision based on a one-sided confidence interval is equivalent to testing a one-sided hypothesis, in that a one-sided confidence interval gives a non-rejection region for a one-tailed test. In other words, rejecting the null hypothesis when the test statistic falls in the rejection region is equivalent to rejecting the null hypothesis when the hypothesized parameter value falls outside the confidence interval.

DETERMINING SAMPLE SIZE

Experimenters are often interested in determining the sample size needed to achieve certain reliable results. This helps the experimenter in planning the experiment and in budgeting its cost. The sample size needed to estimate the parameter within a specified margin of error and the required confidence level can be determined using the formula for the margin of error.

Note: When computing sample size, round up the numerical answer to attain the desired level of accuracy. For example, if the answer is 96.012, then we need at least 97 observations to attain the desired level of accuracy.

Finding Z_α

When determining sample size, you'll often need to find the value for the z-score Z_α, or z-(alpha). As described in the earlier chapter, Z_α = the z-score such that the area under the standard normal distribution beyond the z-score is equal to α. As shown in the accompanying graph, Z_α is the number on the baseline. It is a z-score. The subscript α (of Z_α) gives the area in the right tail.

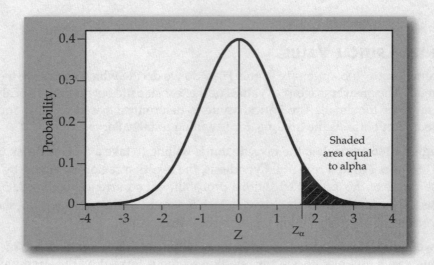

Figure 7: Graphical representation of Z_α

Example 5: Find $Z_{0.05}$.

Solution: As described earlier, $Z_{0.05}$ = the z-score such that the area under the standard normal distribution beyond the z-score is equal to 0.05. In other words, 95 percent of the area under the curve is below $Z_{0.05}$. This makes $Z_{0.05}$ the 95th percentile. So, as shown in the accompanying graph, finding $Z_{0.05}$ is the same as finding a 95th percentile for the standard normal distribution.

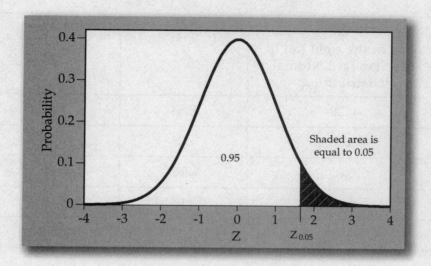

Figure 8: Graphical representation of $Z_{0.05}$

- **Finding $Z_{0.05}$ using the Standard normal table:** Inside the body of the table, locate the number closest to 0.95. It is halfway between 0.9495 and 0.9505. Note that 0.9495 corresponds to the z-score 1.64 and 0.9505 corresponds to the z-score 1.65. So 0.95 corresponds to the z-score 1.645. In other words, $Z_{0.05} = 1.645$.

- **Finding $Z_{0.05}$ using the TI-83:** 2nd → DISTR → 3: invNorm(0.95, 0, 1)

This gives $Z_{0.05} = 1.6448$, which is approximately 1.645.

Example 6: For $\alpha = 0.05$, find $Z_{\alpha/2}$.

Solution: It is given that $\alpha = 0.05$, which means $\alpha/2 = 0.025$. So, as described earlier,

$Z_{\alpha/2} = Z_{0.025}$ = The z-score such that the area under the standard normal distribution beyond the z-score is equal to 0.025.

Therefore, we are interested in finding the 97.5th percentile for the standard normal distribution.

- **Using the Standard normal table:** Inside the body of the table, locate the number closest to 0.975. In this case it is exactly equal to 0.9750 and corresponds to the z-score 1.96. So $Z_{0.025} = 1.96$.

- **Using the TI-83:** 2nd → DISTR → 3: invNorm(0.975, 0, 1)

This gives $Z_{0.025} = 1.95996$, which is approximately 1.96.

Some of the commonly used z-scores and the corresponding tail probabilities are listed in the following table:

α Area in the right tail of the Standard Normal Distribution	Z_α	$Z_{\alpha/2}$
0.20	0.84	1.28
0.10	1.28	1.645
0.05	1.645	1.96
0.02	2.05	2.33
0.01	2.33	2.576

Table 3: z-scores associated with the commonly used values of α

Determining the sample size to estimate population mean μ

- The maximum margin of error to estimate μ is $Z_{\alpha/2}\left(\dfrac{\sigma}{\sqrt{n}}\right)$. First, determine the desired level of confidence and the margin of error. Then estimate n by equating the desired margin of error with this formula.

- By rewriting this formula we can estimate the required sample size as

$$n \geq \left(\frac{Z_{\alpha/2}\,\sigma}{ME}\right)^2$$

- If the population variance is unknown, use the sample variance in place of the population variance.

Determining the sample size to estimate population proportion p

- The maximum margin of error to estimate p is $Z_{\alpha/2}\sqrt{\dfrac{\hat{p}(1-\hat{p})}{n}}$. First, determine the desired level of confidence and the margin of error. Then estimate n by equating the desired margin of error with this formula.

- If an estimate of p is available from past experiments, then estimate the required sample size as

$$n \geq \left(\frac{Z_{\alpha/2}}{ME}\right)^2 \hat{p}(1-\hat{p})$$

- If no information about p is available, then use $\hat{p} = \frac{1}{2}$ and estimate the required sample size as

$$n \geq \left(\frac{Z_{\alpha/2}}{2\ ME} \right)^2$$

This gives a conservative estimate for the sample size in the absence of any prior information about p.

- For a 95 percent confidence level, $Z_{\alpha/2} = 1.96 \cong 2.0$. By substituting this in the above formula, we get

$$n \geq \left(\frac{1}{ME} \right)^2$$

Note that, to cut the margin of error in half, the sample size needs to be quadrupled. It can be easily seen from the above formulas that

- Sample size increases as the desired margin of error increases.
- Sample size increases as the required confidence level increases.
- Sample size increases as the population becomes more diverse (i.e., as the variance increases).

Example 7: A factory cans fresh pineapple in sugar syrup. The manager in charge is interested in estimating the average amount of sugar per can to within 2 mg of the true mean. From previous experiments, he knows that the standard deviation of the sugar content is approximately 15 mg. Each test of measuring the amount of sugar in a can costs $5.00. One thousand dollars have been budgeted for this experiment. Does the manager have enough funds to estimate the average amount of sugar per can with a 95 percent confidence?

Solution: The manager is interested in determining the sample size needed to estimate

μ = the mean amount of sugar per can.

Confidence level = 0.95 $\Rightarrow$ $\alpha = 0.05$ $\Rightarrow$ $Z_{\alpha/2} = Z_{0.025} = 1.96$

The desired ME = 2 mg, and the standard deviation is 15 mg.
So the required sample size is

$$n \geq \left(\frac{Z_{\alpha/2}\ \sigma}{ME} \right)^2 = \left(\frac{1.96(15)}{2} \right)^2 = 216.09$$

The manager should sample at least 217 cans. It will cost him at least 217(5) = $1,085. Since he has a budget of $1,000, he does not have enough money.

Example 8: Officials at a large university want to estimate the proportion of students in favor of changing from a quarter system to a semester system. The estimate is expected to be within 0.04 of the true proportion with a 95 percent confidence level.

(a) Estimate the required sample size if no prior information is available.

(b) Assume that a similar poll was conducted two years ago. It resulted in 35 percent of the students favoring a change from the quarter system to the semester system. Estimate the required sample size.

Solution: The officials are interested in estimating p = the proportion of students in favor of changing from a quarter system to a semester system.

Confidence level = 0.95 $\Rightarrow \alpha = 0.05 \Rightarrow Z_{\alpha/2} = Z_{0.025} = 1.96$

The desired ME = 0.04

(a) Since no prior information is available, use $\hat{p} = \dfrac{1}{2}$ to get a conservative estimate of the required sample size.

$$n \geq \left(\frac{Z_{\alpha/2}}{2 \ ME} \right)^2 = \left(\frac{1.96}{2(0.04)} \right)^2 = 600.25$$

The university officials need to poll at least 601 students at random.

(b) Using information from the prior poll we get $\hat{p} = 0.35$. Then the required sample size is

$$n \geq \left(\frac{Z_{\alpha/2}}{ME} \right)^2 \hat{p}(1-\hat{p}) = \left(\frac{1.96}{0.04} \right)^2 (0.35)(1 - 0.35) = 546.23$$

The university officials need to poll at least 547 students at random.

ESTIMATION AND INFERENCE PROBLEMS

To do well on the AP Statistics exam, you will need to be able to estimate and make inferences about the following parameters: proportion (p), population mean (μ), the difference between two population proportions ($p_1 - p_2$), the difference between two population means ($\mu_1 - \mu_2$), and the slope of the least-squares regression line (β_1).

In addition, you also need to know how to make inferences about categorical data. Estimation procedures, such as constructing confidence intervals, are used to estimate unknown population parameters; whereas inference procedures, such as testing of hypotheses, are used for making inferences about unknown population parameters.

Below are the general steps you need to solve problems involving confidence intervals and the testing of hypotheses. All these steps are covered in detail later in this chapter. Before answering any estimation or inference problem, read the entire question carefully. Some problems may require you to use all the steps listed below, while others may only require a few.

STEPS FOR CONSTRUCTING A CONFIDENCE INTERVAL

1. Set up the problem correctly.

- Identify the parameter of interest—for example, population proportion (p), population mean (μ), difference in population proportions ($p_1 - p_2$), difference in population means, or population mean of differences (μ_d).

- Describe the parameter in the context of the problem. For example, write p = the proportion of voters in Iowa in favor of the governor's position, or μ_d = the mean difference in the cholesterol level of patients before and after taking the new medicine.

2. Identify the appropriate type of confidence interval and check its requirements.

- Give the correct name or formula for the type of confidence interval you've selected. For example, to construct a confidence interval for p = the proportion of voters in Iowa in favor of the governor's position, you could write either:

    (a) Use a large samples z-interval for proportion, or

    (b) The confidence interval for p is constructed as $\hat{p} \pm Z_{\alpha/2} \sqrt{\dfrac{\hat{p}(1-\hat{p})}{n}}$

- Check the requirements for the selected confidence interval. For example, to construct a confidence interval for p, ask yourself whether $n\hat{p} > 10$ and $n(1-\hat{p}) > 10$ (all requirements will be discussed in detail later in this chapter). Show your work. Just stating the assumptions or saying they are satisfied is not enough.

Note: If you use the wrong type of confidence interval, then you will not get any credit for this part of the problem on the AP exam.

3. Provide the correct mechanics to solve the problem.

- Give the correct values obtained from statistical tables or your calculator. For example, for a 95 percent confidence interval for p, give $Z_{\alpha/2} = Z_{0.025} = 1.96$.

- Compute the confidence interval correctly. Show you're plugging in the correct numbers for the formula you already gave in step 2. After you've computed the correct confidence interval, be sure to state it as (lower limit, upper limit).

4. State the correct conclusion in the context of the problem, using your confidence interval.

For example, if your 95 percent interval for p is (0.62, 0.68), then write "we are 95 percent confident that the proportion of voters in Iowa in favor of the governor's position is between 0.62 and 0.68."

STEPS FOR TESTING A HYPOTHESIS

1. State a correct set of hypotheses.

- State the null and alternative hypotheses correctly, defining any notation used.

- State both hypotheses in the context of the problem. For example, write:

    (a) $H_0 : p = 0.5$ against $H_a : p > 0.5$, where p = the proportion of voters in the state of Iowa in favor of the governor's position, or

    (b) $H_0 : \mu_d = 0$ against $H_a : \mu_d > 0$, where μ_d = the mean difference in the cholesterol level of patients before and after taking the new medicine.

Note: If you switch the null and alternative hypotheses around, you will lose all credit for this step on the AP exam.

2. Identify the appropriate statistical test and check the appropriate requirements.

- Give the correct name of the test, or give the correct symbol or formula for the test statistic. For example, to test for p as defined in step 1, write either:

    (a) Use a large samples z-test for proportion, or

    (b) The test statistic is $z = \dfrac{\hat{p} - p_0}{\sqrt{\dfrac{\hat{p}(1 - \hat{p})}{n}}}$

- Check the requirements for the selected test. (Use the same procedure as in step 3 of the estimation problem process, above).

Note: If you use the wrong statistical test (for example, if you use a paired t-test when an independent samples t-test is more appropriate), then you will not get any credit for this part of the problem on the AP exam.

3. Provide the correct mechanics to solve the problem.

- Give the correct numerical value of the test statistic. Be sure to show that you're plugging in the correct numbers into the formula you gave in step 2. For example, write:

$$\text{Test statistic} = z = \frac{\hat{p} - p_0}{\sqrt{\dfrac{p_0(1 - p_0)}{n}}} = \frac{0.64 - 0.5}{\sqrt{\dfrac{0.5(1 - 0.5)}{250}}} = 4.43$$

- At this point there are two ways to do the problem: the **p-value approach** and the **rejection region approach** (again, both are described in detail below). The p-value approach is generally the easier way to go if you're using a TI-83 calculator. The TEST option on the calculator will give the p-value. The rejection region is a bit more complicated, but can be done just by using the tables supplied on the AP Statistics exam—it does not require a calculator. Both approaches are equally acceptable to the AP graders.

4. State the correct conclusion in the context of the problem using the results of your statistical test.

- Use your test results from the earlier step to arrive at the conclusion, using either the p-value approach or the rejection region approach. State clearly the link between the conclusion and the test result. For example, write

  (a) Since p-value = 0.0000047 < any reasonable α, we reject the null and accept the alternative hypothesis; or

  (b) Since the test statistic value 4.43 falls in the rejection region, we reject the null and accept the alternative hypothesis; or

  (c) Since the test statistic value 4.43 > 1.645, we reject the null and accept the alternative hypothesis.

- Write the conclusion in the context of the problem, consistent with the defined hypotheses. In other words, do not stop after saying "reject" or "do not reject" the null hypothesis. For the above example, you should write the following: "There is significant evidence to suggest that the proportion of voters in Iowa in favor of the governor's position is more than 0.5."

ESTIMATION FOR AND INFERENCE ABOUT A POPULATION PROPORTION p

Newspapers, television stations, and manufacturers routinely use public opinion polls to estimate the proportion of a population in favor of a certain issue, candidate, or product.

Parameter of interest: Population proportion p

- Select a random sample of size n.

- For each selected item or subject in the sample, note the presence or absence of the specific criteria of interest.

- Count the number of subjects meeting the required criteria (x).

- The estimated proportion from the sample is $\hat{p} = \dfrac{x}{n}$

$\hat{p}$ is a point estimate of an unknown population proportion. Different random samples of size n from the same population will result in different sample proportions, giving different estimates. The distribution of the estimated proportions from all possible random samples of size n is the sampling distribution of $\hat{p}$.

- The mean of all possible sample proportions is p. Therefore $\hat{p}$ is an unbiased estimator of p.

- The standard deviation of the sampling distribution of $\hat{p}$ is $\sigma_{\hat{p}} = \sqrt{p(1-p)\big/n}$

- For a large n, the sampling distribution of $\hat{p}$ is approximately normally distributed. Therefore, for a large n, we can construct a z-interval or use a z-test. For a small n, we may need to use a different test (which is not in the AP Statistics curriculum).

Estimating p using $(1-\alpha)100\%$

Confidence interval: Large sample case: Construct a z-interval

Margin of Error: $\qquad Z_{\alpha/2}\sigma_{\hat{p}} = Z_{\alpha/2}\sqrt{\dfrac{\hat{p}(1-\hat{p})}{n}}$

Confidence Interval: $\qquad \hat{p} \pm Z_{\alpha/2}\sqrt{\dfrac{\hat{p}(1-\hat{p})}{n}}$

Making an inference about the difference in population means p:
Large sample case: Use a z-test

$H_0: p = p_0$
(specified)

$H_a: p > p_0$ or
$\quad p < p_0$ or
$\quad p \neq p_0$

$$TS = \frac{\hat{p} - p_0}{\sqrt{\dfrac{p_0(1-p_0)}{n}}}$$

	Rejection Rule	
Alternative hypothesis:	Rejection region approach:	p-value approach:
$H_a: p > p_0$ $H_a: p < p_0$ or $H_a: p \neq p_0$	Reject H_0 if $TS > Z_\alpha$ $TS < -Z_\alpha$ $TS > Z_{\alpha/2}\ TS < -Z_{\alpha/2}$	Reject H_0 if p-value $< \alpha$, where p-value $= P(Z > TS)$ p-value $= P(Z < TS)$ p-value $= P(Z > |TS|) + P(Z < -|TS|)$

Conditions:

(a) A random sample of size n is taken from the population.

(b) The sample size is large enough so that the distribution of $\hat{p}$ is approximately normal.

Checking the normality condition (b):
If the following conditions are satisfied, then the sample size is large enough to assume that the distribution of $\hat{p}$ is approximately normal.

- $n\hat{p}$ and $n(1-\hat{p}) \geq 10$ for an estimation problem.

- $np_0 \geq 10$ and $n(1-p_0) \geq 10$ for an inference problem.

Example 9: A bank randomly selected 300 checking accounts from all its checking accounts and found that 45 were overdrawn at least once in the past two years.

(a) Estimate the true proportion of checking accounts at this bank that were overdrawn at least once in the last two years, using a 95 percent confidence interval.

(b) The bank manager reported that the bank has a significantly lower percentage of overdrawn checking accounts compared to the nation as a whole. If 20 percent of accounts nationally are overdrawn, can we believe the bank manager's report?

Solution: (a) Estimation:
Step 1: The bank is interested in estimating
p = The true proportion of checking accounts overdrawn at least once in the last two years.

Step 2: A random sample of $n = 300$ accounts was taken.
Of the sampled accounts, $x = 45$ were overdrawn at least once in the last two years.

The sample proportion is $\hat{p} = \dfrac{x}{n} = \dfrac{45}{300} = 0.15$

Conditions:

(a) It is given that a random sample of accounts was taken.

(b) $n\hat{p} = 300\,(0.15) = 45 > 10$ and $n\,(1 - \hat{p}) = 300\,(1 - 0.15) = 255 > 10$. Therefore, the sample size is large enough to assume that the sampling distribution of $\hat{p}$ is approximately normal.

Both conditions are satisfied, so we can construct a large sample z-interval for proportion.

Step 3: To construct a 95 percent confidence interval, we use $\alpha = 0.05$. Therefore, as we discussed in the section on "Finding Z_α," above, $Z_{\frac{\alpha}{2}} = Z_{\frac{0.05}{2}} = Z_{0.025} = 1.96$

$$\text{The 95 percent ME} = Z_{\frac{\alpha}{2}} \sqrt{\frac{\hat{p}(1-\hat{p})}{n}} = 1.96 \sqrt{\frac{0.15(1-0.15)}{300}} = 0.04$$

So, $\hat{p} \pm \text{ME} \Rightarrow 0.15 \pm 0.04 \Rightarrow (0.11, 0.19)$

Therefore, a 95 percent confidence interval to estimate p is (0.11, 0.19).

Step 4: We are 95 percent confident that the true proportion of checking accounts at this bank that were overdrawn at least once in the last two years is between 0.11 and 0.19. In other words, we are 95 percent confident that 11 percent to 19 percent of checking accounts at this bank were overdrawn at least once in the last two years.

> **TI-83:**
>
> - Choose **STAT** → **TESTS** → **A: 1-PropZInt** II
> - Enter appropriate values
>   1-PropZInt
>   X: 45
>   n: 300
>   C-Level: .95
>   Calculate
> - Highlight Calculate
> - Press **ENTER**

(b) Inference:

Step 1: We are interested in making an inference about

p = the true proportion of checking accounts at this bank overdrawn at least once in the last two years.

Nationally, 20 percent of checking accounts are overdrawn. The manager reported that $p < 0.20$. We are looking for evidence to support the manager's report. Therefore, use $p_0 = 0.20$ and define the null and alternative hypotheses as

$H_0: p = 0.20$ (The proportion of overdrawn accounts at this bank is the same as the national proportion)

$H_a: p < 0.20$ (The proportion of overdrawn accounts at this bank is lower than the national proportion)

Step 2: A random sample of $n = 300$ accounts was taken.
Of the sampled accounts, $x = 45$ were overdrawn at least once in the last two years.
The sample proportion is

$$\hat{p} = \frac{x}{n} = \frac{45}{300} = 0.15$$

Conditions:

(a) It is given that a random sample of accounts was taken.

(b) $n\,p_0 = 300\,(0.20) = 60 > 10$ and $n\,(1 - p_0) = 300\,(1 - 0.20) = 240 > 10$.

Therefore, the sample size is large enough to assume that the sampling distribution of $\hat{p}$ is approximately normal.

The conditions are satisfied, so we can use a large sample z-test for proportion.

Step 3: The alternative hypothesis indicates that this is a left-tailed test. Suppose we are willing to take a 5 percent risk of rejecting the true null hypothesis. In this case, $\alpha = 0.05$.

Using the p-value approach: The rejection rule is "Reject H_0 if p-value < 0.05."
Compute the test statistic value as

$$\text{TS} = \frac{\hat{p} - p_0}{\sqrt{\dfrac{p_0(1 - p_0)}{n}}} = \frac{0.15 - 0.20}{\sqrt{\dfrac{0.20(1 - 0.20)}{300}}} = \frac{-0.05}{0.023} = -2.165$$

Compute the p-value using either the standard normal table or the TI-83.

- Using the standard normal table: The probability corresponding to the z-score of $-2.165 \approx -2.17$ is 0.015

- Using the TI-83: **2nd** $\rightarrow$ **DISTR** $\rightarrow$ **2:normalcdf(-5000, -2.165, 0, 1)**. This gives the figure 0.01519, which is approximately 0.015. Therefore, value $P(Z < -2.165) = 0.015$

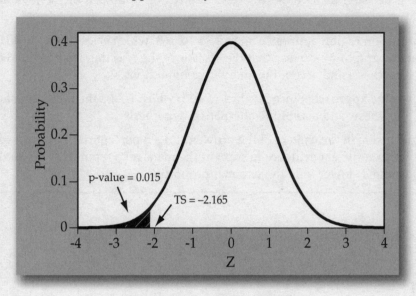

Figure 9: *P*-value approach

Using the rejection region approach:

The rejection rule is "Reject H_0 if TS $< -Z_\alpha = -Z_{0.05} = -1.645$"
The following graph shows the rejection region.

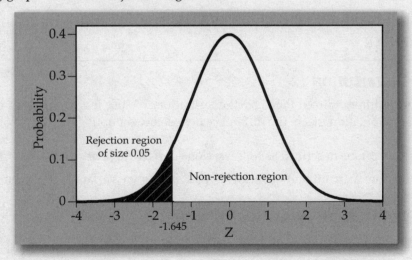

Figure 10: Rejection region and non-rejection region

Compute the test statistic value as

$$TS = \frac{\hat{p} - p_0}{\sqrt{\dfrac{p_0(1 - p_0)}{n}}} = \frac{0.15 - 0.20}{\sqrt{\dfrac{0.20(1 - 0.20)}{300}}} = \frac{-0.05}{0.023} = -2.165$$

Step 4: Make a decision using either the rejection region approach or the *p*-value approach as follows:

The rejection region approach: Since TS = –2.165, which is less than –1.645 (or since, from the above graph, we can see that the TS falls in the rejection region) we should reject the null hypothesis and accept the alternative hypothesis.

The *p*-value approach: Since *p*-value = 0.015, which is less than 0.05, we should reject the null hypothesis and accept the alternative hypothesis.

Now state the conclusion in the context of the problem: At a 5 percent risk of error, we can conclude that the data provides sufficient evidence to support the manager's report that the bank's proportion of overdrawn accounts is lower than the national proportion.

TI-83:

- Choose **STAT** → **TESTS** → **5: 1-PropZTest**
- Enter appropriate values

  1-PropZTest
  p0: 0.20
  x: 45
  n: 300
  prop ≠ p0   < p0   >p0
  Calculate   Draw

- Highlight Calculate
- Press **ENTER**

STUDENT'S *t*-DISTRIBUTION

The *t*-distribution is different from the normal distribution. We use it when making estimates of or inferences about a population mean, the difference between two population means, or the slope of a regression line.

The *t*-distribution can be described as follows: Consider a sample of size *n* taken from a normally distributed population with unknown mean μ and unknown variance σ^2. Then the unknown population variance is estimated using the sample variance S^2. The statistic $t = \dfrac{\overline{X} - \mu}{S/\sqrt{n}}$ is computed from the sample. Different samples of size *n* will result in different values for the statistic. William Gosset, while working for the Guinness brewery, discovered the sampling distribution that the above statistic follows. He published his results under the pen name "student." Since then, this sampling distribution has been known as Student's *t*-distribution.

The characteristics of the *t*-distribution include the following:

- It's a continuous distribution.

- Its mean is 0.

- It's symmetric about its mean.

- It's bell shaped.

- Its shape depends on a parameter, called **degrees of freedom**, denoted by υ. For smaller degrees of freedom, the distribution is more spread out, while as degrees of freedom increase, the distribution becomes more compact. In other words, as the degrees of freedom increase, the variance of the *t*-distribution decreases.

- It approaches the standard normal distribution as the degrees of freedom increase.

- It has a larger variance than the standard normal distribution. In other words, it has thicker tails than the standard normal distribution. As the degrees of freedom increase, the variance of the *t*-distribution approaches 1.

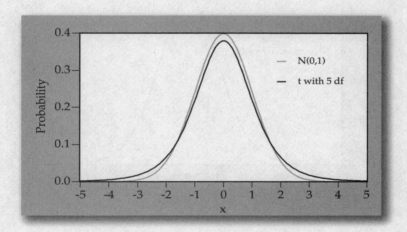

Figure 11: Comparison of standard normal and *t*-distribution

How to read the *t*-table

Each *t*-score is denoted by $t_\alpha(\upsilon)$, where the subscript α gives the area under the *t*-distribution beyond the *t*-score, and υ is the degrees of freedom.

- Determine the required degrees of freedom υ. There are different formulas for degrees of freedom depending on which test or confidence interval you're using (see next page).

- Determine the area in the right tail of the distribution, namely subscript α.

- In the *t*-table, go down to the row that corresponds to the degrees of freedom, and then go across to the column that corresponds to the area in the right tail. Read the number in the cross-section of the selected row and column.

Example 10: (a) Find $t_{0.05}(8)$, **(b)** Find $t_{0.01}(15)$.
Solution:

(a) We are interested in finding $t_{0.05}(8)$. This means we need to find the *t*-score for a *t*-distribution with 8 degrees of freedom such that the area to the right of this *t*-score is equal to 0.05. So read the number in the cross-section of the row corresponding to $\upsilon = 8$ and the column corresponding to $t_{0.05}$. It should read $t_{0.05}(8) = 1.860$.

(b) We are interested in finding $t_{0.01}(15)$. This means we need to find the *t*-score for a *t*-distribution with 15 degrees of freedom such that the area to the right of this *t*-score is equal to 0.01. So read the number in the cross-section of the row corresponding to $\upsilon = 15$ and the column corresponding to $t_{0.01}$. It should read $t_{0.01}(15) = 2.602$.

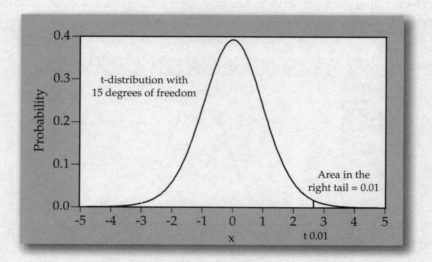

Figure 12: Finding the *t*-score for a specified area in the right tail

ESTIMATION FOR AND INFERENCE ABOUT A POPULATION MEAN μ

Another important parameter is population mean. For example, manufacturers are often interested in estimating the mean amount of a product per box filled by a certain machine, the mean amount of time spent by robots per assembly of specific units, etc. The Department of Education might be interested in the mean amount per child spent by the state on education, the mean amount of time spent by parents on volunteer activities in their children's schools, etc. Local television stations might be interested in the mean amount of time viewers spend watching a particular program.

Parameter of interest: Population mean μ

- Select a random sample of size n.

- For each item or subject in the sample, measure the numerical characteristic of interest, X.

$$\text{Sample: } (x_1, x_2, x_3, \cdots, x_n)$$

- Compute the sample mean $\bar{x} = \dfrac{\sum x_i}{n}$ and sample standard deviation

$$S = \sqrt{\frac{\sum x_i^2 - \left(\sum x_i\right)^2 / n}{n-1}}$$

This sample mean $\overline{X}$ is a point estimate of the unknown population mean. Different random samples of size n from the same population will result in different sample means, giving different estimates. The distribution of means from all possible random samples of size n is the sampling distribution of $\overline{X}$.

- The mean of all possible sample means is m. Therefore $\overline{X}$ is an unbiased estimator of m.

- The standard deviation of the sampling distribution of $\overline{X}$ is $\sigma_{\bar{x}} = \dfrac{\sigma}{\sqrt{n}}$.

- Sampling distribution of $\bar{x}$:

    If the population is normally distributed and the population variance is known, then the sampling distribution of $\bar{x}$ is also a **normal distribution**.

    If the population is normally distributed and the population variance is unknown, then the sampling distribution of $\bar{x}$ is a **t-distribution** with $(n-1)$ degrees of freedom.

    If the sample size is large, then according to the Central Limit Theorem, the sampling distribution of $\bar{x}$ is approximately **normal** regardless of the population distribution.

Construct a confidence interval or make an inference using a normal (Z) or a t- distribution. Decide between a normal and a t-distribution using the following scheme:

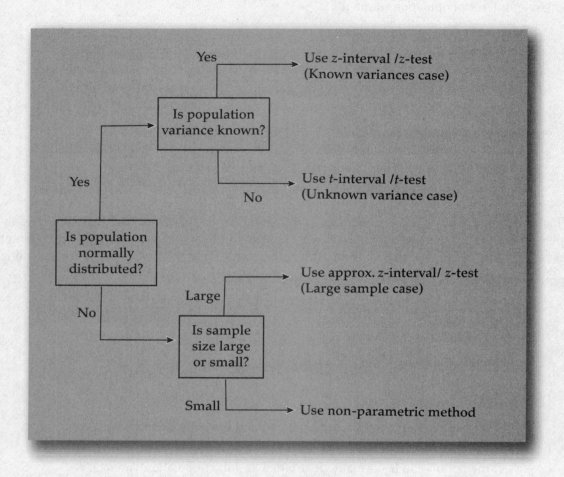

Figure 13: Scheme for selecting *t* or *z* interval for estimation of and inference about sample mean

Known variance case

Population variance σ^2 is known.

Estimating μ using $(1-\alpha)100\%$ confidence interval:

Known variance case:

Construct a *z*-interval Margin of Error: $\quad Z_{\alpha/2}\, \sigma_{\bar{x}} = Z_{\alpha/2}\dfrac{\sigma}{\sqrt{n}}$

Confidence Interval: $\quad \bar{x} \pm Z_{\alpha/2}\dfrac{\sigma}{\sqrt{n}}$

Making an inference about the difference in population means μ:
Known variance case: Use a z-test

H_0: $\mu = \mu_0$

H_a: $\mu > \mu_0$ or

$\qquad \mu < \mu_0$ or

$\qquad \mu \neq \mu_0$

$$TS = \frac{\overline{x} - \mu_0}{\sigma / \sqrt{n}}$$

	Rejection Rule	
Alternative hypothesis:	**Rejection region approach:**	**p-value approach:**
H_a: $\mu > \mu_0$ H_a: $\mu < \mu_0$ or H_a: $\mu \neq \mu_0$	Reject H_0 if $TS > Z_\alpha$ $TS < -Z_\alpha$ $TS > Z_{\alpha/2}$ or $TS < -Z_{\alpha/2}$	Reject H_0 if p-value $< \alpha$, where p-value $= P(Z > TS)$ p-value $= P(Z < TS)$ p-value $= P(Z > |TS|) + P(Z < -|TS|)$

Conditions:

(a) A random sample is taken from the population.

(b) The sampled population is normally distributed.

Checking the normality condition:

- Make a dotplot, histogram, or a stem-and-leaf plot for the sample. Ask yourself whether the distribution is fairly symmetric and bell-shaped, without any outliers. In other words, ask yourself whether the distribution resembles the normal distribution. Alternatively, use a normal probability plot.

Unknown variance case

If the population standard deviation σ is unknown, then estimate it using the sample standard deviation S.

Estimating μ using $(1 - \alpha)100\%$ confidence interval:

Unknown variance case:

Construct a t-interval with $\upsilon = (n - 1)$ degrees of freedom

$\qquad$ Margin of Error: $\qquad t_{\alpha/2}(\upsilon) \, S_{\overline{X}} = t_{\alpha/2}(\upsilon) \dfrac{\sigma}{\sqrt{n}}$

$\qquad$ Confidence Interval: $\qquad \overline{X} \pm t_{\alpha/2}(\upsilon) \dfrac{\sigma}{\sqrt{n}}$

Making an inference about the difference in population means μ:
Unknown variance case: Use a t-test with $\upsilon(n-1)$ degrees of freedom

$H_0: \mu = \mu_0$
$H_a: \mu > \mu_0$ or
  $\mu < \mu_0$ or
  $\mu \neq \mu_0$

$$TS = \frac{\bar{x} - \mu_0}{S/\sqrt{n}}$$

	Rejection Rule	
Alternative hypothesis:	**Rejection region approach:**	**p-value approach:**
$H_a: \mu > \mu_0$ $H_a: \mu < \mu_0$ or $H_a: \mu \neq \mu_0$	Reject H_0 if $TS > t_\alpha(\upsilon)$ $TS < -t_\alpha(\upsilon)$ $TS > t_{\alpha/2}(\upsilon)$ or $TS < -t_{\alpha/2}(\upsilon)$	Reject H_0 if p-value $< \alpha$, where p-value $= P(t(\upsilon) > TS)$ p-value $= P(t(\upsilon) < TS)$ p-value $= P(t(\upsilon) > |TS|) + P(t(\upsilon) < -|TS|)$

Conditions:

(a) A random sample is taken from the population.

(b) The sampled population is normally distributed.

Checking the normality condition:

- Make a dotplot, histogram, or a stem-and-leaf plot for the sample. Ask yourself whether the shape of the distribution is fairly symmetric and bell-shaped, without any outliers. In other words, ask yourself whether the distribution resembles the normal distribution. Alternatively, use a normal probability plot.

Large sample case

If the population standard deviation σ is unknown, then estimate it using the sample standard deviation S.

Estimating μ using $(1-\alpha)100\%$ confidence interval:

Large sample case:
Construct an approximate z-interval

Margin of Error: $\quad Z_{\alpha/2} \, \hat{\sigma}_{\bar{x}} = Z_{\alpha/2} \dfrac{\sigma}{\sqrt{n}}$

Confidence Interval: $\quad \bar{x} \pm Z_{\alpha/2} \dfrac{\sigma}{\sqrt{n}}$

Making an inference about the difference in population means μ: Large sample case: Use a z-test		
$H_0: \mu = \mu_0$ $H_a: \mu > \mu_0$ or $\quad \mu < \mu_0$ or $\quad \mu \neq \mu_0$		$TS = \dfrac{\bar{x} - \mu_0}{S/\sqrt{n}}$
	Rejection Rule	
Alternative hypothesis:	Rejection region approach:	p-value approach:
$H_a: \mu > \mu_0$ $H_a: \mu < \mu_0$ or $H_a: \mu \neq \mu_0$	Reject H_0 if $TS > Z_\alpha$ $TS < -Z_\alpha$ $TS > Z_{\alpha/2}$ or $TS < -Z_{\alpha/2}$	Reject H_0 if p-value $< \alpha$, where p-value $= P(Z > TS)$ p-value $= P(Z < TS)$ p-value $= P(Z > |TS|) + P(Z < -|TS|)$

Conditions:

(a) A random sample is taken from the population.

(b) The sample size is large enough to apply the Central Limit Theorem.

Checking the sample size condition:

- There is no fixed value that determines whether a sample size is large or small. No matter how large the sample, whether the sampling distribution of the sample mean approximates the normal distribution depends on the shape of the sampled population. If there are no outliers, and the population distribution is not extremely skewed, then $n \geq 30$ is large enough to get approximately normal sampling distribution of $\bar{x}$.

Example 11: A company that manufactures bicycles receives steel rods in large shipments from a supplier. From past experience, he knows that s = 0.12 inches and that the lengths are approximately normally distributed. The manager takes a random sample of 10 rods. The lengths of the sampled rods are as follows:

$$11.90, \ 11.94, \ 12.05, \ 12.07, \ 11.97, \ 12.01, \ 12.08, \ 12.05, \ 12.12, \ 12.14$$

(a) The manager wants to estimate the mean length of the rods using a 90 percent confidence interval. Help this manager construct a confidence interval and then interpret it.

(b) The company needs rods with a length of 12 inches in order to assemble the bikes properly. Since too-large and too-small rods are unsuitable, shipments not meeting the requirement are sent back to the supplier. Help this manager determine whether the shipment should be accepted or rejected.

Solution: (a)

Step 1: The manager is interested in estimating

μ = true mean length of rods received in the latest shipment.

Step 2: A random sample of $n = 10$ rods was taken.

For each sampled rod x = the length of the rod in inches.

It is given that the population standard deviation is $\sigma = 0.12$ inches.

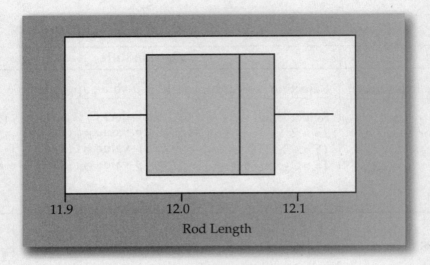

Figure 14: Distribution of rod lengths

Conditions:

(a) It is given that a random sample of rods was taken from the shipment.

(b) It is also given that the lengths of the rods are approximately normally distributed. The boxplot of data shows no outliers. The conditions are therefore satisfied and the population variance is known. So this is a "known variance case," and we can use a z-interval to estimate the population mean.

Step 3: To construct a 90 percent confidence interval, we need $\alpha = 0.10$. Therefore

$$Z_{\alpha/2} = Z_{0.10/2} = Z_{0.05} = 1.645$$

The sample mean is $\bar{x} = \dfrac{\sum x}{n} = \dfrac{120.33}{10} = 12.033$ inches.

The 90 percent ME = $Z_{\alpha/2} \dfrac{\sigma}{\sqrt{n}} = 1.645 \dfrac{0.12}{10} = 0.0624$

$\bar{x} \pm \text{ME} \Rightarrow 12.033 \pm 0.0624 \Rightarrow (11.9706, 12.0954)$

Therefore, the 90 percent confidence interval to estimate μ is (11.97, 12.10) inches.

Step 4: We are 90 percent confident that the true mean length of rods from this shipment is between 11.97 and 12.10 inches.

TI-83:

Using the data

If the actual measurements (the lengths of the rods, for example) are available, then use this option.

- Enter data in list L1

- Choose **STAT** → **TESTS** → **7:ZInterval**

- Highlight Data

- Enter appropriate values

    ZInterval
    Input: Data Stats
    σ: 0.12
    List: L1
    Freq: 1
    C-Level: .90
    Calculate

- Highlight Calculate

- Press **ENTER**

TI-83:

Using summary statistics

If the actual measurements are not available, but the sample mean and the population standard deviation are available, then use this option.

- Choose **STAT** → **TESTS** → **7:ZInterval**

- Highlight Stats

- Enter appropriate values

    ZInterval
    Input: Data Stats
    σ: 0.12
    $\bar{x}$: 12.033
    n: 10
    C-Level: .90
    Calculate

- Highlight Calculate

- Press **ENTER**

(b) Making an inference about the mean.

Step 1: $\mu =$ the true mean length of rods received in the latest shipment.

The manager is interested in making an inference about the mean length of the rods in this shipment—in other words, he wants to test

$$H_0 : \mu = 12 \text{ inches (accept the shipment)}$$

against $H_a : \mu \neq 12$ inches (reject the shipment)

Step 2: A random sample of $n = 10$ rods was taken.

For each sampled rod, $x =$ the length of the rod measured in inches.

It is given that the population standard deviation $\sigma = 0.12$ inches.

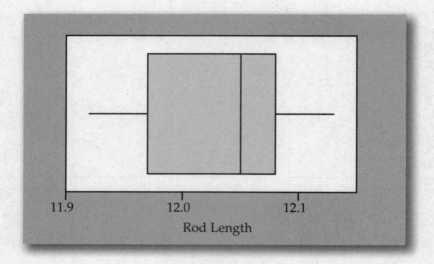

Figure 15: Distribution of rod lengths

Conditions: It is given that a random sample of rods is taken from the shipment. It is also given that the lengths are approximately normally distributed. The boxplot of data shows no outliers. The conditions are satisfied and the population variance is known. So this is a "known variance case," and we can use a z-test for mean.

Step 3: Let's use $\alpha = 0.10$. $Z_{\alpha/2} = Z_{0.10/2} = Z_{0.05} = 1.645$

The rejection rule is

- Reject the null hypothesis if p-value < 0.10 [using a p-value approach].

- Reject the null hypothesis if TS > 1.645 or if TS < −1.645 [using the rejection rule approach].

The sample mean is $\bar{x} = 12.033$ inches.

$$\text{TS} = \frac{\bar{X} - \mu_0}{\sigma / \sqrt{n}} = \frac{12.033 - 12}{0.12 / \sqrt{10}} = 0.87$$

$$p\text{-value} = P(Z > 0.87) + P(Z < -0.87) = 0.3843$$

Step 4: Since p-value = 0.3843 > 0.10 (or if using the rejection region approach, since $-1.645 <$ TS < 1.6450), we do not reject the null hypothesis. The manager should not reject the shipment. Note that p-value = 0.3843 indicates that, if the manager rejects the shipment, then there is a 38.43 percent chance that he is rejecting a shipment that meets specifications. Since the manager is only willing to take a 10 percent risk of rejecting the true null hypothesis, he must not reject the shipment.

TI-83:
Using the data
If the actual measurements are available, then use this option.

- Enter data in list L1
- Choose **STAT** → **TESTS** → **1: Z-Test**
- Highlight Data
- Enter appropriate values

 Z Test
 Input: Data Stats
 μo: 12
 σ: 0.12
 List: L1
 Freq: 1
 μ: ≠ μo < μo > μo
 Calculate   Draw

- Highlight Calculate
- Press **ENTER**

TI-83:
Using summary statistics
If the actual measurements are not available, but the sample mean and the population standard deviation are available, then use this option.

- Choose **STAT** → **TESTS** → **1: Z-Test**
- Highlight Stats
- Enter appropriate values
 Z Test
 Input: Data Stats
 μo: 12
 σ: 0.12
 $\bar{x}$: 12.033
 n: 10 μ: ≠ μo < μo > μo
 Calculate   Draw

- Highlight Calculate
- Press **ENTER**

Example 12: Consider a vending machine that is supposed to dispense 8 ounces of a soft drink. A sample of 20 cups taken over a one-week period contained the following amounts in ounces:

| 8.1 | 7.7 | 7.9 | 8.0 | 7.7 | 7.8 | 7.9 | 8.0 | 7.6 | 7.9 |
| 8.0 | 7.9 | 7.6 | 7.5 | 8.1 | 7.8 | 7.8 | 7.9 | 8.2 | 7.5 |

(a) Estimate the true mean amount dispensed by the machine, using a 95 percent confidence level.

(b) Is there significant evidence to conclude that the machine is dispensing less than 8 ounces?

Solution: (a) Estimation:

Step 1: We are interested in estimating

μ = the true mean amount of soft drink per cup dispensed by the machine.

Step 2: A random sample of $n = 20$ cups was taken.

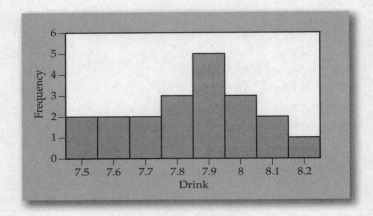

Figure 16: Histogram of amount of drink dispensed per cup

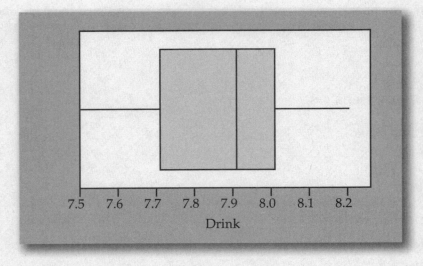

Figure 17: Boxplot of amount of drink dispensed per cup

Conditions:

(a) It is given that a random sample of cups was examined. Since the cups were filled over a period of one week, we can assume that the amounts filled are independent.

(b) Let's use a histogram and a boxplot to summarize the data. There are no outliers, and the distributions are fairly symmetric. Therefore, the above plots show that it is reasonable to assume that the amounts dispensed per cup by the machine are approximately normally distributed.

The amount of soft drink dispensed per cup is approximately normally distributed, but the population variance of the distribution of the amount of drink per cup is unknown. Therefore, we should construct a t-interval for the mean.

Step 3: Compute the sample mean and sample standard deviation, using the formulas we already learned in chapter 4.

$$\bar{x} = 7.845 \text{ and } s = 0.1986$$

With a sample of size 20, the degrees of freedom = 20 − 1 = 19.

To construct a 95 percent confidence interval, use $\alpha = 0.05$. Using the t-table for 19 degrees of freedom we get

$$\Rightarrow t_{\alpha/2}(19) = t_{0.05/2}(19) = t_{0.025}(19) = 2.093$$

$$95 \text{ percent ME} = t_{0.025}(19)\left(\frac{s}{\sqrt{n}}\right) = 2.093\left(\frac{0.1986}{\sqrt{20}}\right) = 0.0929 \text{ ounces}$$

$$\bar{x} \pm \text{ME} \Rightarrow 7.845 \pm 0.0929 \Rightarrow (7.752, 7.938)$$

The 95 percent confidence interval to estimate μ is (7.75, 7.94).

Step 4: Interpretation.
- We are 95 percent confident that the true mean amount dispensed by the machine is between 7.75 ounces and 7.94 ounces.
- We are 95 percent confident that our best estimate of 7.845 ounces is within 0.0929 ounces of the true mean amount dispensed by the machine.

TI-83:
Using the data

- Enter the data into L1
- Choose **STAT** → **TESTS** → **8: T Interval**
- Highlight **Data**
- Enter the appropriate values
  TInterval
  Inpt: Data Stats
  List: L1
  Freq: 1
  C-Level: .95
  Calculate
- Highlight Calculate
- Press **ENTER**

TI-83:
Using summary statistics
If the actual measurements are not available, but the sample mean and the sample standard deviation are available, then use this option.

- Enter the data into L1
- Choose **STAT** → **TESTS** → **8: T Interval**
- Highlight **Data**
- Enter the appropriate values

  TInterval
  Inpt: Data Stats
  $\bar{x}$: 7.845
  Sx: 0.1986
  n: 20
  C-Level: .95
  Calculate
- Highlight Calculate
- Press **ENTER**

(b) Inference:

Step 1: We are interested in testing the hypothesis about

μ = The true mean amount of soft drink dispensed by the machine.

H_0: $\mu = 8$ ounces (The true mean amount of soft drink dispensed by the machine is 8 ounces.)

H_a: $\mu < 8$ ounces (The true mean amount of soft drink dispensed by the machine is less than 8 ounces.)

Step 2: A random sample of $n = 20$ cups was taken.

Conditions:

(a) It is given that a random sample of cups filled was examined.

(b) Let's use a histogram and boxplot to summarize the data (see the previous histogram and boxplot). The amount of soft drink dispensed per cup is approximately normally distributed, but the population variance of the distribution of the amount of soft drink per cup is unknown. Therefore, we should use a t-test for the mean.

Step 3: Compute the sample mean and sample standard deviation, using the formulas already learned in chapter 4.

$$\bar{x} = 7.845 \text{ and } s = 0.1986$$
$$\text{With a sample of size 20, df} = 20 - 1 = 19$$

Suppose we use $\alpha = 0.05$. Then, using a t-table for 19 degrees of freedom, we get

$$t_\alpha(19) = t_{0.05}(19) = 1.73$$

So the rejection rule is to reject the null hypothesis and accept the alternative hypothesis if:

- TS < -1.73 (rejection region approach)

- p-value < 0.05 (p-value approach)

Compute the test statistic (and p-value if using p-value approach)

$$TS = \frac{\left(\bar{X} - \mu\right)}{S/\sqrt{n}} = \frac{(7.845 - 8.000)}{0.1986/\sqrt{20}} = -3.49$$

$$p\text{-value} = P(t < -3.49) = 0.0012$$

Step 4: Write a conclusion.

- Using the **p-value approach:** Since p-value $= 0.0012 < \alpha = 0.05$, we should reject the null hypothesis and accept the alternative hypothesis.

- Using the **rejection region approach:** Since t $= -3.49 < -1.73$ (in other words, the test statistic falls in the rejection region), we should reject the null hypothesis and accept the alternative hypothesis.

Conclusion: At 5 percent level of significance, there is sufficient evidence to conclude that the true mean amount dispensed by the machine is less than 8 ounces.

TI-83:
Using the data
If the actual measurements are available, then use this option.

- Enter the data into L1

- Choose **STAT** → **TESTS** → **2:** *T* **Test**

- Highlight **Data**

- Enter appropriate values

  T Test
  Inpt: Data Stats
  $\mu 0$: 8.0
  List: L1
  Freq: 1
  $\mu: \neq \mu 0 < \mu 0 > \mu 0$
  Calculate Draw

- Highlight **Calculate**

- Press **ENTER**

TI-83:
Using summary statistics
If the actual measurements are not available, but the sample mean and standard deviation are available, then use this option.

- Enter the data into L1

- Choose **STAT** → **TESTS** → **2:** *T* **Test**

- Highlight **Stats**

- Enter appropriate values

  T Test
  Inpt: Data Stats
  $\mu 0$: 8.0
  $\bar{x}$: 7.845
  Sx: 0.1986
  n: 20
  $\mu: \neq \mu 0 < \mu 0 > \mu 0$
  Calculate Draw

- Highlight **Calculate**

- Press **ENTER**

Example 13: A bottling plant fills spring water in bottles labeled 12 oz. The floor supervisor noticed that in the past couple of days the plant had had several bottles overflow during the filling process. Suspecting that the mean filling-process amount had increased, he took a random sample of 40 bottles from those filled in the last eight-hour shift and measured the contents of each selected bottle (in oz). The amounts are as follows:

13.19	12.87	12.20	11.97	12.05	12.68	12.41	13.30
12.89	12.23	12.39	13.13	12.74	13.17	12.40	11.97
12.39	12.67	12.07	13.37	12.74	12.26	12.47	12.16
12.24	12.86	12.11	12.60	12.03	12.19	12.92	12.35
12.53	12.30	12.64	12.52	13.22	12.84	13.09	12.20

(a) Estimate the filling-process mean using a 90 percent confidence interval.

(b) Is there significant evidence to support the supervisor's suspicions? Justify your answer using statistical evidence.

Solution: (a) Estimating the filling-process mean:

Step 1: The supervisor is interested in estimating

μ = the true mean amount of spring water filled per bottle (in oz.).

Step 2: A random sample of $n = 40$ bottles was taken.

For each sampled bottle x = the amount of water per bottle measured in ounces.

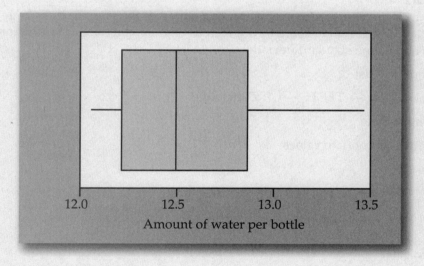

Figure 18: Boxplot of the amount of water filled per bottle

Conditions:

(a) It is given that a random sample of bottles was taken from those filled in the last eight-hour shift.

(b) A boxplot of the data shows no outliers. We do not know the distribution of the amount filled per bottle, but the sample size is large enough that we can apply the Central Limit Theorem and assume that $\bar{x}$ is approximately normally distributed. Therefore, we can use a z-interval to estimate the population mean.

Step 3: To construct a 90 percent confidence interval, we need $\alpha = 0.10$. Therefore,

$$Z_{\alpha/2} = Z_{0.10/2} = Z_{0.05} = 1.645$$

The sample mean $\bar{x} = \dfrac{502.36}{40} = 12.559$ oz.

The sample standard deviation is

$$S = \sqrt{\frac{6315.52 - \left(502.36^2/40\right)}{40-1}} = 0.405 \text{ oz.}$$

Then

$$90 \text{ percent ME} = Z_{\alpha/2}\frac{S}{\sqrt{n}} = 1.645\frac{0.405}{\sqrt{40}} = 0.105 \text{ oz.}$$

So, $\bar{x} \pm \text{ME} \Rightarrow 12.559 \pm 0.105 \Rightarrow (12.454, 12.664)$.

Therefore, the 90 percent confidence interval to estimate μ is (12.45, 12.66) oz.

Step 4: We are 90 percent confident that the true mean amount per bottle filled is between 12.45 and 12.66 oz.

TI-83:

Using the data

If the actual measurements are available, use this option. If the sample size is large and the population standard deviation is unknown, then use the sample standard deviation to estimate the population standard deviation.

- Enter data in list L1
- Choose **STAT** → **TESTS** → **1: ZInterval**
- Highlight Data
- Enter the appropriate values

  Zinterval
  Input: Data Stats
  σ: 0.405
  List: L1
  Freq: 1
  C-Level: .90
  Calculate

- Highlight Calculate
- Press **ENTER**

If the actual measurements are not available, but the sample mean and the population standard deviation are available, then use this option. If the sample size is large and the population standard deviation is unknown, then use the sample standard deviation to estimate the population standard deviation.

- Choose **STAT** → **TESTS** → **1: ZInterval**

- Highlight Stats

- Enter the appropriate values

  ZInterval
  Input: Data Stats
  σ: 0.405
  $\bar{x}$: 12.559
  n: 40
  C-Level: .90
  Calculate

- Highlight Calculate

- Press **ENTER**

(b) The supervisor is interested in determining whether the filling-process mean has increased.

Step 1: The filling-process mean is

μ = true mean amount of spring water filled per bottle (in oz).

In order to decide whether the filling-process mean has increased, the supervisor will test

H_0: μ = 12 oz (The plant is still filling on the average 12 oz per bottle.)

H_a: μ > 12 oz (On the average, the plant is filling more than 12 oz per bottle.)

Step 2: A random sample of n = 40 bottles was taken.

For each sampled bottle, x = the amount of water per bottle measured in ounces.

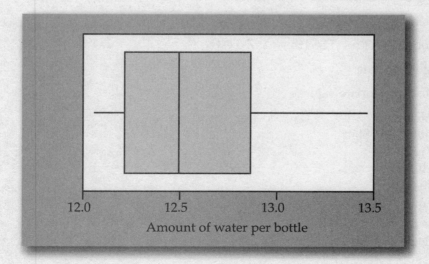

Figure 19: Boxplot of the amount of water filled per bottle

Conditions:

(a) It is given that a random sample of bottles was taken from the bottles filled in the last eight-hour shift.

(b) A boxplot of the data shows no outliers. We do not know the distribution of the amount filled per bottle, but the sample size is large enough so that we can apply the Central Limit Theorem and assume that $\bar{x}$ is approximately normally distributed. Therefore, we can use a z-test to make an inference about the filling-process mean.

Step 3: Suppose we use $\alpha = 0.05$. Then

$$CV = Z_\alpha = Z_{0.05} = 1.645$$

The sample mean is $\bar{x} = 12.559$ oz and the sample standard deviation is $S = 0.405$ oz. The rejection rule is "Reject the null hypothesis if p-value < 0.05" (or, "reject the null hypothesis if TS > 1.645," if using a rejection region approach).

Compute the test statistic value (and compute the p-value, if using a p-value approach).

$$TS = \frac{\bar{x} - \mu_0}{S/\sqrt{n}} = \frac{12.559 - 12}{0.405/\sqrt{40}} = 8.74$$

$$p\text{-value} = P(Z > 8.74) = \text{almost } 0$$

Step 4: Since the p-value < 0.05 (or TS = 8.74 > CV = 1.645), reject the null hypothesis and accept the alternative hypothesis. At a 5 percent risk of rejecting the true null hypothesis, we can conclude that the filling-process mean has increased.

TI-83:

Using the data

If the actual measurements are available, use this option. If the sample size is large and the population standard deviation is unknown, then use the sample standard deviation to estimate the population standard deviation.

- Enter data in list L1

- Choose **STAT** → **TESTS** → **1: Z-Test**

- Highlight Data

- Enter appropriate values

   Zinterval
   Input: Data Stats
   μ_0: 12
   σ: 0.405
   List: L1
   Freq: 1

   $\mu \neq \mu_0 < \mu_0 < \mu_0$
   Calculate   Draw

- Highlight Calculate

- Press **ENTER**

ESTIMATION OF AND INFERENCE ABOUT THE DIFFERENCE IN POPULATION PROPORTIONS ($p_1 - p_2$)

LARGE SAMPLES CASE

Often we are interested in comparing proportions from two different populations. For example:

- Comparing the proportion of residents of Mobile county in favor of using tax money to rebuild private beaches to the proportion of residents of Baldwin county in favor of the same proposal

- Comparing the proportion of Florida residents who support the patient's bill of rights to that of Texas residents who support the bill

- Comparing the proportion of Visa cardholders assessed late-payment penalties to that of Master Card cardholders assessed late-payment penalties

Let

$$p_1 = \text{the proportion of interest in population 1}$$
$$p_2 = \text{the proportion of interest in population 2}$$

In the situations described above, we are interested in estimating the difference between two population proportions.

Parameter of interest: Difference between two population proportions $(p_1 - p_2)$

- Select a random sample of size n_1 from population 1.
- Select a random sample of size n_2 from population 2.
- Be sure to select the two samples independently of each other.
- For each item or subject in the sample, note the presence or absence of the specific criteria of interest.
- Count the number of subjects meeting required criteria (x_1) from sample 1.
- Count the number of subjects meeting required criteria (x_2) from sample 2.

The estimated proportion from sample 1 is $\hat{p}_1 = \dfrac{x_1}{x_2}$

The estimated proportion from sample 2 is $\hat{p}_2 = \dfrac{x_2}{n_2}$

$\hat{p}_1$ and $\hat{p}_2$ respectively, provide point estimates of the unknown population proportions p_1 and p_2. The difference $(\hat{p}_1 - \hat{p}_2)$ gives a point estimate of $(p_1 - p_2)$. Different random samples of the same size from the same population will result in different sample proportions, giving different estimates. Therefore, the difference $(\hat{p}_1 - \hat{p}_2)$ is a random variable. The distribution of estimated differences from all possible random samples of sizes n_1 and n_2 is the sampling distribution of $(\hat{p}_1 - \hat{p}_2)$.

- The mean of the sampling distribution of $(\hat{p}_1 - \hat{p}_2)$ is $(p_1 - p_2)$. Therefore,

$$(\hat{p}_1 - \hat{p}_2) \text{ is an unbiased estimator of } (p_1 - p_2)$$

- The standard deviation of the sampling distribution of $(\hat{p}_1 - \hat{p}_2)$ is

$$\sigma_{(\hat{p}_1 - \hat{p}_2)} = \sqrt{\frac{p_1(1 - p_1)}{n_1} + \frac{p_2(1 - p_2)}{n_2}}$$

- For large sample sizes, the sampling distribution of $(\hat{p}_1 - \hat{p}_2)$ is approximately normally distributed.

Estimating $(p_1 - p_2)$ **using** $(1 - \alpha)100\%$ **confidence interval**:
Large samples case: Construct a z-interval
Margin of Error:

$$Z_{\alpha/2}\hat{\sigma}_{(\hat{p}_1 - \hat{p}_2)} = Z_{\alpha/2}\sqrt{\frac{\hat{p}_1(1 - \hat{p}_1)}{n_1} + \frac{\hat{p}_2(1 - \hat{p}_2)}{n_2}}$$

Confidence Interval:

$$(\hat{p}_1 - \hat{p}_2) \pm Z_{\alpha/2}\sqrt{\frac{\hat{p}_1(1 - \hat{p}_1)}{n_1} + \frac{\hat{p}_2(1 - \hat{p}_2)}{n_2}}$$

> **Making an inference about the difference in population proportions ($\hat{p}_1 - \hat{p}_2$):**
> **Large samples case: Use a z-test**
>
> $H_0: p_1 - p_0 =$ (D_0 is "specified difference in proportions")
>
> $H_a: p_1 - p_0 > D_0$ or $\text{TS} = \dfrac{(\hat{p}_1 - \hat{p}_2) - D_0}{\sqrt{\hat{p}(1 - \hat{p}_c)\,\dfrac{1}{n_1} + \dfrac{1}{n_2}}}$ where $\hat{p}_c = \dfrac{X_1 + X_2}{n_1 + n_2}$
> $\quad\ p_1 - p_0 < D_0$ or
> $\quad\ p_1 - p_0 \neq D_0$
>
> | | Rejection Rule | |
> |---|---|---|
> | **Alternative hypothesis:** | **Rejection region approach:** | **p-value approach:** |
> | $H_a:\ p_1 > p_2$
 $H_a:\ p_1 < p_2$
 $H_a:\ p_1 \neq p_0$ | Reject H_0 if
 $\text{TS} > Z_\alpha$
 $\text{TS} < -Z_\alpha$
 $\text{TS} > Z_{\alpha/2}\ \text{TS} < -Z_{\alpha/2}$ | Reject H_0 if p-value $< \alpha$, where
 $p\text{-value} = P(Z > \text{TS})$
 $p\text{-value} = P(Z < \text{TS})$
 $p\text{-value} = P(Z > |\text{TS}|) + P(Z < -|\text{TS}|)$ |

Conditions:

(a) Random samples are taken from both the populations.

(b) The samples are taken independently.

(c) Both sample sizes are large enough that the distribution of $\left(\hat{p}_1 - \hat{p}_2\right)$ is approximately normal.

Checking the normality condition:

If $n_1\hat{p}_1 > 10$, $n_1\left(1 - \hat{p}_1\right) > 10$, $n_2\hat{p}_2 > 10$ and $n_2\left(1 - \hat{p}_2\right) > 10$, then it is reasonable to assume that the distribution of $\left(\hat{p}_1 - \hat{p}_2\right)$ is approximately normal.

Example 14: A large manufacturer of jeans has two factories, one in Mexico and one in the Philippines. At the end of the assembly lines, the quality of each finished pair of jeans is inspected and classified as either good or defective. The business manager wants to compare the proportion of defective jeans produced by the two factories. From one day's production, he randomly selects 500 jeans from the factory in Mexico and finds 25 defective. Similarly, he randomly selects 350 jeans from the factory in the Philippines and finds 27 defective. Estimate the difference in the proportion of defective jeans produced by the two factories, using a 98 percent confidence interval.

Solution:

Step 1: The business manager wants to estimate $\left(p_1 - p_2\right)$, where

$\qquad p_1$ = The true proportion of defective jeans manufactured at the plant in Mexico.

$\qquad p_2$ = The true proportion of defective jeans manufactured at the plant in the Philippines.

Step 2: A random sample of $n_1 = 500$ jeans was taken from the plant in Mexico.

Of the sampled jeans $x_1 = 25$ were defective.

The sample proportion is $\hat{p}_1 = {x_1}/{n_1} = {25}/{500} = 0.05$

A random sample of $n_2 = 350$ jeans was taken from the plant in the Philippines.

Of the sampled jeans $x_2 = 27$ were defective.

The sample proportion is $\hat{p}_2 = {x_2}/{n_2} = {27}/{350} = 0.077$

Conditions:

(a) It is given that random samples of jeans were taken. It is reasonable to assume that both samples were taken independently.

(b) $n_1 \hat{p}_1 = 500\,(0.05) = 25 > 10$ and $n_1\,(1 - \hat{p}_1) = 500\,(1 - 0.05) = 450 > 10$. $n_2 \hat{p}_2 = 350$ $(0.077) = 27 > 10$ and $n_2\,(1 - \hat{p}_2) = 350\,(1 - 0.077) = 323 > 10$. Therefore the sample sizes are large enough that we can assume that the sampling distribution of $(\hat{p}_1 - \hat{p}_2)$ is approximately normal.

The conditions are satisfied and we can therefore use a large-samples z-interval for proportion.

Step 3: To construct a 98 percent confidence interval, we use $\alpha = 0.02$

$$Z_{\alpha/2} = Z_{0.02/2} = Z_{0.01} = 2.33$$

$$(\hat{p}_1 - \hat{p}_2) = 0.05 - 0.077 = -0.027$$

$$98\% \text{ ME} = Z_{\alpha/2} \sqrt{\frac{\hat{p}_1(1 - \hat{p}_1)}{n_1} + \frac{\hat{p}_2(1 - \hat{p}_2)}{n_2}}$$

$$= 2.33 \sqrt{\frac{0.05(1 - 0.05)}{500} + \frac{0.077(1 - 0.077)}{350}}$$

$$= 0.04$$

$$(\hat{p}_1 - \hat{p}_2) \pm \text{ME} \Rightarrow -0.027 \pm 0.04 \Rightarrow (-0.067, 0.013)$$

Therefore, a 98 percent confidence interval to estimate $(p_1 - p_2)$ is $(-0.067, 0.013)$.

Step 4: We are 98 percent confident that the difference between the proportion of defective jeans produced by the plant in Mexico and the proportion of defective jeans produced by the plant in the Philippines is between -0.067 and 0.013.

Since 0 falls in this interval, we can conclude that $p_1 - p_2 = 0$. In other words, there is no significant difference between the proportion of defective jeans produced by the factory in Mexico and the proportion produced by the factory in the Philippines.

ESTIMATION OF AND INFERENCE ABOUT THE DIFFERENCE IN POPULATION MEANS ($\mu_1 - \mu_2$)

We are often interested in comparing the means of two different populations. For example:

- Comparing the mean lifetimes of two comparable brands of tires

- Comparing the mean costs of education at two state universities

- Comparing the mean grades of students taught using two different methods

- Comparing the mean number of asthma attacks per month before and after patients are given a new medication

- Comparing the mean cost of long distance calls per minute using two different companies

In each of the above examples we want to compare the means of two populations. In order to make such a comparison, we need to take a random sample from each of the two populations and compare their sample means. But notice that in some cases the two samples are independent, whereas in others the samples are dependent. By dependence, we mean that there is some kind of matching involved between the first sample and the second sample. Data collected from independent samples is analyzed differently from data collected from dependent samples.

- **Independent samples.** To compare the effect of two different teaching methods (traditional and new) on students' grades, take a group of students with similar educational backgrounds. Assign these students randomly to one of two different groups. Teach the students in group 1 using the traditional method and those in group 2 using the new method. At the end of the course, give the same exam to both groups and measure the students' grades. In this situation, there is no specific matching between the students in one group and the students in the other group. So the two samples are independent or unpaired.

- **Dependent samples.** To compare the effectiveness of a new diet, select a group of patients and measure their cholesterol levels before starting on a new diet. Then measure the cholesterol levels of the same patients after they've been put on the diet for three months. In this situation, note that there is a specific match between the "before diet" cholesterol level sample and the "after diet" cholesterol level sample. Both samples are taken from the same patients. It does not make sense to compare the "before diet" cholesterol level for Bob with the "after diet" cholesterol level for Ann. Dependence does not neccesarily mean taking measurements on the same item or person, however.

CASE OF INDEPENDENT OR UNPAIRED SAMPLES

Two samples are considered independent if the selection of one sample has no bearing on the selection of the other sample. For example, to compare the lifetime of Goodyear tires to the lifetime of Firestone tires, we could select a sample of tires from Goodyear's production line and a sample from Firestone's. Which tires get selected in one sample has no connection to which tires get selected in the other sample.

Let

μ_1 = The mean of population 1, and σ_1^2 = the variance of population 1.

μ_2 = The mean of population 2, and σ_2^2 = the variance of population 2.

Suppose we are interested in estimating the difference between two population means.

Parameter of interest: Difference between two population means $(\mu_1 - \mu_2)$.

- Select a random sample of size n_1 from population 1.

- Select a random sample of size n_2 from population 2.

- Select the two samples independently of each other.

- For each selected item, measure the specific variable of interest. Let $x_{11}, x_{12}, ..., x_{1n_1}$ be the measurements from the first sample and $x_{21}, x_{22}, ..., x_{2n_2}$ be the measurements from the second sample.

- Compute both sample means.

- The mean of sample 1 is $\bar{x}_1 = \sum x_{1i} / n_1$. The mean of sample 2 is $\bar{x}_2 = \sum x_{2i} / n_2$. Note that $\bar{x}_1$ estimates μ_1 and $\bar{x}_2$ estimates μ_2. The difference $(\bar{x}_1 - \bar{x}_2)$ gives a point estimate of the difference $(\mu_1 - \mu_2)$. Different random samples of the same size from the same population will result in different sample means, giving different estimates. Therefore, the difference $(\bar{x}_1 - \bar{x}_2)$ is a random variable. The distribution of the estimated differences in sample means from all possible random and independent samples of sizes n_1 and n_2 is the sampling distribution of $(\bar{x}_1 - \bar{x}_2)$.

- The mean of the sampling distribution of $(\bar{x}_1 - \bar{x}_2)$ is $(\mu_1 - \mu_2)$. Therefore $(\bar{x}_1 - \bar{x}_2)$ is an unbiased estimator of $(\mu_1 - \mu_2)$.

- Since the samples were taken independently, the standard deviation of the sampling distribution of $\left(\overline{x}_1 - \overline{x}_2\right)$ is

$$\sigma_{\left(\overline{x}_1 - \overline{x}_2\right)} = \sqrt{\frac{\sigma_1^2}{n_1} + \frac{\sigma_2^2}{n_2}}$$

- Note the following about the sampling distribution of $\left(\overline{x}_1 - \overline{x}_2\right)$:

If both the populations are normally distributed and the population variances are known, then the sampling distribution of $\left(\overline{x}_1 - \overline{x}_2\right)$ is also a **normal distribution.**

If both the populations are normally distributed and the population variances are unknown but equal, then the sampling distribution of $\left(\overline{x}_1 - \overline{x}_2\right)$ is a *t*-distribution with $\left(n_1 + n_2 - 2\right)$ degrees of freedom.

If both the populations are normally distributed and the population variances are unknown and unequal, then the sampling distribution of $\left(\overline{x}_1 - \overline{x}_2\right)$ is an approximate *t*-distribution with degrees of freedom equal to

$$\upsilon = \frac{\left(\dfrac{S_1^2}{n_1} + \dfrac{S_2^2}{n_2}\right)^2}{\dfrac{\left(S_1^2/n_1\right)^2}{n_1 - 1} + \dfrac{\left(S_2^2/n_2\right)^2}{n_2 - 1}}$$

In most cases this formula gives a fractional value for the required degrees of freedom. We would therefore need computers or calculators to find the true corresponding *t* values. When using tables, use the next smallest degree of freedom. For example if the above formula gives degrees of freedom equal to 17.35, then use 18 degrees of freedom in the *t*-distribution table.

If both the sample sizes are large, then according to the Central Limit Theorem, the sampling distribution of $\left(\overline{x}_1 - \overline{x}_2\right)$ is approximately **normal**, regardless of the population distributions.

- Construct a confidence interval using a normal or a *t*-distribution. Decide between the two distributions using the following scheme:

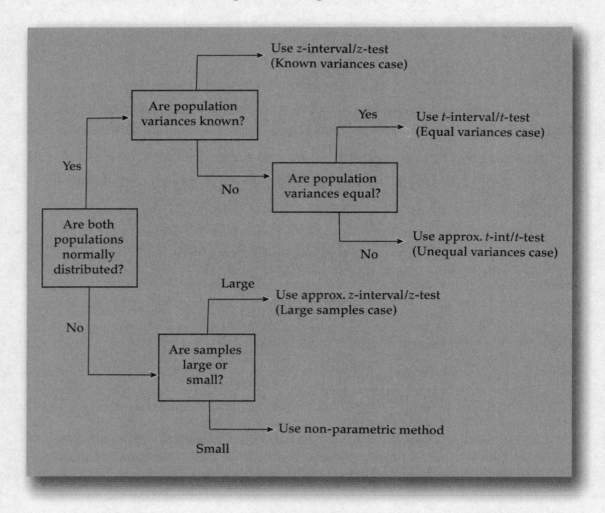

Figure 20: Scheme for selecting a confidence interval or test for difference of population means

Known variances case

The two population variances σ_1^2 and σ_2^2 are known.

Estimating $(\mu_1 - \mu_2)$ **using** $(1-\alpha)100\%$ **confidence interval**:

Known variances case: Construct a z-interval

Margin of Error:
$$Z_{\alpha/2}\sigma_{(\bar{x}_1 - \bar{x}_2)} = Z_{\alpha/2}\sqrt{\frac{\sigma_1^2}{n_1} + \frac{\sigma_2^2}{n_2}}$$

Confidence Interval:
$$(\bar{x}_1 - \bar{x}_2) \pm Z_{\alpha/2}\sqrt{\frac{\sigma_1^2}{n_1} + \frac{\sigma_2^2}{n_2}}$$

Making an inference about the difference in population means $(\mu_1 - \mu_2)$:
Known variances case: Use a z-test

$H_0: \mu_1 - \mu_2 = D_0$

$H_a: \mu_1 - \mu_2 > D_0$ or

$\quad \mu_1 - \mu_2 < D_0$ or

$\quad \mu_1 - \mu_2 \neq D_0$

$$TS = \frac{(\bar{x}_1 - \bar{x}_2) - D_0}{\sqrt{\frac{\sigma_1^2}{n_1} + \frac{\sigma_2^2}{n_2}}}$$

	Rejection Rule	
Alternative hypothesis:	Rejection region approach:	p-value approach:
$H_a:\ \mu_1 - \mu_2 > D_0$ $H_a:\ \mu_1 - \mu_2 < D_0$ $H_a:\ \mu_1 - \mu_2 \neq D_0$	Reject H_0 if $TS > Z_\alpha(\upsilon)$ $TS < -Z_\alpha(\upsilon)$ $TS > Z_{\alpha/2}$ or $TS < -Z_{\alpha/2}$	Reject H_0 if p-value $< \alpha$, where p-value $= P(Z > TS)$ p-value $= P(Z < TS)$ p-value $= P(Z > |TS|) + P(Z < -|TS|)$

Conditions:

(a) Random samples are taken from both the populations.

(b) The samples are taken independently.

(c) The sampled populations are normally distributed.

Checking the normality condition:

Make a dotplot, histogram, or stem-and-leaf plot for each sample. Ask yourself whether each distribution is fairly symmetric and bell-shaped, without any outliers. In other words, ask yourself whether the distribution resembles the normal distribution. Alternatively, use a normal probability plot.

Equal variances case

Two population variances σ_1^2 and σ_2^2 are unknown, but the variances are equal. Let's say $\sigma_1^2 = \sigma_2^2 = \sigma^2$. Compute sample variances from each sample. Let S_1^2 be the variance computed from sample 1 and S_2^2 the variance computed from sample 2. We know that S_1^2 estimates σ_1^2 and S_2^2 estimates σ_2^2. But remember that $\sigma_1^2 = \sigma_2^2 = \sigma^2$. So we have two estimates (S_1^2 and S_2^2) for one unknown quantity σ^2. By pooling information from both samples, we can get an improved estimate of σ^2. The pooled estimate of σ^2 is computed as

$$S_p^2 = \frac{(n_1 - 1)S_1^2 + (n_2 - 1)S_2^2}{(n_1 - 1) + (n_2 - 1)}$$

Estimating $(\mu_1 - \mu_2)$ using $(1-\alpha)100\%$ confidence interval:

Equal variances case: Construct a t-interval with υ degrees of freedom, where $\upsilon = (n_1 + n_2 - 2)$.

Margin of Error:
$$t_{\alpha/2}(\upsilon)\, \hat{\sigma}_{(\bar{x}_1 - \bar{x}_2)} = t_{\alpha/2}(\upsilon)\, S_p \sqrt{\frac{1}{n_1} + \frac{1}{n_2}}$$

Where
$$S_p = \sqrt{\frac{(n_1 - 1)S_1^2 + (n_2 - 1)S_2^2}{(n_1 - 1) + (n_2 - 1)}}$$

Confidence Interval:
$$(\bar{x}_1 - \bar{x}_2) \pm t_{\alpha/2}(\upsilon)\, S_p \sqrt{\frac{1}{n_1} + \frac{1}{n_2}}$$

Making an inference about the difference in population means $(\mu_1 - \mu_2)$:
Equal variances case: Use a t-test with $\upsilon = (n_1 + n_2 - 2)$ degrees of freedom

H_0: $\mu_1 - \mu_2 = D_0$
(specified difference)

H_a: $\mu_1 - \mu_2 > D_0$ or
$\quad \mu_1 - \mu_2 < D_0$ or
$\quad \mu_1 - \mu_2 \neq D_0$

$$TS = \frac{\bar{x}_1 - \bar{x}_2 - D_0}{S_p = \sqrt{\frac{1}{n_1} + \frac{1}{n_2}}}$$

where
$$S_p = \sqrt{\frac{(n_1 - 1)S_1^2 + (n_2 - 1)S_2^2}{(n_1 - 1) + (n_2 - 1)}}$$

	Rejection Rule	
Alternative hypothesis:	**Rejection region approach:**	**p-value approach:**
H_a: $\mu_1 - \mu_2 > D_0$	Reject H_0 if	Reject H_0 p-value $< \alpha$, where
H_a: $\mu_1 - \mu_2 < D_0$	$TS > t_\alpha(\upsilon)$	p-value $= P(t(\upsilon) > TS)$
H_a: $\mu_1 - \mu_2 \neq D_0$	$TS < -t_\alpha(\upsilon)$	p-value $= P(t(\upsilon) < TS)$
	$TS > t_{\alpha/2}(\upsilon)$ or $TS < -t_{\alpha/2}(\upsilon)$	p-value $= P(t(\upsilon) > |TS|) + P(t(\upsilon) < -|TS|)$

Conditions:

(a) Random samples are taken from both the populations.

(b) The samples are taken independently.

(c) The sampled populations are normally distributed.

(d) The population variances are equal $(\sigma_1^2 = \sigma_2^2)$

Checking the normality condition:

Make a dotplot, histogram, or stem-and-leaf plot for each sample. Ask yourself whether each distribution is fairly symmetric and bell-shaped, without any outliers. In other words, ask yourself whether the distribution resembles the normal distribution. Alternatively, use a normal probability plot.

Checking the condition of equal variances:

Make a dotplot or histogram and visually compare the spread of the measurements. If they are fairly comparable, without any outliers, then it is reasonable to assume that the variances are equal. Alternatively, use a two-tailed F-test for equality of variances (you may have learned how to do this in your statistics class).

Unequal variances case

Two population variances σ_1^2 and σ_2^2 are unknown and $\sigma_1^2 \neq \sigma_2^2$.

Estimate the unknown population variances using the sample variances S_1^2 and S_2^2.

Estimating $(\mu_1 - \mu_2)$ **using** $(1-\alpha)100\%$ **confidence interval**:

Unequal variances case: Construct a t-interval with

$$\upsilon = \frac{\left(\dfrac{S_1^2}{n_1} + \dfrac{S_2^2}{n_2}\right)^2}{\dfrac{\left(S_1^2/n_1\right)^2}{n_1 - 1} + \dfrac{\left(S_2^2/n_2\right)^2}{n_2 - 1}} \text{ degrees of freedom}$$

Margin of Error: $\quad t_{\alpha/2}(\upsilon)\,\hat{\sigma}_{(\bar{x}_1 - \bar{x}_2)} = t_{\alpha/2}(\upsilon)\sqrt{\dfrac{S_1^2}{n_1} + \dfrac{S_2^2}{n_2}}$

Confidence Interval: $\quad (\bar{x}_1 - \bar{x}_2) \pm t_{\alpha/2}(\upsilon)\sqrt{\dfrac{S_1^2}{n_1} + \dfrac{S_2^2}{n_2}}$

Making an inference about the difference in population means ($\mu_1 - \mu_2$):

Unequal variances case: Use a t-test with $\upsilon = \dfrac{\left(\dfrac{S_1^2}{n_1} + \dfrac{S_2^2}{n_2}\right)^2}{\dfrac{(S_1^2/n_1)^2}{n_1 - 1} + \dfrac{(S_2^2/n_2)^2}{n_2 - 1}}$ degrees of freedom

H_0: $\mu_1 - \mu_2 = D_0$ (specified difference)

H_a: $\mu_1 - \mu_2 > D_0$ or

$\quad \mu_1 - \mu_2 < D_0$ or

$\quad \mu_1 - \mu_2 \neq D_0$

$$TS = \frac{\bar{x}_1 - \bar{x}_2 - D_0}{\sqrt{\dfrac{S_1^2}{n_1} + \dfrac{S_2^2}{n_2}}}$$

	Rejection Rule	
Alternative hypothesis:	**Rejection region approach:**	**p-value approach:**
H_a: $\mu_1 - \mu_2 > D_0$	Reject H_0 if	Reject H_0 p-value $< \alpha$, where
H_a: $\mu_1 - \mu_2 < D_0$	$TS > t_\alpha(\upsilon)$	p-value $= P(t(\upsilon) > TS)$
H_a: $\mu_1 - \mu_2 \neq D_0$	$TS < -t_\alpha(\upsilon)$	p-value $= P(t(\upsilon) < TS)$
	$TS > t_{\alpha/2}(\upsilon)$ or $TS < -t_{\alpha/2}(\upsilon)$	p-value $= P(t(\upsilon) > |TS|) + P(t(\upsilon) < -|TS|)$

Conditions:

(a) Random samples are taken from both the populations.

(b) The samples are taken independently.

(c) The sampled populations are normally distributed.

Checking the normality condition:

Make a dotplot, histogram, or stem-and-leaf plot for each sample. Ask yourself whether the shape of each distribution is fairly symmetric and bell-shaped, without any outliers. In other words, ask yourself whether the distribution resembles the normal distribution. Alternatively, use a normal probability plot.

Checking the condition of unequal variances:

In most cases, if the ratio of sample variances is larger than 4, then it is safe to assume that the variances are unequal. Alternatively, use a two-tailed F-test for equality of variances (you may have learned how to do this in your statistics class).

Large samples case

Both samples are large.

If the population variances (σ_1^2 and σ_2^2) are unknown, estimate them using the sample variances (S_1^2 and S_2^2).

Estimating $(\mu_1 - \mu_2)$ **using** $(1 - \alpha)100\%$ **confidence interval:**
Large samples case: Construct a z-interval

Margin of Error: $\qquad Z_{\alpha/2} \sigma_{(\bar{x}_1 - \bar{x}_2)} = Z_{\alpha/2} \sqrt{\dfrac{\sigma_1^2}{n_1} + \dfrac{\sigma_2^2}{n_2}}$

Confidence Interval: $\qquad (\bar{x}_1 - \bar{x}_2) \pm Z_{\alpha/2} \sqrt{\dfrac{\sigma_1^2}{n_1} + \dfrac{\sigma_2^2}{n_2}}$

Making an inference about the difference in population means $(\mu_1 - \mu_2)$**:**
Large samples case: Use a z-test

$H_0: \mu_1 - \mu_2 = D_0$
$H_a: \mu_1 - \mu_2 > D_0$ or
$\quad \mu_1 - \mu_2 < D_0$ or
$\quad \mu_1 - \mu_2 \neq D_0$
(D_0 is specified difference)

$$TS = \dfrac{\bar{x}_1 - \bar{x}_2 - D_0}{\sqrt{\dfrac{\sigma_1^2}{n_1} + \dfrac{\sigma_2^2}{n_2}}}$$

	Rejection Rule	
Alternative hypothesis:	**Rejection region approach:**	**p-value approach:**
$H_a: \mu_1 - \mu_2 > D_0$ $H_a: \mu_1 - \mu_2 < D_0$ $H_a: \mu_1 - \mu_2 \neq D_0$	Reject H_0 if $TS > Z_\alpha$ $TS < -Z_\alpha$ $TS > Z_{\alpha/2}$ or $TS < -Z_{\alpha/2}$	Reject H_0 if p-value $< \alpha$, where p-value $= P(Z > TS)$ p-value $= P(Z < TS)$ p-value $= P(Z > |TS|) + P(Z < -|TS|)$

Conditions:

(a) Random samples are taken from both the populations.

(b) The samples are taken independently.

(c) The samples are large enough so that the distribution for $(\bar{x}_1 - \bar{x}_2)$ is approximately normal.

Checking the normality condition:
There is no unique value that determines whether a sample size is large or small. No matter how large the sample size, whether the sampling distribution of the sample mean approximates the normal distribution depends on the shape of the distribution of the sampled population. If there are no outliers and the population distributions are not extremely skewed, then $n_1 \geq 30$ and $n_2 \geq 30$ are large enough to get approximately normal sampling distributions for $\bar{x}_1$ and $\bar{x}_2$, and consequently for $(\bar{x}_1 - \bar{x}_2)$.

Example 15: An economist wants to compare the hourly rates charged by automobile mechanics in two suburbs. She randomly selects auto repair facilities from both suburbs and records their hourly rates (in dollars). The data is as follows:

Suburb 1	40.0	38.0	38.0	37.0	36.0	39.0	41.5	38.0	39.5	37.5	35.0	40.0
Suburb 2	35.0	37.0	31.0	39.0	31.5	35.0	32.5	34.0	39.0	36.0		

Is there sufficient evidence to indicate a difference in the mean hourly rates for these two suburbs?

Solution: The economist wants to make an inference about the hourly rates charged by auto mechanics.

Step 1: Let

μ_1 = the mean rate charged by mechanics in suburb 1

μ_2 = the mean rate charged by mechanics in suburb 2

We are interested in the difference $(\mu_1 - \mu_2)$. Since the economist wants to determine whether there is a difference in the two population means, we should use a two-tailed test.

H_0: $(\mu_1 - \mu_2) = 0$ (there is no difference in the mean rates charged in the two suburbs)

H_a: $(\mu_1 - \mu_2) \neq 0$ (there is a difference in the mean rates charged in the two suburbs).

Step 2: The sample sizes n_1 = 12 and n_2 = 10 are both small. Let us plot both the samples.

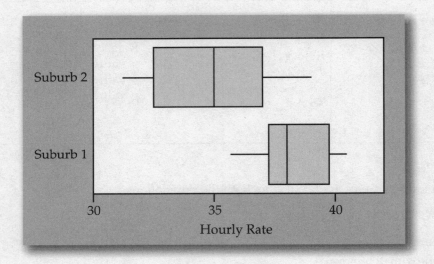

Figure 21: Boxplots of mechanics' hourly rates

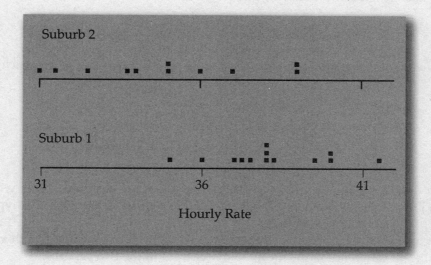

Figure 22: Parallel dotplots showing distribution of hourly rates

Conditions:

(a) It is given that random samples of auto repair facilities were obtained.

(b) There is no reason for the selection of facilities in one suburb to have any bearing on the selection of facilities in another suburb. Therefore, it is reasonable to assume that the samples were selected independently of each other.

(c) The above graphs show that the distributions of hourly rates are fairly symmetric, with no outliers. It is reasonable to assume that both the populations are approximately normally distributed.

All the conditions for a t-test are satisfied. Since the population variances are unknown, but the dotplots show a similar spread for both samples, it is reasonable to assume equal population variances and to use an equal variances t-test.

Step 3: Suppose we use a 5 percent level of significance. The degrees of freedom

$$\upsilon = 12 + 10 - 2 = 20 \text{ and } t_{\alpha/2}(\upsilon) = t_{0.025}(20) = 2.086$$

The rejection rule is "reject the null hypothesis if p-value < 0.05" (or, if using the rejection region approach, "reject the null hypothesis if TS < –2.086 or TS > 2.086").

Compute sample means and variances, using the formulas we've learned before:

	N	Average	Standard Deviation
Suburb 1	12	38.29	1.83
Suburb 2	10	35.0	2.84

The pooled estimate of the standard deviation is

$$S_p = \sqrt{\frac{(12-1)1.83^2 + (10-1)2.84^2}{12+10-2}} = 2.34$$

Compute the test statistic value (and the p-value, if using the p-value approach).

$$TS = \frac{(\bar{x}_1 - \bar{x}_2) - 0}{S_p\sqrt{\left(\frac{1}{n_1} + \frac{1}{n_2}\right)}} = \frac{38.29 - 35.00}{2.34\sqrt{\left(\frac{1}{12} + \frac{1}{10}\right)}} = 3.29$$

$$p\text{-value} = P(t(20) < -3.29) + P(t(20) > 3.29) = 0.0037$$

Step 4: Since p-value = 0.0037 < 0.05 (or, if using the rejection region approach, since the TS = 3.29 falls in the rejection region, or TS = 3.29 > 2.086), we should reject the null hypothesis and accept the alternative hypothesis.

At a 5 percent risk of making the wrong decision, we can conclude that there is a significant difference in the mean hourly charges in the two suburbs.

Since $\bar{x}_1 > \bar{x}_2$, we can say that the mean rates charged in suburb 1 are higher than the mean rates charged in suburb 2.

TI-83:

Inference using data

If the actual measurements are available, use this option.

- Enter data in 2 columns, say Suburb 1 in L1 and Suburb 2 in L2
- **Choose STAT → TESTS → 4: 2-SampTTest**
- Press **ENTER**
- Highlight Data
- Press **ENTER**
- Enter appropriate values

  2-SampTTest

  Inpt: Data   Stats

  List1: L1

  List2: L2

  Freq1: 1

  Freq2: 1

  $\mu_1: \neq \mu 2 < \mu_2 > \mu 2$

  Pooled: No   Yes

  Calculate   Draw

- Highlight Calculate
- Press **ENTER**

TI-83:

Estimation using data

If the actual measurements are available, use this option.

- Enter data in 2 columns, say Suburb 1 in L1 and Suburb 2 in L2
- **Choose STAT → TESTS → 0: 2-SampTInt**
- Press **ENTER**
- Highlight Data
- Press **ENTER**
- Enter appropriate values

  2-SampTInt
  Inpt: Data Stats
  List1: L1
  List2: L2
  Freq1: 1
  Freq2: 1
  C-Level: .95
  Pooled: No Yes
  Calculate

- Highlight Calculate
- Press **ENTER**

Example 16: Students in a course at a large university felt that using a calculator would give them an advantage on an exam. Their instructor decided to check it out. Since she was teaching 2 of the 18 sections of this course and students were assigned randomly to different sections, she decided to allow one section to use calculators on the test and not the other. The students' scores on the test are approximately normally distributed. The average class scores and variances of the class scores are as follows:

	n	Class Average	Class Variance
Calculators	23	80.7	49.5
No Calculators	22	78.9	60.4

Is it advantageous for students to use calculators on the test? Justify using statistical evidence.

Solution: The instructor wants to compare two population means, namely, the mean test score of students using a calculator and the mean test score of students not using a calculator.

Step 1: Let

μ_1 = the mean score of students using a calculator

μ_2 = the mean score of students not using a calculator

We are interested in making an inference about $(\mu_1 - \mu_2)$.

H_0: $\mu_1 = \mu_2$ or $\mu_1 - \mu_2 = 0$
(There's no difference between the mean scores of the two groups)

H_a: $\mu_1 > \mu_2$ or $\mu_1 - \mu_2 > 0$
(The mean score of the students using a calculator is higher)

Step 2: It is given that the students are assigned randomly to different sections. So it is reasonable to assume that the selected students are random, independent samples of all students taking this course. Also, it is given that the scores are approximately normally distributed.

The sample variances are fairly close to each other, and we can assume that the unknown population variances are equal. We should use the equal variances t-test with $v = 23 + 22 - 2 = 43$ degrees of freedom. Let's use a 5 percent error rate.

The rejection rule is to "reject null if p-value < 0.05" (or, if using the rejection region approach, "reject null if TS > 1.681").

The pooled estimate of the standard deviation is

$$S_p = \sqrt{\frac{(23-1)49.5 + (22-1)60.4}{23 + 22 - 2}} = 7.40$$

Compute the test statistic value (and p-value if using p-value approach).

$$TS = \frac{(\bar{x}_1 - \bar{x}_2) - 0}{S_p \sqrt{\left(\frac{1}{n_1} + \frac{1}{n_2}\right)}} = \frac{80.7 - 78.9}{7.40\sqrt{\left(\frac{1}{23} + \frac{1}{22}\right)}} = 0.815$$

p-value = $P(t(43) > 0.815) = 0.2097$, or if it were not reasonable to assume equal population variances, then we could use the unequal variances t-test with

$$v = \frac{\left(\frac{S_1^2}{n_1} + \frac{S_2^2}{n_2}\right)^2}{\frac{\left(S_1^2/n_1\right)^2}{n_1 - 1} + \frac{\left(S_2^2/n_2\right)^2}{n_2 - 1}} = \frac{\left(\frac{49.5}{23} + \frac{60.4}{22}\right)^2}{\frac{(49.5/23)^2}{23 - 1} + \frac{(60.4/22)^2}{22 - 1}} = 42.12$$

Again, use a 5 percent error rate. The rejection rule is to "reject null if p-value < 0.05" (or, if using the rejection region approach, reject null if TS > 1.682).

Compute the test statistic value (and p-value if using p-value approach).

$$TS = \frac{(\bar{x}_1 - \bar{x}_2) - 0}{\sqrt{\left(\frac{S_1^2}{n_1} + \frac{S_2^2}{n_2}\right)}} = \frac{80.7 - 78.9}{\sqrt{\left(\frac{49.5}{23} + \frac{60.4}{22}\right)}} = 0.813$$

p-value = $P(t(42.12) > 0.813) = 0.2103$

Step 4: Since, in both cases, the p-value > 0.05 (or the TS falls in the non-rejection region), we do not reject the null hypothesis. At a 5 percent risk, we can conclude that there is no evidence to suggest that the use of calculators improves the mean student grade.

TI-83:

Inference using summary statistics

If the actual measurements are not available, but the sample means and sample standard deviations are available, then use this option.

- Choose **STAT** → **TESTS** → **4: 2-SampTTest**

- Press **ENTER**

- Highlight Stats

- Press Enter

- Enter appropriate values

  2-SampTTest
  Inpt: Data   Stats
  $\overline{x}$1: 80.7
  Sx1: 2nd → $\sqrt{49.5}$
  n1: 23
  $\overline{x}$2: 78.9
  Sx2: 2nd → $\sqrt{60.4}$
  n2: 22
  μ_1: $\neq \mu_2$ $< \mu_2$ $> \mu_2$
  Pooled: No   Yes
  Calculate   Draw

- Highlight Calculate

- Press **ENTER**

Note:

- For equal variances case choose

    Pooled : Yes

- For unequal variances case choose

    Pooled: No

TI-83:

Estimation using summary statistic

If the actual measurements are not available, but the sample means and sample standard deviations are available, then use this option.

- Choose **STAT** → **TESTS** → **0: 2-SampTInt**

- Press **ENTER**

- Highlight Stats

- Press **ENTER**

- Enter appropriate values
  2-SampTInt
  Inpt: Data   Stats
  $\bar{x}1$: 80.7
  Sx1: 2nd → $\sqrt{49.5}$
  n1: 23
  $\bar{x}2$: 78.9
  Sx2: 2nd → $\sqrt{60.4}$
  n2: 22
  C-Level: .95
  Pooled: No   Yes
  Calculate

- Highlight Calculate

- Press **ENTER**

  Note:

- For equal variances case choose

     Pooled : Yes

- For unequal variances case choose

     Pooled: No

Example 17: A student waiting tables at a restaurant near a university in Chicago felt that customers tend to tip female waiters better than they tip male waiters. To confirm his suspicion, he contacted 50 female students and 75 male students that waited tables at different restaurants near the university and asked them to keep a record of tips received for one week. At the end of the week, he compiled the data in terms of the mean amount of tips received per hour worked by each student and summarized the data as follows:

	n	Average	Standard Deviation
Females	50	15.50	4.25
Males	75	12.25	3.20

(a) Estimate the difference in the mean amount of tips received hourly by female and male waiters. Use $\alpha = 0.10$.

(b) Does this data provide evidence to justify the student's suspicions?

(c) Would you do anything differently in this experiment if you repeated it? Why?

Solution:

(a) We are interested in the difference in the mean amount of tips received by female and male waiters.

Step 1: Let

μ_1 = The mean amount of tips received by female waiters per hour

μ_2 = The mean amount of tips received by male waiters per hour

We are interested in estimating

$(\mu_1 - \mu_2)$ = the difference in the mean amount of tips received by female and male waiters.

Step 2: The sample sizes are large enough so that we can apply the Central Limit Theorem and use a z-interval. Let us assume that

- There are no outliers in the data. (Since there is no data available, we cannot check.)
- All male and female waiters were selected randomly and independently.

Step 3: Using $\alpha = 0.10$, we get $Z_{\alpha/2} = 1.645$. The population variances are unknown, so we estimate them using the sample variations.

The 90 percent ME = $Z_{\alpha/2}\sqrt{\dfrac{S_1^2}{n_1} + \dfrac{S_2^2}{n_2}} = 1.645\sqrt{\dfrac{4.25^2}{50} + \dfrac{3.20^2}{75}} = 1.16$

$(\bar{x}_1 - \bar{x}_2) \pm \text{ME} \Rightarrow (15.50 - 12.25) \pm 1.16 \Rightarrow (2.09, 4.41)$

The 90 percent confidence interval to estimate $(\mu_1 - \mu_2)$ is (2.09, 4.41) dollars.

Step 4: We are 90 percent confident that the difference in mean amounts of tips received per hour by female and male waiters is between \$2.09 and \$4.41.

(b) Refer to the confidence interval constructed in part (a). Note that the interval does not contain zero. Therefore, at a 10 percent risk we can conclude that there is a significant difference in the mean amount of tips received by female and male waiters.

Also note that the entire interval for $(\mu_1 - \mu_2)$ lies above 0. So, we can conclude that $(\mu_1 - \mu_2) > 0$. In other words, the mean amount of tips received by female waiters is significantly higher than the mean amount of tips received by male waiters.

Alternatively, we could test

$$H_0: (\mu_1 - \mu_2) = 0$$

(There is no difference in the mean amount of tips received by male and female waiters).

$$H_a: (\mu_1 - \mu_2) > 0$$

(Female waiters receive on the average higher tips than male waiters).

The large samples z-test results in TS = 4.60, p-value = 0.000002 (almost 0).

For this p-value we should reject the null for any reasonable level of significance and conclude that there is evidence to support the student's suspicions. The data suggests that, on average, female waiters tend to receive higher tips than male waiters.

(c) A better way to do the study would be to take a random sample of waiters, regardless of whether or not they're students. It is not clear if these samples were selected at random. Since only student waiters were included in the experiment, the results will only be applicable to student waiters at this particular university, rather than all male and female waiters.

CASE OF DEPENDENT OR PAIRED SAMPLES

Sometimes it's either not possible to take independent samples, or the results from the independent samples are insufficient to answer the questions at hand. For example, when checking the effectiveness of a certain weight loss program, you need to measure and compare the weights of the same participants before starting on the program and after completing the program. Comparison of Bill's "before" weight with Leslie's "after" weight is meaningless. We need to compare Bill's "before" and "after" program weights, and Leslie's "before" and "after" weights. Therefore, we have to use dependent or paired measurements.

Pairing or matching does not necessarily mean taking both measurements on the same subject. For example, suppose we are interested in comparing two different brands of calculators (say, TI and HP) in terms of ease of computation. If we did some computations on TI calculators and some other computations on HP calculators, then it's possible that some of the differences in the ease of computation would be due to the differences in the types of computations performed. The responses would not be comparable. The best way to perform this experiment would be to do the same type of computations on both calculators, and to do each calculation in random order, to avoid giving any specific calculator the advantage of the practice effect. This would result in the matching or pairing of samples. The samples would therefore not be independent. Is this a problem? No. It just means that the data would need to be analyzed differently.

Some of the ways in which pairing or matching can be achieved are the following:

- Take both measurements on the same subject, such as we discussed in the diet example above.

- Use naturally occurring pairs (such as twins, or husbands and wives) and assign the two subjects in each pair to two different groups, using some kind of randomization scheme. Then take measurements on both groups and compare.

- Match subjects by some characteristics, the effect of which might otherwise obscure the difference in responses. For example, to compare the effects of two headache medicines, we could match patients by their ages, since the effect of the medicine may differ depending on the patient's age. Two patients in the same age group could each be given a different medicine and then the medicine's effects could be compared. The age effect would not then be confounded with the medicine effect.

Let μ_X be the mean of one population and μ_Y be the mean of the other. All the members of the X-population are paired in some way with all the members of the Y-population. We are interested in the differences $(X - Y)$. Parameter of interest: Population mean of differences μ_d.

Here, $\mu_d = \mu_X - \mu_Y$, but this case differs from that of the two-samples cases described earlier in that the two populations are not independent, so the responses of the subjects will not be independent either.

- Select a random sample of size n items (or n pairs of items).

- For each selected item, measure the characteristic of interest, resulting in a sample of pairs of measurements.

Sample: $(x_1, y_1), (x_2, y_2), (x_3, y_3), \cdots, (x_n, y_n)$

- Compute the differences $d_i = x_i - y_i$, $i = 1, 2, \cdots, n$. Note that the two-sample case reduces to a one-sample case.

Compute the mean difference and the standard deviation of the differences

$$\bar{d} = \frac{\sum d_i}{n} \text{ and } S_d = \sqrt{\frac{\sum d_i^2 - \left(\sum d_i\right)^2 / n}{n-1}}$$

This sample mean $\bar{d}$ is a point estimate of the unknown population mean μ_d. Different random samples of size n from the same population will result in different sample means, giving different estimates. The distribution of means from all possible random samples of n differences is the sampling distribution of $\bar{d}$.

- The mean of all possible sample means is μ_d. Therefore $\bar{d}$ is an unbiased estimator of μ_d.

- The standard deviation of the sampling distribution of $\bar{d}$ is $\sigma_{\bar{d}} = \frac{\sigma_d}{\sqrt{n}}$, where σ_d is the standard deviation of the population of differences.

- If the population of differences is normally distributed and the population variance σ_d is unknown, then the sampling distribution of $\bar{d}$ is a t-distribution with $(n - 1)$ degrees of freedom.

Estimating μ_d using $(1-\alpha)100\%$ **confidence interval**:

Construct a t-interval with $\upsilon = (n-1)$ degrees of freedom

Margin of Error: $\quad t_{\alpha/2}(\upsilon)\, S_{\bar{d}} = t_{\alpha/2}(\upsilon)\dfrac{S_d}{\sqrt{n}}$

Confidence Interval: $\quad \bar{d} \pm t_{\alpha/2}(\upsilon)\dfrac{S_d}{\sqrt{n}}$

Making an inference about the difference in population means μ_d:
Use a t-test with $\upsilon = (n-1)$ degrees of freedom

$H_0: \mu_d = \mu_0$ (Specified)

$H_a: \ \mu_d > \mu_0$ or

$\quad \mu_d < \mu_0$ or

$\quad \mu_d \neq \mu_0$

$$\text{TS} = \frac{\bar{d} - \mu_{d0}}{S_d/\sqrt{n}}$$

	Rejection Rule	
Alternative hypothesis:	Rejection region approach:	p-value approach:
$H_a: \ \mu_d > \mu_0$ $H_a: \ \mu_d < \mu_0$ or $H_a: \ \mu_d \neq \mu_0$	Reject H_0 if $TS > t_\alpha(\upsilon)$ $TS < -t_\alpha(\upsilon)$ $TS > t_{\alpha/2}(\upsilon)$ or $TS < -t_{\alpha/2}(\upsilon)$	Reject H_0 if p-value $< \alpha$, where p-value $= P(t(\upsilon) > TS)$ p-value $= P(t(\upsilon) < TS)$ p-value $=$ $P(t(\upsilon) > |TS|) + P(Z < -|TS|)$

Conditions:

(a) A random sample of differences is taken from the population differences.

(b) The sampled population of differences is normally distributed.

Checking the normality condition:

Make a dotplot, histogram, or stem-and-leaf plot for the sample of differences. Ask yourself whether the distribution is fairly symmetric and bell-shaped, without any outliers. In other words, ask yourself whether the distribution of differences resembles the normal distribution. Alternatively, use a normal probability plot.

Example 18: Workers at a factory asked their supervisor to provide music during their shift. The supervisor wanted to know whether the music really helped improve the workers' performance. Since all the workers were assigned to different rooms at random, the supervisor randomly selected one room. For one week, he provided music in this room, and for one week, he provided none. He flipped a coin to determine which week to provide music. Afterward, he recorded the productivity of the workers, using the average number of items assembled per day:

	n	Class Average	Class Variance
Calculators	23	80.7	49.5
No Calculators	22	78.9	60.4

(a) Estimate the difference between the workers' performance in the presence of music and their performance in the absence of music, using a 95 percent level of confidence.

(b) Does music improve the performance of workers as measured by the mean number of items assembled per day? Give statistical evidence.

Solution: (a) Estimation.

Step 1: Let X = the performance with music

Y = the performance without music

Let μ_X = the mean performance with music

μ_Y = the mean performance without music

We are interested in $\mu_d = \mu_X - \mu_Y$ = the mean difference in performance.

Step 2: Since the performances "with music" and "without music" are measured on the same group of workers, this is a dependent samples case. The specific person's effect on the performance will be nullified when we look at the differences.

Define difference $d = X - Y$. Compute the differences in the performance of each worker.

With Music	29.38	31.53	27.45	27.76	29.31	27.69	29.07	27.48	29.83	28.96
Without Music	24.55	25.59	23.17	24.71	25.26	24.88	24.34	26.13	25.57	26.63
Difference	4.83	5.94	4.28	3.05	4.05	2.81	4.73	1.35	4.26	2.33

Plot the differences. A random sample of one room with $n = 10$ workers is taken.

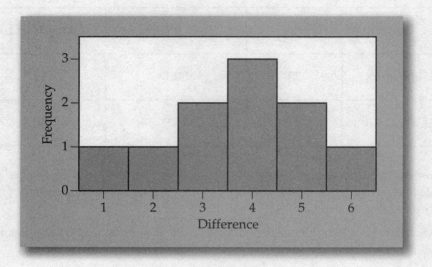

Figure 23: Histogram of the differences in performance

Conditions:

(a) It is given that a random sample of one room was taken. Since the workers are randomly assigned to different rooms, workers in the selected room where the sample was taken can be assumed to be a random sample of all workers at this factory.

(b) A histogram of the differences shows that there are no outliers and its shape suggests it is reasonable to assume that the differences in performance are approximately normally distributed.

Since the population variance of the differences is unknown, we should construct a t-interval for the mean.

Step 3: Now the two-sample problem has been reduced to a one-sample problem. Compute the sample mean and standard deviation of the differences.

$$\bar{d} = 3.767 \text{ items per day, and } S_d = 1.362 \text{ items per day}$$

With a sample of size 10, degrees of freedom = $10 - 1 = 9$

To construct a 95 percent confidence interval, use $\alpha = 0.05$. Using a t-table for 9 degrees of freedom we get

$$t_{\frac{\alpha}{2}}(9) = t_{\frac{0.05}{2}}(9) = t_{0.025}(9) = 2.262$$

The 95 percent ME = $t_{0.025}(9)\left(\dfrac{s_d}{\sqrt{n}}\right) = 2.262\left(\dfrac{1.362}{\sqrt{10}}\right) = 0.974$ items/day

$$\bar{d} \pm \text{ME} \Rightarrow 3.767 \pm 0.974 \Rightarrow (2.793, 4.741)$$

The 95 percent confidence interval to estimate μ_d is (2.79, 4.74).

Step 4: Interpretation:

We are 95 percent confident that the true mean difference in performance is between 2.79 and 4.74 items per day.

We are 95 percent confident that our best estimate of the difference, 3.767 items per day, is within 0.974 items of the true mean difference in performance.

Note that the confidence interval falls entirely above zero. Therefore, we can conclude that the mean difference in performance is significant and that the mean number of items produced per day with music is higher than the mean number produced without music.

TI-83:

Using data

- Enter the data into two lists, "with music" in L1, and "without music" in L2

- Move cursor to the column labeled L3

- Type L1-L2

- Press **ENTER** (all the differences should appear in list L3)

- Choose **STAT** → **TESTS** → **8: T Interval**

- Highlight **Data**

- Press **ENTER**

- Enter appropriate values

  TInterval
  Inpt: Data Stats
  List: L3
  Freq: 1
  C-Level: .95
  Calculate

- Highlight Calculate

- Press **ENTER**

(b) Inference.

Step 1: We are interested in testing a hypothesis about

μ_d = The true mean difference in performance of workers as measured by the number of items assembled per day = mean with music – mean without music.

H_0: $\mu_d = 0$ (There is no difference in the performance of workers with and without music.)

H_a: $\mu_d > 0$ (Music improves performance, i.e., the mean performance is better with music than without music.)

Step 2: A random sample of $n = 10$ workers was taken.

Since the performances "with music" and "without music" were measured on the same group of workers, this is a dependent samples case. The specific person's effect on the performance will be nullified when we look at the differences.

Define difference $d = X - Y$. Compute the differences in performance of each worker.

With Music	29.38	31.53	27.45	27.76	29.31	27.69	29.07	27.48	29.83	28.96
Without Music	24.55	25.59	23.17	24.71	25.26	24.88	24.34	26.13	25.57	26.63
Difference	4.83	5.94	4.28	3.05	4.05	2.81	4.73	1.35	4.26	2.33

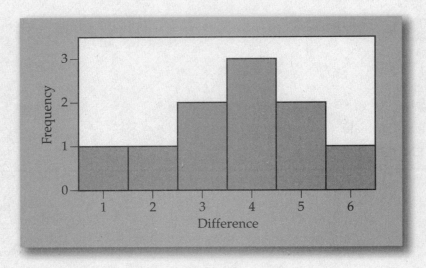

Figure 24: Histogram of difference in performance

Conditions:

(a) It is given that a random sample of one room was taken. Since the workers are randomly assigned to different rooms, workers in the selected room can be assumed to be a random sample of all workers at this factory.

(b) A histogram of differences shows that there are no outliers and its shape suggests it is reasonable to assume that the differences in performance are approximately normally distributed.

Since the population variance of the differences is unknown, we should use a t-test for the mean.

Step 3: Now the two-sample problem has been reduced to a one-sample problem. Compute the sample mean and standard deviation of the differences.

$$\bar{d} = 3.767 \text{ items per day, and } S_d = 1.362$$

With a sample of size 10, degrees of freedom = $10 - 1 = 9$
Suppose we use $\alpha = 0.05$. Then, using the t-table for 9 degrees of freedom, we get

$$t_\alpha(9) = t_{0.05}(9) = 1.833$$

The rejection rule is to reject the null hypothesis and accept the alternative hypothesis if

- TS < -1.73 (rejection region approach)
- p-value < 0.05 (p-value approach)

Compute the test statistic (and p-value if using p-value approach)

$$TS = \frac{(\bar{x} - \mu)}{S/\sqrt{n}} = \frac{(3.767 - 0)}{1.362/\sqrt{10}} = 8.746$$

$$p\text{-value} = P(t > 8.746) = \text{almost } 0$$

Step 4: Write conclusion.

- Using p-value approach:
  Since the p-value is almost 0, for any reasonable α we should reject the null hypothesis and accept the alternative hypothesis.

- Using the rejection region approach:
  Since t = 8.746 > 1.833 (or the test statistic falls in the rejection region), we should reject the null hypothesis and accept the alternative hypothesis.

Conclusion: At a 5 percent level of significance, there is sufficient evidence to conclude that the performance of workers has improved in the presence of music.

MAKING AN INFERENCE USING CATEGORICAL DATA

A categorical variable is a variable that classifies the outcomes of an experiment into different categories. These categories can be numerical or non-numerical. For example:

- A teacher classifies students according to the student status (freshman, sophomore, junior, and senior).

- A biologist classifies crossbred varieties of flowers according to the color of petals (white, red, or pink).

- A doctor classifies patients by gender (male, female).

- A factory classifies each item produced by its status (good, minor defect, major defect).

- A postal worker classifies letters by the state of the addressee (AL, ... WA).

- To issue tax rebates in 2001, the Internal Revenue Service divided taxpayers according to the last two digits of their social security numbers (00, 01, ... 99). This grouping was used to determine in which week each taxpayer would receive a check.

Suppose there are k different groups into which the measurements are categorized. These groups are typically referred to as cells. The observed frequency, count of a cell, or a category is the number of measurements from one experiment falling into that particular cell. The observed counts of cells, 1 through k, are denoted by $O_1, O_2, \cdots, O_k$. If n observations are taken in one experiment, then

$$O_1 + O_2 + \cdots + O_k = n$$

Often, we devise a theory about the distribution of measurements into different categories, and we wish to check out our theory by conducting an experiment. The expected frequency, count of a cell, or a category is the number of measurements expected to fall into that cell according to our theory. The expected counts for cells 1 through k are denoted by

$$E_1, E_2, \cdots, E_k, \text{ and } E_1 + E_2 + \cdots + E_k = n$$

For example, a biologist might suspect that when two varieties of a flowering plant are crossbred the result would be 20, 30, and 50 percent of the plants bearing white, red, or pink flowers, respectively. Then, to check her theory, the biologist might crossbreed and grow, say, 150 plants and classify each one by the resulting color of flowers that it produces. Suppose the experiment results in 28 plants bearing white flowers, 46 bearing red, and 76 bearing pink. In this case, 28, 46, and 76 are the observed counts. The theoretical proportions of 20, 30, and 50 percent lead to the expected counts in 150 plants as 30 bearing white flowers, 45 bearing red, and 75 bearing pink.

The question of interest here is whether the observed counts seem to agree with the expected counts, or how likely the observed counts would be if the truth were really described by the expected counts. The test statistic value that determines the extent of agreement between the observed and expected counts is computed as

$$TS = \sum_{\text{all cells}} \frac{\left(O_i - E_i\right)^2}{E_i}$$

The smaller the value of the test statistic, the higher the agreement between the expected and observed counts. Larger values of the test statistic indicate more discrepancy between the observed and expected counts. This test statistic follows an approximate χ^2 (chi-square) distribution.

THE CHI-SQUARE DISTRIBUTION

Another commonly used sampling distribution, besides the t-distribution and the standard normal, is the χ^2 (or "chi-square") distribution. This distribution is commonly observed when using inferential procedures for categorical data. It has the following properties:

- It is a continuous distribution.

- It is a distribution of the sums of squared normal random variables. So the chi-square variable takes only positive values.

- It is a right-skewed distribution.

- The shape of the chi-square distribution, like that of the t-distribution, depends on its degrees of freedom (υ). The graph below shows how the shape of the distribution changes with the degrees of freedom.

- The mean of the chi-square distribution = υ. Note, in the graph on the next page, that the center of the distribution shifts to the right as degrees of freedom increase.

- The standard deviation of the chi-square distribution = $\sqrt{2\upsilon}$.

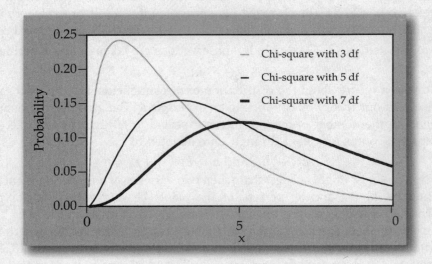

Figure 25: Chi-square distribution for different degrees of freedom

Reading a chi-square table

χ_α^2: A chi-square value such that the area to the right under the distribution is equal to α.

- To find $\chi_{0.05}^2$ with 10 degrees of freedom from the table, go down to the row corresponding to 10 degrees of freedom and then go across to the column corresponding to the right-tail area 0.05. Read the number in the cross section of the row for 10 degrees of freedom and the column for right-tail area 0.05. It gives $\chi_{0.05}^2(10) = 18.3$.

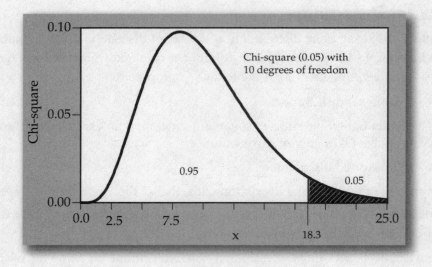

Figure 26: Chi-square (0.05) with 10 degrees of freedom

- To find $\chi^2_{0.01}(10)$, read the number in the cross section of the row corresponding to 10 degrees of freedom and the column corresponding to the right-tail area 0.01. It gives $\chi^2_{0.01}(10) = 23.21$.

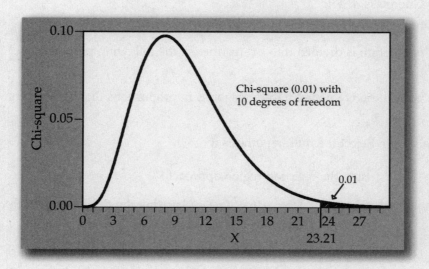

Figure 27: Chi-square (0.01) with 10 degrees of freedom

THE TEST OF GOODNESS OF FIT

This test is used to check whether the observed data counts confirm the expected distribution of counts into different categories.

- Suppose the population is divided into k different categories.

- Let the expected proportion of the population in these categories be given by p_1, p_2, $\cdots$, p_k. This is the same as saying that the probability of an item belonging to the ith category is p_i, where $i = 1,2,\ldots, k$.

- Take a random sample of size n from the population of interest.

- Classify each selected item of the sample into one of the k categories.

- Count the number of items in each category. These are the observed counts, $O_1, O_2, \cdots, O_k$.

- With a sample of size n, the expected counts are
$$E_i = np_i \quad (i = 1,2,\cdots,k)$$

- Compute the test statistic $TS = \sum\limits_{\text{all cells}} \dfrac{\left(O_i - E_i\right)^2}{E_i}$

- For a sufficiently large random sample, the distribution of the test statistic is approximately a chi-square with $\upsilon = (k-1)$ degrees of freedom.

χ^2 Test of Goodness of Fit:

Use a chi-square test with $\upsilon = (k-1)$ degrees of freedom.

H_0: The population is divided into k categories in the following proportions:
$p_1, p_2, \cdots, p_k$.

H_a: The population is divided into k categories in proportions that differ from $p_1, p_2, \cdots, p_k$.

The rejection rule: Reject the null hypothesis if

- $TS > \chi^2(\upsilon)$ (using the rejection region approach)

- p-value $< \alpha$, where p-value $= P(\chi^2(\upsilon) > TS)$ (using the p-value approach).

Conditions:

(a) A random sample of size n is taken.

(b) The sample size n is large enough to get an approximate chi-square distribution for the test statistic.

Checking the condition of a large n:

If all expected counts are greater than 5 ($E_i \geq 5$) then we have a large enough sample to use a chi-square approximation. If some cells have $E_i < 5$, then such cells should be combined with other adjoining cells in a logical manner to satisfy the requirement of expected counts.

Example 19: An accounting firm in Mississippi has clients from various states. The chief accountant knew that last year the firm had the following distribution of clients from different states.

State of residence	Mississippi	Alabama	Louisiana	Arkansas	Florida	Tennessee
Proportion of clients	0.60	0.15	0.15	0.04	0.03	0.03

But the accountant thought that the distribution had changed this year. So he took a random sample of 400 clients and classified them according to their state of residence. The summarized data is as follows:

State of residence	Mississippi	Alabama	Louisiana	Arkansas	Florida	Tennessee
Number of clients	200	87	68	27	8	20

What does the data suggest? Is the distribution of clients the same as last year or has it changed?

Solution: The clients are classified by their state of residence, which is a categorical variable.

Step 1: We are interested in testing

H_0: The proportion of clients from Mississippi, Alabama, Louisiana, Arkansas, Florida, and Tennessee is the same this year as last year.

H_a: This year, at least two proportions have changed from those of last year.

Step 2: Use a chi-square test of goodness of fit. Compute the expected counts as $400p_i$, where p_i is the proportion of clients from the ith state. For example, last year, 60 percent of clients were from Mississippi. If the proportions this year are the same, then out of 400, 60 percent of clients—i.e., $400(0.60) = 240$ clients—should be from Mississippi.

State of residence	Mississippi	Alabama	Louisiana	Arkansas	Florida	Tennessee
Number of clients (O_i)	200	87	68	27	8	20
Number of clients (E_i)	240	60	60	16	12	10

A random sample of clients was selected. All the expected counts are higher than 5. Therefore, it is reasonable to use the chi-square test.

Step 3: The firm's clients are from 6 different states. So for $k = 6$, we get $\upsilon = k - 1 = 5$ degrees of freedom. Suppose we use 0.05-level of significance.

The rejection rule is to "reject the null hypothesis if p-value < 0.05" (or, if using rejection region approach, "reject the null hypothesis if TS > $\chi^2_{0.05}(5) = 11.1$").

$$TS = \sum_{i=1}^{6} \frac{(O_i - E_i)^2}{E_i}$$

$$= \frac{(200-240)^2}{240} + \frac{(87-60)^2}{60} + \frac{(68-60)^2}{60} + \frac{(27-16)^2}{16} + \frac{(8-12)^2}{12} + \frac{(20-10)^2}{10}$$

$$= 6.67 + 12.15 + 1.07 + 7.56 + 1.33 + 10$$

$$= 38.78$$

The p-value $= P(\chi^2(5) > 38.78) = 0.000022$, which is almost 0.

Step 4: Since p-value $= 0.000022 < 0.05$ (or TS $= 38.78 > 11.1$, if using the rejection region approach), we should reject the null hypothesis and accept the alternative hypothesis. The p-value indicates that if this year, the proportion of clients had remained the same as last year, then the probability of observing the test statistic value of 38.78 or higher is 0.000022. Therefore we can conclude that the data suggests that the proportions have changed from those of last year.

TI-83:

- Clear lists L1, L2, and L3
- Enter the observed counts in L1
- Enter the expected counts in L2
- Define list L3 to be (L1-L2)2/L2
- Bring the cursor to the list heading L3

  Type (L1-L2)2/L2

- Press **ENTER**
- Choose 2nd → LIST → MATH → 5: sum(
- Press **ENTER**

  Sum(L3)

- Press **ENTER**

To compute the p-value:
Use the chi-square CDF from the distribution menu to compute the area between the TS value (given by the sum command as described above) and infinity (simulated using some large number).

- Choose 2nd → DISTR → 7: χ^2cdf
- Press **ENTER**

  χ^2cdf(29.11, 1e50, 5)

- Press **ENTER**

Example 20: A nursery ships plants by truck in trays of 12 plants each. At the end of one such journey, one hundred randomly selected trays were inspected and the number of plants in each tray that did not survive the journey was counted. The data was recorded as follows:

Number of plants that did not survive the journey	0	1	2	3	4
Number of trays	31	44	15	8	2

Is the binomial distribution an appropriate model for this data?

Solution: There are 12 plants per tray, i.e., $n = 12$ trials. There is a total of $12 \times 100 = 1{,}200$ plants. Associated with each plant are two possible outcomes, namely, "surviving the journey" and "not surviving the journey." If we define success as "not surviving the journey", then the probability of success associated with each plant is estimated as follows:

Out of 1,200 plants inspected, $(31(0) + 44(1) + 15(2) + 8(3) + 4(2)) = 106$ did not survive the journey.

So the estimated probability of not surviving the journey = $\hat{p} = 106/1200 = 0.088$.

Step 1: Here we are interested in testing the following hypotheses:

H_0: A binomial distribution with $n = 12$ and $p = 0.088$ is an appropriate model to describe this data.

H_a: A binomial distribution with $n = 12$ and $p = 0.088$ is not an appropriate model to describe this data.

Step 2: We can use the chi-square goodness of fit test to check the appropriateness of the binomial distribution to describe the data above. Assuming that the null hypothesis is true, i.e., assuming that the data comes from a binomial population with $n = 12$, and $p = 0.088$, compute the likelihood of 0, 1, 2, 3, etc., plants not surviving the journey. For example:

$$P(X = 2 \text{ survive the journey}) = \binom{12}{2} 0.088^2 (1 - 0.088)^{10} = 0.2034$$

Number of plants that did not survive the journey (x)	0	1	2	3	4	5 or more
$P(X = x)$	0.3311	0.3834	0.2034	0.0654	0.0142	0.0025

Using these probabilities, compute the expected number of trays with the number of plants not surviving the journey equal to 0, 1, 2, etc., as $100 \times P(x)$. This gives the expected counts as follows:

Number of plants that did not survive the journey (x)	0	1	2	3	4	5 or more
$P(X = x)$	0.3311	0.3834	0.2034	0.0654	0.0142	0.0025
Expected counts	33.11	38.34	20.34	6.54	1.42	0.25

Since the expected counts for the last two categories are less than 5, the chi-square test cannot be applied successfully. So let us combine the last three cells to give the expected counts as follows:

Number of plants that did not survive the journey (x)	0	1	2	3 or more
Observed counts (O_i)	31	44	15	10
Expected counts (E_i)	33.11	38.34	20.34	8.21

All the expected counts are larger than 5, and all trays were selected at random. So, the conditions for the chi-square test are satisfied.

Step 3: With four categories in the table, degrees of freedom = $\upsilon = 3$. If we are willing to take a 5 percent risk of rejecting the true null hypothesis, then the rejection rule is "reject the null hypothesis if p-value < 0.05" (or if using the rejection region approach, "reject the null hypothesis if the TS > $\chi^2_{0.05}(3) = 7.81$").

Compute the test statistic value (and p-value if using a p-value approach).

$$TS = \sum_{i=1}^{4} \frac{(O_i - E_i)^2}{E_i}$$
$$= \frac{(31 - 33.11)^2}{33.11} + \frac{(44 - 38.34)^2}{38.34} + \frac{(15 - 20.34)^2}{20.34} + \frac{(10 - 8.21)^2}{8.21}$$
$$= 2.76$$

The p-value = $P(\chi^2(3) > 2.76) = 0.4301$

Step 4: Since p-value = 0.4301 > 0.05 (or since TS = 2.76 < $\chi^2_{0.05}(3) = 7.81$), we fail to reject the null hypothesis. So, we can conclude that there is no evidence against the null hypothesis. In other words, it is reasonable to assume that the data follows a binomial model with $n = 12$ and $p = 0.088$.

CONTINGENCY TABLES

In many experiments, data is classified by two different factors, each factor with two or more categories. Such a classification of data results in a table with two or more rows and columns, where rows represent categories of one factor and columns represent categories of the other factor. For example, students might be classified by gender and academic major, athletes by athletic specialty (track, football, gymnastics, etc.) and the type of injury sustained, or patients classified by gender and race.

An $r \times c$ Contingency Table is an arrangement of data into a table with r rows and c columns, creating a total of rc cells, where each cell gives its count.

Test of independence

Often scientists are interested in determining whether two different categorical variables are independent or dependent. For example, television stations might want to know whether the type of program a viewer watches is associated with his or her gender, sociologists might want to know whether children's behavior patterns are associated with the marital status of parents, and marine biologists might want to know whether the behavior patterns of dolphins are associated with the time of year.

- Identify two factors of interest and their categories.

- Take a random sample of n items from the population of interest.

- Determine the category of each of two factors to which each item in the sample belongs.

- Summarize the observed data into an $r \times c$ contingency table, where

    r = the number of rows = the number of categories of interest for factor 1
    c = the number of columns = the number of categories of interest for factor 2

- Count the number of items in each cell. These are the observed counts O_{ij}

    $(i = 1, 2, \cdots, r, \text{ and } j = 1, 2, \cdots, c)$.

		Columns				Row Total R_i
		1	2	...	c	
Rows	1	O_{11}	O_{12}	...	O_{1c}	R_i
	2	O_{21}	O_{22}	...	O_{2c}	R_2
	$\vdots$	$\vdots$	$\vdots$		$\vdots$	$\vdots$
	r	O_{r1}	O_{r2}	...	O_{rc}	R_r
Column Totals C_j		C_1	C_2	...	C_c	n

Table 4: r × c contingency table of observed counts

- Compute the row totals

$$\left(R_i = \sum_{j=1}^{c} O_{ij} \right), \ i = 1, 2, \cdots, r$$

and the column totals

$$\left(C_j = \sum_{i=1}^{r} O_{ij} \right), \ j = 1, 2, \cdots, c. \text{ Note that, } \sum_{i=1}^{r} R_i = \sum_{j=1}^{c} C_j = n$$

- If the two factors of interest are independent, then

$$P\left(\text{a randomly selected item belongs to the } (i, j)^{th} \text{ cell}\right)$$

$$= P\left(\text{it belongs to the } i^{th} \text{ category of factor 1}\right) \times P\left(\text{it belongs to the } j^{th} \text{ category of factor 2}\right)$$

Therefore, out of n observations, the $(i, j)^{th}$ cell is expected to contain

$$E_{ij} = \frac{R_i C_j}{n} \text{ observations}$$

Compute the expected counts for all cells.

		Columns				Row Total R_i
		1	2	...	c	
Rows	1	$O_{11} (E_{11})$	$O_{12} (E_{12})$	...	$O_{1c} (E_{1c})$	R_1
	2	$O_{21} (E_{21})$	$O_{22} (E_{22})$	...	$O_{2c} (E_{2c})$	R_2
	$\vdots$	$\vdots$	$\vdots$		$\vdots$	$\vdots$
	r	$O_{r1} (E_{r1})$	$O_{r2} (E_{r2})$	...	$O_{rc} (E_{rc})$	R_r
Column Totals C_j		C_1	C_2	...	C_c	n

Table 5: $r \times c$ contingency table of observed and (expected) counts

- Compute the test statistic value as

$$TS = \sum_{j=1}^{c} \sum_{i=1}^{r} \frac{\left(O_{ij} - E_{ij}\right)^2}{E_{ij}}$$

- For a sufficiently large n, the test statistic follows a chi-square distribution with $\upsilon = (r-1)(c-1)$ degrees of freedom.

χ^2 Test of Independence:

Use a chi-square test with $\upsilon = (r-1)(c-1)$ degrees of freedom.

H_0: The two factors of interest are independent. Or, there is no association between two factors of interest.

H_a: Two factors of interest are not independent. Or, there is an association between two factors of interest.

$$TS = \sum_{j=1}^{c} \sum_{i=1}^{r} \frac{\left(O_{ij} - E_{ij}\right)^2}{E_{ij}}$$

$$\text{where } E_{ij} = \frac{R_i \, C_j}{n}$$

The rejection rule: Reject the null hypothesis if

- $TS > \chi^2(\upsilon)$ (using the rejection region approach)

- p-value $< \alpha$, where p-value $= P(\chi^2(\upsilon) > TS)$ (using the p-value approach)

Conditions:

(a) A random sample of size n is taken.

(b) The sample size n is large enough to get an approximate chi-square distribution for the test statistic.

Checking the assumption of a large n:

If all expected counts are greater than 5—in other words, if

$E_{ij} \geq 5 \ (i=1,2,\cdots,r, \text{ and } j=1,2,\cdots,c)$, then we have a large enough sample to use the

chi-square approximation. If some cells have $E_i < 5$, then the corresponding rows and/or columns should be combined with other rows and/or columns in a logical manner to satisfy the requirement of expected counts.

Example 21: The State Department of Education wants to see whether there is any connection between the education level of fathers and sons. A random sample of 1,000 father-son pairs was selected from the available census data for the state of Alabama and the level of education for both father and son was recorded as "less than high school (< HS)," "high school (HS)," or "more than high school (> HS)." The resulting data is summarized in the following table.

		Father's Education Level		
		<HS	HS	>HS
Son's Education Level	<HS	120	80	25
	HS	210	170	60
	>HS	110	140	85

Does this data provide significant evidence of an association between a father's education level and his son's education level?

Solution:

Step 1:

H_0: There is no association between a father's education level and his son's education level.

H_a: There is an association between a father's education level and his son's education level.

Or

H_0: A father's education level and his son's education level are independent.

H_a: A father's education level and his son's education level are not independent.

Step 2: Use a chi-square test for independence. Compute all row totals and column totals. Then compute the expected cell counts as

$$\text{Expected count for a cell} = \frac{(\text{Row total})(\text{Column Total})}{1,000}$$

Below is a table of observed and expected counts, with the expected counts in parentheses.

		Father's Education Level			
		<HS	HS	>HS	Total
Son's Education Level	<HS	120 (99.0)	80 (87.7)	25 (38.3)	225
	HS	210 (193.6)	170 (171.6)	60 (74.8)	440
	>HS	110 (147.4)	140 (130.7)	85 (56.9)	335
	Total	440	390	170	1000

All expected counts are greater than or equal to 5. So the chi-square test of independence is appropriate.

Step 3: This is a 3 x 3 contingency table. So the degrees of freedom = $(3 - 1)(3 - 1) = 4$. Suppose we use $\alpha = 0.05$. The rejection rule is "reject null if p-value $< \alpha$" (or if using the rejection region approach, "reject null if TS $> \chi^2_{0.05}(4) = 9.49$").

Compute the test statistic (and p-value if using the p-value approach).

$$TS = \sum_{i=1}^{3} \sum_{j=1}^{3} \frac{\left(O_{ij} - E_{ij}\right)^2}{E_{ij}}$$

$$= \frac{\left(120 - 99\right)^2}{99} + \frac{\left(80 - 87.7\right)^2}{87.7} + \cdots + \frac{\left(85 - 56.9\right)^2}{56.9}$$

$$= 38.03576$$

$$p\text{-value} = P(\chi^2 > 38.03576) = 0.00000011 \approx 0$$

Step 4: Since the p-value is too small for any reasonable level of significance (or since TS = 38.035 > 9.49, if using the rejection region approach), we should reject the null hypothesis and accept the alternative hypothesis. There is significant evidence to conclude that there is an association between a father's education level and his son's education level.

TI-83:

- Choose **2nd** → **MATRX** → **EDIT**
- Select 1: [A]
- Press **ENTER**
- 3 ▷ ▷ 3
- Press **ENTER**
- Enter observed counts in a 3X3 matrix
- Choose **STAT** → **TESTS** → **C: χ^2- Test**
- Press **ENTER**

  χ^2- Test
  Observed: [A]
  Expected: [B]
  Calculate   Draw

- Highlight Calculate
- Press **ENTER**

To get the expected counts:

- Choose **MATRX** → **EDIT**
- Select 2: [B]
- Press **ENTER**

TEST FOR HOMOGENEITY OF PROPORTIONS

To compare two or more populations, we use the chi-square test for homogeneity of proportions—which is an extension of the large-samples z-test for the difference of two independent proportions $(p_1 - p_2)$. In the chi-square test, independent samples are taken from two or more populations of interest. When comparing only two population proportions, the two-tailed z-test gives the same results as the chi-square test. The procedure for the test of homogeneity of proportions is similar to the procedure for the test of independence, except for one criterion. In the test of homogeneity, since the samples are taken from different populations of interest, row or column totals are fixed in the resulting contingency table.

- Identify k populations of interest, for which we are interested in comparing the proportions $p_1, p_2, \cdots, p_k$, where p_i is the proportion for ith population of interest $(i = 1, 2, \cdots, k)$.

- We want to make an inference about the equality of $p_1, p_2, \cdots, p_k$.

- Take a random sample from each population of interest. Take the samples independently. Let the sample sizes be equal to $n_1, n_2, \cdots, n_k$ respectively, from k populations. The total number of observations is $n = n_1 + n_2 + \cdots + n_k$.

- Count the number of items in favor of and against the criteria of interest from each sample. These are the observed counts
$$O_{ij} \ (i = 1, 2, \cdots, k \text{ and } j = 1, 2)$$

- Summarize the observed data into a $k \times 2$ contingency table, where in each row, the number in the first column indicates the number in favor and the number in the second column indicates the number against the criterion of interest in that sample.

- The row totals are equal to the sample sizes, i.e.,
$$R_i = n_i, \ (i = 1, 2, \cdots, k)$$

- Compute the column totals
$$C_j = \sum_{i=1}^{k} O_{ij}, \ j = 1, 2$$

Note that
$$\sum_{i=1}^{k} R_i = \sum_{j=1}^{2} C_j = n$$

- If all k population proportions are equal, then the expected count in each cell of the table (in favor of and against the criterion in each sample) can be computed as
$$E_{ij} = \frac{R_i C_j}{n}$$

So compute the expected counts for all cells.

- Compute the test statistic value as
$$TS = \sum_{j=1}^{2} \sum_{i=1}^{k} \frac{\left(O_{ij} - E_{ij}\right)^2}{E_{ij}} \ (i = 1, 2, \cdots, k \text{ and } j = 1, 2)$$

- For a sufficiently large n, the test statistic follows a chi-square distribution with $\upsilon = (k - 1)$ degrees of freedom.

χ^2 **Test for homogeneity of proportions:**

Use a chi-square test with $\upsilon = (k-1)$ degrees of freedom.

H_0: $p_1 = p_2 = \cdots = p_k$, i.e., all population proportions are equal

H_a: At least two population proportions are different.

$$TS = \sum_{j=1}^{2} \sum_{i=1}^{k} \frac{(O_{ij} - E_{ij})^2}{E_{ij}}$$

$$\text{where } E_{ij} = \frac{R_i\, C_j}{n}$$

The rejection rule: Reject the null hypothesis if

- $TS > \chi^2(\upsilon)$ (using the rejection region approach)

- p-value $< \alpha$, where p-value $= P(\chi^2(\upsilon) > TS)$ (using the p-value approach).

Assumptions:

(a) Each sample is selected at random from the population.

(b) All samples are taken independently of each other.

(c) The sample size n is large enough to get an approximate chi-square distribution for the test statistic.

Checking the assumption of a large n:
If all expected counts are greater than 5—i.e., $E_{ij} \geq 5$ $(i = 1, 2, \cdots, r$, and $j = 1, 2, \cdots, c)$—then we have a large enough sample to use the chi-square approximation. If some cells have $E_i < 5$, then the corresponding rows can be combined with other rows in a logical manner to satisfy the requirement of expected counts.

Example 22: On the campus of a large boarding school, students are housed in Alpha, Beta, Gamma, and Delta dormitories respectively, according to their grade levels (9, 10, 11, and 12). The school officials had heard several complaints about the food services for the dormitories, but felt that the complaints differed across the four dormitories. To get student input, a random sample of students was selected from each dormitory (100 students each from Alpha and Beta dormitories, and 75 students each from Gamma and Delta dormitories). Each selected student was asked, "Are the current food services in your dormitory satisfactory?" The answers were recorded as "satisfactory" or "not satisfactory." The results were summarized as follows:

	Satisfactory	Sample Size
Alpha	78	100
Beta	72	100
Gamma	49	75
Delta	44	75

Is there significant evidence to indicate whether the proportion of students satisfied with the current food services differs in different dormitories?

Solution: Here we are interested in comparing four proportions,

p_1 = The proportion of students from Alpha dormitory satisfied with the food services.

p_2 = The proportion of students from Beta dormitory satisfied with the food services.

p_3 = The proportion of students from Gamma dormitory satisfied with the food services.

p_4 = The proportion of students from Delta dormitory satisfied with the food services.

Step 1: Define the null and alternative hypothesis as follows:

H_0: $p_1 = p_2 = p_3 = p_4$, i.e., the proportion of students satisfied with the food services is the same across all four dormitories.

H_a: At least two dormitories differ in the proportion of students satisfied with the food services.

Step 2: Use a chi-square test of homogeneity of proportions.
Complete the table of observed counts and then compute the row and column totals.

	Satisfactory	Not Satisfactory	Row Totals ($R_i = n_i$)
Alpha	78	22	100
Beta	72	28	100
Gamma	49	26	75
Delta	44	31	75
Column Total (C_j)	243	107	$n = 350$

Compute the expected counts as

$$E_{ij} = \frac{R_i \, C_j}{n}$$

For example:

The expected number of students satisfied with the food services from the Alpha dormitory

$$= \frac{(100)(243)}{350} = 69.43$$

The following table shows the observed and expected counts, with the expected counts in parentheses.

	Satisfactory	Not Satisfactory
Alpha	78 (69.429)	22 (30.571)
Beta	72 (69.429)	28 (30.571)
Gamma	49 (52.071)	26 (22.929)
Delta	44 (52.071)	31 (22.929)

All the students were selected at random. All four samples were taken independently of each other. All the cell counts are larger than 5. Therefore, the conditions for the chi-square test of homogeneity are satisfied.

Step 3: Suppose we are using a 5 percent level of significance. With $k = 4$ population proportions to compare, the degrees of freedom $= \upsilon = 3$. The rejection rule is "reject the null hypothesis if p-value < 0.05" (or if using the rejection region approach, "reject the null hypothesis if

$$TS > \chi^2_{0.05}(3) = 7.81").$$

Compute the test statistic (and the p-value if using the p-value approach).

$$TS = \sum_{i=1}^{4} \sum_{j=1}^{2} \frac{\left(O_{ij} - E_{ij}\right)^2}{E_{ij}}$$

$$= \frac{(78 - 69.429)^2}{69.429} + \frac{(22 - 30.571)^2}{30.571} + \cdots + \frac{(31 - 22.929)^2}{22.929}$$

$$= 8.45$$

$$p\text{-value} = P(\chi^2 > 8.45) = 0.037$$

Step 4: Since p-value $= 0.037 < 0.05$ (or if using the rejection region approach, since $TS = 8.45 > 7.81$), we should reject the null hypothesis and conclude that at least two dormitories differ in terms of the proportion of students satisfied with the current food services.

INFERENCE FOR THE SLOPE OF A LEAST SQUARES LINE

It's common practice to estimate the relation between correlated variables and use the estimation to predict a response for a given value of an independent variable. Some examples are: car manufacturers estimate the mean miles per gallon given by a model of a car from the weight of the car; real estate agents estimate the price of a house using the age and/or the location of the house; colleges estimate the grade point average of prospective students at graduation using their scores on college entrance examinations; and crime labs use the dimensions of bones to estimate the age of a victim.

A linear relation between two variables X (the independent variable) and Y (the response variable) is a relation described by a line. Suppose the true linear relation between X and Y is given by

$$Y = \beta_0 + \beta_1 X + e, \text{ where}$$

$$\beta_0 = \text{intercept of the line}$$

$$\beta_1 = \text{slope of the line}$$

$$e = \text{random error}$$

Using the **least squares regression technique**, the slope and the intercept can be estimated from n pairs of measurements as

$$\hat{\beta}_1 = b = \frac{SS_{xy}}{SS_{xx}} \text{ and } \hat{\beta}_0 = a = \bar{y} - b\bar{x}$$

where $SS_{xx} = \sum x^2 - \frac{(\sum x)^2}{n}$ and $SS_{xy} = \sum xy - \frac{(\sum x)(\sum y)}{n}$

The **error (residual)** is the difference between the observed response and the response predicted by the estimated regression line, i.e., $e = (y - \hat{y})$, where $\hat{y} = a + bx$. The standard deviation of all the error terms denoted by S_e is computed as

$$S_e = \sqrt{\frac{\sum_{i=1}^{n} e_i^2}{n-2}} = \sqrt{\frac{SS_{yy} - bSS_{xy}}{n-2}}$$

$$\text{where } SS_{yy} = \sum Y^2 - \frac{(\sum Y)^2}{n}$$

Then the question that arises is: Is there a significant relationship between Y and X? In other words: Does Y depend significantly on X? Or: Does X provide enough information for us to predict Y?

If the slope of the line of true relation is 0—i.e., if the relation between Y and X is a horizontal line—then there is no relation between Y and X. A line of slope 0 gives the same value for Y regardless of the value of X. In other words, the value of Y does not depend on the value of X. The scatterplot of such population data will show a cloud of measurements with no specific direction; however, in a sample this may not be true. Even with a population with $\beta_1 = 0$, the slope estimated from the sample (and not computed from the whole population) will not necessarily be equal to zero, due to the sampling variation involved. If the estimated slope is non-zero, then the following questions arise:

- Is $b \neq 0$, because the slope of true relation is non-zero, i.e., $\beta_1 \neq 0$?

- Is $b \neq 0$ due just to sampling variation, when in fact $\beta_1 = 0$?

How much variation among b values can be explained away as a chance variation? That can be determined using the sampling distribution of b. To check the likelihood of b from a population with a specified β_1 (of zero or non-zero value), use the **t-test for slope**.

- Take a random sample of n pairs of observations from the population of interest, or take a random sample of n objects from the population, and make a pair of measurements on each selected object.

$$(x_1, y_1), (x_2, y_2), \cdots (x_n, y_n)$$

- Assume that random variables X and Y are linearly related. Make a scatterplot of the n pairs of observations. A quick review of the scatterplot will indicate whether an assumption of linear relation between X and Y is reasonable.

- If the assumption of linear relation is reasonable, then estimate the slope of the line of best fit (also known as "the least squares regression line").

$$b = \frac{n\sum xy - (\sum x)(\sum y)}{n\sum x^2 - (\sum x)^2}$$

- Different random samples of size n will result in different estimates b. If for any fixed value of X, the responses are normally distributed with the same variance σ, then the sampling distribution of b is also a normal distribution, with a mean of β_1 and a standard deviation:

$$\sigma_{\hat{\beta}_1} = \frac{\sigma}{\sigma_x \sqrt{n-1}}$$

Since the standard deviation of errors s and the standard deviation of s_x are unknown, estimate them using S and S_x respectively. Then the ratio b/S_b follows a t-distribution with $\upsilon = (n-2)$ degrees of freedom.

Estimating β_1 using $(1-\alpha)100\%$ confidence interval:

Construct a t-interval with $\upsilon = (n-2)$ degrees of freedom.

Margin of Error:
$$t_{\alpha/2}(\upsilon)\hat{\sigma}_b = t_{\alpha/2}(\upsilon)\frac{S_e}{\sqrt{SS_{xx}}}$$

$$\text{where } S_e = \sqrt{\frac{SS_{yy}-bSS_{xy}}{n-2}}$$

Confidence Interval:
$$b \pm t_{\alpha/2}(\upsilon)\frac{S_e}{\sqrt{SS_{xx}}}$$

Making an inference about the difference in population means β_1:
Use a t-test with $\upsilon = (n-2)$ degrees of freedom

$H_0: \beta_1 = \beta_{10}$ (β_{10} Specified)
$H_a: \beta_1 > \beta_{10}$ or
$\quad \beta_1 < \beta_{10}$ or
$\quad \beta_1 \neq \beta_{10}$

$$TS = \frac{b - \beta_{10}}{S_e/\sqrt{SS}} \quad \text{where } S_e = \sqrt{\frac{SS_{yy} - bSS_{xy}}{n-2}}$$

	Rejection Rule	
Alternative hypothesis:	**Rejection region approach:**	**p-value approach:**
$H_a: \beta_1 > \beta_{10}$ $H_a: \beta_1 < \beta_{10}$ $H_a: \beta_1 \neq \beta_{10}$	Reject H_0 if $TS > t_\alpha(\upsilon)$ $TS < -t_\alpha(\upsilon)$ $TS > t_{\alpha/2}(\upsilon)$ or $TS < -t_{\alpha/2}(\upsilon)$	Reject H_0 if p-value $< \alpha$, where p-value $= P(t(\upsilon) > TS)$ p-value $= P(t(\upsilon) < TS)$ p-value $=$ $P(t(\upsilon) > |TS|) + P(Z < -|TS|)$

Conditions:

(a) A random sample of n pairs is obtained.

(b) The errors are normally distributed.

(c) The mean error is 0.

(d) The standard deviation of errors, σ, is the same for all values of X.

(e) The errors are independent.

Checking the conditions:

(a) From the description of the experiment, determine if it is reasonable to assume that the sample was randomly selected from the population of interest.

(b) Make a histogram or stem-and-leaf plot of the errors. If the distribution is fairly symmetric and bell shaped, then it is reasonable to assume that the errors are normally distributed. Alternatively, use a normal probability plot to make the decision.

(c) Plot the errors to get a residual plot. If all the errors are scattered around 0, then it is reasonable to assume that the mean is 0.

(d) If the residual plot shows a somewhat similar spread of errors across all values of X, then it is reasonable to assume a constant standard deviation.

(e) If the residual plot shows no specific trends or patterns, it is reasonable to assume that the errors are independent.

Example 23: Some of the members of the faculty of the College of Education believe that reading performance is related to the point size of the letters in the document read. A group of randomly selected students were given a test. They were asked to read certain passages in different point sizes on a computer. The letter sizes were randomized. The average time (in minutes) required for the subjects to read the passages was determined. The data is given in the following table.

Letter Size	7	8	9	10	11	12	13	14
Average Reading Time (in minutes)	7.10	7.14	6.50	6.78	6.44	6.94	6.30	6.46

The regression analysis performed on the data by a computer gave the following results:

Predictor	Coef	StDev	T
P			
Constant	7.6700	0.4225	18.15
0.000			
Letter size	-0.09167	0.03931	-2.33
0.058			

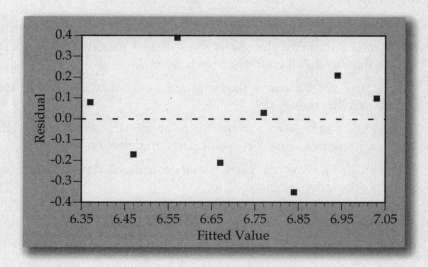

Figure 28: Residual plot

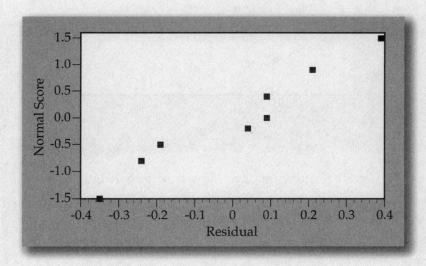

Figure 29: Normal probability plot for residuals

Is there a significant relation between the letter point size and the reading performance as measured by average reading time?

Solution:

Step 1: The faculty are interested in determining whether average reading time depends on the point size of the letter. So test

H_0: There is no relation between average reading time and letter size,

or $\beta_1 = 0$ or $\rho = 0$

H_a: There is a relation between average reading time and letter size,

or $\beta_1 \neq 0$ or $\rho \neq 0$

Step 2: Use the *t*-test for slope (or a *t*-test for correlation coefficient).

(a) A random sample of students was used.

(b) The normal probability plot shows a fairly linear pattern. So it is reasonable to assume that the distribution of errors is normal.

(c) The residual plot shows that the errors are scattered around 0. It is reasonable to assume that the mean is 0.

(d) The residual plot shows a somewhat similar spread of errors across all values of X. It is reasonable to assume a constant standard deviation.

(e) The residual plot shows no specific trends or patterns. It is reasonable to assume that the errors are independent.

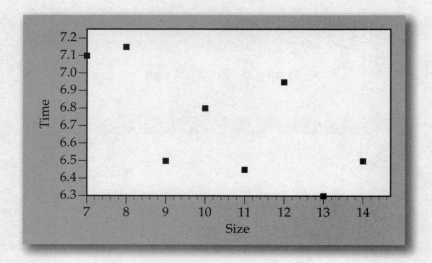

Figure 30: Scatterplot of reading time versus letter size

This scatterplot indicates a slightly downward trend. It is reasonable to assume that a linear relation exists between the reading time and the letter point size.

Step 3: With n = 8 pairs of measurements, degrees of freedom = n – 2 = 6.

Suppose we use α = 0.10, then

$$t_{\alpha/2}(\upsilon) = t_{0.10/2}(6) = t_{0.05}(6) = 1.943$$

The rejection rule is to "reject null if *p*-value < 0.10" (or "reject null if TS > 1.943 or TS < 1.943," if using the rejection region approach).

From the results of the regression analysis provided we get

b = –0.092, TS = –2.33 and *p*-value = 0.058

Step 4: Since *p*-value = 0.058 < 0.10 (or, if using the rejection region approach, TS = –2.33, which falls in the rejection region), reject the null hypothesis and accept the alternative hypothesis. At a 10 percent error rate, we can conclude that there is a linear relation between letter size and reading performance.

Confidence Interval:		Point Estimate $\pm$ Multiplier $\times$ Standard Error	
Test Statistic		$\dfrac{\text{Point Estimate} - \text{Hypothesized value}}{\text{Standard Error}}$	
Parameter of Interest	**Point Estimate**	**Multiplier & Test with DF**	**Standard Error (SE)**
p	$\hat{p} = \dfrac{x}{n}$	Approx. z-interval Approx. z-test	$\hat{\sigma}_{\hat{p}} = \sqrt{\hat{p}(1-\hat{p})\Big/ n}$ (for estimation) $\sigma_{\hat{p}} = \sqrt{p_0(1-p_0)\Big/ n}$ (for inference)
μ	$\hat{\mu} = \overline{X}$	Known variance case z-interval z-test	$\sigma_{\overline{X}} = \dfrac{\sigma}{\sqrt{n}}$
		Unknown variance case $t_{\alpha/2}\,(v)$ t-test with $(n-1)$ df	$\hat{\sigma}_{\overline{X}} = \dfrac{S}{\sqrt{n}}$
		Large sample case Approx. z-interval Approx. z-test	$\sigma_{\overline{X}} = \dfrac{\sigma}{\sqrt{n}}$ Estimate σ using S if σ is unknown
$(p_1 - p_2)$	$(\hat{p}_1 - \hat{p}_2)$ $= \left(\dfrac{x_1}{n_1}\right) - \left(\dfrac{x_2}{n_2}\right)$	Approx. z-interval Approx. z-test	$\hat{\sigma}_{(\hat{p}_1 - \hat{p}_2)} = \sqrt{\dfrac{\hat{p}_1(1-\hat{p}_1)}{n_1} + \dfrac{\hat{p}_2(1-\hat{p}_2)}{n_2}}$ (for estimation) $\sigma_{(\hat{p}_1 - \hat{p}_2)} = \sqrt{p_c(1-p_c)\left(\dfrac{1}{n_1} + \dfrac{1}{n_2}\right)}$ where $p_c = \dfrac{x_1 + x_2}{n_1 + n_2}$ (for inference)

Parameter of Interest	Point Estimate	Multiplier & Test with DF	Standard Error (SE)
$\mu_1 - \mu_2$	$\hat{\mu}_1 - \hat{\mu}_2$ $= (\bar{x}_1 - \bar{x}_2)$ Independent samples	Known variances case z-interval z-test	$\sigma_{(\bar{x}_1 - \bar{x}_2)} = \sqrt{\dfrac{\sigma_1^2}{n_1} + \dfrac{\sigma_2^2}{n_2}}$
		Equal variances case t-interval t-test with $\upsilon = (n_1 + n_2 - 2)$ df	$\hat{\sigma}_{(\bar{x}_1 - \bar{x}_2)} = S_p \sqrt{\dfrac{1}{n_1} + \dfrac{1}{n_2}}$ where the pooled standard deviation is $S_p = \sqrt{\dfrac{(n_1 - 1) S_1^2 + (n_2 - 1) S_2^2}{n_1 + n_2 - 2}}$
		Unequal variances case Approx. t-interval Approx. t-test with df $\dfrac{\left(\dfrac{S_1^2}{n_1} + \dfrac{S_2^2}{n_2}\right)^2}{\dfrac{(S_1^2/n_1)^2}{n_1 - 1} + \dfrac{(S_2^2/n_2)^2}{n_2 - 1}}$	$\hat{\sigma}_{(\bar{x}_1 - \bar{x}_2)} = \sqrt{\dfrac{S_1^2}{n_1} + \dfrac{S_2^2}{n_2}}$
		Large samples case Approx. z-interval Approx. z-test	$\sigma_{(\bar{x}_1 - \bar{x}_2)} = \sqrt{\dfrac{\sigma_1^2}{n_1} + \dfrac{\sigma_2^2}{n_2}}$ If σ_1^2 and σ_2^2 are not known, then estimate them using S_1^2 and S_2^2 respectively.
$\mu_d = \mu_1 - \mu_2$	$\hat{\mu}_d = \bar{d}$ $= \dfrac{\sum d_i}{n}$ Dependent samples	t-interval t-test with $\upsilon = n - 1$ df	$\hat{\sigma}_{\bar{d}} = \dfrac{S_d}{\sqrt{n}}$
β_1	$\hat{\beta}_1 = b = \dfrac{SS_{xy}}{SS_{xx}}$	t-interval t-test with $\upsilon = n - 2$ df	$\hat{\sigma}_{\bar{d}} = \dfrac{S_e}{\sqrt{SS_{xx}}}$ where $S_e = \sqrt{\dfrac{SS_{yy} - \hat{\beta}_1 SS_{xy}}{n - 2}}$

Table 6: Summary of formulas for estimation and inference

PART **III**

Practice Tests and Explanations

8

THE PRINCETON REVIEW
AP STATISTICS
PRACTICE TEST 1

STATISTICS

Three hours are allotted for this examination: 1 hour and 30 minutes for Section I, which consists of multiple-choice questions, and 1 hour and 30 minutes for Section II, which consists of longer problems. In determining your grade, the two sections are given equal weight. Section I is printed in this examination booklet; Section II is in a separate booklet.

SECTION I

Time—1 hour and 30 minutes

Number of questions—40

Percent of total grade—50

Section I of this examination contains 40 multiple-choice questions. Please be careful to fill in only the ovals that are preceded by numbers 1 through 40 on your answer sheet.

General Instructions

DO NOT OPEN THIS BOOKLET UNTIL YOU ARE INSTRUCTED TO DO SO.

INDICATE ALL YOUR ANSWERS TO QUESTIONS IN SECTION I ON THE SEPARATE ANSWER SHEET ENCLOSED. No credit will be given for anything written in this examination booklet, but you may use the booklet for notes or scratchwork. After you have decided which of the suggested answers is best, COMPLETELY fill in the corresponding oval on the answer sheet. Give only one answer to each question. If you change an answer, be sure that the previous mark is erased completely.

Example: Sample Answer

What is the median of the set of numbers 4, 5, 6, and 7?   Ⓐ ● Ⓒ Ⓓ Ⓔ

(A) 5

(B) 5.5

(C) 6

(D) 6.6

(E) 7

Many candidates wonder whether or not to guess the answers to questions about which they are not certain. In this section of the examination, as a correction for haphazard guessing, one-fourth of the number of questions you answer incorrectly will be subtracted from the number of questions you answer correctly. It is improbable, therefore, that mere guessing will improve your score significantly; it may even lower your score, and it does take time. If, however, you are not sure of the best answer but have some knowledge of the questions and are able to eliminate one or more answer choices as wrong, your chance of getting the right answer is improved, and it may be to your advantage to answer such a question.

Use your time effectively, working as rapidly as you can without losing accuracy. Do not spend too much time on questions that are too difficult. Go on to other questions and come back to the difficult ones if you have time. It is not expected that everyone will be able to answer all the multiple-choice questions.

Formulas begin on page 386.

Tables begin on page 389.

STATISTICS

SECTION I

Time—1 hour and 30 minutes

Number of questions—40

Percent of total grade—50

<u>Directions</u>: Solve each of the following problems, using the available space for scratchwork. Decide which is the best of the choices given and fill in the corresponding oval on the answer sheet. No credit will be given for anything written in the test book. Do not spend too much time on any one problem.

1. An outlier is an observation that

   (A) is seen more frequently than the other observations in the data set.
   (B) is seen less frequently than the other observations in the data set.
   (C) is always smaller than the other observations in the data set.
   (D) is always larger than the other observations in the data set.
   (E) is significantly different from the other observations in the data set.

GO ON TO THE NEXT PAGE

2. During flu season, a city medical center needs to keep a large supply of flu shots. A nurse's aid compiles data on the number of flu shots given per day in the past few years during flu season. A cumulative probability chart of the collected data is as follows:

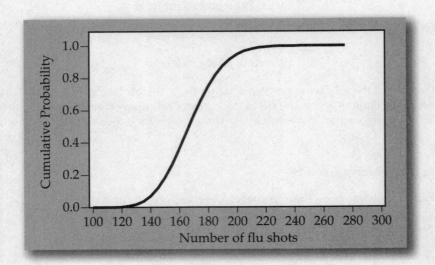

How many flu shots should the center store every day to meet the demand on 95 percent of the days?

(A) At most 190

(B) At most 140

(C) Exactly 170

(D) At least 150

(E) At least 200

GO ON TO THE NEXT PAGE

3. A large company has offices in two locations, one in New Jersey and one in Utah. The mean salary of office assistants in the New Jersey office is $28,500. The mean salary of office assistants in the Utah office is $22,500. The New Jersey office has 128 office assistants and the Utah office has 32 office assistants. What is the mean salary paid to the office assistants in this company?

(A) $22,500
(B) $23,700
(C) $25,500
(D) $27,300
(E) $28,500

GO ON TO THE NEXT PAGE

4. In the northern U.S., schools are sometimes closed during winter due to severe snowstorms. At the end of the school year, schools have to make up for the days missed. The following graph shows the frequency distribution of the number of days missed due to snowstorms per year, using data collected from the past 75 years.

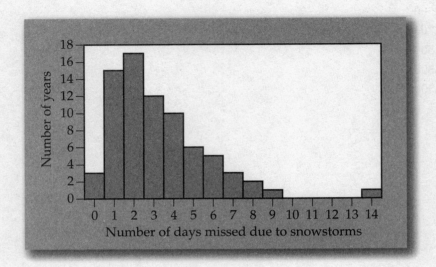

Which of the following should be used to describe the center of this distribution?

(A) Mean, because it is an unbiased estimator.

(B) Median, because the distribution is skewed.

(C) IQR, because it excludes outliers and includes only the middle 50 percent of data.

(D) First quartile, because the distribution is left skewed.

(E) Standard deviation, because it is unaffected by the outliers.

GO ON TO THE NEXT PAGE

5. The probability that a car will skid on a bridge on a rainy day is 0.75. Today the weather station announced that there is a 20 percent chance of rain. What is the probability that it will rain today and that a car will skid on the bridge?

(A) 0.0300
(B) 0.0375
(C) 0.1500
(D) 0.3000
(E) 0.9500

---

6. A nursery guarantees that it will replace all the plants it sells that do not survive one year from the purchase date. From past experience the manager knows that 95 percent of plants sold survive more than a year. Suppose your school purchased 200 plants from this nursery to beautify the campus. How many plants do you expect will be replaced in the next year?

(A) 5
(B) 10
(C) 20
(D) 95
(E) 190

GO ON TO THE NEXT PAGE

7. The average number of calories in Yum-Yum Good candy bars is 210, with a standard deviation of 10. If the number of calories per candy bar is approximately normally distributed, what percent of candy bars contain more than 225 calories?

    (A) 66.8%
    (B) 47.7%
    (C) 43.3%
    (D) 6.68%
    (E) 3.34%

8. A publisher used standard boxes for shipping books. The mean weight of books packed per box is 25 pounds, with a standard deviation of 2 pounds. The mean weight of the boxes is 1 pound, with a standard deviation of 0.15 pounds. The mean weight of the packing material used per box is 2 pounds, with a standard deviation of 0.25 pounds. What is the standard deviation of the weights of the packed boxes?

    (A) 28.000 pounds
    (B) 5.290 pounds
    (C) 4.085 pounds
    (D) 2.400 pounds
    (E) 2.021 pounds

GO ON TO THE NEXT PAGE

9. The principal of a school is interested in estimating the average income per family of her students. She selects a random sample of students and collects information about their family income. A 95 percent confidence interval computed from this data for the mean income per family is ($35,095, $45,005). Which of the following provides the best interpretation of this confidence interval?

(A) 95 percent of the students in her school are from families whose income is between $35,095 and $45,005.

(B) We are 95 percent confident that the mean income per family of the students in this school is between $35,095 and $45,005.

(C) We are 95 percent confident that the families of all the students in this school have an income of between $35,095 and $45,005.

(D) 95 percent of students in her school have a mean family income between $35,095 and $45,005.

(E) If we take many samples of the same size from this school, collect data, and construct 95 percent confidence intervals, then 95 percent of those intervals will contain the true mean income of families of students in her school.

---

10. The Department of Health plans to test the lead level in a specific park. Since a high lead level is harmful to children, the park will be closed if the lead level exceeds the allowed limit. The department randomly selects several locations in the park, gets soil samples from those locations, and tests the samples for their lead levels. Which of the following decisions would result from the type I error?

(A) Closing the park when the lead levels are within the allowed limit.
(B) Keeping the park open when the lead levels are in excess of the allowed limit.
(C) Closing the park when the lead levels are in excess of the allowed limit.
(D) Keeping the park open when the lead levels are within the allowed limit.
(E) Closing the park because of the increased noise level in the neighborhood.

GO ON TO THE NEXT PAGE

11. Extra study sessions were offered to students after the midterm to help improve their understanding of statistics. Student scores on the midterm and the final exam were recorded. The following scatterplot shows final test scores against the midterm test scores.

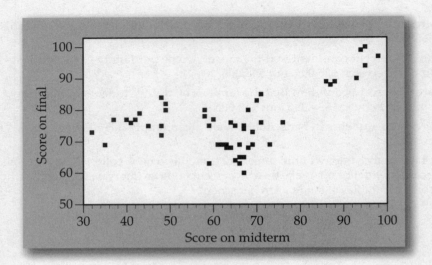

Which of the following statement correctly interprets the scatterplot?

(A) All students have shown significant improvement in the final exam scores as a result of the extra study sessions.

(B) The extra study sessions were of no help. Each student's final exam score was about the same as his or her score on the midterm.

(C) The extra study sessions further confused students. All student scores decreased from midterm to final exam.

(D) Students that scored below 55 on the midterm showed considerable improvement on the final exam; those who scored between 55 and 80 on the midterm showed minimal improvement on the final exam; and those who scored above 80 on the midterm showed almost no improvement on the final exam.

(E) Students that scored below 55 on the midterm showed minimal improvement on the final exam; those who scored between 55 and 80 on the midterm showed moderate improvement on the final exam; and those who scored above 80 on the midterm showed considerable improvement on the final exam.

GO ON TO THE NEXT PAGE

12. A resident of Auto Town was interested in finding the cheapest gas prices at nearby gas stations. On randomly selected days over a period of one month, he recorded the gas prices (in dollars) at four gas stations near his house. The box plots of gas prices are as follows:

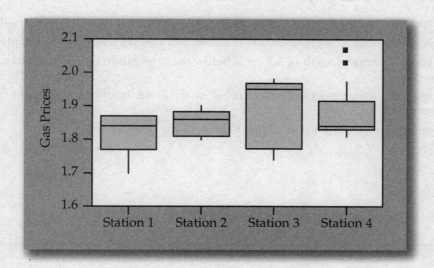

Which station has more consistent gas prices?

(A) Station 1
(B) Station 2
(C) Station 3
(D) Station 4
(E) Station 4 without the outlier

GO ON TO THE NEXT PAGE

13. A botanist is interested in testing $H_0: \mu = 3.5$cm versus $H_0: \mu > 3.5$, where μ = the mean petal length of one variety of flowers. A random sample of 50 petals gives significant results at a 5 percent level of significance. Which of the following statements about the confidence interval to estimate the mean petal length is true?

(A) The specified mean length of 3.5 cm is within a 90 percent confidence interval.

(B) The specified mean length of 3.5 cm is not within a 90 percent confidence interval.

(C) The specified mean length of 3.5 cm is below the lower limit of a 90 percent confidence interval.

(D) The specified mean length of 3.5 cm is below the lower limit of a 95 percent confidence interval.

(E) Not enough information is available to answer the question.

---

14. A filling machine puts an average of 4 ounces of coffee in jars, with a standard deviation of 0.25 ounces. Forty jars filled by this machine are selected at random. What is the probability that the mean amount per jar filled in the sampled jars is less than 3.9 ounces?

(A) 0.0057

(B) 0.0225

(C) 0.0250

(D) 0.0500

(E) 0.3446

GO ON TO THE NEXT PAGE

15. The number of customers served per day by a large department store is approximately normally distributed, with a mean of 3,250 customers and a standard deviation of 320. Find the range of customers served on the middle 50 percent of days.

(A) (3,035, 3,464)

(B) (2,930, 3,570)

(C) (2,610, 3,890)

(D) (2,450, 4,050)

(E) (2,290, 4,210)

16. Which of the following statements describes the 35th percentile for the distribution of random variable X?

(A) $P(X < x_0) = 0.35$

(B) $P(X > x_0) = 0.35$

(C) $P(X < 0.35) = x_0$

(D) $P(X > 0.35) = x_0$

(E) $P(-x_0 < X < x_0) = 0.35$

GO ON TO THE NEXT PAGE

17. The run times of a marathon runner are approximately normally distributed. The z-score for his run this week is -2. Which one of the following statements is a correct interpretation of his z-score?

(A) This week his time was 2 minutes lower than his time last week.

(B) This week his time was 2 minutes lower than his best time ever.

(C) This week his time was 2 minutes lower than his average time.

(D) This week his time was 2 standard deviations lower than his average time.

(E) This week his time was 2 standard deviations lower than his time last week.

---

18. Which of the following is an outcome of a binomial experiment?

(A) Getting both spades on the first two draws from a standard deck of cards, when the first card is not replaced before the second card is drawn.

(B) Getting three spades out of the first seven draws from a standard deck of cards, when each card drawn is not replaced before the next card is drawn.

(C) Getting three spades out of the first seven draws from a standard deck of cards, when each card drawn is replaced before the next card is drawn.

(D) Getting three spades and four hearts out of the first seven draws from a standard deck of cards, when each card is not replaced before the next card is drawn.

(E) Getting three spades and four hearts out of the first seven draws from a standard deck of cards, when each card is replaced before the next card is drawn.

GO ON TO THE NEXT PAGE

19. A dentist has noticed that about 2 kids in every 7 that he sees professionally develop cavities before they turn 10 years old. Last week he examined the teeth of 5 unrelated children younger than 10. Let X be the number of children who develop cavities before turning 10. Which of the following gives the probability that at least one will develop a cavity before turning 10?

(A) $P(X = 2, 3, 4, 5, 6, 7)$
(B) $P(X = 2$ out of $7)$
(C) $P(X = 1)$
(D) $1 - P(X = 0)$
(E) $P(X = 0, 1)$

20. The probability that Ted will enroll in an English class is 1/3. If he does enroll in an English class, the probability that he would enroll in a mathematics class is 1/5. What is the probability that he enrolls in both classes?

(A) 1/15
(B) 2/15
(C) 7/15
(D) 3/5
(E) 13/15

GO ON TO THE NEXT PAGE

21. Two dice are rolled simultaneously. If both dice show 6, then the player wins $20; otherwise the player loses the game. It costs $2.00 to play the game. What is the expected gain or loss for the game?

(A) The player will gain about $0.55.

(B) The player will gain about $1.44.

(C) The player will lose about $0.55.

(D) The player will lose about $1.44.

(E) The player will lose about $2.00.

22. According to the central limit theorem, the sample mean $\overline{X}$ is approximately normally distributed

(A) for a large sample, regardless of the distribution of random variable X.

(B) for a large sample, provided the random variable X is normally distributed.

(C) regardless of the sample size.

(D) for a small sample, regardless of the distribution of random variable X.

(E) for a small sample, provided the random variable X is normally distributed.

GO ON TO THE NEXT PAGE

23. A department store at a large mall claims that over 60 percent of the mall's visitors shop at that store. Let p = the proportion of the mall's visitors that shop at the store. Which of the following pair of hypotheses should be used to support this claim?

(A) $H_0 : p = 0.60$ and $H_a : p > 0.60$

(B) $H_0 : p = 0.60$ and $H_a : p \neq 0.60$

(C) $H_0 : p = 0.60$ and $H_a : p < 0.60$

(D) $H_0 : p > 0.60$ and $H_a : p \leq 0.60$

(E) $H_0 : p < 0.60$ and $H_a : p \geq 0.60$

---

24. A random sample of 16 light bulbs of one brand was selected to estimate the mean lifetime of that brand of bulbs. The sample mean was 1,025 hours, with a standard deviation of 130 hours. Assuming that the lifetimes are approximately normally distributed, which of the following will give a 95 percent confidence interval to estimate the mean lifetime?

(A) $1,025 \pm 1.96 \sqrt{\dfrac{130}{16}}$

(B) $1,025 \pm 1.96 \sqrt{130}$

(C) $1,025 \pm 1.96 \dfrac{130}{\sqrt{16}}$

(D) $1,025 \pm 2.13 \dfrac{130}{\sqrt{16}}$

(E) $1,025 \pm 2.13 \sqrt{\dfrac{130}{16}}$

GO ON TO THE NEXT PAGE

25. A school committee member is lobbying for an increase in the gasoline tax to support the county school system. The local newspaper conducted a survey of county residents to assess their support for such an increase. What is the population of interest here?

(A) All school-aged children

(B) All county residents

(C) All county residents with school-aged children

(D) All county residents with children in the county school system

(E) All county school system teachers

---

26. A manufacturer of ready-bake cake mixes is interested in designing a study to test the effects of 4 different temperature levels (300, 325, 350, and 375 degrees F), 2 different types of pans (glass and metal), and 3 different types of ovens (gas, electric, and microwave) on the texture of its cakes. How many different treatment combinations are to be used in this study?

(A) 3

(B) 9

(C) 18

(D) 20

(E) 24

GO ON TO THE NEXT PAGE

27. Which one of the following distributions could have a mean of approximately 12 and a standard deviation of approximately 2?

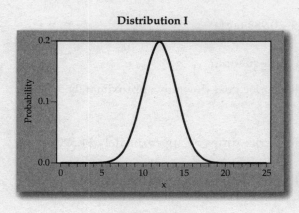

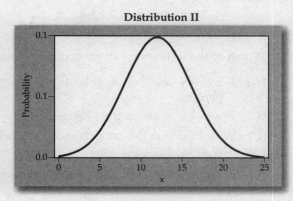

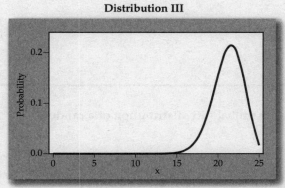

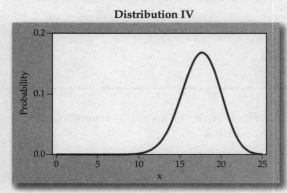

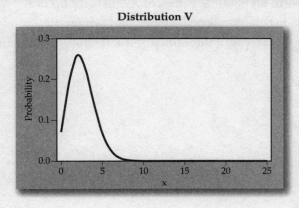

(A) Distribution I
(B) Distribution II
(C) Distribution III
(D) Distribution IV
(E) Distribution V

GO ON TO THE NEXT PAGE

28. The relation between the selling price of a car (in $1,000) and its age (in years) is estimated from a random sample of cars of a specific model. The relation is given by the following formula:

$$\text{Selling price} = 15.9 - 0.983\,(\text{age})$$

Which of the following can we conclude from this equation?

(A) For every year the car gets older, the selling price goes down by approximately 9.83 percent.

(B) A new car costs on the average $9,830.

(C) For every year the car gets older, the selling price drops by approximately $1,590.

(D) A new car costs $16,883.

(E) For every year the car gets older, the selling price drops by approximately $983.

---

29. Which of the following is true about any discrete probability distribution of a random variable X?

(A) The expected value of $X=np$.

(B) The sum of all possible values of X is equal to 1.

(C) The probabilities of all possible values of X must add up to 1.

(D) The probability distribution is bell-shaped and symmetric.

(E) Approximately 95 percent of the values of X fall within 2 standard deviations of the mean.

GO ON TO THE NEXT PAGE

30. Which of the following is <u>not</u> a random variable?

   (A) The number of students present in a class.

   (B) The amount of water released through the Hoover Dam every day.

   (C) The number of credits a student gets for completing English 101.

   (D) The time it takes to complete a lap in the Indy 500.

   (E) The number of questions answered by a student on the final exam.

31. After a frost warning was issued, the owner of a large orange grove asked his workers to spray all his trees with water. The water was supposed to freeze and form a protective covering of ice around the orange blossom. Nevertheless, the owner suspected that some trees suffered considerable damage due to the frost. To estimate the proportion of trees that suffered more than 50 percent damage due to the frost, he took a random sample of 100 trees from his grove. What constitutes an observation (measurement) in this experiment?

   (A) The proportion of trees that suffered more than 50 percent damage due to frost.

   (B) The number of trees affected by the frost.

   (C) The number of trees sampled from the grove.

   (D) For each sampled tree, whether it was sprayed with water or not sprayed with water.

   (E) For each sampled tree, whether it suffered more than 50 percent damage or at most 50 percent damage.

GO ON TO THE NEXT PAGE

32. For which of the following purposes would it be most unreasonable to use a census?

(A) To determine the proportion of students with a learning disability in a small rural area high school.

(B) To determine the proportion of red snappers with a high mercury level in the Gulf of Mexico.

(C) To determine the difference between the proportion of engineering professors and the proportion of business professors in favor of the new teaching initiative at a large university.

(D) To determine the mean wage earned by construction workers in a small town.

(E) To determine the mean selling price of houses in your neighborhood.

---

33. A student organization at a university is interested in estimating the proportion of students in favor of showing movies biweekly instead of monthly. How many students should be sampled to get a 90 percent confidence interval with a width of at most 0.08?

(A) 27
(B) 64
(C) 106
(D) 256
(E) 423

GO ON TO THE NEXT PAGE

34. A small kiosk at the Atlanta airport carries souvenirs in the price range of $3.99 to $29.99, with a mean price of $14.75. The airport authorities decide to increase the rent charged for a kiosk by 5 percent. To make up for the increased rent, the kiosk owner decides to increase the prices of all items by 50 cents. As a result, which of the following will happen?

(A) The mean price and the range of prices will increase by 50 cents.

(B) The mean price will remain the same, but the range of prices will increase by 50 cents.

(C) The mean price and the standard deviation of prices will increase by 50 cents.

(D) The mean price will increase by 50 cents, but the standard deviation of prices will remain the same.

(E) The mean price and the standard deviation will remain the same.

---

35. Two hundred students were classified by gender and hostility level (low, medium, high), as measured by an HLT-test. The results were the following:

	Hostility Level		
	Low	Medium	High
Male	35	40	5
Female	62	50	8

If the hostility level among students were independent of their gender, then how many female students would we expect to show the medium HLT score?

(A) 25
(B) 45
(C) 54
(D) 60
(E) 75

GO ON TO THE NEXT PAGE

36. After receiving several complaints from his customers about the store being closed on Sundays, a storekeeper decided to conduct a survey. He randomly selected 100 female customers and 120 male customers, and asked them, "Are you interested in shopping at this store on Sundays?" He counted the number of customers answering "yes" and constructed a 95 percent confidence interval for the difference in the proportions of male and female customers in favor of shopping on Sundays. The resulting interval was (–0.23, –0.18). Which of the following is a correct interpretation of the interval?

(A) We are 95 percent confident that the proportion of women interested in shopping on Sundays exceeds the proportion of men interested in shopping on Sundays.

(B) We are 95 percent confident that the proportion of men interested in shopping on Sundays exceeds the proportion of women interested in shopping on Sundays.

(C) We are 95 percent confident that the proportion of women interested in shopping on Sundays is equal to the proportion of men interested in shopping on Sundays.

(D) Because the interval contains negative values, it is invalid and should not be interpreted.

(E) Because the interval does not contain zero, the interval is invalid, and should not be interpreted.

37. A company is interested in comparing the mean sales revenue per salesperson at two different locations. The manager takes a random sample of 10 salespersons from each location independently and records the sales revenue generated by each person during the last 4 weeks. He decides to use a t-test to compare the mean sales revenue at the two locations. Which of the following assumptions is necessary for the validity of the t-test?

(A) The population variances at both locations are equal.

(B) The population variances at both locations are not equal.

(C) The population variances at both locations are known.

(D) The population of the sales records at each location is normally distributed.

(E) The population of the difference in sales records computed by pairing one salesperson from each location is normally distributed.

GO ON TO THE NEXT PAGE

38. A skeptic decides to conduct an experiment in ESP in which a blindfolded subject calls out the color of a card dealt from a regular deck of cards (half the cards are red; the other half, black). One hundred cards are dealt from a well-shuffled pack, with each card being replaced after a deal. Using a 5 percent level of significance, what is the lowest number of cards that the subject needs to call out correctly in order to show that he is doing better than he would if he were simply guessing?

(A) 51
(B) 59
(C) 75
(D) 95
(E) 98

39. A manufacturer of motor oil is interested in testing the effects of a newly developed additive on the lifespan of an engine. Twenty-five different engine types are selected at random and each one is tested using oil with the additive and oil without the additive. What type of analysis will yield the most useful information?

(A) Matched pairs comparison of population proportions.
(B) Matched pairs comparison of population means.
(C) Independent samples comparison of population proportions.
(D) Independent samples comparison of population means.
(E) *Chi-square* test of homogeneity.

GO ON TO THE NEXT PAGE

40. A test of independence is to be performed on a 3×4 contingency table. Which of the following assumptions needs to be satisfied for the *chi-square* test to be valid?

(A) All expected counts are at least 5.

(B) All observed counts are at least 5.

(C) The *chi-square* test statistic is at least 5.

(D) The total number of observations is at least 5.

(E) The number of categories is at least 5.

END OF SECTION I

IF YOU FINISH BEFORE TIME IS CALLED, YOU MAY
CHECK YOUR WORK ON SECTION I.
DO NOT GO ON TO SECTION II UNTIL YOU ARE TOLD TO DO SO.

STATISTICS

SECTION II

Time — 1 hour and 30 minutes

Number of problems — 6

Percent of total grade — 50

GENERAL INSTRUCTIONS

There are two parts to this section of the examination. Part A consists of five equally weighted problems that represent 75 percent of the total weight of this section. Spend about 65 minutes on this part of the exam. Part B consists of one longer problem that represents 25 percent of the total weight of this section. Spend about 25 minutes on this part of the exam. Since it is not expected that everyone will be able to complete all parts of all problems, you may wish to look over all the problems before you begin to work. The questions are printed in the booklet and on the green insert: it may be easier for you to look over all the problems on the insert. Statistical tables and useful formulas are printed in the green insert. When you are told to begin, open your booklet, carefully tear out the green insert, and start your work.

- You should write all work for each part of each problem in the space provided for that part in this booklet. Be sure to write clearly and legibly. If you make an error, you may save time by crossing it out rather than trying to erase it. Erased or crossed-out work will not be graded. No credit will be given for any work shown on the green insert.

- Show all your work. Indicate clearly the methods you use because you will be graded on the correctness of your methods as well as the accuracy of your final answers. Correct answers without supporting work may not receive credit.

STATISTICS

SECTION II

Part A

Questions 1-5

Spend about 65 minutes on this part of the exam.

Percent of Section II grade—75

Show all your work. Indicate clearly the methods you use, because you will be graded on the correctness of your method as well as on the accuracy of your results and explanation.

1. A state park has campsites available for pitching tents. Visitors are allowed to pitch tents only at the designated campsites. In addition to campsites, the park also has some log cabins for rent. The demand for cabins and campsites changes from month to month. The renting records for year 2001 are as follows:

Month	Number of cabins rented	Number of campsites rented
Jan	21	3
Feb	16	5
Mar	12	8
Apr	10	15
May	8	18
Jun	10	25
Jul	12	28
Aug	10	30
Sep	10	25
Oct	24	15
Nov	22	8
Dec	10	4

(a) Display the data graphically to compare the pattern of cabin rentals with that of campsite rentals.

(b) Examine your graphical display. Write a few sentences describing the rental history of cabins and campsites.

GO ON TO THE NEXT PAGE

2. The lifetimes of zip drives marketed by ZipZap, Inc. are normally distributed, with a mean lifetime of 18 months and a standard deviation of 3 months. The company plans to offer a new warranty guaranteeing the replacement of failed zip drives during the warranty period. The replacement of failed drives is costly, however, and the company can afford to replace only up to 2 percent of its drives. How many months of warranty should the company offer with these zip drives? Round your answer to the nearest month.

GO ON TO THE NEXT PAGE

3. A company executive is interested in purchasing printers for his division. He contacts a wholesaler, who shows him two printers comparable in quality and price made by two different manufacturers. Both printers are suitable for the kind of printing generally done in his division. To help him decide between these two printers, the wholesaler offers to loan him a printer of each kind for one day. Since the printers' printing time per page depends on the type of document printed, the executive selects 25 different documents of varying size and complexity for printing. Help this executive design an experiment to compare the mean printing times of the two printers.

GO ON TO THE NEXT PAGE

4. A nutritionist wants to confirm her suspicion that women tend to prefer chocolate for dessert more often than men. She decides that it will be convenient to collect data on customers of a large and popular restaurant owned by her family. The restaurant has a practice of showing the daily selection of desserts on a tray to the customers. For 500 customers selected randomly over a one week period, the nutritionist notes the gender of the customer and the choice of dessert. The data is summarized in the table below.

	Gender	
	Male	Female
Dessert with chocolate	140	150
Dessert without chocolate	160	50

(a) Identify the target and sampled populations in this experiment. Are they the same or different? Discuss how their sameness or difference will affect the conclusions drawn from this experiment.

GO ON TO THE NEXT PAGE

(b) The nutritionist is considering using a *chi-square* test of independence to analyze this data. Why is this test inappropriate to justify her suspicions?

(c) Which test would be more appropriate to gather evidence to support her suspicions? Can the test you named be done using this data? Justify your answer.

GO ON TO THE NEXT PAGE

5. A large security-system management company with clients in Los Angeles and San Francisco installs and monitors security systems in houses and on business premises. The system's alarm sounds at the central monitoring location if there is any security break-in, smoke, or fire at any of the client premises. Tests have indicated that in approximately 3 percent of incidences the alarms are false, and in approximately 0.5 percent of incidences, the system fails to sound an alarm. The records indicate that about 0.1 percent of the company's clients have true break-in/fire/smoke incidents.

(a) Suppose a client is selected at random. What is the probability that the alarm will sound at this client's premises?

(b) Suppose the alarm is sounded at a client's premises. What is the probability that there was no break-in/smoke/or fire incident?

GO ON TO THE NEXT PAGE

STATISTICS

SECTION II

Part B

Question 6

Spend about 25 minutes on this part of the exam.

Percent of Section II grade—25

6. A physician who has delivered babies for over 20 years claims that babies tend to weigh more at birth than their next older sibling. In other words, a parent's second child tends to have a higher birthweight than the first child, the third child tends to have higher birthweight than the second child, and so on. To verify the doctor's statement, her office assistant gets a random sample of mothers with at least two children from the hospital records, and records the birthweights of the first two children. The birthweights for the children of 19 mothers are given in the table below.

Mother	Birth weight of first child (in pounds)	Birth weight of second child (in pounds)
1	5.13	6.43
2	5.25	5.83
3	6.71	7.78
4	4.71	5.27
5	3.77	4.45
6	5.81	6.61
7	8.29	9.51
8	6.36	7.01
9	6.08	8.49
10	4.91	5.62
11	3.19	4.04
12	5.64	6.10
13	6.37	7.25
14	5.90	6.58
15	4.73	5.28
16	5.60	7.49
17	4.68	5.43
18	7.79	8.76
19	4.18	4.85

(a) Does this data provide any evidence to support the physician's theory? Justify your
answer using statistical evidence.

GO ON TO THE NEXT PAGE

(b) The scatterplot of birthweights of first-born children and second-born children is given below.

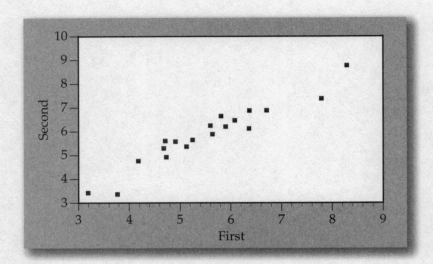

Write a few sentences describing the relation between the birthweights of first-born children and the birthweights of second-born children.

(c) The regression analysis of the data resulted in the following outcome.

```
Predictor        Coef        StDev          T          P
Constant       0.5626      0.3966        1.42      0.174
first          0.95939     0.06996      13.71      0.000

S = 0.3772        R-Sq = 91.7%      R-Sq(adj) = 91.2%
```

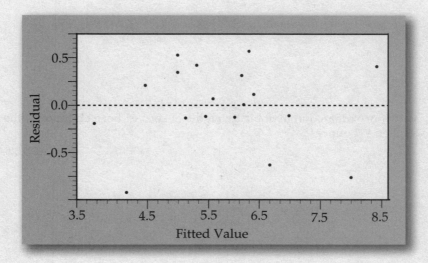

Is there a significant relation between the birthweights of first-born children and the birthweights of second-born children? Justify your answer using statistical evidence.

GO ON TO THE NEXT PAGE

(d) Suppose the doctor is getting ready to deliver the second child of a mother whose first child weighed 7.2 ounces. Predict the birthweight of this second child.

(e) What is an approximate range of birthweights of second-born children, if the first-born child weighed 7.2 ounces?

END OF EXAMINATION

9

ANSWERS AND EXPLANATIONS TO PRACTICE TEST 1

Multiple Choice

1. **Answer: E**

    An "outlier" is an observation that is significantly different from the other observations in the data set. It is not necessarily just the largest or the smallest observation, since it is possible to have more than one outlier in a given data set.

2. **Answer: E**

    Look closely at the chart. For example, the point (160, 0.4) indicates that on 40 percent of the days, up to 160 shots were given. To find the number of shots needed to meet the demand on

95 percent of the days, we need to find the 95th percentile. Draw a horizontal line from the cumulative probability of 0.95 to the curve. From the point at which the line meets the curve, draw a vertical line down to the X-axis, and then read the number of flu shots given there. It should be approximately 200.

3. **Answer: D**
The total amount paid in salaries to the office assistants is 128(28,500) + 32(22,500) = $95,808,000. This total amount is paid to 128 + 32 = 160 office assistants. The mean salary paid

$$\text{to office assistants} = \frac{\text{total}}{\text{number of assistants}} = \frac{95,808,000}{160} = \$27,300.$$

4. **Answer: B**
IQR, first quartile, and standard deviation are not measures of central tendency. Median and mean are measures of central tendency. Mean is affected by extreme observations—large observations tend to make the mean higher. Since this distribution is skewed, the median should be used to describe the center of the distribution.

5. **Answer: C**
It is given that P(car will skid | it rains) = 0.75 and P(it will rain) = 0.20.
Use the multiplication rule:
P(it will rain <u>and</u> the car will skid on the bridge) = P(car will skid | it rains) P(it will rain)

$$= 0.75(0.20)$$
$$= 0.15$$

6. **Answer: B**
This is a binomial situation. With each plant there are two possibilities: (i) the plant will survive and there will be no need to replace it or (ii) the plant will not survive and will need to be replaced. The probability that the plant will survive is equal to 0.95. A total of n = 200 plants were purchased. So the expected number of plants that will need to be replaced = np = 200 (0.05) = 10.

7. **Answer: D**
It is given that the random variable X = number of calories per bar. Now we need to find $P(\text{Number of calories} > 225)$.

$$P(X > 225) = P\left(Z > \frac{225 - 210}{10}\right) = P(Z < 1.5) = 1 - 0.9332 = 0.668$$

[Hint: On the TI 83, use the normalcdf function from the DISTR menu]

8. **Answer: E**
Note that the weight of a packed box = weight of books + weight of box + weight of packing material used.
It is given that $\sigma_{\text{books}} = 2$, $\sigma_{\text{box}} = 0.15$, and $\sigma_{\text{packing material}} = 0.25$. So, the standard deviation of the weights of the packed boxes is

$$\sigma_{\text{packed boxes}} = \sqrt{\sigma^2_{\text{books}} + \sigma^2_{\text{box}} + \sigma^2_{\text{packing material}}} = \sqrt{2^2 + 0.15^2 + 0.25^2} = 2.021$$

9. **Answer: B**

Since this is a 95 percent confidence interval, we can only be 95 percent confident that the population mean is within the confidence interval computed using the sample mean.

10. **Answer: A**

The hypotheses tested here are

H_0: The true mean lead level is within the allowed limit

H_a: The true mean lead level exceeds the allowed limit

The type I error is the error of rejecting the null hypothesis when the null hypothesis is true. In this case, the type I error would be concluding that the mean lead levels are in excess of the allowed limit—and therefore, that the park should be closed—when in fact the levels are within the allowed limit.

11. **Answer: D**

The scatterplot shows three different groups. The group of students on the far left of the scatterplot scored lowest on the midterm, in a range of 30-50, but then scored in a range of 65-85 on the final, showing considerable improvement. The middle group scored between 55-80 on the midterm and then between 60-85 on the final, showing very little improvement. The third group, the one on the far right of the scatterplot, scored above 85 on the midterm and then above 85 on the final, showing almost no improvement.

12. **Answer: B**

The station with the lowest variation is the one with the most consistent gas prices. Variation is measured by the spread of prices. Of the four gas stations, Station 2 shows the least variation in gas prices.

13. **Answer: C**

The right-tailed test is used. So there is a 5 percent area in the rejection region in the right tail of the sampling distribution. If we construct a 90 percent confidence interval, then the upper confidence limit will match with the critical value. If the test of hypothesis is rejected at a 5 percent level of significance, then the test statistic fell in the rejection region. In other words, the hypothesized value of mean did not belong to the 90 percent confidence interval.

14. **Answer: A**

The sample of 40 jars is large enough for us to apply the Central Limit Theorem and get an approximately normal distribution of the sample mean, with $\mu_{\bar{x}} = 4$ ounces and

$$\sigma_{\bar{x}} = \frac{\sigma}{\sqrt{n}} = \frac{0.25}{\sqrt{40}} = 0.0395. \text{ So, } P(\bar{X} < 3.9) = P\left(Z < \frac{3.9 - 4.0}{0.0395}\right) = P(Z < -2.53) = 0.0057$$

[Hint: On the TI-83, use the normalcdf function from the DISTR menu]

15. **Answer: A**

Find the first and third quartiles of the distribution, since the middle 50 percent of the data falls between the first and the third quartile.

$$P(X < Q_1) = 0.25 \implies Q_1 = \mu - Z_{0.25}\sigma = 3,250 - 0.67(320) = 3,035$$
$$P(X < Q_3) = 0.75 \implies Q_3 = \mu - Z_{0.25}\sigma = 3,250 + 0.67(320) = 3,464$$

16. **Answer: A**

The 35th percentile is the value of x—say, (x_0)—such that 35 percent of the x-values are smaller than x_0, or such that 35 percent of the distribution falls below x_0.

17. **Answer: D**

The z-score $= \dfrac{X - \mu}{\sigma}$. A negative z-score indicates that the x-value is below the average. The value of the score represents the difference between the x-value and the mean in terms of the number of standard deviations.

18. **Answer: C**

Sampling without replacement in a finite population does not result in a binomial distribution, since the probability of success on each successive trial changes. So we can rule out answers A, B, and D. In binomial distribution, each trial has only two possible outcomes. Answer E indicates 3 possible outcomes (a spade, a heart, and a non-spade and non-heart card). So we can rule out answer E. In answer C, sampling is carried out with replacement, keeping the probability of success constant on each card drawn. Also, there are two possible outcomes for each card drawn: spade or non-spade.

19. **Answer: D**

The probability that at least 1 child will develop a cavity is equal to the probability that 1, 2, 3, 4, or 5 children will develop cavities. Since X, the number of children developing cavities in a sample of 5 children, takes values 0, 1, 2, 3, 4, 5, and the sum of their probabilities is equal to 1, then the probability that 1, 2, 3, 4, or 5 children will develop cavities is equal to 1 minus the probability that no child develops cavities.

20. **Answer: A**

It is given that $P(\text{Ted enrolls in English class}) = P(E) = \dfrac{1}{3}$

It is also given that

$P(\text{Ted enrolls in Math class} \mid \text{he does not enroll in English class}) = P(M \mid E) = \dfrac{1}{5}$

So using the multiplication rule we get

$P(\text{Ted enrolls in English \underline{and} Math class}) = P(E \cap M) = P(M \mid E)P(E) = \left(\dfrac{1}{5}\right)\left(\dfrac{1}{3}\right) = \dfrac{1}{15}$

21. **Answer: D**

$P(\text{Both dice roll 6}) = \dfrac{1}{36}$. So there is a 1 out of 36 chance that the player will win \$20, and a $\dfrac{35}{36}$ chance that the player will win nothing. So, the expected amount won by the player is $20\left(\dfrac{1}{36}\right) = \$0.56$. But note that it costs the player \$2.00 to play the game. Therefore, the expected gain or loss for the game is $0.56 - 2.00 = -1.44$. In other words, on average the player will lose \$1.44.

22. **Answer: B**

The Central Limit Theorem states that for a large sample, the sampling distribution of the sample mean will be approximately normally distributed.

23. **Answer: A**

If we're trying to support the claim that more than 60 percent of mallgoers visit the store, we need to make this statement the alternative hypothesis. The null hypothesis should be that the proportion of visitors to the store is equal to 0.60.

24. **Answer: D**

The population variance is unknown, and the lifetimes are normally distributed. Therefore, we should use a t-interval to estimate the mean lifetime. With a sample of 16 bulbs, we get 15 degrees of freedom. To construct a 95 percent confidence interval, use $\alpha = 0.05$. Therefore, using a t-table, find $t_{\alpha/2}(\upsilon) = t_{0.025}(15) = 2.1$. The confidence interval for the mean lifetime is

$$\bar{x} \pm t_{\alpha/2}(\upsilon)\frac{s}{\sqrt{n}} = 1,025 \pm 2.13\frac{130}{\sqrt{16}}$$

25. **Answer: B**

All county residents will be affected by the gasoline tax increase, regardless of whether they have school-aged children or where their children go to school.

26. **Answer: E**

There are three factors involved in this experiment, each with a different number of levels.
    Factor 1: Temperature setting. This has 4 levels.
    Factor 2: Type of pan. This has 2 levels.
    Factor 3: Type of oven. This has 3 levels.
So the total number of treatment combinations in this experiment is 4(2)(3) = 24.

All 24 combinations are listed on the next page. Each triplet indicates temperature setting, type of pan, and type of oven.

(300, Glass, Gas)	(350, Glass, Gas)
(300, Glass, Electric)	(350, Glass, Electric)
(300, Glass, Microwave)	(350, Glass, Microwave)
(300, Metal, Gas)	(350, Metal, Gas)
(300, Metal, Electric)	(350, Metal, Electric)
(300, Metal, Microwave)	(350, Metal, Microwave)
(325, Glass, Gas)	(375, Glass, Gas)
(325, Glass, Electric)	(375, Glass, Electric)
(325, Glass, Microwave)	(375, Glass, Microwave)
(325, Metal, Gas)	(375, Metal, Gas)
(325, Metal, Electric)	(375, Metal, Electric)
(325, Metal, Microwave)	(375, Metal, Microwave)

27. **Answer: A**

The distribution with a mean of 12 will be centered around 12. So rule out Distributions III and IV, which have higher means. Also rule out Distribution V, which has a lower mean. Distributions I and II are centered around 12. A fairly symmetric and mound-shaped distribution with mean 12 and standard deviation 2 should have an approximate spread between 6 and 18 (3 standard deviations around mean, $12 - 3(2) = 6$ and $12 + 3(2) = 18$). Distribution II has a higher spread, so rule it out. Distribution I is centered around 12 and has an approximate spread between 6 and 18.

28. **Answer: E**

In the given equation, Y-intercept = 15.9 and slope = -0.983. Note that the car prices are recorded in $1,000. The slope is negative, which means the price goes down as the age increases. The amount of change in price for every unit change in age is equal to 0.983 (in $1,000), i.e., $983. So for every year the car gets older, the selling price goes down by approximately $983.

29. **Answer: C**

For any discrete probability distribution to be valid, one of the two conditions that need to be satisfied is $\sum_{\text{all possible values of X}} P(X_i) = 1$

30. **Answer: C**

The number of credits a student gets for completing any course is a constant. It does not differ from student to student.

31. **Answer: E**

For each sampled tree, one of two possible outcomes will be noted: (i) the tree suffered more than 50 percent damage, or (ii) the tree suffered at most 50 percent damage.

32. **Answer: B**

It would be impossible to catch all the red snappers in the Gulf of Mexico and measure their mercury levels.

33. **Answer: E**

The margin of error = $\dfrac{\text{width}}{2} = \dfrac{0.08}{2} = 0.04$.

For a 90 percent confidence interval, we need to use $\alpha = 0.05$ and find

$$Z_{\alpha/2} = Z_{0.10/2} = Z_{0.05} = 1.645$$

Since no prior estimate for p is available, we should use $p = \dfrac{1}{2}$. Then,

$$n \geq \left(\dfrac{1.645}{0.04}\right)^2 \left(\dfrac{1}{2}\right)\left(\dfrac{1}{2}\right) = 422.82$$

At least 423 students should be sampled.

[Hint: On the TI-83, use the invNorm function from the DISTR menu to find $Z_{\alpha/2}$]

34. **Answer: D**

The range and the standard deviation remain unaffected by the constant increment in all the measurements, but the mean will increase by 50 cents.

35. **Answer: C**

The total number of females in the sample = 120.
The total number of students with medium HLT score = 90.
The total number of students in the sample = 200.
The expected number of females with medium HLT score

$$= \dfrac{(\text{Number of female students})(\text{Number of students with medium HLT score})}{\text{The total number of students}}$$

$$= \dfrac{(120)(90)}{200}$$

$$= 54$$

36. **Answer: A**

The entire interval for $(p_M - p_F)$ falls below 0. This indicates that $(p_M - p_F) < 0$, which means that it is likely that $p_M < p_F$.

37. **Answer: D**

Equality of variances is not necessary for a t-test to be valid. One of the conditions of a t-test is that the underlying populations must be normally distributed.

38. **Answer: B**

The hypotheses used in this experiment are

H_0: The subject is guessing, i.e., $p = 0.50$

H_a: The subject is not guessing, i.e., $p > 0.50$

where p = the proportion of correct answers. Using $\alpha = 0.05$, the null hypothesis will be rejected if

$$TS = \frac{\hat{p} - p_0}{\sqrt{\dfrac{p_0(1 - p_0)}{n}}} Z_\delta$$

i.e., if $TS = \dfrac{\hat{p} - 0.50}{\sqrt{\dfrac{0.50(1 - 0.50)}{100}}} > 1.645$

i.e., if $\hat{p} > 0.50 + 1.645\sqrt{\dfrac{0.50(1 - 0.50)}{100}} = 0.5823$

The subject needs to identify at least 58.23 percent correctly. Since 100 cards are dealt, the subject needs to identify at least 59 cards correctly.

[Hint: On the TI-83, use the invNorm function from the DISTR menu to find Z_α]

39. **Answer: B**

Both engine oils, with the additive and without the additive, are tested on each car. Therefore, each car is acting as a block, or in other words, each car is matched with itself.

40. **Answer: A**

The chi-square test can only be used if the expected counts are at least 5.

Free Response

1. **(a)** You should first construct a bar or line graph identifying the two groups clearly. Each graph should include scales, labels, axis titles, and legends.

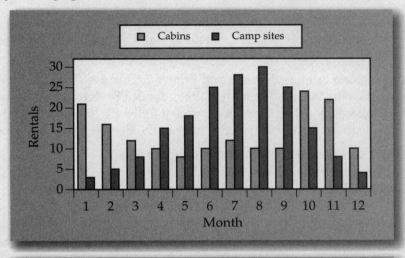

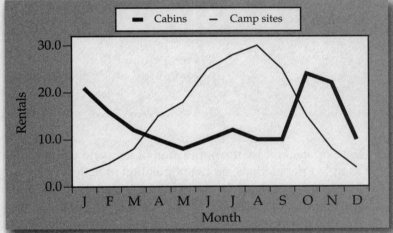

(b) In general, more campsites are rented during the summer months, with rentals peaking in August. The cabin rentals are higher during the fall and winter months, except in December. Both cabin and campsite rentals are down in December.

2. Let random variable X = the lifetime of zip drives.

In this case, X is normally distributed, with a mean of 18 months and a standard deviation of 3 months.

We need to find the warranty period W, such that only 2 percent of the zip drives have a lifetime below W—in other words, to find W such that $P(X < W) = 0.02$, since

$$\Rightarrow P\left(Z \; \frac{W-18}{3}\right) = 0.02$$

From the standard normal distribution we get $Z_{0.02} = 2.054$. Therefore,

$$\frac{W - 18}{3} = -2.054$$

$$W = 18 - 3(3.054) = 11.838 \approx 12 \text{ months}$$

The company should consider offering a 12-month warranty on its zip drives.
[Hint: On the TI-83, use the invNorm function from the DISTR menu]

3. Let's label the two printers Printer 1 and Printer 2. Then we should list the 25 selected documents in a random order. The order can be determined using a random number table. Then for each document in the list, toss a coin, and use the following rule to decide in which order to print the document on the two printers.

Heads: Print on Printer 1 first and then on Printer 2.
Tails: Print on Printer 2 first and then on Printer 1.
      For each document, measure the printing time, and compare.

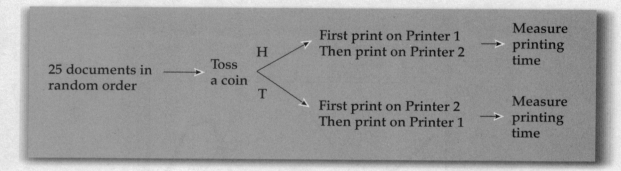

4. (a)   The target populations are the population of men and the population of women. The sampled populations are the population of male and female customers at this restaurant who order desserts and the population of female customers at this restaurant who order desserts. Obviously, the sampled populations are different from the target populations. Since the nutritionist has taken a sample of dessert-ordering customers at this restaurant only, the conclusion will be applicable only to the customers of this restaurant who order desserts, not to all men and women in general.

(b)   The nutritionist is interested in testing a one-sided alternative—specifically, that the proportion of women preferring chocolate is higher than the proportion of men preferring chocolate. But the chi-square test of independence will only tell the nutritionist whether the preference for chocolate is gender-dependent. This test is incapable of making the required determination, because it is not a one-sided test.

(c)   In order to find evidence to support her theory, the nutritionist needs to do a large sample z-test for difference of proportions with a one-sided alternative. She cannot do a z-test on this data, since the samples of men and women were not drawn independently of each other.

5. Let's define "fire" as an incident of fire, security break-in, or smoke.

It is given that $P(\text{false alarm}) = P(\text{alarm} \mid \text{no fire}) = 0.03$,

$P(\text{no alarm} \mid \text{fire}) = 0.005$, and $P(\text{fire}) = 0.001$.

$P(\text{alarm} \mid \text{fire}) = 1 - 0.005 = 0.995$.

(a) $P(\text{alarm}) = P(\text{alarm} \mid \text{fire})P(\text{fire}) + P(\text{alarm} \mid \text{no fire})P(\text{no fire})$

$\qquad = 0.995\,(0.001) + 0.03\,(0.999)$

$\qquad = 0.030965 \approx 0.031$

(b) $P(\text{no fire} \mid \text{alarm}) = \dfrac{P(\text{alarm} \mid \text{no fire})P(\text{no fire})}{P(\text{alarm})} = \dfrac{0.03(0.999)}{0.031} = 0.967$

Or

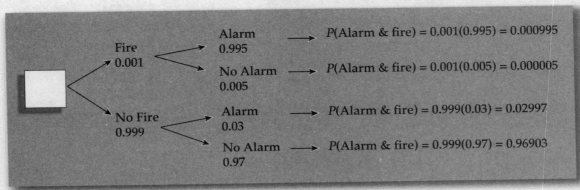

Using this tree diagram we get

(a) $P(\text{alarm}) = 0.000995 + 0.02997 = 0.030965 \approx 0.031$

(b) $P(\text{no fire} \mid \text{alarm}) = \dfrac{0.0299}{0.03} = 0.967$

6. **(a)** Let μ_1 = The mean birthweight of the first child

$\qquad \mu_2$ = The mean birthweight of the second child

We are interested in

$\qquad \mu_d = (\mu_1 - \mu_2) = 0$ The mean difference in birthweights of first and second children.

We want to test

$\qquad H_a : \mu_d = 0$ (there is no difference in the mean birthweights of first and second children)

$\qquad H_a : \mu_d < 0$ (the mean birthweight of the second child is higher than the mean birthweight of the first child)

The data is collected on siblings, so it is paired data. Let d_i = (weight of first child – weight of second child) in the ith pair. Then plot all the differences. Use any one of the following graphs or charts to argue for the normality of the population of differences in birthweights of first and second children.

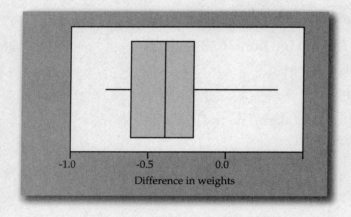

Difference in weights

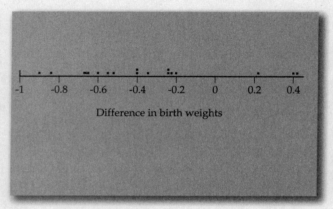

Difference in birth weights

Character Stem-and-Leaf Display
Stem-and-leaf of diff-wt
N = 19
Leaf Unit = 0.10

```
 2   -0 98
 5   -0 666
 8   -0 554
(6)  -0 333222
 5   -0 11
 3    0
 3    0 2
 2    0 44
```

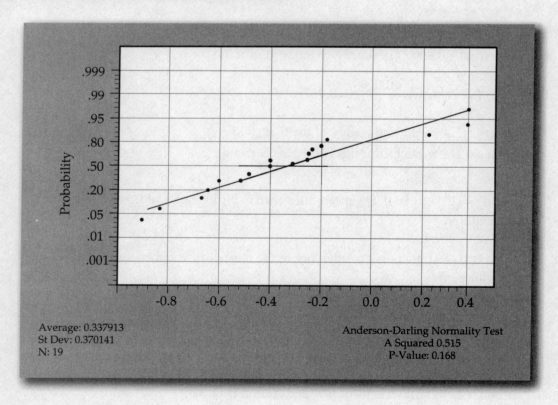

Average: 0.337913
St Dev: 0.370141
N: 19

Anderson-Darling Normality Test
A Squared 0.515
P-Value: 0.168

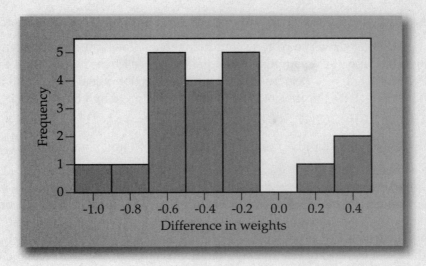

The pairs of siblings were selected at random, and from the above plots it is reasonable to assume the normality of the population of differences in weights. The variance of the population of differences is unknown, so we should use the paired t-test.

With n = 19 observations, we get 18 degrees of freedom. Let's use a 5 percent level of significance. The rejection rule will be "reject null hypothesis if p-value < α = 0.05."

(If you chose to use the rejection-region approach, then the rule would be "reject null hypothesis if the $TS < -t_\alpha(\upsilon) = -t_{0.05}(18) = -1.734$.")

$$\bar{d} = -0.3379, \text{ and } S_d = 0.3701$$

$$TS = \frac{\bar{d} - 0}{S_d / \sqrt{n}} = \frac{-0.3379 - 0}{0.3701 / \sqrt{19}} = -3.98$$

$$p\text{-value} = P\big(t(18) < -3.598\big) < 0.001$$

With p-value < 0.001 < 0.05 (or since $TS = -3.98$ falls in the rejection region), we can reject the null hypothesis and accept the alternative hypothesis. At a 5 percent level of significance, we should conclude that this data provides significant evidence supporting the physician's statement that, on average, the second child tends to weigh more than the first one at birth.

[Hint: On the TI-83, use the t-test function from the STAT→TESTS menu using the differences in birthweights. You could also use the calculator's graphing capability to make your graphs. Don't forget to copy the graphs from the calculator screen to your exam paper.]

(b) There appears to be a strong positive linear relation between the birthweights of first and second children.

(c) Let β_1 = the slope of the regression line for the weight of the second child as a function of the weight of the first child.

To test $H_0: \beta_1 = 0$ versus $H_a: \beta_1 \neq 0$, let's use a 5 percent level of significance.

The residual plot shows no patterns, indicating that a line is an appropriate model for this data. Also, the assumption of constant variance is reasonable. Use a t-test for slope, with $(19 - 2) = 17$ degrees of freedom. The rejection rule is "reject null hypothesis if p-value < 0.05" (or if using p-value approach, "reject null hypothesis if

$$TS > t_{\alpha/2}(\upsilon) = t_{0.025}(17) = 2.110 \text{ or } TS < t_{\alpha/2}(\upsilon) = -t_{0.025}(17) = 2.110.")$$

The regression output provided shows that $TS = 13.71$ and p-value < 0.001.

Since p-value $< 0.001 < 0.05$ (or the TS falls in the rejection region, or $TS > 2.110$) we should reject the null hypothesis and accept the alternative hypothesis. At a 5 percent level of significance, we can conclude that there is sufficient evidence indicating that the slope of the regression between the birthweights of first and second children is not zero. In other words, there is sufficient evidence to indicate that there is a significant relation between the weights of first and second children.

[Hint: On the TI-83, use the LinRegTTest function from the STAT → TESTS menu]

(d) From the regression output, we can write the equation of the line of best fit as follows:
Weight of a second child = 0.5626 + 0.95939 (weight of a first child)
Use this equation to predict the weight of a second child.
Weight of a second child = 0.5626 + 0.95939 (7.2) = 7.47 ounces.
The second child is expected to weigh about 7.47 ounces.

(e) From the regression output, we get an estimated standard deviation of $S = 0.3772$. If the first child weighed 7.2 ounces, then most of the second children should weigh in the range $7.47 \pm 3(0.3772)$, i.e., in the range (6.34, 8.60) ounces.

10

THE PRINCETON REVIEW
AP STATISTICS
PRACTICE TEST 2

STATISTICS

Three hours are allotted for this examination: 1 hour and 30 minutes for Section I, which consists of multiple-choice questions, and 1 hour and 30 minutes for Section II, which consists of longer problems. In determining your grade, the two sections are given equal weight. Section I is printed in this examination booklet; Section II is in a separate booklet.

SECTION I

Time—1 hour and 30 minutes

Number of questions—40

Percent of total grade—50

Section I of this examination contains 40 multiple-choice questions. Please be careful to fill in only the ovals that are preceded by numbers 1 through 40 on your answer sheet.

General Instructions

DO NOT OPEN THIS BOOKLET UNTIL YOU ARE INSTRUCTED TO DO SO.

INDICATE ALL YOUR ANSWERS TO QUESTIONS IN SECTION I ON THE SEPARATE ANSWER SHEET ENCLOSED. No credit will be given for anything written in this examination booklet, but you may use the booklet for notes or scratchwork. After you have decided which of the suggested answers is best, COMPLETELY fill in the corresponding oval on the answer sheet. Give only one answer to each question. If you change an answer, be sure that the previous mark is erased completely.

Example: Sample Answer

What is the median of the set of numbers 4, 5, 6, and 7?   Ⓐ ● Ⓒ Ⓓ Ⓔ

   (A) 5
   (B) 5.5
   (C) 6
   (D) 6.6
   (E) 7

Many candidates wonder whether or not to guess the answers to questions about which they are not certain. In this section of the examination, as a correction for haphazard guessing, one-fourth of the number of questions you answer incorrectly will be subtracted from the number of questions you answer correctly. It is improbable, therefore, that mere guessing will improve your score significantly; it may even lower your score, and it does take time. If, however, you are not sure of the best answer but have some knowledge of the questions and are able to eliminate one or more answer choices as wrong, your chance of getting the right answer is improved, and it may be to your advantage to answer such a question.

Use your time effectively, working as rapidly as you can without losing accuracy. Do not spend too much time on questions that are too difficult. Go on to other questions and come back to the difficult ones if you have time. It is not expected that everyone will be able to answer all the multiple-choice questions.

Formulas begin on page 386.

Tables begin on page 389.

STATISTICS

SECTION I

Time—1 hour and 30 minutes

Number of questions—40

Percent of total grade—50

<u>Directions</u>: Solve each of the following problems, using the available space for scratchwork. Decide which is the best of the choices given and fill in the corresponding oval on the answer sheet. No credit will be given for anything written in the test book. Do not spend too much time on any one problem.

1. Fifty oranges of one variety were selected at random and weighed. A 95 percent confidence interval computed from the sample weights to estimate the mean weight of these oranges is (7.58, 8.72) ounces. Which of the following statement is true with respect to the confidence level used?

    (A) In repeated samplings of the same size, 95 percent of the intervals constructed will contain the true mean weight of the oranges.

    (B) In repeated samplings of the same size, 95 percent of the intervals constructed will contain the sampled mean weight of the oranges.

    (C) Ninety-five percent of the oranges in this sample weigh between 7.58 and 8.72 ounces.

    (D) Ninety-five percent of the oranges of this variety weigh between 7.58 and 8.72 ounces.

    (E) There is a 95 percent chance that the mean weight of another sample of 50 oranges from this variety will be between 7.58 and 8.72 ounces.

---

2. In the jury pool available for this week, 30 percent of potential jurors are women. If a jury of 12 is to be selected at random, what is the expected number of men in the group?

    (A) $12(0.30)$

    (B) $12(0.50)$

    (C) $12(0.70)$

    (D) $12(0.30)(0.70)$

    (E) $\sqrt{12(0.30)(0.70)}$

GO ON TO THE NEXT PAGE

3. The mean daily demand for bread at a popular bakery is 2,500 loaves, with a standard deviation of 225 loaves. Every morning the bakery bakes 3,000 loaves. What is the probability that today they will run out of bread?

(A) 0.8333

(B) 0.1667

(C) 0.9869

(D) 0.013

(E) 0.0900

4. A medicine is known to produce side effects in 1 in 5 patients taking it. Suppose a doctor prescribes the medicine to 4 unrelated patients. What is the probability that none of the patients will develop side effects?

(A) 0.8000

(B) 0.4096

(C) 0.2500

(D) 0.2000

(E) 0.0016

GO ON TO THE NEXT PAGE

5. An automobile service station performs only oil changes and tire replacements. Eighty percent of its customers request an oil change. Of those who request an oil change, only 20 percent request a tire replacement. What is the probability that the next customer will request both an oil change and a tire replacement?

(A) 0.16

(B) 0.20

(C) 0.25

(D) 0.80

(E) 0.85

6. The following boxplot summarizes the prices of books at a bookstore.

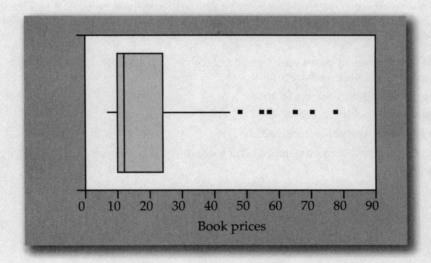

Book prices

Which of the following is true about the prices of books at this store?

(A) This store mostly carries high-priced books.

(B) This store mostly carries low-priced books.

(C) This store carries about the same number of books at different prices in the entire price range.

(D) The mean price of books at this store is the same as the median price of books.

(E) The mean price of books at this store is lower than the median price of books.

GO ON TO THE NEXT PAGE

7. Random variable X is normally distributed, with a mean of 25 and a standard deviation of 4. Which of the following is closest to the inter-quartile range for this distribution?

   (A) $25.00 - 22.30 = 2.70$
   (B) $27.70 - 22.30 = 5.40$
   (C) $27.70/22.30 = 1.24$
   (D) $2.00(4.00) = 8.00$
   (E) $37.00 - 13.00 = 24.00$

8. An experiment was designed to test the effects of 3 different types of paint on the durability of wooden toys. Since boys and girls tend to play differently with toys, a randomly selected group of children was divided into 2 groups by gender. Which of the following statements about this experiment is true?

   (A) There are 3 types of paint and 2 gender groups, giving a total of 6 treatment combinations in this experiment.
   (B) Type of paint is a blocking factor.
   (C) Gender is a blocking factor.
   (D) This is a completely randomized design.
   (E) This is a matched-pairs design in which one boy and one girl are matched by age to form a pair.

GO ON TO THE NEXT PAGE

9. The following graph summarizes data collected on annual rainfall in two cities for the past 150 years.

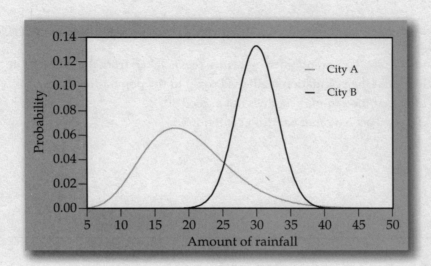

Which of the following conclusions can be made from this graph?

(A) The cities have different mean annual rainfalls, but the range of their annual rainfalls is approximately the same.

(B) On average, City B gets more rain than City A, but has a smaller range of annual rainfall.

(C) On average, City B gets more rain than City A, but has a larger range of annual rainfall.

(D) On average, City A gets more rain than City B, but has a smaller range of annual rainfall.

(E) On average, City A gets more rain than City B, but has a larger range of annual rainfall.

GO ON TO THE NEXT PAGE

10. According to the Central Limit Theorem, regardless of the population distribution, the sample mean $\overline{X}$ is approximately normally distributed with $\mu_{\overline{X}} = \mu_X$ and $\sigma_{\overline{X}} = \frac{\sigma_X}{\sqrt{n}}$,

(A) provided that a large number of random samples of the same size are selected from the population.
(B) provided that a large random sample of size n is taken from the population.
(C) provided that the population median is equal to the population mean.
(D) provided that the sample size does not exceed 30.
(E) It is always true. No other condition is required.

11. Which of the following is a discrete random variable?

(A) The number of times a student guesses the answers to questions on a certain test.
(B) The amount of gasoline purchased by a customer.
(C) The amount of mercury found in fish caught in the Gulf of Mexico.
(D) The height of water-oak trees.
(E) The time elapsed until the first field goal at home football games.

GO ON TO THE NEXT PAGE

12. A random sample of 300 shoppers was selected to estimate the proportion of customers satisfied with the floor displays of merchandise throughout the store. What is the maximum error in estimation if a 90 percent confidence interval is to be constructed?

(A) 0.0033

(B) 0.0475

(C) 0.0566

(D) 0.0949

(E) 0.1132

---

13. Which of the following statements correctly describes the relation between a t-distribution and a standard normal distribution?

(A) The standard normal distribution is centered at 0, while the t-distribution is centered at $(n - 1)$.

(B) As the sample size increases, the difference between the t-distribution and the standard normal distribution increases.

(C) The standard normal is just another name for the t-distribution.

(D) The standard normal distribution has a larger variance than the t-distribution.

(E) The t-distribution has a larger variance than the standard normal distribution.

GO ON TO THE NEXT PAGE

14. Suppose that two independent samples of sizes 7 and 9 are taken in order to test
    $H_0 : \mu_1 = \mu_2$ versus $H_a : \mu_1 \neq \mu_2$. Suppose also that the assumption of $\sigma_1^2 = \sigma_2^2$ is reasonable regarding unknown population variances. Which of the following is the best approach to use in this situation in testing the hypotheses?

    (A) Use a paired difference t-test.
    (B) Compute pooled estimates of common variance using sample variances.
    (C) Use a large-samples z-test for difference in population means.
    (D) Use a *chi-square* test for proportions.

    (E) Estimate the correlation between μ_1 and μ_2.

---

15. Scores on the take-home part of a test are approximately normally distributed, with a mean of 40 and a standard deviation of 3. Scores on the in-class part of the same test are also approximately normally distributed, with a mean of 34 and a standard deviation of 6. The final score on the test is the sum of the score on the take-home part plus the score on the in-class part. What is the mean and standard deviation of the final test scores?

    (A) Mean 74 and standard deviation 4.50
    (B) Mean 37 and standard deviation 6.71
    (C) Mean 37 and standard deviation 4.50
    (D) Mean 74 and standard deviation 6.71
    (E) Mean 74 and standard deviation 3.00

GO ON TO THE NEXT PAGE

16. On a modified boxplot, an observation is classified as an outlier if

(A) it is smaller than $\overline{X} - 3S$ or larger than $\overline{X} + 3S$.

(B) it is larger than $\overline{X} - 3S$ and smaller than $\overline{X} + 3S$.

(C) it is smaller than Q_1 or larger than Q_3.

(D) it is smaller than $Q_1 - 1.5IQR$ or larger than $Q_3 + 1.5IQR$.

(E) it is larger than $Q_1 - 1.5IQR$ and smaller than $Q_3 + 1.5IQR$.

---

17. The following cumulative graph gives the electricity demand of a certain town.

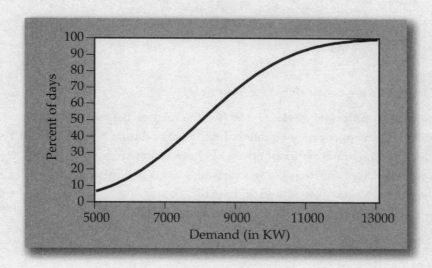

The power plant that provides electricity to this town is capable of generating 12,000 KW daily. On what percent of days will the power plant not be able to meet the demand for electricity?

(A) About 3 percent
(B) About 60 percent
(C) About 80 percent
(D) About 92 percent
(E) About 97 percent

GO ON TO THE NEXT PAGE

18. Sixty pairs of measurements were taken at random to estimate the relation between variables X and Y. A least squares regression line was fitted to the collected data. The resulting residual plot is as follows:

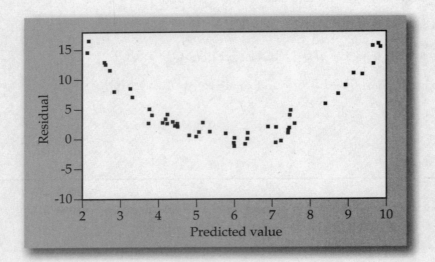

Which of the following conclusions is appropriate?

(A) A line is an appropriate model to describe the relation between X and Y.

(B) A line is not an appropriate model to describe the relation between X and Y.

(C) The assumption of normality of errors has been violated.

(D) The assumption of constant sample variances has been violated.

(E) The variables X and Y are not related at all.

GO ON TO THE NEXT PAGE

19. A consumer awareness group has received several complaints that the price of an asthma medicine has significantly increased in recent years. Two years ago the mean price for this medicine was estimated to be $78.00, and the price at different pharmacies was approximately normally distributed. The group decides to select 10 pharmacies at random and record the price of the medicine at each of the pharmacies. Assuming a 5 percent level of significance, which of the following decision rules should be used to test the hypotheses below?

H_0: The mean price of medicine is $78.00.

H_a: The mean price of medicine is higher than $78.00.

(A) Reject the null hypothesis if p-value > 0.05.
(B) Reject the null hypothesis if p-value > 0.025.

(C) Reject the null hypothesis if $\overline{X} > 78.00$.
(D) Reject the null hypothesis if the test statistic > 1.812.
(E) Reject the null hypothesis if the test statistic > 1.833.

---

20. A team of engineers at the research center of a car manufacturer performs crash tests to determine the proportion of times the cars' airbags fail to operate in a crash. With the airbag system's new modified design, the team expected to reduce the failed proportion to below the last year's proportion of 0.08. They decided to test $H_0: p = 0.08$ versus $H_a: p < 0.08$, where p = the proportion of failed airbags during crash tests. If 300 crashes performed in the lab resulted in 18 failures, which of the following is the test statistic for this test?

(A) $$TS = \frac{0.06 - 0.08}{\sqrt{\dfrac{0.08(1-0.08)}{300}}}$$

(B) $$TS = \frac{0.06 - 0.08}{\sqrt{\dfrac{0.06(1-0.06)}{300}}}$$

(C) $$TS = \frac{0.06 - 0.08}{\sqrt{300(0.08)(1-0.08)}}$$

(D) $$TS = \frac{0.06 - 0.08}{\sqrt{300(0.06)(1-0.06)}}$$

(E) $$TS = \frac{0.06 - 0.08}{\sqrt{\dfrac{0.06(1-0.08)}{300}}}$$

GO ON TO THE NEXT PAGE

21. A farmer wants to know whether a new fertilizer has increased the mean weight of his apples. With the old fertilizer, the mean weight was 4.0 ounces per apple. The farmer decides to test $H_0 : \mu = 4.0$ versus $H_a : \mu > 4.0$ ounces, at a 5 percent level of significance, where μ = the mean weight of apples using the new fertilizer. The weights of apples are approximately normally distributed. The farmer takes a random sample of 16 apples and computes a mean of 4.3 ounces and a standard deviation of 0.6 ounces. Which of the following gives the p-value for this test?

   (A) $P(Z > 2)$
   (B) $P(Z < 2)$
   (C) $P(t > 2)$ with 15 degrees of freedom
   (D) $P(t < 2)$ with 15 degrees of freedom
   (E) $P(t > 2)$ with 16 degrees of freedom

22. Tina's science fair project was to estimate the mean amount of chemicals in her city's water supply. At first she had decided to use a random sample of 15 observations. But her teacher asked her to take 35 observations. The mean and standard deviation from 35 observations turned out to be approximately the same as those from 15 observations. Is there any advantage in using 35 observations instead of 15 observations?

   (A) There is no advantage. Since the mean and the standard deviation are about the same, the confidence interval computed using 35 observations should be approximately the same as that computed using 15 observations.

   (B) There is no advantage. In fact, the 20 extra observations will increase the likelihood of error.

   (C) There is no advantage. Since she took 35 observations instead of 15 observations, the confidence interval using 35 observations will be wider than that using 15 observations.

   (D) There is some advantage. Since she took 35 observations instead of 15 observations, the confidence interval using 35 observations will be narrower than that using 15 observations.

   (E) There is some advantage. With 35 observations, she will be able to compute an exact z-confidence interval instead of an approximate t-confidence interval.

GO ON TO THE NEXT PAGE

23. The Hardcore Construction Company has two offices, one in Atlanta, GA and one in New Orleans, LA. Fifteen engineers work in the Atlanta office, and 14 engineers work in the New Orleans office. The business manager decided to use a 2-sample t-test to compare the mean salaries of engineers in the two offices. Since there were only 15 and 14 engineers, he used the salaries of all the engineers in the computation. Is the 2-sample t-test an appropriate inferential technique in this situation?

(A) Yes, because he is comparing the means of two small groups.

(B) Yes. Both Atlanta and New Orleans are large cities, so the salaries are comparable.

(C) Yes. Since Atlanta and New Orleans are about 500 miles apart, the two groups of engineers can be assumed to be independent.

(D) No, because the number of engineers in the two offices is different.

(E) No, because the entire population information was used from both offices. Since no samples were taken, a t-test should not be used.

---

24. The distribution of salaries of a county school system with 4,752 employees is known to be right skewed, with the superintendent's salary an outlier on the higher side. A random sample of 20 employees was taken and their salaries recorded. A 95 percent t-confidence interval for the mean salary of the county school system employees is ($15,360, $32,470). The t-confidence interval is not appropriate in this situation because

(A) the sample size is too small compared to the number of employees in the system to give a fair representation.

(B) the skewed salary distribution tells us that assumption of normality of the sampled population will not be satisfied.

(C) the population variance of the salaries of employees of this county school system is not known.

(D) the teacher salaries are not negotiable, but the superintendent's salary is negotiable, so the superintendent's salary should be excluded from the population sampled.

(E) the salaries depend on the number of years of experience, which is not taken into account here.

GO ON TO THE NEXT PAGE

25. A random sample of families was taken in order to estimate the relation between fertility and level of education (measured in number of years). A confidence interval needs to be constructed for the slope of the regression line. The social worker in charge of the project is debating whether to use a 90 percent or a 95 percent confidence interval. Which of the following statements about the length of these intervals is true?

(A) The 95 percent confidence interval will be wider than the 90 percent confidence interval.

(B) The 95 percent confidence interval will be narrower than the 90 percent confidence interval.

(C) Both intervals will be of the same length, since they are computed from the same sample.

(D) The length of the confidence interval will depend on the sample size, not on the confidence level.

(E) The length of the confidence interval will depend on the sample variance, not on the confidence level.

26. An insurance agent is successful in selling a life insurance policy to 20 percent of the customers he contacts. He decides to construct a simulation to estimate the mean number of customers he needs to contact before being able to sell a policy. Which of the following schemes should he use to do the simulation?

(A) Assign numbers "0, 1" to successfully selling a policy to a customer and numbers "2, 3, 4, 5, 6, 7, 8, 9" to failing to sell a policy to a customer.

(B) Assign numbers "0, 1" to successfully selling a policy to a customer and numbers "2, 3, 4" to failing to sell a policy to a customer.

(C) Assign number "0" to successfully selling a policy to a customer and numbers "0, 1" to failing to sell a policy to a customer.

(D) Assign numbers "0, 1, 2, 3, 4" to successfully selling a policy to a customer and numbers "5, 6, 7, 8, 9" to failing to sell a policy to a customer.

(E) Assign number "20" to successfully selling a policy to a customer and numbers "1, 3, 5, 7, 9, 11, 13, 15, 17, 19" to failing to sell a policy to a customer.

GO ON TO THE NEXT PAGE

27. The mean height of adult men is 70 inches, with a standard deviation of 4 inches. The mean height of adult women is 66 inches, with a standard deviation of 3 inches. Between a 74-inches-tall man and a 70-inches-tall woman, who should be considered taller within the respective gender group?

(A) It cannot be determined, because the mean heights for the two groups are different.

(B) It cannot be determined, because the standard deviations of the heights for the two groups are different.

(C) The man, because he is 74 inches tall and the woman is only 70 inches tall.

(D) Both should be considered equally tall, because both of them are 4 inches taller than the average height of their respective gender groups.

(E) The woman, because her height is 1.33 standard deviations above the mean height of all women, whereas the man's height is only one standard deviation above the mean height of all men.

28. The amount of rainfall per month in a certain city is approximately normally distributed, with a mean of 6 inches and a standard deviation of 1.6 inches. Which of the following is the highest amount of rainfall this city could have this month for the month to be among the 10 percent driest months the city has seen?

(A) 8.05
(B) 7.60
(C) 3.95
(D) 3.37
(E) 2.28

GO ON TO THE NEXT PAGE

29. A large city was interested in annexing part of the surrounding county. In a survey conducted by the local newspaper, 58 percent of respondents said they were against the annexation. During the actual vote, not all eligible voters voted, but 56 percent of the respondents voted against the annexation. Which of the following best describes the difference in the percentages obtained from the newspaper poll and the vote itself?

(A) It is an example of non-response bias, the systematic tendency of individuals with particular characteristics to refuse to answer a survey question.

(B) It is the systematic difference between a statistic and parameter caused by the non-random selection of surveyed persons.

(C) It is the difference between the same statistics computed from two different samples.

(D) It is the difference between the statistic and the truth due to use of a random sample.

(E) It was caused by the large number of newspaper subscribers in the county.

---

30. In a clinical trial, 30 sickle-cell patients are randomly assigned to two groups. One group receives the currently marketed medicine, and the other group receives the experimental medicine. Each week patients report to the clinic where blood tests are conducted. The lab technician is unaware of the kind of medicine the patient is taking. This design can be described as

(A) a completely randomized design, with the currently marketed medicine and the experimental medicine as two treatments.

(B) a matched-pairs design, with the currently marketed medicine and the experimental medicine forming a pair.

(C) a randomized block design, with the currently marketed medicine and the experimental medicine as two blocks.

(D) a randomized block design, with the currently marketed medicine and the experimental medicine as two treatments.

(E) a stratified design with two strata, patients with sickle-cell disease forming one stratum and those without sickle-cell disease forming the other stratum.

GO ON TO THE NEXT PAGE

31. The registrar's office at a university has noticed that a large number of students fail to report a change of address. The registrar decides to take a random sample of 150 students from the current directory of students and determine the number of students with the correct addresses on record. He then uses this information to construct a 95 percent confidence interval. Which of the following statements must be true?

(A) The true proportion of students at this university with the correct address on record is within the confidence interval constructed.

(B) 95 percent of students at this university have the correct address on record.

(C) The true proportion of students at this university with the correct addresses on records is within the confidence interval 95 percent of the time.

(D) The sample proportion of students at this university with the correct address on record is within the confidence interval 95 percent of the time.

(E) The sample proportion of students at this university with the correct address on record is within the confidence interval.

32. In which of the following situations is a binomial not an appropriate model to describe the outcome?

(A) The number of heads in three tosses of a coin.
(B) The number of rainy days in a given week.
(C) The number of girls in a family of 5 children.
(D) The number of students present in a class of 22.
(E) The number of defective computer monitors out of 7 purchased.

33. Which of the following statements about any two events A and B is true?

(A) $P(A \cup B) = P(A)$ implies events A and B are independent.

(B) $P(A \cup B) = 1$ implies events A and B are mutually exclusive.

(C) $P(A \cap B) = 0$ implies events A and B are independent.

(D) $P(A \cap B) = 0$ implies events A and B are mutually exclusive.

(E) $P(A \cap B) = P(A) - P(B)$ implies A and B are equally likely events.

---

34. A newspaper reporter examined police reports of accidents during the past 12 months to collect data about the speed of a car and its stopping distance. The reporter then constructed a scatterplot and computed a correlation coefficient to show the relation between a car's speed and its stopping distance. This is an example of

(A) a double blind study.
(B) a single blind study.
(C) a study involving no blinding at all.
(D) an observational study.
(E) a well-designed experiment.

GO ON TO THE NEXT PAGE

35. A company with offices in five different countries is interested in estimating the proportion of its employees in favor of banning smoking on the office premises. It is known that the views of people from different countries on issues like smoking tend to vary due to the influence of different local social structures. Which of the following is an appropriate sampling technique to use in this situation, and why?

(A) Stratified sample, because the population is divided into five strata—namely, five offices in five different countries.

(B) Stratified sample, because people in different countries use different languages and thus will not be able to communicate to each other the results of a simple random sample.

(C) Simple random sample, because the study has not been attempted before.

(D) Simple random sample, because this is the only method that gives unbiased results.

(E) Simple random sample, because this is the only method for which inferential techniques are available.

36. In a clinic, 50 patients with sleep disorders are randomly assigned to one of two different groups. Patients in one group are given medication before bedtime. Patients in the other group are given blindfolds and played soft music at bedtime. Each patient is attached to a machine that records breathing patterns. From the patterns, it is possible to determine if the patient is awake or asleep. The data will be used to decide which method is more effective in helping patients with sleep disorders. Which of the following statements is correct in the context of this experiment?

(A) This is a single blind experiment, because only one group uses blindfolds.

(B) This is a single blind experiment, because only patients and not doctors use blindfolds.

(C) This is a double blind experiment, since patients are blindfolded and the doctor does not know which patient receives which treatment.

(D) This experiment cannot be a single blind experiment, because many patients do not like to be blindfolded.

(E) This experiment cannot be a double blind experiment, because patients will know which treatment they are receiving, although the examining doctor might not.

GO ON TO THE NEXT PAGE

37. Data was collected on two variables X and Y and a least squares regression line was fitted to the data. The estimated equation for this data is $\left[y = -2.29 + 1.70x\right] = -2.29 + 1.70x$. What is the residual for point (5, 6)?

(A) 7.91
(B) 6.21
(C) 0.21
(D) −0.21
(E) −2.91

38. The relation between car speed (in miles per hour) and gas consumption (in miles per gallon) was estimated from a random sample to be

$$mpg = 39.43 - 0.18 \, (speed)$$

How will gas consumption change with a 10 mile-per-hour increase in the car's speed?

(A) Gas consumption will increase by 37.63 mpg.
(B) Gas consumption will increase by 1.8 mpg.
(C) Gas consumption will remain unchanged.
(D) Gas consumption will decrease by 1.8 mpg.
(E) Gas consumption will decrease by 37.63 mpg.

GO ON TO THE NEXT PAGE

39. A group of scientists wanted to estimate the proportion of geese returning to the same site for the next breeding season. Suppose they decided to increase the sample size from 200 to 2,000. How will this affect the distribution of the sample proportion?

(A) The distribution of the sample proportion will be more spread out.

(B) The distribution of the sample proportion will be less spread out.

(C) The spread of the distribution of the sample proportion will remain unaffected.

(D) The distribution of the sample proportion will more closely resemble the binomial distribution.

(E) The distribution of the sample proportion will more closely resemble the *chi-square* distribution.

40. A company has 400 employees. Their mean income is $20,500, and the standard deviation of their incomes is $3,750. The distribution of incomes is skewed. How many of the 400 employees do you expect to have an income of between $13,000 and $28,000?

(A) 50

(B) 100

(C) 200

(D) 300

(E) 400

END OF SECTION I

IF YOU FINISH BEFORE TIME IS CALLED, YOU MAY
CHECK YOUR WORK ON SECTION I.
DO NOT GO ON TO SECTION II UNTIL YOU ARE TOLD TO DO SO.

STATISTICS

SECTION II

Time — 1 hour and 30 minutes

Number of problems — 6

Percent of total grade — 50

GENERAL INSTRUCTIONS

There are two parts to this section of the examination. Part A consists of five equally weighted problems that represent 75 percent of the total weight of this section. Spend about 65 minutes on this part of the exam. Part B consists of one longer problem that represents 25 percent of the total weight of this section. Spend about 25 minutes on this part of the exam. Since it is not expected that everyone will be able to complete all parts of all problems, you may wish to look over all the problems before you begin to work. The questions are printed in the booklet and on the green insert: it may be easier for you to look over all the problems on the insert. Statistical tables and useful formulas are printed in the green insert. When you are told to begin, open your booklet, carefully tear out the green insert, and start your work.

- You should write all work for each part of each problem in the space provided for that part in this booklet. Be sure to write clearly and legibly. If you make an error, you may save time by crossing it out rather than trying to erase it. Erased or crossed-out work will not be graded. No credit will be given for any work shown on the green insert.

- Show all your work. Indicate clearly the methods you use because you will be graded on the correctness of your methods as well as the accuracy of your final answers. Correct answers without supporting work may not receive credit.

GO ON TO THE NEXT PAGE

STATISTICS

SECTION II

Part A

Question 1-5

Spend about 65 minutes on this part of the exam.

Percent of Section II grade—75

Show all your work. Indicate clearly the methods you use, because you will be graded on the correctness of your method as well as on the accuracy of your results and explanation.

1. A short-term parking facility allows cars to be parked for a maximum of 4 hours. For any fraction of an hour a car is parked, the facility charges for the full hour. For example, if a person parks at this facility for 1 hour and 25 minutes, then the person is charged for 2 full hours. The probability distribution of the parking time at this short-term parking facility, as measured in full hours, is as follows:

Hours	1	2	3	4
Probability	0.15	0.25	0.45	0.15

(a) What is the mean parking time in this facility?

(b) The facility charges $3.00 for the first hour of parking and $2.50 per hour thereafter. What is the mean parking fee paid by the customers?

GO ON TO THE NEXT PAGE

2. Scientists have suspected that animals, when deficient in certain chemicals, tend to ingest natural resources that have high concentrations of those chemicals to offset the deficiency. In a study, scientists drained saliva from the parotid gland of sheep in order to make them sodium deficient. Then they offered these sheep a solution of sodium bicarbonate and measured the sheep's sodium intake. The sodium deficiency and the sodium intake, both measured in millimoles, are recorded as follows:

Sodium Deficit (in millimoles)	Sodium Intake (in millimoles)
100	110
200	180
570	610
850	790
700	750
425	390
375	420
325	380
450	300
850	790

The summary statistics and the regression output for this data are as follows:

Variable	N	Mean	Median	StDev	Q1	Q3
Deficit	10	484.5	437.5	256.4	293.7	737.5
Intake	10	472.0	405.0	250.0	270.0	760.0

Predictor	Coef	StDev	T	P
Constant	15.55	47.94	0.32	0.754
Deficit	0.94211	0.08843	10.65	0.000

GO ON TO THE NEXT PAGE

(a) Does the line appear to be a reasonable model for this data? Explain your answer.

(b) State and interpret the slope in terms of the problem.

GO ON TO THE NEXT PAGE

(c) Estimate the correlation between sodium deficit and sodium intake. Interpret your answer in the context of this problem.

(d) Estimate the amount of a sheep's sodium intake if the sheep is found to be deficient in sodium by 800 millimoles.

GO ON TO THE NEXT PAGE

3. A university offers degrees in the following four areas:

- Arts and Sciences (A & S)
- Engineering (Eng)
- Business and Management (B & M)
- Computer Science (Comp)

Incoming freshmen apply for majors in A&S, Eng, B&M, and Comp in a ratio of approximately $5:6:6:8$. But many students change their major during the course of study. The university officials are interested in determining whether the distribution of majors among graduating students differs from that of incoming students. They took a random sample of 200 graduating students and classified them according to their majors. The distribution of graduating students in this sample is given in the table below.

	Major			
	A&S	Eng	B&M	Comp
Number of students	60	30	60	50

Is the distribution of majors among graduating students different from that of incoming students? Provide statistical justification for your answer.

GO ON TO THE NEXT PAGE

4. An education professor is interested in getting students involved in a tutoring program for area schools. The participating students are paid through a grant from the city. This year, the city has agreed to provide funds to support three students in this program. The professor has found that about 4 out of 5 students that he interviews are not able to participate in the program due to other commitments.

(a) Describe how you would use a random number table to carry out simulations to determine the number of students the professor needs to interview to fill the three spots in the tutoring program. Describe what each random number represents in your simulation.

25211	75049	70678	24646	96329	63547	37255	51013	25211	75049
97077	82384	33078	59574	34916	09422	85700	74202	97077	82384
82641	66179	30341	40674	51778	97680	84707	88808	82641	66179
60675	60254	16308	70130	29610	27658	94288	88752	60675	60254
53860	97861	34625	85190	38477	60503	34561	04360	53860	97861

GO ON TO THE NEXT PAGE

(b) Run two trials of your simulation. Use the random number table provided to illustrate your simulation.

(c) Suppose the professor did 100 simulations to estimate the number of students that he needs to interview to find 3 students willing to work for the tutoring program. The results of the simulations are shown below.

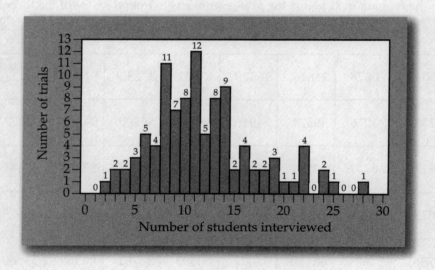

Estimate the probability that the professor has to interview more than 20 students before he finds 3 willing to work for the tutoring program.

GO ON TO THE NEXT PAGE

5. A resident at a medical college was interested in showing that exercising regularly helps reduce cholesterol levels. Over a period of one month, he selected a random sample of 50 patients who came to his clinic for their annual physical examination. He asked the patients if they exercised regularly, and noted down the answers as "Exercises regularly" or "Does not exercise regularly." He also recorded their current cholesterol levels and their cholesterol levels from the previous year's physical examination, as noted in their medical records. He summarized the data on their cholesterol levels as shown in the table below.

	Exercises regularly		Does not exercise regularly	
	Last year	This year	Last year	This year
Number of patients	18	18	32	32
Mean	223.80	189.75	268.35	265.53
Standard deviation	15.88	18.77	32.81	28.17
Difference in mean cholesterol levels (Last year – this year)	34.05		2.82	

(a) The resident included the following in his report:

"On the average, the group that exercises regularly has experienced a larger decrease in cholesterol level as compared to the group that does not exercise regularly. Since the observed difference is considerably large, we can conclude that exercising regularly reduces cholesterol level."

Why is such a causal conclusion not allowed from this data? Explain your answer.

GO ON TO THE NEXT PAGE

(b) Design an experiment that will allow the resident to draw such a conclusion.

STATISTICS

SECTION II

Part B

Question 6

Spend about 25 minutes on this part of the exam.

Percent of Section II grade—25

6. Pam and Dave decided to buy a small house and move out of their apartment. After looking around, they decided that they both liked two neighborhoods, Sunshine Estates and Pinewoods Estates, and wanted to buy a house in one of those two neighborhoods if they could afford it. Their real estate agent selected a random sample of houses sold in the last 12 months from each neighborhood and found out how much the houses sold for. The summary statistics for the selling prices (in $1,000) of houses in both neighborhoods are as follows:

	Sunshine Estates	Pinewoods Estates
Sample size	14	15
Mean selling price	113.357	124.333
Standard deviation of selling price	3.296	14.181
Minimum selling price	107.000	97.000
1st Quartile selling price	111.000	112.000
Median selling price	113.500	121.000
3rd Quartile selling price	116.000	133.000
Maximum selling price	119.000	149.000

(a) Make parallel box plots to compare the selling prices of houses in Sunshine Estates and Pinewoods Estates. Write a few sentences describing the selling prices in these two neighborhoods.

GO ON TO THE NEXT PAGE

(b) Assume the selling prices of houses in these two neighborhoods are approximately normally distributed. Construct a 95 percent confidence interval to compare the mean prices in the two neighborhoods. Interpret your interval.

(c) Pam and Dave decide that they could afford to spend about $120,000 on their new house. What percent of houses in Sunshine Estates are within their budget?

GO ON TO THE NEXT PAGE

(d) In which neighborhood are they are more likely to find a house within their budget? Justify your answer.

(e) Using the information available, can we support the assumption that the prices of the houses are distributed normally? Explain your answer.

END OF EXAMINATION

11

ANSWERS AND EXPLANATIONS TO PRACTICE TEST 2

Multiple Choice

1. **Answer: A**
Note that this question asks for an interpretation of the confidence level, and not of the confidence interval. The example uses a confidence level of 0.95. This means that if lots of random samples of 50 oranges are taken and a 95 percent confidence interval is constructed from each selected sample, then 95 percent of those confidence intervals constructed will contain the true mean weight of the oranges.

2. **Answer: C**

Thirty percent of the members of the jury pool are women. The remaining 70 percent must be men. A jury of 12 is selected at random. This results in a binomial distribution with 12 trials: P(a woman is selected) = 0.30 and P(a man is selected) = 0.70. Therefore, the expected number of men selected in this group is equal to $np = 12\ (0.70)$.

3. **Answer: D**

It is given that the demand for bread is N(2,500, 225). We need to find the probability that the demand will exceed the supply. If 3,000 loaves are available today, compute

$$P(\text{Demand for bread} > 3000)$$
$$= P\left(Z > \frac{3000 - 2500}{225}\right)$$
$$= P(Z > 2.22)$$
$$= 1 - P(Z < 2.22)$$
$$= 1 - 0.9867$$
$$= 0.0131$$

[Hint: On the TI-83, use the normalcdf function from the DISTR menu]

4. **Answer: B**

This is a binomial situation. Since four patients are trying the medicine, that means there are four trials. The probability that a patient will develop side effects is 1 out of 5, i.e., $1/5 = 0.20$. The probability that a patient will not develop side effects $= 4/5 = 0.80$. So the probability that

none of the four patients will develop side effects is $P(0) = \binom{4}{0}\left(\frac{1}{5}\right)^0\left(\frac{4}{5}\right)^4 = 0.80^4 = 0.4096$

[Hint: On the TI-83, use the binomcdf function from the DISTR menu]

5. **Answer: A**

It is given that P(oil change) = 0.80, so P(Tires service | Oil change) = 0.20. Using the multiplication rule, we get

P(Oil change <u>and</u> Tires service)
$= P$(Tires service | Oil change) P(Oil change)
$= 0.20\ (0.80)$
$= 0.16$

6. **Answer: B**

This box plot is highly right-skewed. The book prices range from about $8 to $80, but the median price is around $12. This means that about 50 percent of the books are priced around $12 or lower. Even the third quartile is around $25, which means that about 75 percent of the books are priced at $25 or below. Therefore, we can conclude that the bookstore carries mostly low-priced books.

7. **Answer: B**

The first quartile of the distribution is Q_1 such that $P(X < Q_1) = 0.25$. Thus

$$Q_1 = 25 - Z_{0.25}(4) = 25 - 0.67(4) = 22.32$$

The third quartile of the distribution is Q_3 such that

$$P(X < Q_3) = 0.75 \text{ or } P(X > Q_3) = 0.25$$

Thus

$$Q_1 = 25 + Z_{0.25}(4) = 25 + 0.67(4) = 27.68$$

Therefore, the interquartile range = $Q_3 - Q_1 = 27.68 - 22.32$
[Hint: On the TI-83, use invNorm function from DISTR menu]

8. **Answer: C**

In this experiment, gender is a blocking factor and the three different types of paint make up three treatments. Children are divided into two groups by gender. There is no matching involved. The experiment is therefore a randomized block design, not a completely randomized design.

9. **Answer: B**

The approximate range of annual rainfall for City A is 5 to 45 inches, with a mean of approximately 23 inches. The approximate range of annual rainfall for City B is 20 to 40 inches, with a mean of approximately 30 inches. This means that on the average City B gets more rain than City A, but the range for City A is larger than for City B.

10. **Answer: B**

The Central Limit Theorem is applicable to samples of large size.

11. **Answer: A**

A discrete variable takes only countable values. The number of test questions a student guesses the answers to is a random variable with possible values 0, 1, 2, ... n, where n is the number of questions on the test.

12. **Answer: B**

For a 90 percent confidence interval, $Z_{\alpha/2} = Z_{0.05} = 1.645$. Since $\hat{p}$ is not given, use $\hat{p} = \dfrac{1}{2} = 0.5$.

The maximum 90 percent margin of error is

$$Z_{\alpha/2}\sqrt{\frac{\hat{p}(1-\hat{p})}{n}} = 1.645\sqrt{\frac{0.5(1-0.5)}{300}} = 0.0475$$

[Hint: On the TI-83, use the invNorm function from the DISTR menu or the 1-propZInt function from the STAT→TESTS menu]

13. **Answer: E**

In general the t-distribution has a larger variance then the standard normal distribution. As sample size increases, the difference between the t-distribution and the standard normal distribution decreases.

14. **Answer: B**

Since the population variances are the same, we should pool information from both the samples to get a better estimate of the unknown common population variance.

15. **Answer: D**

It is given that take-home grades $\sim N(40,3)$ and in-class grades $\sim N(34,6)$.
The test grade = take-home grade + in-class grade.

Thus, $\mu_{\text{Test grade}} = \mu_{\text{Take-home grade}} + \mu_{\text{In-class grade}} = 40 + 34 = 74$, and $\sigma_{\text{Test grade}} =$

$$\sqrt{\sigma^2_{\text{Take-home grade}} + \sigma^2_{\text{In-class grade}}} = \sqrt{3^2 + 6^2} = 6.71$$

16. **Answer: D**

Any observation that falls 1.5(IQR) beyond the first and third quartiles is considered an outlier.

17. **Answer: A**

In this cumulative graph, we need to find $P(\text{demand} > 12,000)$, because that is the point at which the power company will not be able to meet the demand for electricity. Draw a vertical line at 12,000 until it reaches the curve. From the point at which it crosses the curve, draw a horizontal line to the Y-axis. The line reaches the Y-axis at approximately 97 percent, which means that on 97 percent of days the demand for electricity will be, at most, 12,000. In other words, at about 3 percent of days, the power plant will have more demand for electricity than what they produce.

18. **Answer: B**

The curvature in the residual plot indicates that a line is not an appropriate model to describe the relation between X and Y. If a line is an appropriate model, then the residual plot will show randomly scattered residuals without any pattern.

19. **Answer: E**

The alternative hypothesis indicates that we need to use a right-tailed test. And since the population variance is unknown, and the population is normally distributed, a t-test is the best option. Sample size 10 gives 9 degrees of freedom, and $\alpha = 0.05$ is used. Therefore, the rejection region is

$$\text{TS} > t_\alpha(\upsilon) = t_{0.05}(9) = 1.833$$

20. **Answer: A**

It is given that the hypothesized value of the proportion is $p_0 = 0.08$. The estimated proportion from a sample of size 300 is

$$\hat{p} = \frac{18}{300} = 0.06$$

Therefore the test statistic used to test the given hypotheses is

$$TS = \frac{\hat{p} - p_0}{\sqrt{\dfrac{p_0(1 - p_0)}{n}}} = \frac{0.06 - 0.08}{\sqrt{\dfrac{0.08(1 - 0.08)}{300}}}$$

21. **Answer: C**

The population variance is unknown and the weights are normally distributed. So we should use a t-test for the mean. The test statistic value is

$$TS = \frac{\bar{x} - \mu_0}{S/\sqrt{n}} = \frac{4.3 - 4.0}{0.6/\sqrt{16}} = 2.0$$

Since we are using a right-tailed test, the p-value is the area in the right tail of the t-distribution with 15 degrees of freedom, beyond 2.0.

[Hint: On the TI-83, use the t-test function from the STAT →TESTS menu]

22. **Answer: D**

Note that $ME = t_{\alpha/2}(\upsilon)\dfrac{S}{\sqrt{n}}$. The margin of error is inversely proportional to the sample size; in other words, it will be smaller for a larger sample size. So, the confidence interval will be narrower.

23. **Answer: E**

The number of engineers working for the company is so small that the mean salaries were computed using the salaries of all the engineers. Since no samples were taken, whatever difference was observed between the mean salaries is the real difference. There is no probability statement associated with the difference. Therefore, there is no inference.

24. **Answer: B**

It is given that the distribution is skewed with an outlier. Therefore, the distribution cannot be normal, since the normal distribution is symmetric. So the assumption of normality required for a t-test is not satisfied.

25. **Answer: A**

For a confidence interval with a higher confidence level, the probability of overestimating or underestimating the result is lower. Therefore, there is less area under the sampling distribution beyond the confidence limits. Hence the confidence interval with a higher confidence level will be wider.

26. **Answer: A**

It is given that P(successfully selling insurance policy) = 0.20, which means that P(failing to sell a policy) = 0.80. If we are using one digit numbers, then there are total of 10 digits available for selection. If "0, 1" are designated for "selling a policy," then we have P(selling a policy) = 0.20, and if the remaining eight digits are designated as "failing to sell a policy," then P(failing to sell a policy) = 0.80 as desired.

27. **Answer: E**

Since the distributions of heights differ for men and women, we cannot compare their heights directly. Let's compute the z-scores for the height of each one within their respective populations.

$$Z_M = \frac{74 - 70}{4} = 1$$

This means that the 74-inches-tall man is one standard deviation taller than the mean height of men.

$$Z_W = \frac{70 - 66}{3} = \frac{4}{3} = 1.33$$

This means that the 70-inches-tall woman is 1.33 standard deviations taller than the mean height of women. Therefore, the woman should be considered taller within her population group.

28. **Answer: C**

X = the amount of rainfall $\sim N(6, 1.6)$.

We need to find amount H such that $P(X < H) = 0.10$.

$$H = \mu - Z_{0.10}\sigma = 6 - 1.28(1.6) = 3.95$$

[Hint: On the TI-83, use the invNorm function from the DISTR menu]

29. **Answer: ~~D~~ C**

If we take different samples from the same population, the estimates from the different samples will be different. The difference in percentages is simply due to sampling variation.

30. **Answer: A**

This experiment consists of two treatments, the currently marketed medicine and the experimental medicine. Patients are not matched, and no blocks are formed. Only patients with the sickle-cell disease are involved in the experiment.

31. **Answer: E**

Confidence intervals are constructed as Statistic ± Margin of Error. Therefore, the statistic is always right in the center of the confidence interval.

32. **Answer: B**

One requirement of the binomial distribution is that trials must be independent. The weather in a given week is not independent from day to day—if there's rain on Monday, there's more likely to be rain on Tuesday (more likely than if Monday were sunny).

33. **Answer: D**

If the probability of the intersection of two events is 0, then those two events cannot intersect each other. They are disjoint.

34. **Answer: D**

This is an example of observational study. The reporter collected the data but had no control over the factor (the car's speed).

35. **Answer: A**

It is given that the population is divided into five groups, and there may be differences among these five groups. In order to ensure representation from all five groups in the sample, stratified sampling should be used.

36. **Answer: E**

In a double blind experiment, both the subject and the person measuring the subject's response are unaware of the treatment given to the subject. In a single blind experiment, only the subject is unaware of the treatment received. Since the patients will know whether they have been given a blindfold or played soft music, they will know what treatment they have received. Therefore, the experiment cannot be double blind.

37. **Answer: D**

The predicted value of Y for $X = 5$ is $\hat{y} = -2.29 + 1.70(5) = 6.21$. The residual is $y - \hat{y} = 6 - 6.21 = -0.21$.

38. **Answer: D**

The slope of the regression line gives the average amount of decrease in miles per gallon for every unit increase in speed. So, if the speed is increased by 10 miles per hour, then the miles per gallon will decrease by $10(0.18) = 1.8$.

39. **Answer: B**

The variance of the sampling distribution of the sample proportion is given by $\dfrac{\hat{p}(1-\hat{p})}{n}$.

Therefore, the variance decreases as the sample size increases. In other words, the distribution becomes less spread out as the sample size increases.

40. **Answer: D**

According to Chebyshev's rule, at least 75 percent of the data falls within 2 standard deviations of the mean. $20,500 - 2(3,750) = 13,000$, and $20,500 + 2(3,750) = 28,000$. So $(13,000, 28,000)$ gives a 2 standard deviation interval from the mean. Therefore, by Chebyshev's rule, 75 percent of data—$0.75(400) = 300$ observations—should fall within the given limits.

Free Response

1. You should identify this as a discrete probability distribution problem.
   (a) $E(\text{Time}) = 1(0.15) + 2(0.25) + 3(0.45) + 4(0.15) = 2.6$
       The mean parking time in this facility is 2.6 hours.
   (b) $E(\text{Charge}) = 1(3.0) + 1.6(2.50) = 7.00$

   Or

Hours	Probability	Parking Charge
1	0.15	$3.00
2	0.25	$5.50
3	0.45	$8.00
4	0.15	$10.50

$E(\text{Charge}) = 3(0.15) + 5.5(0.25) + 8(0.45) + 10.5(0.15) = 7.00$

The mean parking charge paid by customers is $7.00.

2. Let D = Sodium deficit and I = Sodium intake.
   (a) Prepare a scatterplot, or a residual plot. Here are examples of each:

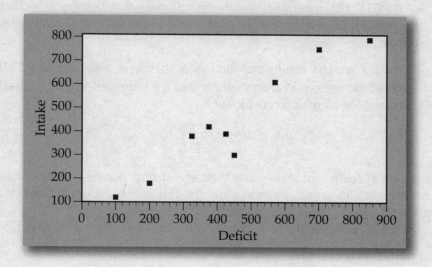

Figure 1: Scatterplot of intake versus deficit

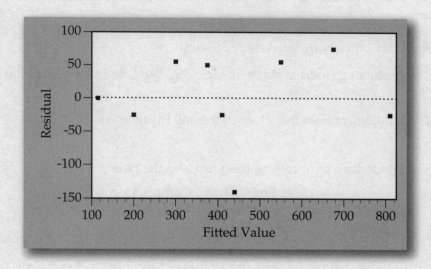

Figure 2: Residual plot for intake as a function of deficit

Using the scatterplot, you could argue that a line appears to be a reasonable model to describe the relation between sodium deficiency and sodium intake.

Using the residual plot, you could argue that the residuals are scattered randomly (they show no patterns or trends), so a line appears to be a reasonable model to describe the relation between sodium deficiency and sodium intake.

[Hint: On the TI-83, use the graph function to make a scatterplot or the regression diagnostics to make a residual plot. Then copy the graph or plot from the calculator screen to the exam paper.]

(b) From the regression output, estimate the slope of the line of best fit as $b = 0.94211$. This means that for every millimole of deficiency in sodium the sheep will take in approximately (or on the average) 0.94211 millimoles of sodium.

(c) The basic summary results provided show that $S_D = 256.4$ and $S_I = 250.0$. The results of the regression analysis show that the estimated slope $b = 0.94211$. Therefore, the correlation coefficient is

$$r = b \frac{S_D}{S_I} = 0.94211 \left(\frac{256.4}{250.0} \right) = 0.966$$

This correlation coefficient shows that there is a strong, positive, linear correlation between the amount of sodium intake and the amount of sodium deficiency among the sheep.

(d) The regression results show that the relation between intake and deficiency is

Intake = 15.55 + 0.94211 (deficit)
= 15.55 + 0.94211 (800)
= 769.238 millimoles.

A sheep with 800 millimoles deficiency will take in about 769.2 millimoles of sodium.

3. The university officials are interested in testing

H_0: The graduating students major in A&S, Eng, B&M, and Comp in a ratio of 5 : 6 : 6 : 8.

H_a: The ratio differs from that given in the null hypothesis.

The major preference for incoming freshmen is in the ratio

A&S : Eng : B&M : CompSci
5 : 6 : 6 : 8

In other words,

P(a new freshman applies for A&S major) $= 5/(5+6+6+8) = 5/25 = 0.20$

P(a new freshman applies for Eng major) $= 6/(5+6+6+8) = 6/25 = 0.24$

P(a new freshman applies for B&M major) $= 6/(5+6+6+8) = 6/25 = 0.24$

P(a new freshman applies for Comp major) $= 8/(5+6+6+8) = 8/25 = 0.32$

A total of 200 students were sampled. If the null hypothesis were true, then the officials would expect approximately 200(0.20) = 40 students to graduate with a degree in A&S. The numbers of students expected to graduate in each of the above majors if the null hypothesis were true are as follows:

Major				
Expected counts	A&S	Eng	B&M	Comp
	40	48	48	64

A random sample of students is taken and all the expected counts are larger than five. So the chi-square test for goodness of fit is appropriate.

Major				
	A&S	Eng	B&M	Comp
Expected counts (E_i)	40	48	48	64
Observed counts (O_i)	60	30	60	50

Degrees of freedom = $\upsilon = (4 - 1) = 3$. Let's use a 5 percent level of significance. The rejection rule is "reject the null hypothesis if p-value < 0.05"

(or if using the rejection region approach, "reject the null hypothesis if TS > $\chi^2_{0.05}(3) = 7.82$").

$$TS = \sum \frac{(O_i - E_i)^2}{E_i}$$
$$= \frac{(60 - 40)^2}{40} + \frac{(30 - 48)^2}{48} + \frac{(60 - 48)^2}{48} + \frac{(50 - 64)^2}{64}$$
$$= 22.81$$

p-value = $P(\chi^2 > 22.81) = 0.000044$ with 3 degrees of freedom.

Since the p-value of 0.000044 is smaller than any reasonable level of significance (or if using the rejection region approach, since TS = 22.81 > 7.82, or since the TS falls in the rejection region), we should reject the null hypothesis and accept the alternative hypothesis. At a 5 percent level of significance, we can conclude that the distribution of majors among the graduating students is different from that of the incoming students.

4. Approximately 4 out of 5 students that the professor interviews are not able to participate in the program. This means,

P(Student is not able to participate) = 4/5 = 0.80

P(Student is able to participate) = 1/5 = 0.20

 (a) To simulate the situation, consider ten 1-digit random numbers
   0, 1, 2, 3, 4, 5, 6, 7, 8, 9.

Designate them as follows:

- Assign "0, 1" to "Student is able to participate."

- Assign "2, 3, ..., 9" to "Student is not able to participate."

Start at the beginning of the table and read random numbers consecutively, one number for each student contacted. Numbers 0 or 1 mean that the student contacted is able to participate in the program, while numbers 2 through 9 mean the student contacted is not able to participate in the program. Continue until 3 students who are able to participate in the program are found.

(b) Suppose we start the first simulation at the beginning of the table.

2 5 2 [1][1]	7 5 [0] 4 9	7 0 6 7 8	2 4 6 4 6	9 6 3 2 9	6 3 5 4 7	3 7 2 5 5	5 1 0 1 3	2 5 2 1 1	7 5 0 4 9

Our first simulation results in interviewing 8 students before finding 3 students who are able to participate in the program.

Suppose we start the second simulation at the beginning of the second line.

9 7 [0] 7 7	8 2 3 8 4	3 3 [0] 7 8	5 9 5 7 4	3 4 9 [1] 6	0 9 4 2 2	8 5 7 0 0

Our second simulation results in interviewing 24 students before identifying 3 students who are able to participate in the program.

Note that the answer to this question depends on how the simulation is designed as well as where in the table one starts the simulation.

(c) From the chart, we can see 9 simulations that resulted in interviewing more than 20 students before 3 students were found.

P(Interviewing more than 20 students) = 9/100 = 0.09.

There is a 9 percent chance that the professor will have to interview more than 20 students before he can recruit 3.

5.

 (a) This is an observational study, not a designed experiment. Therefore, casual conclusions are not appropriate from this data.

(b) Recruit a group of patients with high cholesterol levels. Randomly assign the selected patients to two groups. Instruct patients in Group 1 to do specifically assigned exercises regularly. Monitor their exercising activities closely. Instruct patients in Group 2 not to do regular exercises. After one year, measure the cholesterol levels of both groups and compare. In order to avoid confounding factors, make sure that none of the patients are on a cholesterol-reducing diet or medicine.

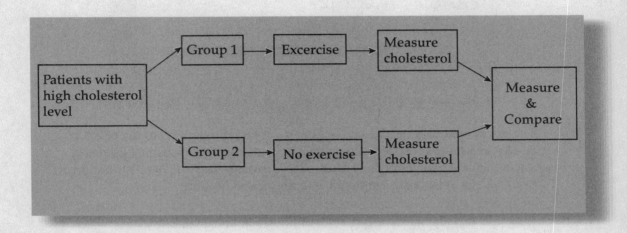

Figure 3: Schematic diagram showing the design of this experiment

6. First, organize the information as follows.

	Sunshine Estates	Pinewoods Estates
Q_1	111.000	112.000
Q_3	116.000	133.000
$IQR = Q_3 - Q_1$	5.000	21.000
Length of Whiskers = (1.5) IQR	7.500	31.500
$Q_1 - (1.5) IQR$	103.500	80.500
$Q_3 - (0.5) IQR$	123.500	164.500

(a) Then use this information to create the following box plots.

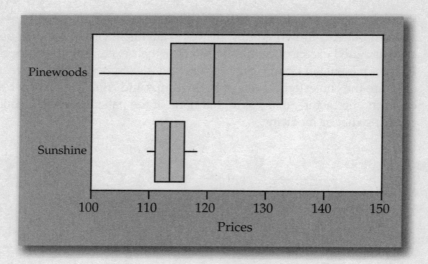

The prices of houses in Pinewoods Estates vary a lot compared to the prices of houses in Sunshine Estates. The median price of houses in Sunshine Estates is lower than the median price of houses in Pinewoods Estates. The distribution of prices seems to be fairly symmetric in both the subdivisions.

(b) Let μ_S = the mean selling price of houses in Sunshine Estates

and μ_P = the mean selling price of houses in Pinewoods Estates

$(\mu_S - \mu_P)$ = the difference in mean selling prices of houses in Sunshine and Pinewoods estates

It is given that the selling prices are approximately normally distributed. The population variances are unknown, but the boxplots indicate that the population variances are more likely to be unequal. So use an unequal variances t-interval to estimate $(\mu_S - \mu_P)$.

$$\upsilon = \frac{\left(\dfrac{S_S^2}{n_S} + \dfrac{S_P^2}{n_P}\right)^2}{\dfrac{\left(S_S^2/n_S\right)^2}{n_S - 1} + \dfrac{\left(S_P^2/n_P\right)^2}{n_P - 1}} = \frac{\left(\dfrac{10.8626}{14} + \dfrac{201.095}{15}\right)^2}{\dfrac{\left(10.8626/14\right)^2}{14 - 1} + \dfrac{\left(201.095/15\right)^2}{15 - 1}} = 15.611$$

Use 15 degrees of freedom.

$$t_{0.025}(15) = 2.131$$

$$95\% \ ME = t_{\alpha/2}(\upsilon)\sqrt{\frac{S_S^2}{n_S} + \frac{S_P^2}{n_P}} = 2.131\sqrt{\frac{10.8626}{14} + \frac{201.095}{15}} = 8.025$$

Therefore, the 95 percent confidence interval for $(\mu_S - \mu_P)$ is

$$\left(\overline{X}_S - \overline{X}_P\right) \pm ME \Rightarrow (113.357 - 124.333) \pm 8.025 \Rightarrow -10.976 \pm 8.025$$

In other words, 95 percent CI for $(\mu_S - \mu_P)$ is $(-19.001, -2.951)$

We are 95 percent confident that the true difference in mean prices of houses in Sunshine Estates and Pinewoods Estates is between \$2,951 and \$19,001, with houses in Pinewoods estate on the average being more expensive.

[Hint: On the TI-83, use the 2-SampTInt function from the STAT→TESTS menu]

    (c)   The prices in Sunshine Estates are approximately normally distributed, with a mean price of \$113,357 and a standard deviation of 3,296. Pam and Dave can afford to spend about \$120,000.

P(Pam and Dave can afford to buy a house in Sunshine Estates)

$$= P(X < 120) = P\left(Z < \frac{120 - 113.357}{3.296} \right) = P(Z < 2.015) = 0.9780$$

About 97.8 percent of the houses in Sunshine Estates are within Pam and Dave's budget.

[Hint: On the TI-83, use the normalcdf function from the DISTR menu]

    (d)   The prices in Pinewoods Estates are approximately normally distributed, with a mean price of 124.333 and a standard deviation of 14,181. Pam and Dave can afford to spend about \$120,000.

P(Pam and Dave can afford to buy a house in Pinewoods Estates)

$$= P(X < 120) = P\left(Z < \frac{120 - 124.333}{14.181} \right) = P(Z < -0.3055) = 0.3800$$

About 38 percent of the houses in Pinewood Estates are within Pam and Dave's budget. From the answer to (c) we know that about 97.8 percent of houses in Sunshine Estates are within Pam and Dave's budget. Comparing these two, we can say that Pam and Dave are more likely to find a house within their budget in Sunshine Estates.

[Hint: On the TI-83, use the normalcdf function from the DISTR menu]

    (e)   This can be argued using several different methods. Some are listed below.

-         The box plots reveal no outliers and the distributions seem symmetric. Median prices are almost the same as mean prices. Therefore, the prices are most likely fairly normally distributed.

- Suppose we computed z-scores for the minimum and the maximum prices in both subdivisions. Then we would get:

	Sunshine Estates	Pinewoods Estates
Minimum	z–score $= \dfrac{107 - 113.357}{3.296} = -1.93$	z–score $= \dfrac{119 - 113.357}{3.296} = 1.74$
Maximum	z–score $= \dfrac{97 - 124.333}{14.181} = -1.93$	z–score $= \dfrac{149 - 124.333}{14.181} = 1.74$

Note that in both Estates, the highest and the lowest prices are less than 2 standard deviations away. In a normal distribution, almost all observations fall within 3 standard deviations from the mean. This could indicate that the prices may not be normally distributed.

- We can still use the z-scores and argue that only about 5 percent of the observations are expected to be beyond 2 standard deviations from the mean. Since we have only 14 and 15 observations, it is possible to get no z-scores in the intervals (–2, –3) and (2, 3) in such a small data set when sampling from a normal population. The box plots reveal no outliers and the distributions seem symmetrical. The median prices are almost the same as the mean prices. So the prices should be fairly normally distributed.

FORMULAS AND TABLES

I. Descriptive Statistics

$$\overline{x} = \frac{\sum x_i}{n}$$

$$s_x = \sqrt{\frac{1}{n-1}\sum (x_i - \overline{x})^2}$$

$$s_p = \sqrt{\frac{(n_1 - 1)s_1^2 + (n_2 - 1)s_2^2}{(n_1 - 1) + (n_2 - 1)}}$$

$$\hat{y} = b_0 + b_1 x$$

$$b_1 = \frac{\sum (x_i - \overline{x})(y_i - \overline{y})}{\sum (x_i - \overline{x})^2}$$

$$b_0 = \overline{y} - b_1\overline{x}$$

$$r = \frac{1}{n-1}\sum \left(\frac{x_i - \overline{x}}{s_x}\right)\left(\frac{y_i - \overline{y}}{s_y}\right)$$

$$b_1 = r\frac{s_y}{s_x}$$

$$s_{b_1} = \frac{\sqrt{\dfrac{\sum (y_i - \hat{y}_i)^2}{n-2}}}{\sqrt{\sum (x_i - \overline{x})^2}}$$

II. Probability

$$P(A \cup B) = P(A) + P(B) - P(A \cap B)$$

$$P(A|B) = \frac{P(A \cap B)}{P(B)}$$

$$E(X) = \mu_x = \sum x_i p_i$$

$$Var(X) = \sigma_x^2 = \sum (x_i - \mu_x)^2 p_i$$

If X has a binomial distribution with parameters n and p, then:

$$P(X = k) = \binom{n}{k} p^k (1 - p)^{n-k}$$

$$\mu_x = np$$

$$\sigma_x = \sqrt{np(1 - p)}$$

$$\mu_{\hat{p}} = p$$

$$\sigma_{\hat{p}} = \sqrt{\frac{p(1 - p)}{n}}$$

If $\bar{x}$ is the mean of a random sample of size n from an infinite population with mean μ and standard deviation σ, then:

$$\mu_{\bar{x}} = \mu$$

$$\sigma_{\bar{x}} = \frac{\sigma}{\sqrt{n}}$$

III. Inferential Statistics

Standardized test statistic: $\dfrac{\text{statistic} - \text{parameter}}{\text{standard deviation of statistic}}$

Confidence interval: statistic $\pm$ (critical value) $\cdot$ (standard deviation of statistic)

Single-Sample

Statistic	Standard Deviation of Statistic
Sample Mean	$\dfrac{\sigma}{\sqrt{n}}$
Sample Proportion	$\sqrt{\dfrac{p(1-p)}{n}}$

Two-Sample

Statistic	Standard Deviation of Statistic
Difference of sample means	$\sqrt{\dfrac{\sigma_1^2}{n_1} + \dfrac{\sigma_2^2}{n_2}}$ Special case when $\sigma_1 = \sigma_2$ $\sigma\sqrt{\dfrac{1}{n_1} + \dfrac{1}{n_2}}$
Difference of sample proportions	$\sqrt{\dfrac{p_1(1-p_1)}{n_1} + \dfrac{p_2(1-p_2)}{n_2}}$ Special case when $p_1 = p_2$ $\sqrt{p(1-p)}\ \sqrt{\dfrac{1}{n_1} + \dfrac{1}{n_2}}$

$$\text{Chi-square test statistic} = \sum \frac{(\text{observed} - \text{expected})^2}{\text{expected}}$$

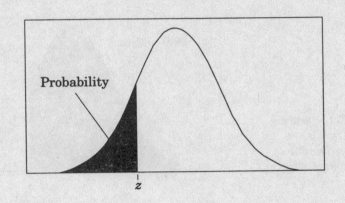

Table entry
for z is the
probability
lying below z.

Probability

z

Table A   Standard normal probabilities

z	.00	.01	.02	.03	.04	.05	.06	.07	.08	.09
−3.4	.0003	.0003	.0003	.0003	.0003	.0003	.0003	.0003	.0003	.0002
−3.3	.0005	.0005	.0005	.0004	.0004	.0004	.0004	.0004	.0004	.0003
−3.2	.0007	.0007	.0006	.0006	.0006	.0006	.0006	.0005	.0005	.0005
−3.1	.0010	.0009	.0009	.0009	.0008	.0008	.0008	.0008	.0007	.0007
−3.0	.0013	.0013	.0013	.0012	.0012	.0011	.0011	.0011	.0010	.0010
−2.9	.0019	.0018	.0018	.0017	.0016	.0016	.0015	.0015	.0014	.0014
−2.8	.0026	.0025	.0024	.0023	.0023	.0022	.0021	.0021	.0020	.0019
−2.7	.0035	.0034	.0033	.0032	.0031	.0030	.0029	.0028	.0027	.0026
−2.6	.0047	.0045	.0044	.0043	.0041	.0040	.0039	.0038	.0037	.0036
−2.5	.0062	.0060	.0059	.0057	.0055	.0054	.0052	.0051	.0049	.0048
−2.4	.0082	.0080	.0078	.0075	.0073	.0071	.0069	.0068	.0066	.0064
−2.3	.0107	.0104	.0102	.0099	.0096	.0094	.0091	.0089	.0087	.0084
−2.2	.0139	.0136	.0132	.0129	.0125	.0122	.0119	.0116	.0113	.0110
−2.1	.0179	.0174	.0170	.0166	.0162	.0158	.0154	.0150	.0146	.0143
−2.0	.0228	.0222	.0217	.0212	.0207	.0202	.0197	.0192	.0188	.0183
−1.9	.0287	.0281	.0274	.0268	.0262	.0256	.0250	.0244	.0239	.0233
−1.8	.0359	.0351	.0344	.0336	.0329	.0322	.0314	.0307	.0301	.0294
−1.7	.0446	.0436	.0427	.0418	.0409	.0401	.0392	.0384	.0375	.0367
−1.6	.0548	.0537	.0526	.0516	.0505	.0495	.0485	.0475	.0465	.0455
−1.5	.0668	.0655	.0643	.0630	.0618	.0606	.0594	.0582	.0571	.0559
−1.4	.0808	.0793	.0778	.0764	.0749	.0735	.0721	.0708	.0694	.0681
−1.3	.0968	.0951	.0934	.0918	.0901	.0885	.0869	.0853	.0838	.0823
−1.2	.1151	.1131	.1112	.1093	.1075	.1056	.1038	.1020	.1003	.0985
−1.1	.1357	.1335	.1314	.1292	.1271	.1251	.1230	.1210	.1190	.1170
−1.0	.1587	.1562	.1539	.1515	.1492	.1469	.1446	.1423	.1401	.1379
−0.9	.1841	.1814	.1788	.1762	.1736	.1711	.1685	.1660	.1635	.1611
−0.8	.2119	.2090	.2061	.2033	.2005	.1977	.1949	.1922	.1894	.1867
−0.7	.2420	.2389	.2358	.2327	.2296	.2266	.2236	.2206	.2177	.2148
−0.6	.2743	.2709	.2676	.2643	.2611	.2578	.2546	.2514	.2483	.2451
−0.5	.3085	.3050	.3015	.2981	.2946	.2912	.2877	.2843	.2810	.2776
−0.4	.3446	.3409	.3372	.3336	.3300	.3264	.3228	.3192	.3156	.3121
−0.3	.3821	.3783	.3745	.3707	.3669	.3632	.3594	.3557	.3520	.3483
−0.2	.4207	.4168	.4129	.4090	.4052	.4013	.3974	.3936	.3897	.3859
−0.1	.4602	.4562	.4522	.4483	.4443	.4404	.4364	.4325	.4286	.4247
−0.0	.5000	.4960	.4920	.4880	.4840	.4801	.4761	.4721	.4681	.4641

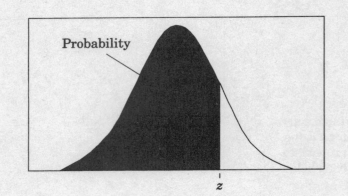

Table entry for z is the probability lying below z.

Table A *(Continued)*

z	.00	.01	.02	.03	.04	.05	.06	.07	.08	.09
0.0	.5000	.5040	.5080	.5120	.5160	.5199	.5239	.5279	.5319	.5359
0.1	.5398	.5438	.5478	.5517	.5557	.5596	.5636	.5675	.5714	.5753
0.2	.5793	.5832	.5871	.5910	.5948	.5987	.6026	.6064	.6103	.6141
0.3	.6179	.6217	.6255	.6293	.6331	.6368	.6406	.6443	.6480	.6517
0.4	.6554	.6591	.6628	.6664	.6700	.6736	.6772	.6808	.6844	.6879
0.5	.6915	.6950	.6985	.7019	.7054	.7088	.7123	.7157	.7190	.7224
0.6	.7257	.7291	.7324	.7357	.7389	.7422	.7454	.7486	.7517	.7549
0.7	.7580	.7611	.7642	.7673	.7704	.7734	.7764	.7794	.7823	.7852
0.8	.7881	.7910	.7939	.7967	.7995	.8023	.8051	.8078	.8106	.8133
0.9	.8159	.8186	.8212	.8238	.8264	.8289	.8315	.8340	.8365	.8389
1.0	.8413	.8438	.8461	.8485	.8508	.8531	.8554	.8577	.8599	.8621
1.1	.8643	.8665	.8686	.8708	.8729	.8749	.8770	.8790	.8810	.8830
1.2	.8849	.8869	.8888	.8907	.8925	.8944	.8962	.8980	.8997	.9015
1.3	.9032	.9049	.9066	.9082	.9099	.9115	.9131	.9147	.9162	.9177
1.4	.9192	.9207	.9222	.9236	.9251	.9265	.9279	.9292	.9306	.9319
1.5	.9332	.9345	.9357	.9370	.9382	.9394	.9406	.9418	.9429	.9441
1.6	.9452	.9463	.9474	.9484	.9495	.9505	.9515	.9525	.9535	.9545
1.7	.9554	.9564	.9573	.9582	.9591	.9599	.9608	.9616	.9625	.9633
1.8	.9641	.9649	.9656	.9664	.9671	.9678	.9686	.9693	.9699	.9706
1.9	.9713	.9719	.9726	.9732	.9738	.9744	.9750	.9756	.9761	.9767
2.0	.9772	.9778	.9783	.9788	.9793	.9798	.9803	.9808	.9812	.9817
2.1	.9821	.9826	.9830	.9834	.9838	.9842	.9846	.9850	.9854	.9857
2.2	.9861	.9864	.9868	.9871	.9875	.9878	.9881	.9884	.9887	.9890
2.3	.9893	.9896	.9898	.9901	.9904	.9906	.9909	.9911	.9913	.9916
2.4	.9918	.9920	.9922	.9925	.9927	.9929	.9931	.9932	.9934	.9936
2.5	.9938	.9940	.9941	.9943	.9945	.9946	.9948	.9949	.9951	.9952
2.6	.9953	.9955	.9956	.9957	.9959	.9960	.9961	.9962	.9963	.9964
2.7	.9965	.9966	.9967	.9968	.9969	.9970	.9971	.9972	.9973	.9974
2.8	.9974	.9975	.9976	.9977	.9977	.9978	.9979	.9979	.9980	.9981
2.9	.9981	.9982	.9982	.9983	.9984	.9984	.9985	.9985	.9986	.9986
3.0	.9987	.9987	.9987	.9988	.9988	.9989	.9989	.9989	.9990	.9990
3.1	.9990	.9991	.9991	.9991	.9992	.9992	.9992	.9992	.9993	.9993
3.2	.9993	.9993	.9994	.9994	.9994	.9994	.9994	.9995	.9995	.9995
3.3	.9995	.9995	.9995	.9996	.9996	.9996	.9996	.9996	.9996	.9997
3.4	.9997	.9997	.9997	.9997	.9997	.9997	.9997	.9997	.9997	.9998

Table entry for p and C is the point t^* with probability p lying above it and probability C lying between $-t^*$ and t^*.

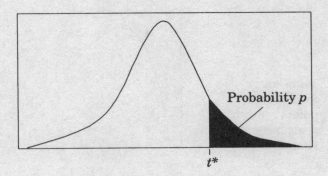

Probability p

t^*

Table B $\qquad$ t distribution critical values

df	.25	.20	.15	.10	.05	.025	.02	.01	.005	.0025	.001	.0005
1	1.000	1.376	1.963	3.078	6.314	12.71	15.89	31.82	63.66	127.3	318.3	636.6
2	.816	1.061	1.386	1.886	2.920	4.303	4.849	6.965	9.925	14.09	22.33	31.60
3	.765	.978	1.250	1.638	2.353	3.182	3.482	4.541	5.841	7.453	10.21	12.92
4	.741	.941	1.190	1.533	2.132	2.776	2.999	3.747	4.604	5.598	7.173	8.610
5	.727	.920	1.156	1.476	2.015	2.571	2.757	3.365	4.032	4.773	5.893	6.869
6	.718	.906	1.134	1.440	1.943	2.447	2.612	3.143	3.707	4.317	5.208	5.959
7	.711	.896	1.119	1.415	1.895	2.365	2.517	2.998	3.499	4.029	4.785	5.408
8	.706	.889	1.108	1.397	1.860	2.306	2.449	2.896	3.355	3.833	4.501	5.041
9	.703	.883	1.100	1.383	1.833	2.262	2.398	2.821	3.250	3.690	4.297	4.781
10	.700	.879	1.093	1.372	1.812	2.228	2.359	2.764	3.169	3.581	4.144	4.587
11	.697	.876	1.088	1.363	1.796	2.201	2.328	2.718	3.106	3.497	4.025	4.437
12	.695	.873	1.083	1.356	1.782	2.179	2.303	2.681	3.055	3.428	3.930	4.318
13	.694	.870	1.079	1.350	1.771	2.160	2.282	2.650	3.012	3.372	3.852	4.221
14	.692	.868	1.076	1.345	1.761	2.145	2.264	2.624	2.977	3.326	3.787	4.140
15	.691	.866	1.074	1.341	1.753	2.131	2.249	2.602	2.947	3.286	3.733	4.073
16	.690	.865	1.071	1.337	1.746	2.120	2.235	2.583	2.921	3.252	3.686	4.015
17	.689	.863	1.069	1.333	1.740	2.110	2.224	2.567	2.898	3.222	3.646	3.965
18	.688	.862	1.067	1.330	1.734	2.101	2.214	2.552	2.878	3.197	3.611	3.922
19	.688	.861	1.066	1.328	1.729	2.093	2.205	2.539	2.861	3.174	3.579	3.883
20	.687	.860	1.064	1.325	1.725	2.086	2.197	2.528	2.845	3.153	3.552	3.850
21	.686	.859	1.063	1.323	1.721	2.080	2.189	2.518	2.831	3.135	3.527	3.819
22	.686	.858	1.061	1.321	1.717	2.074	2.183	2.508	2.819	3.119	3.505	3.792
23	.685	.858	1.060	1.319	1.714	2.069	2.177	2.500	2.807	3.104	3.485	3.768
24	.685	.857	1.059	1.318	1.711	2.064	2.172	2.492	2.797	3.091	3.467	3.745
25	.684	.856	1.058	1.316	1.708	2.060	2.167	2.485	2.787	3.078	3.450	3.725
26	.684	.856	1.058	1.315	1.706	2.056	2.162	2.479	2.779	3.067	3.435	3.707
27	.684	.855	1.057	1.314	1.703	2.052	2.158	2.473	2.771	3.057	3.421	3.690
28	.683	.855	1.056	1.313	1.701	2.048	2.154	2.467	2.763	3.047	3.408	3.674
29	.683	.854	1.055	1.311	1.699	2.045	2.150	2.462	2.756	3.038	3.396	3.659
30	.683	.854	1.055	1.310	1.697	2.042	2.147	2.457	2.750	3.030	3.385	3.646
40	.681	.851	1.050	1.303	1.684	2.021	2.123	2.423	2.704	2.971	3.307	3.551
50	.679	.849	1.047	1.299	1.676	2.009	2.109	2.403	2.678	2.937	3.261	3.496
60	.679	.848	1.045	1.296	1.671	2.000	2.099	2.390	2.660	2.915	3.232	3.460
80	.678	.846	1.043	1.292	1.664	1.990	2.088	2.374	2.639	2.887	3.195	3.416
100	.677	.845	1.042	1.290	1.660	1.984	2.081	2.364	2.626	2.871	3.174	3.390
1000	.675	.842	1.037	1.282	1.646	1.962	2.056	2.330	2.581	2.813	3.098	3.300
∞	.674	.841	1.036	1.282	1.645	1.960	2.054	2.326	2.576	2.807	3.091	3.291
	50%	60%	70%	80%	90%	95%	96%	98%	99%	99.5%	99.8%	99.9%

Confidence level C

Table entry for p is the point (χ^2) with probability p lying above it.

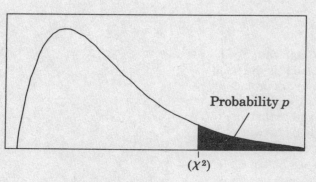

Probability p

(χ^2)

Table C χ^2 critical values

					Tail probability p						
df	.25	.20	.15	.10	.05	.025	.02	.01	.005	.0025	.001
1	1.32	1.64	2.07	2.71	3.84	5.02	5.41	6.63	7.88	9.14	10.83
2	2.77	3.22	3.79	4.61	5.99	7.38	7.82	9.21	10.60	11.98	13.82
3	4.11	4.64	5.32	6.25	7.81	9.35	9.84	11.34	12.84	14.32	16.27
4	5.39	5.99	6.74	7.78	9.49	11.14	11.67	13.28	14.86	16.42	18.47
5	6.63	7.29	8.12	9.24	11.07	12.83	13.39	15.09	16.75	18.39	20.51
6	7.84	8.56	9.45	10.64	12.59	14.45	15.03	16.81	18.55	20.25	22.46
7	9.04	9.80	10.75	12.02	14.07	16.01	16.62	18.48	20.28	22.04	24.32
8	10.22	11.03	12.03	13.36	15.51	17.53	18.17	20.09	21.95	23.77	26.12
9	11.39	12.24	13.29	14.68	16.92	19.02	19.68	21.67	23.59	25.46	27.88
10	12.55	13.44	14.53	15.99	18.31	20.48	21.16	23.21	25.19	27.11	29.59
11	13.70	14.63	15.77	17.28	19.68	21.92	22.62	24.72	26.76	28.73	31.26
12	14.85	15.81	16.99	18.55	21.03	23.34	24.05	26.22	28.30	30.32	32.91
13	15.98	16.98	18.20	19.81	22.36	24.74	25.47	27.69	29.82	31.88	34.53
14	17.12	18.15	19.41	21.06	23.68	26.12	26.87	29.14	31.32	33.43	36.12
15	18.25	19.31	20.60	22.31	25.00	27.49	28.26	30.58	32.80	34.95	37.70
16	19.37	20.47	21.79	23.54	26.30	28.85	29.63	32.00	34.27	36.46	39.25
17	20.49	21.61	22.98	24.77	27.59	30.19	31.00	33.41	35.72	37.95	40.79
18	21.60	22.76	24.16	25.99	28.87	31.53	32.35	34.81	37.16	39.42	42.31
19	22.72	23.90	25.33	27.20	30.14	32.85	33.69	36.19	38.58	40.88	43.82
20	23.83	25.04	26.50	28.41	31.41	34.17	35.02	37.57	40.00	42.34	45.31
21	24.93	26.17	27.66	29.62	32.67	35.48	36.34	38.93	41.40	43.78	46.80
22	26.04	27.30	28.82	30.81	33.92	36.78	37.66	40.29	42.80	45.20	48.27
23	27.14	28.43	29.98	32.01	35.17	38.08	38.97	41.64	44.18	46.62	49.73
24	28.24	29.55	31.13	33.20	36.42	39.36	40.27	42.98	45.56	48.03	51.18
25	29.34	30.68	32.28	34.38	37.65	40.65	41.57	44.31	46.93	49.44	52.62
26	30.43	31.79	33.43	35.56	38.89	41.92	42.86	45.64	48.29	50.83	54.05
27	31.53	32.91	34.57	36.74	40.11	43.19	44.14	46.96	49.64	52.22	55.48
28	32.62	34.03	35.71	37.92	41.34	44.46	45.42	48.28	50.99	53.59	56.89
29	33.71	35.14	36.85	39.09	42.56	45.72	46.69	49.59	52.34	54.97	58.30
30	34.80	36.25	37.99	40.26	43.77	46.98	47.96	50.89	53.67	56.33	59.70
40	45.62	47.27	49.24	51.81	55.76	59.34	60.44	63.69	66.77	69.70	73.40
50	56.33	58.16	60.35	63.17	67.50	71.42	72.61	76.15	79.49	82.66	86.66
60	66.98	68.97	71.34	74.40	79.08	83.30	84.58	88.38	91.95	95.34	99.61
80	88.13	90.41	93.11	96.58	101.9	106.6	108.1	112.3	116.3	120.1	124.8
100	109.1	111.7	114.7	118.5	124.3	129.6	131.1	135.8	140.2	144.3	149.4

ABOUT THE AUTHOR

Madhuri S. Mulekar received her Ph.D. in Statistics from Oklahoma State University in 1988. She is currently a Professor of Statistics at the University of South Alabama. She has been involved with AP Statistics since 1997 as both a reader and a table leader. She has given several lectures and workshops on teaching AP Statistics. She also wrote several refereed publications on such topics as statistical education, selection and raking procedures, estimation and inferential procedures for overlap coefficients, and medical applications. Dr. Mulekar has received grants from the National Science Foundation and the Alabama Center for Estuarine Studies (Environmental Protection Agency).

Completely darken bubbles with a No. 2 pencil. If you make a mistake, be sure to erase mark completely. Erase all stray marks.

1. YOUR NAME: _____
(Print)   Last   First   M.I.

SIGNATURE: _____ **DATE:** ____ / ____ / ____

HOME ADDRESS: _____
(Print)   Number and Street

_____
City   State   Zip Code

PHONE NO. : _____
(Print)

IMPORTANT: Please fill in these boxes exactly as shown on the back cover of your test book.

2. TEST FORM

3. TEST CODE

4. REGISTRATION NUMBER

6. DATE OF BIRTH

Month	Day		Year	
○ JAN				
○ FEB				
○ MAR	⓪	⓪	⓪	⓪
○ APR	①	①	①	①
○ MAY	②	②	②	②
○ JUN	③	③	③	③
○ JUL		④	④	④
○ AUG		⑤	⑤	⑤
○ SEP		⑦	⑦	⑦
○ OCT		⑧	⑧	⑧
○ NOV		⑨	⑨	⑨
○ DEC				

Test Code bubbles: ⓪①②③④⑤⑦⑧⑨ with letters Ⓐ Ⓑ Ⓒ Ⓓ Ⓔ Ⓕ Ⓖ

7. SEX

○ MALE
○ FEMALE

The Princeton Review

© 1996 Princeton Review L.L.C.
FORM NO. 00001-PR

5. YOUR NAME

First 4 letters of last name | FIRST INIT | MID INIT

Ⓐ Ⓑ Ⓒ Ⓓ Ⓔ Ⓕ Ⓖ Ⓗ Ⓘ Ⓙ Ⓚ Ⓛ Ⓜ Ⓝ Ⓞ Ⓟ Ⓠ Ⓡ Ⓢ Ⓣ Ⓤ Ⓥ Ⓦ Ⓧ Ⓨ Ⓩ

Section ①   Start with number 1 for each new section.
If a section has fewer questions than answer spaces, leave the extra answer spaces blank.

1. Ⓐ Ⓑ Ⓒ Ⓓ Ⓔ   31. Ⓐ Ⓑ Ⓒ Ⓓ Ⓔ   61. Ⓐ Ⓑ Ⓒ Ⓓ Ⓔ
2. Ⓐ Ⓑ Ⓒ Ⓓ Ⓔ   32. Ⓐ Ⓑ Ⓒ Ⓓ Ⓔ   62. Ⓐ Ⓑ Ⓒ Ⓓ Ⓔ
3. Ⓐ Ⓑ Ⓒ Ⓓ Ⓔ   33. Ⓐ Ⓑ Ⓒ Ⓓ Ⓔ   63. Ⓐ Ⓑ Ⓒ Ⓓ Ⓔ
4. Ⓐ Ⓑ Ⓒ Ⓓ Ⓔ   34. Ⓐ Ⓑ Ⓒ Ⓓ Ⓔ   64. Ⓐ Ⓑ Ⓒ Ⓓ Ⓔ
5. Ⓐ Ⓑ Ⓒ Ⓓ Ⓔ   35. Ⓐ Ⓑ Ⓒ Ⓓ Ⓔ   65. Ⓐ Ⓑ Ⓒ Ⓓ Ⓔ
6. Ⓐ Ⓑ Ⓒ Ⓓ Ⓔ   36. Ⓐ Ⓑ Ⓒ Ⓓ Ⓔ   66. Ⓐ Ⓑ Ⓒ Ⓓ Ⓔ
7. Ⓐ Ⓑ Ⓒ Ⓓ Ⓔ   37. Ⓐ Ⓑ Ⓒ Ⓓ Ⓔ   67. Ⓐ Ⓑ Ⓒ Ⓓ Ⓔ
8. Ⓐ Ⓑ Ⓒ Ⓓ Ⓔ   38. Ⓐ Ⓑ Ⓒ Ⓓ Ⓔ   68. Ⓐ Ⓑ Ⓒ Ⓓ Ⓔ
9. Ⓐ Ⓑ Ⓒ Ⓓ Ⓔ   39. Ⓐ Ⓑ Ⓒ Ⓓ Ⓔ   69. Ⓐ Ⓑ Ⓒ Ⓓ Ⓔ
10. Ⓐ Ⓑ Ⓒ Ⓓ Ⓔ   40. Ⓐ Ⓑ Ⓒ Ⓓ Ⓔ   70. Ⓐ Ⓑ Ⓒ Ⓓ Ⓔ
11. Ⓐ Ⓑ Ⓒ Ⓓ Ⓔ   41. Ⓐ Ⓑ Ⓒ Ⓓ Ⓔ   71. Ⓐ Ⓑ Ⓒ Ⓓ Ⓔ
12. Ⓐ Ⓑ Ⓒ Ⓓ Ⓔ   42. Ⓐ Ⓑ Ⓒ Ⓓ Ⓔ   72. Ⓐ Ⓑ Ⓒ Ⓓ Ⓔ
13. Ⓐ Ⓑ Ⓒ Ⓓ Ⓔ   43. Ⓐ Ⓑ Ⓒ Ⓓ Ⓔ   73. Ⓐ Ⓑ Ⓒ Ⓓ Ⓔ
14. Ⓐ Ⓑ Ⓒ Ⓓ Ⓔ   44. Ⓐ Ⓑ Ⓒ Ⓓ Ⓔ   74. Ⓐ Ⓑ Ⓒ Ⓓ Ⓔ
15. Ⓐ Ⓑ Ⓒ Ⓓ Ⓔ   45. Ⓐ Ⓑ Ⓒ Ⓓ Ⓔ   75. Ⓐ Ⓑ Ⓒ Ⓓ Ⓔ
16. Ⓐ Ⓑ Ⓒ Ⓓ Ⓔ   46. Ⓐ Ⓑ Ⓒ Ⓓ Ⓔ   76. Ⓐ Ⓑ Ⓒ Ⓓ Ⓔ
17. Ⓐ Ⓑ Ⓒ Ⓓ Ⓔ   47. Ⓐ Ⓑ Ⓒ Ⓓ Ⓔ   77. Ⓐ Ⓑ Ⓒ Ⓓ Ⓔ
18. Ⓐ Ⓑ Ⓒ Ⓓ Ⓔ   48. Ⓐ Ⓑ Ⓒ Ⓓ Ⓔ   78. Ⓐ Ⓑ Ⓒ Ⓓ Ⓔ
19. Ⓐ Ⓑ Ⓒ Ⓓ Ⓔ   49. Ⓐ Ⓑ Ⓒ Ⓓ Ⓔ   79. Ⓐ Ⓑ Ⓒ Ⓓ Ⓔ
20. Ⓐ Ⓑ Ⓒ Ⓓ Ⓔ   50. Ⓐ Ⓑ Ⓒ Ⓓ Ⓔ   80. Ⓐ Ⓑ Ⓒ Ⓓ Ⓔ
21. Ⓐ Ⓑ Ⓒ Ⓓ Ⓔ   51. Ⓐ Ⓑ Ⓒ Ⓓ Ⓔ   81. Ⓐ Ⓑ Ⓒ Ⓓ Ⓔ
22. Ⓐ Ⓑ Ⓒ Ⓓ Ⓔ   52. Ⓐ Ⓑ Ⓒ Ⓓ Ⓔ   82. Ⓐ Ⓑ Ⓒ Ⓓ Ⓔ
23. Ⓐ Ⓑ Ⓒ Ⓓ Ⓔ   53. Ⓐ Ⓑ Ⓒ Ⓓ Ⓔ   83. Ⓐ Ⓑ Ⓒ Ⓓ Ⓔ
24. Ⓐ Ⓑ Ⓒ Ⓓ Ⓔ   54. Ⓐ Ⓑ Ⓒ Ⓓ Ⓔ   84. Ⓐ Ⓑ Ⓒ Ⓓ Ⓔ
25. Ⓐ Ⓑ Ⓒ Ⓓ Ⓔ   55. Ⓐ Ⓑ Ⓒ Ⓓ Ⓔ   85. Ⓐ Ⓑ Ⓒ Ⓓ Ⓔ
26. Ⓐ Ⓑ Ⓒ Ⓓ Ⓔ   56. Ⓐ Ⓑ Ⓒ Ⓓ Ⓔ   86. Ⓐ Ⓑ Ⓒ Ⓓ Ⓔ
27. Ⓐ Ⓑ Ⓒ Ⓓ Ⓔ   57. Ⓐ Ⓑ Ⓒ Ⓓ Ⓔ   87. Ⓐ Ⓑ Ⓒ Ⓓ Ⓔ
28. Ⓐ Ⓑ Ⓒ Ⓓ Ⓔ   58. Ⓐ Ⓑ Ⓒ Ⓓ Ⓔ   88. Ⓐ Ⓑ Ⓒ Ⓓ Ⓔ
29. Ⓐ Ⓑ Ⓒ Ⓓ Ⓔ   59. Ⓐ Ⓑ Ⓒ Ⓓ Ⓔ   89. Ⓐ Ⓑ Ⓒ Ⓓ Ⓔ
30. Ⓐ Ⓑ Ⓒ Ⓓ Ⓔ   60. Ⓐ Ⓑ Ⓒ Ⓓ Ⓔ   90. Ⓐ Ⓑ Ⓒ Ⓓ Ⓔ

Completely darken bubbles with a No. 2 pencil. If you make a mistake, be sure to erase mark completely. Erase all stray marks.

1. YOUR NAME:
(Print) _____
　　　　Last　　　　　　First　　　　　　M.I.

SIGNATURE: _____ DATE: _____ / ____ / ____

HOME ADDRESS: _____
(Print)
　　　　　　　Number and Street
_____
　　City　　　　　　State　　　　　Zip Code
PHONE NO. : _____
(Print)

5. YOUR NAME

First 4 letters of last name				FIRST INIT	MID INIT
Ⓐ	Ⓐ	Ⓐ	Ⓐ	Ⓐ	Ⓐ
Ⓑ	Ⓑ	Ⓑ	Ⓑ	Ⓑ	Ⓑ
Ⓒ	Ⓒ	Ⓒ	Ⓒ	Ⓒ	Ⓒ
Ⓓ	Ⓓ	Ⓓ	Ⓓ	Ⓓ	Ⓓ
Ⓔ	Ⓔ	Ⓔ	Ⓔ	Ⓔ	Ⓔ
Ⓕ	Ⓕ	Ⓕ	Ⓕ	Ⓕ	Ⓕ
Ⓖ	Ⓖ	Ⓖ	Ⓖ	Ⓖ	Ⓖ
Ⓗ	Ⓗ	Ⓗ	Ⓗ	Ⓗ	Ⓗ
Ⓘ	Ⓘ	Ⓘ	Ⓘ	Ⓘ	Ⓘ
Ⓙ	Ⓙ	Ⓙ	Ⓙ	Ⓙ	Ⓙ
Ⓚ	Ⓚ	Ⓚ	Ⓚ	Ⓚ	Ⓚ
Ⓛ	Ⓛ	Ⓛ	Ⓛ	Ⓛ	Ⓛ
Ⓜ	Ⓜ	Ⓜ	Ⓜ	Ⓜ	Ⓜ
Ⓝ	Ⓝ	Ⓝ	Ⓝ	Ⓝ	Ⓝ
Ⓞ	Ⓞ	Ⓞ	Ⓞ	Ⓞ	Ⓞ
Ⓟ	Ⓟ	Ⓟ	Ⓟ	Ⓟ	Ⓟ
Ⓠ	Ⓠ	Ⓠ	Ⓠ	Ⓠ	Ⓠ
Ⓡ	Ⓡ	Ⓡ	Ⓡ	Ⓡ	Ⓡ
Ⓢ	Ⓢ	Ⓢ	Ⓢ	Ⓢ	Ⓢ
Ⓣ	Ⓣ	Ⓣ	Ⓣ	Ⓣ	Ⓣ
Ⓤ	Ⓤ	Ⓤ	Ⓤ	Ⓤ	Ⓤ
Ⓥ	Ⓥ	Ⓥ	Ⓥ	Ⓥ	Ⓥ
Ⓦ	Ⓦ	Ⓦ	Ⓦ	Ⓦ	Ⓦ
Ⓧ	Ⓧ	Ⓧ	Ⓧ	Ⓧ	Ⓧ
Ⓨ	Ⓨ	Ⓨ	Ⓨ	Ⓨ	Ⓨ
Ⓩ	Ⓩ	Ⓩ	Ⓩ	Ⓩ	Ⓩ

IMPORTANT: Please fill in these boxes exactly as shown on the back cover of your test book.

2. TEST FORM

3. TEST CODE　　**4. REGISTRATION NUMBER**

Test Code column: ⓪ Ⓐ ① ② ③ ④ ⑤ ⑥ ⑦ ⑧ ⑨ with A–G letters (Ⓐ Ⓑ Ⓒ Ⓓ Ⓔ Ⓕ Ⓖ)

Digit columns (0–9 bubbles): ⓪①②③④⑤⑥⑦⑧⑨

6. DATE OF BIRTH

Month	Day		Year	
◯ JAN				
◯ FEB				
◯ MAR	⓪	⓪	⓪	⓪
◯ APR	①	①	①	①
◯ MAY	②	②	②	②
◯ JUN	③	③	③	③
◯ JUL		④	④	④
◯ AUG		⑤	⑤	⑤
◯ SEP		⑦	⑦	⑦
◯ OCT		⑧	⑧	⑧
◯ NOV		⑨	⑨	⑨
◯ DEC				

7. SEX
◯ MALE
◯ FEMALE

The Princeton Review
© 1996 Princeton Review L.L.C.
FORM NO. 00001-PR

Section ①　Start with number 1 for each new section.
If a section has fewer questions than answer spaces, leave the extra answer spaces blank.

1. Ⓐ Ⓑ Ⓒ Ⓓ Ⓔ
2. Ⓐ Ⓑ Ⓒ Ⓓ Ⓔ
3. Ⓐ Ⓑ Ⓒ Ⓓ Ⓔ
4. Ⓐ Ⓑ Ⓒ Ⓓ Ⓔ
5. Ⓐ Ⓑ Ⓒ Ⓓ Ⓔ
6. Ⓐ Ⓑ Ⓒ Ⓓ Ⓔ
7. Ⓐ Ⓑ Ⓒ Ⓓ Ⓔ
8. Ⓐ Ⓑ Ⓒ Ⓓ Ⓔ
9. Ⓐ Ⓑ Ⓒ Ⓓ Ⓔ
10. Ⓐ Ⓑ Ⓒ Ⓓ Ⓔ
11. Ⓐ Ⓑ Ⓒ Ⓓ Ⓔ
12. Ⓐ Ⓑ Ⓒ Ⓓ Ⓔ
13. Ⓐ Ⓑ Ⓒ Ⓓ Ⓔ
14. Ⓐ Ⓑ Ⓒ Ⓓ Ⓔ
15. Ⓐ Ⓑ Ⓒ Ⓓ Ⓔ
16. Ⓐ Ⓑ Ⓒ Ⓓ Ⓔ
17. Ⓐ Ⓑ Ⓒ Ⓓ Ⓔ
18. Ⓐ Ⓑ Ⓒ Ⓓ Ⓔ
19. Ⓐ Ⓑ Ⓒ Ⓓ Ⓔ
20. Ⓐ Ⓑ Ⓒ Ⓓ Ⓔ
21. Ⓐ Ⓑ Ⓒ Ⓓ Ⓔ
22. Ⓐ Ⓑ Ⓒ Ⓓ Ⓔ
23. Ⓐ Ⓑ Ⓒ Ⓓ Ⓔ
24. Ⓐ Ⓑ Ⓒ Ⓓ Ⓔ
25. Ⓐ Ⓑ Ⓒ Ⓓ Ⓔ
26. Ⓐ Ⓑ Ⓒ Ⓓ Ⓔ
27. Ⓐ Ⓑ Ⓒ Ⓓ Ⓔ
28. Ⓐ Ⓑ Ⓒ Ⓓ Ⓔ
29. Ⓐ Ⓑ Ⓒ Ⓓ Ⓔ
30. Ⓐ Ⓑ Ⓒ Ⓓ Ⓔ

31. Ⓐ Ⓑ Ⓒ Ⓓ Ⓔ
32. Ⓐ Ⓑ Ⓒ Ⓓ Ⓔ
33. Ⓐ Ⓑ Ⓒ Ⓓ Ⓔ
34. Ⓐ Ⓑ Ⓒ Ⓓ Ⓔ
35. Ⓐ Ⓑ Ⓒ Ⓓ Ⓔ
36. Ⓐ Ⓑ Ⓒ Ⓓ Ⓔ
37. Ⓐ Ⓑ Ⓒ Ⓓ Ⓔ
38. Ⓐ Ⓑ Ⓒ Ⓓ Ⓔ
39. Ⓐ Ⓑ Ⓒ Ⓓ Ⓔ
40. Ⓐ Ⓑ Ⓒ Ⓓ Ⓔ
41. Ⓐ Ⓑ Ⓒ Ⓓ Ⓔ
42. Ⓐ Ⓑ Ⓒ Ⓓ Ⓔ
43. Ⓐ Ⓑ Ⓒ Ⓓ Ⓔ
44. Ⓐ Ⓑ Ⓒ Ⓓ Ⓔ
45. Ⓐ Ⓑ Ⓒ Ⓓ Ⓔ
46. Ⓐ Ⓑ Ⓒ Ⓓ Ⓔ
47. Ⓐ Ⓑ Ⓒ Ⓓ Ⓔ
48. Ⓐ Ⓑ Ⓒ Ⓓ Ⓔ
49. Ⓐ Ⓑ Ⓒ Ⓓ Ⓔ
50. Ⓐ Ⓑ Ⓒ Ⓓ Ⓔ
51. Ⓐ Ⓑ Ⓒ Ⓓ Ⓔ
52. Ⓐ Ⓑ Ⓒ Ⓓ Ⓔ
53. Ⓐ Ⓑ Ⓒ Ⓓ Ⓔ
54. Ⓐ Ⓑ Ⓒ Ⓓ Ⓔ
55. Ⓐ Ⓑ Ⓒ Ⓓ Ⓔ
56. Ⓐ Ⓑ Ⓒ Ⓓ Ⓔ
57. Ⓐ Ⓑ Ⓒ Ⓓ Ⓔ
58. Ⓐ Ⓑ Ⓒ Ⓓ Ⓔ
59. Ⓐ Ⓑ Ⓒ Ⓓ Ⓔ
60. Ⓐ Ⓑ Ⓒ Ⓓ Ⓔ

61. Ⓐ Ⓑ Ⓒ Ⓓ Ⓔ
62. Ⓐ Ⓑ Ⓒ Ⓓ Ⓔ
63. Ⓐ Ⓑ Ⓒ Ⓓ Ⓔ
64. Ⓐ Ⓑ Ⓒ Ⓓ Ⓔ
65. Ⓐ Ⓑ Ⓒ Ⓓ Ⓔ
66. Ⓐ Ⓑ Ⓒ Ⓓ Ⓔ
67. Ⓐ Ⓑ Ⓒ Ⓓ Ⓔ
68. Ⓐ Ⓑ Ⓒ Ⓓ Ⓔ
69. Ⓐ Ⓑ Ⓒ Ⓓ Ⓔ
70. Ⓐ Ⓑ Ⓒ Ⓓ Ⓔ
71. Ⓐ Ⓑ Ⓒ Ⓓ Ⓔ
72. Ⓐ Ⓑ Ⓒ Ⓓ Ⓔ
73. Ⓐ Ⓑ Ⓒ Ⓓ Ⓔ
74. Ⓐ Ⓑ Ⓒ Ⓓ Ⓔ
75. Ⓐ Ⓑ Ⓒ Ⓓ Ⓔ
76. Ⓐ Ⓑ Ⓒ Ⓓ Ⓔ
77. Ⓐ Ⓑ Ⓒ Ⓓ Ⓔ
78. Ⓐ Ⓑ Ⓒ Ⓓ Ⓔ
79. Ⓐ Ⓑ Ⓒ Ⓓ Ⓔ
80. Ⓐ Ⓑ Ⓒ Ⓓ Ⓔ
81. Ⓐ Ⓑ Ⓒ Ⓓ Ⓔ
82. Ⓐ Ⓑ Ⓒ Ⓓ Ⓔ
83. Ⓐ Ⓑ Ⓒ Ⓓ Ⓔ
84. Ⓐ Ⓑ Ⓒ Ⓓ Ⓔ
85. Ⓐ Ⓑ Ⓒ Ⓓ Ⓔ
86. Ⓐ Ⓑ Ⓒ Ⓓ Ⓔ
87. Ⓐ Ⓑ Ⓒ Ⓓ Ⓔ
88. Ⓐ Ⓑ Ⓒ Ⓓ Ⓔ
89. Ⓐ Ⓑ Ⓒ Ⓓ Ⓔ
90. Ⓐ Ⓑ Ⓒ Ⓓ Ⓔ

NOTES

NOTES

NOTES

The Princeton Review

Find the Right School

BEST 331 COLLEGES
2002 EDITION
The Smart Buyer's Guide to College
0-375-76201-9 • $20.00

COMPLETE BOOK OF COLLEGES
2002 EDITION
0-375-76202-7 • $26.95

COMPLETE BOOK OF
DISTANCE LEARNING SCHOOLS
0-375-76204-3 • $21.00

POCKET GUIDE TO COLLEGES
2002 EDITION
0-375-76203-5 • $11.95

AFRICAN AMERICAN STUDENT'S
GUIDE TO COLLEGE
Making the Most of College:
Getting In, Staying In, and
Graduating
0-679-77878-0 • $17.95

Get in

CRACKING THE SAT & PSAT/NMSQT
2002 EDITION
0-375-76207-8 • $18.00

CRACKING THE SAT & PSAT/NMSQT
WITH SAMPLE TESTS ON CD-ROM
2002 EDITION
0-375-76192-6 • $29.95

MATH WORKOUT FOR THE SAT
2ND EDITION
0-375-76177-2 • $14.95

VERBAL WORKOUT FOR THE SAT
2ND EDITION
0-375-76176-4 • $14.95

CRACKING THE ACT
2002 EDITION
0-375-76233-7 • $19.00

CRACKING THE ACT WITH
SAMPLE TESTS ON CD-ROM
2002 EDITION
0-375-76234-5 • $29.95

CRASH COURSE FOR THE ACT
10 Easy Steps to Higher Score
0-375-75326-5 • $9.95

CRASH COURSE FOR THE SAT
10 Easy Steps to Higher Score
0-375-75324-9 • $9.95

Get Help Paying for it

DOLLARS & SENSE FOR COLLEGE STUDENTS
How Not to Run Out of Money by Midterms
0-375-75206-4 • $10.95

PAYING FOR COLLEGE WITHOUT GOING BROKE
2002 EDITION
Insider Strategies to Maximize Financial Aid
and Minimize College Costs
0-375-76211-6 • $18.00

THE SCHOLARSHIP ADVISOR
5TH EDITION
0-375-76210-8 • $26.00

Make the Grade with Study Guides for the AP and SAT II Exams

AP Exams

CRACKING THE AP BIOLOGY
2002-2003 EDITION
0-375-76221-3 • $18.00

CRACKING THE AP CALCULUS
AB & BC
2002-2003 EDITION
0-375-76222-1 • $19.00

CRACKING THE AP CHEMISTRY
2002-2003 EDITION
0-375-76223-X • $18.00

CRACKING THE AP ECONOMICS
(MACRO & MICRO)
2002-2003 EDITION
0-375-76224-8 • $18.00

CRACKING THE AP ENGLISH
LITERATURE
2002-2003 EDITION
0-375-76225-6 • $18.00

CRACKING THE AP EUROPEAN
HISTORY
2002-2003 EDITION
0-375-76226-4 • $18.00

CRACKING THE AP PHYSICS
2002-2003 EDITION
0-375-76227-2 • $19.00

CRACKING THE AP PSYCHOLOGY
2002-2003 EDITION
0-375-76228-0 • $18.00

CRACKING THE AP SPANISH
2002-2003 EDITION
0-375-76229-9 • $18.00

CRACKING THE AP U.S.
GOVERNMENT AND POLITICS
2002-2003 EDITION
0-375-76230-2 • $18.00

CRACKING THE AP U.S. HISTORY
2002-2003 EDITION
0-375-76231-0 • $18.00

SAT II Exams

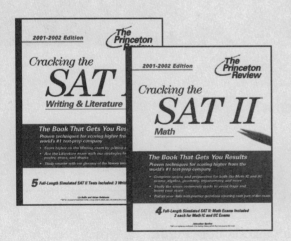

CRACKING THE SAT II: BIOLOGY
2001-2002 EDITION
0-375-76181-0 • $18.00

CRACKING THE SAT II: CHEMISTRY
2001-2002 EDITION
0-375-76182-9 • $17.00

CRACKING THE SAT II: FRENCH
2001-2002 EDITION
0-375-76184-5 • $17.00

CRACKING THE SAT II:
WRITING & LITERATURE
2001-2002 EDITION
0-375-76183-7 • $17.00

CRACKING THE SAT II: MATH
2001-2002 EDITION
0-375-76186-1 • $18.00

CRACKING THE SAT II: PHYSICS
2001-2002 EDITION
0-375-76187-X • $18.00

CRACKING THE SAT II: SPANISH
2001-2002 EDITION
0-375-76188-8 • $17.00

CRACKING THE SAT II:
U.S. & WORLD HISTORY
2001-2002 EDITION
0-375-76185-3 • $18.00

 The Princeton Review

Available at Bookstores Everywhere.
www.review.com